Shoe Reels

Film and Fashions

Series editor Pamela Church Gibson

This series explores the complex and multi-faceted relationship between cinema, fashion and design. Intended for all scholars and students with an interest in film and in fashion itself, the series not only forms an important addition to the existing literature around cinematic costume, but advances the debates by moving them forward into new, unexplored territory and extending their reach beyond the parameters of Western cinema alone.

edinburghuniversitypress.com/series/faf

Shoe Reels

The History and Philosophy of Footwear in Film

Edited by Elizabeth Ezra and Catherine Wheatley

EDINBURGH
University Press

Edinburgh University Press is one of the leading university presses in the UK. We publish academic books and journals in our selected subject areas across the humanities and social sciences, combining cutting-edge scholarship with high editorial and production values to produce academic works of lasting importance. For more information visit our website: edinburghuniversitypress.com

Edinburgh University Press Ltd
The Tun – Holyrood Road
12 (2f) Jackson's Entry
Edinburgh EH8 8PJ

First published in hardback by Edinburgh University Press 2020

Typeset in 12/14 Arno and Myriad by
IDSUK (Dataconnection) Ltd,
and printed and bound by CPI Group (UK) Ltd,
Croydon, CR0 4YY

A CIP record for this book is available from the British Library

ISBN 978 1 4744 5140 6 (hardback)
ISBN 978 1 4744 5141 3 (paperback)
ISBN 978 1 4744 5142 0 (webready PDF)
ISBN 978 1 4744 5143 7 (epub)

Contents

List of figures   vii
Acknowledgements   ix
Notes on contributors   x
Foreword   xiv

Introduction: foot notes   1
Elizabeth Ezra and Catherine Wheatley

1 Max's stylish shoes   18
   Margaret C. Flinn
2 A girl and a shoe: Marcel Fabre's *Amor pedestre*   26
   Malgorzata Bugaj
3 'An intensive study of – *feet*!' in two films by Lois Weber:
   Shoes and *The Blot*   38
   Pamela Hutchinson
4 Magic shoes: Dorothy, Cinderella, Carrie   49
   Elizabeth Ezra
5 The ruby slippers at the V&A: an odyssey   62
   Keith Lodwick
6 Blood-red shoes?   68
   Ian Christie
7 The two textures of invisibility: shoes as liminal questionings
   in *Sullivan's Travels*   78
   Kelli Fuery
8 How to see through a shoe: the fashion show sequence in
   How to Marry a Millionaire   94
   Ana Salzberg
9 Frenetic footwear and lively lace-ups: the spectacle of shoes in
   Golden Age Hollywood animation   103
   Christopher Holliday

10 Ferragamo's shoes: from silent cinema to the present   125
    Eugenia Paulicelli

11 Feet of strength: the sword-and-sandals film   136
    Robert A. Rushing

12 Men in boots: on spectacular masculinity and its desublimation   148
    Louise Wallenberg

13 'The brunette with the legs': the significance of footwear in *Marnie*   166
    Lucy Bolton

14 The sole of Africa: shoes in three African films   180
    Rachael Langford

15 Slippers and heels: *In the Mood for Love* and sartorial investigation   198
    Tyler Parks

16 Sex, corruption and killer heels: footwear in the Korean
    corporate crime drama   213
    Kate Taylor-Jones

17 It's gotta be the shoes: Nike in the Spike-o-sphere   229
    Jeff Scheible

18 'Nice shoes': Will Smith, mid-2000s (post) racial discourse
    and the symbolic significance of shoes in *I, Robot* and
    The Pursuit of Happyness   248
    Hannah Hamad

19 'Whoa! Look at all her Louboutins!' Girlhood and shoes in
    the films of Sofia Coppola   261
    Fiona Handyside

20 Isabelle's espadrilles, or *les chaussures d'Huppert*   279
    Catherine Wheatley

Index   293

Figures

I.1 The pile of empty shoes in *Nuit et brouillard*   7

I.2 Lee Daniels and Fred Astaire in *The Band Wagon*'s
shoeshine number   8

I.3 Chaplin eats his boots in *The Gold Rush*   9

I.4 A stiletto heel drips blood in *Single White Female*   12

3.1 Eva draws her tattered shoes out of sight in the park   42

3.2 One of the Olsen children plays in the yard wearing
$18 high heels   44

3.3 The hungry cat gives away the secret of Rev Gates'
goose-grease shoe polish   45

4.1 All wrong for the witch   52

4.2 Dorothy and her new friends   59

5.1 The ruby slippers   63

7.1 The valet presents Sully the shoes with the hidden identity card
in the sole   82

7.2 The replacement shoes left to Sully by the homeless man   88

8.1 Behind the scenes   100

8.2 The fashion show   101

9.1 The spectacle and musicality of collective labour in
The Shoemaker and the Elves   107

9.2 Comedic performance and slapstick shoe production in
Holiday for Shoestrings   109

9.3 Mammy Two Shoes' ill-fitting footwear, *A Mouse in The House*   119

10.1 Décolleté, 1959–60, upper and heel covered by Swarovski
crystals; designed for Marilyn Monroe   132

10.2 Salvatore Ferragamo, sandal, 1938, heel and platform
covered by suede; created for Judy Garland   133

10.3 Rainbow Future, Fall/Winter Collection 2018–19, handmade,
      crocheted sandal in organic cotton, heel and platform in wood
      covered with the same material   134
11.1 *Hercules*   137
11.2 *The Fury of Hercules*   142
11.3 *300*   146
12.1 Hal's leather boots, inherited from his father, in *Picnic*   153
12.2 Joe Buck's decorative cowboy boots in *Midnight Cowboy*   156
12.3 Cooper, Tone and Cromwell desublimising normative
      masculinity in *The Lives of a Bengal Lancer*   159
13.1 The shoe as tool, disposing of Marion Holland's key   172
13.2 The shoe as traitor, threatening to expose Marnie's crime   173
13.3 The boot as surrender, buckling in the grip of Rutland patriarchy   174
15.1 Homely pink slippers are contrasted with dark angular heels   203
15.2 Mrs Chan's woven-toed pumps suggest a relaxation of the rigid
      boundaries of her identity   208
16.1 Na-mi's strappy designer footwear contrasts with the basic black
      stilettos the maids wear   217
16.2 Eva is unable to fight back against the vengeful Geum-ok   223
17.1 Mookie with Oscar, in hang time pose   230
17.2 Mars Blackmon introduced in *She's Gotta Have It*   234
17.3 Mars standing on Jordan's shoulders, Hang Time Air Jordan III
      commercial   236
18.1 and 18.2   Blackness and masculinity are collapsed into the
      sartorial signifier of Del Spooner's Chuck Taylor Converse
      All Stars in *I, Robot*   252
18.3 'Where's my shoe?!' Chris Gardner loses a key signifier of his
      'bootstrap' aspirationalism   257
19.1 and 19.2   *The Bling Ring*'s sequence shows cast members' names
      superimposed over shoes   263
19.3 Marie Antoinette's lavender blue Converse high-tops sit
      alongside Manolo Blahnik-designed high heels   267
20.1 Huppert at Cannes, 2015   285
20.2 Nathalie wears brown espadrilles while teaching in the park   287
20.3 Nathalie's shoes bear her forward   288

Acknowledgements

The editors of the book would above all like to thank Gillian Leslie for her unwavering enthusiasm and support for the project from its inception. Our thanks also go to Pamela Church-Gibson for her encouragement, Zoë Ross for her eagle-eyed copy-editing and Richard Strachan for steering the book through to completion.

Shoe Reels has been a terrifically fun book to edit. But when we were plotting this book in sunny Gothenburg, sporting sandals and sneakers, we had no idea that we would be finishing the final edits from our respective homes, outdoor shoes long abandoned, feet entrenched in well-worn slippers. We are grateful to all our contributors for their professionalism and good humour, even during a global pandemic.

Notes on contributors

Lucy Bolton is Reader in Film Studies at Queen Mary University of London. She is the author of *Film and Female Consciousness: Irigaray, Cinema and Thinking Women*, and *Contemporary Cinema and the Philosophy of Iris Murdoch*, as well as the co-editor of *Lasting Screen Stars: Images that Fade and Personas that Endure*. She is currently working on an anthology of feminist film philosophy and a monograph on philosophy and film stardom.

Malgorzata Bugaj is a teaching fellow of Film Media and Contemporary Cultures at the University of Edinburgh's Centre for Open Learning. She teaches courses on twentieth century avant-garde film, European cinema, film theory, female filmmakers and cinema and the five senses. Her recent publications include journal articles and book chapters on synaesthesia in film, intermediality and auteurs of Polish and Russian cinema.

Ian Christie is Anniversary Professor of Film and Media History at Birkbeck, University of London and also teaches for Gresham College and the National Film and Television School. He has curated and written extensively on Powell and Pressburger, with audio commentaries on *The Red Shoes* and *A Canterbury Tale*, and on Sergei Eisenstein and Russian cinema and culture. His most recent work has been on the origins of British cinema, with a multi-strand project on Robert Paul in 2019 and a forthcoming co-edited collection *The Eisenstein Universe*.

Elizabeth Ezra is Professor of Cinema and Culture at the University of Stirling. She is the author of *The Cinema of Things: Globalization and the Posthuman Object* and *The Colonial Unconscious: Race and Culture in Interwar France*, as well as books on the work of Georges Méliès and Jean-Pierre Jeunet. She has edited books on European cinema, transnational cinema (with Terry

Rowden), and film and French national identity (with Sue Harris). She is also a children's author and does practice-led research in the field of children's literature and cinema.

Margaret C. Flinn is Associate Professor in the Department of French and Italian and the Program in Film Studies at The Ohio State University. She is the author of *The Social Architecture of French Cinema, 1929–39*, as well as articles and book chapters on a variety of topics in twentieth and twenty-first century French and Francophone cinema studies, comics studies and new media art.

Kelli Fuery is Associate Professor of Film Studies in Dodge College of Film and Media Arts at Chapman University, California. Her publications include: *Visual Cultures and Critical Theory* (co-authored), *New Media: Culture and Image* (2008) and *Wilfred Bion, Thinking and Emotional Experience with Moving Images* (2018). Her current project examines Simone de Beauvoir's theory of ambiguity in relation to women's filmmaking. She is the Special Issues editor for the North American undergraduate research journal *Film Matters*.

Hannah Hamad is Senior Lecturer in Media and Communication at Cardiff University, School of Journalism, Media and Culture. She is the author of *Postfeminism and Paternity in Contemporary Hollywood Film: Framing Fatherhood* and is working on a book on film, feminism and rape culture in the Yorkshire Ripper years.

Fiona Handyside is Associate Professor of Film Studies at the University of Exeter. She has written *Cinema at the Shore: The Beach in French Film* and *Sofia Coppola: A Cinema of Girlhood*. She edited *Eric Rohmer: Interviews* and co-edited *International Cinema and the Girl: Local Issues, Global Contexts* with Kate Taylor-Jones. She has recently completed a special edition of the journal *Film Studies* on the topic of 'Difficult Women' with Lavinia Brydon.

Christopher Holliday teaches Film Studies and Liberal Arts at King's College London specialising in Hollywood cinema, animation and contemporary digital media. He has published several book chapters and articles on digital technology and computer animation, including work in *Animation Practice, Process & Production* and *animation: an interdisciplinary journal*. He is the author of *The Computer-Animated Film: Industry, Style and Genre* and co-editor of *Fantasy/Animation: Connections Between Media, Mediums and Genres* and *Snow White and the Seven Dwarfs: New Perspectives on Production, Reception, Legacy*. He is also the co-creator and curator of *fantasy-animation.org*

Pamela Hutchinson is a freelance writer, critic and film historian who contributes regularly to *Sight & Sound*, *The Guardian*, Criterion, Indicator and the BBC, specialising in silent and classic cinema and women in film. She is a guest lecturer at the National Film and Television School, and a member of both Fipresci and the London Film Critics' Circle. She has written essays for several edited collections and is the author of the BFI Film Classic on *Pandora's Box* and the editor of *30-Second Cinema*. She also writes the silent cinema website Silent London.

Rachael Langford is Professor of French Studies and Pro Vice-Chancellor and Dean of the Faculty of Humanities and Social Sciences at Oxford Brookes University. She holds an MA from Oxford University and a PhD from Cambridge University and was formerly head of the School of Modern Languages at Cardiff University. She teaches and publishes on French and Francophone colonial cultures and on Francophone African visual cultures, particularly film and photography.

Keith Lodwick is Curator of Theatre and Screen Arts at the V&A. Keith curated the touring exhibition *Vivien Leigh: Public Faces, Private Lives* and was the V&A curator for the major V&A exhibition *Hollywood Costume*, one of the most successful exhibitions in the museum's history. Keith has contributed to the following publications: *Diaghilev and the Golden Age of the Ballets Russes*; *Oliver Messel: In the Theatre of Design*; *Hollywood Costume*; *Alexander McQueen: Savage Beauty*; and *Vivien Leigh: Actress and Icon*.

Tyler Parks is an Associate Lecturer of Film Studies at the University of St Andrews, where he teaches film history and film theory as well as modules on Eco-cinema, Film Noir and Political Aesthetics. His research focuses on the politics and ethics of alternative cinematic practices; landscape, history and place in the 'avant-doc'; and film style in East Asian Cinemas.

Eugenia Paulicelli is Professor of Italian, Comparative Literature and Women's and Gender Studies at the Graduate Center and Queens College, CUNY. At the Graduate Center she founded and coordinates the Concentration in Fashion Studies in the Master of Arts in Liberal Studies (MALS). Her latest publications include: *Italian Style: Fashion & Film from Early Cinema to the Digital Age*; (co-editor) *Film and Fashion in the 1960s*; and *Moda e Cinema in Italia. Dal Muto ai giorni nostri*. She is founder and director of the film festival 'Italian Cinema CUNY' (IC-CUNY: https://iccuny.commons.gc.cuny.edu/)

Robert A. Rushing is Professor of Italian and Professor and Director of the Program in Comparative Literature at the University of Illinois, Urbana-Champaign. He is the author of *Resisting Arrest: Detective Fiction and Popular*

Culture and *Descended from Hercules: Biopolitics and the Muscled Male Body on Screen*. He is co-editor of two volumes on television, one on *Mad Men* and one on *Orphan Black*. He has published widely on Italian cinema, especially popular genres, and literature from Ovid to Italo Calvino.

Ana Salzberg is a Lecturer in Film Studies and Visual Culture at the University of Dundee. She is the author of *Beyond the Looking Glass: Narcissism and Female Stardom in Studio-Era Hollywood* and *Produced by Irving Thalberg: Theory of Studio-Era Filmmaking*.

Jeff Scheible is a Lecturer in Film Studies at King's College London, where he teaches on American cinema, race, new media, television and contemporary film. He is the author of *Digital Shift: The Cultural Logic of Punctuation* and the co-editor of *Deep Mediations*.

Kate Taylor-Jones is Professor of East Asian Cinema at the University of Sheffield. She has published on topics including colonial Japanese and Korean cinema, cinema and landscape in East Asia and domestic violence and the sex trade. She is author of *Divine Work: Japanese Colonial Cinema and its Legacy* and editor-in-chief of the East Asian Journal of Popular Culture. She is co-editor of *International Cinema and the Girl: Local Issues, Transnational Contexts* and *Prostitution and Sex Work in Global Cinema: New Takes on Fallen Women*.

Louise Wallenberg holds a PhD in Cinema Studies from Stockholm University, Sweden. Between 2007 and 2013 she was the establishing Director at the Centre for Fashion Studies and currently she is Professor of Fashion Studies in the Department of Media Studies at that same university. She has published on cinema, gender, sexuality and fashion and is currently writing a book on women filmworkers' experiences in the Swedish film industry and co-editing one book on fashion ethics and aesthetics, and one on Ingmar Bergman's film at the crossroads between theory and practice.

Catherine Wheatley is Senior Lecturer in Film Studies at King's College London. Her books include *Stanley Cavell and Film: Scepticism and Self-Reliance at the Cinema, Michael Haneke's Cinema: The Ethic of the Image*, the BFI Film Classics book on *Caché* and, with Lucy Mazdon, *Sex, Art and Cinephilia: French Cinema in Britain*. Catherine also writes regularly for *Sight & Sound* magazine and is a contributor to the BFI's Philosophical Screens series.

Foreword by the series editor

Film and Fashions is a new series, designed to address a particular gap within contemporary critical literature. The use of the word 'fashions', the plural rather than the singular, indicates a wish that the series will extend its reach beyond the clothes we see on screen to wider considerations of style and culture; the influence of cinema was not confined to clothes and hairstyles.

I am delighted that this particular anthology, *Shoe Reels: The History and Philosophy of Footwear in Film*, which meets these hopes, is to open the series. It is an impressive work of scholarship, eclectic in its reach and diverse in its content. The editors have brought together a distinguished group of scholars from the fields of film and fashion; the breadth and variety of the chosen topics is both impressive and refreshing. Ranging across cinema from its infancy to the present day, it also covers diverse cinematic forms and spans the globe. In short, it sets a benchmark for the series.

Pamela Church Gibson

Introduction: foot notes

Elizabeth Ezra and Catherine Wheatley

> [T]here is something undeniably intimate, romantic even, to the humble shoe. In shoes we trudge, often along lowly paths, through detritus and debris, and yet they can solicit the highest praise. They are capable of elevating us in every sense.
>
> Shahidha Bari, *Dressed: The Secret Life of Clothes*

'Everything begins with the feet.' So writes Bernard Stiegler in the first volume of *Technics and Time* (Stiegler 1998: 112). Undoubtedly the directors of films such as *Strangers on a Train* (Alfred Hitchcock, USA, 1951), *Saturday Night Fever* (John Badham, USA, 1977) and *Footloose* (Herbert Ross, USA, 1984) would agree: after all, the opening sequences of these films convey a great deal of information by focusing attention on the shoes worn by their protagonists. So, too, would Carrie Bradshaw of the television franchise *Sex and the City* (Darren Star, USA, 1998–2004), perhaps the screen's most famous lover of shoes. But as Christian Louboutin told Lauren Collins in an article for *The New Yorker*, 'a shoe has so much more to offer than just to walk' (Collins 2011).

So what is it that shoes actually *do*? They are necessary for many types of work, dance and sport. Besides protecting the feet, they contribute to the performance of gender; they indicate aspects of personality, sexuality, race, ethnicity and social class; and they serve as tools of seduction.

Shoes have also contributed to expressions of national identity. In August 1918 production began in France of the '*chaussure nationale*' ('national shoe') in order to combat rising prices and presumably as a way of uniting a war-ravaged country around the shared benefits of affordable footwear. Leather was provided for this purpose by the Ministry of Industrial Reconstruction, the production of which was overseen by the War Ministry (Hertz 1920: 49). Although manufacture ceased in April of the following year, the national shoe played a small role in helping France get back on its feet after the war. Indeed, the cultural valency of shoes and their symbolism in the modern age have been demonstrated at the highest levels of state. One-time Philippines First Lady Imelda Marcos's shoe collection, reportedly comprising more than 1,000 pairs, was long cited as an emblem of political kleptocracy. More recently, former British Prime Minister Theresa May's leopard-print kitten heels made waves in the news media for their suggestion of rebellious femininity and whiff of hedonism, while former Scottish Conservative Party leader Ruth Davidson raised eyebrows by tweeting a photo of Gillian Anderson in stilettos, with the words 'Right. I'm off for a fortnight. In the mean time [*sic*], here's @GillianA just sitting round the house in stilettos and seamed stockings. As you do.' Shoes, especially women's shoes, often act as a lightning rod, invoking (or distracting from) larger political and cultural debates.

Shoes are also ripe for metaphorical appropriation in the English language. To 'put oneself in another person's shoes' is widely used as an expression of empathy, 'filling another person's shoes' suggests taking over for someone, and the 'dropping of shoes' indicates bad news. A 'goody two-shoes', named after the heroine of an eighteenth-century children's story, is someone who ostentatiously does no wrong. 'Pulling oneself up by one's bootstraps' is an essential component of the American Dream, signifying the overcoming of adversity by dint of hard work and a can-do attitude. 'Riding roughshod', an expression linked to horseshoes affixed with projecting nails, connotes brutal disregard for the best interests of someone or something; if something is 'slipshod', which originally meant to wear slippers or loose shoes, it is careless or negligent; and the term 'down-at-heel', meaning destitute, comes from the image of worn-down shoes. Doing things 'backwards and in high heels' refers to Ginger Rogers' position in her dances with Fred Astaire and is a metaphor for the double standard faced by women having to do everything men do, with the added obstacle of sexist objectification (the line originally comes from a 1982 Frank and Ernest cartoon). Shoes, perhaps more than any other item of clothing (with the possible exception of hats), are almost endlessly expressive, floating signifiers of the fashion world. They would say a lot even if they didn't have tongues.

Certainly shoes exert a powerful hold on the imagination of some of our greatest thinkers and artists. Karl Marx and Vincent Van Gogh in the nineteenth century, Walter Benjamin, Martin Heidegger, Charlie Chaplin and Walker Evans in the twentieth, are amongst those who have 'tracked aesthetic value, social standing and the meaning of labour through the boots of workers' (Rabinowitz 2011a: 185). Meanwhile, following Sigmund Freud's consideration of the shoe as fetish object, thinkers such as Simone de Beauvoir, Frantz Fanon, Virginia Woolf and Naomi Wolf have understood that shoes can signal freedom or constraint, work or leisure, depending on the context in which they are worn. Perhaps this is because shoes facilitate mobility – both literal mobility and social mobility. Shoes thus come to serve as emblems of both labour and of fashion: 'a commercial industry producing and selling material commodities; a socio-cultural force bound up with the dynamics of modernity and post-modernity; and an intangible system of signification' (Rocamora and Smelik 2016: 2).

For Marx, the birth of fashion coincides with the birth of modernity. In his *Communist Manifesto*, Marx depicts 'the shock of the new', when social and class relations were no longer determined by a fixed hierarchy but instead by the concept of social mobility based on financial capital. Alongside this change in social behaviours came a change in habits and significance of dress: a competitive cycle of fashionable emulation and symbolic distinction developed. Marx's particular interest in fashion was connected to the exploitation of human labour in the production of these fashion commodities. In volume one of *Capital* he examines the textile industry, arguing that no matter how beautiful or practical the fashion item might be, it is always produced at the cost of 'deformity' for the worker (Rocamora and Smelik 2016: 37). This is an argument revived by contemporary debates surrounding the use of child labour and exploitation of workers in the production of high street fashion, as made manifest, for example, in Stacey Dooley's BBC documentary *Blood, Sweat and T-shirts*.

Commodity fetishism is a belief in the power of objects themselves, sold to consumers as goods that can change their lives. In order to illustrate commodity fetishism, Marx gives the example of boots (Ibid.: 72). Footwear becomes the quintessential example of a product once worn in order to work which becomes a product separated from use-value and becomes instead an object that masks the labour that has gone into its own production. Walter Benjamin describes such a fetishised commodity as a

> phantasmagoria . . . a consumer item in which there is no longer anything that is supposed to remind us how it came into being. It becomes a magical object, insofar as the labor stored up in it comes to seem supernatural and sacred at the very moment when it can no longer be recognised as labor. (Benjamin 1999: 669)

Again taking shoes as a key example of such transformation, he quotes (Ibid.: 594) from Leon Halevy's poem, *La Chaussure*:

> This people, whose head and hand you fear,
> Must march, must march – no halting!
> It's when you stop their steps
> They notice the holes in their shoes.

As shoes become a fetishised commodity, they are transformed from clothing – a 'stable and functional form of dress that alters only gradually' – into fashion, which 'thrives on novelty and change' (Arnold 2009: 3). We dismiss fashion at our peril, for as Rocamora and Smelik astutely note, fashion is 'the most specific manifestation of capitalism's will-to-change' (Rocamora and Smelik 2016: 82). Fashion can be homogenising, encouraging everyone to dress in a certain way. At the same time, it often hinges on a search for individuality and self-expression. It is characterised by an inherent self-contradiction, 'obsessed with the new, yet it constantly harks back to the past' (Arnold 2009: 2).

Arnold's words would seem an apposite description not only of fashion but of Hollywood, another capitalist machine running in constant pursuit of novelty yet nostalgic for a time before. The two industries coalesce in Budd Schulberg's novel *What Makes Sammy Run* (1941), an elegant satire of Hollywood first published in 1941. Here the progression of Sammy Glick's cut-throat ascent to the top of a Golden Age studio is marked by his ever-changing and increasingly expensive footwear. Sammy's story is narrated by Al Manheim, a journalist-turned-screenwriter whose career Sammy hijacks. Sammy's venality is first signalled when he hoodwinks four dollars out of Manheim, money that ends up on his feet:

> They were brand new the way only shoes can be new, stiff and shiny and still in the window. They were a highly polished yellow-brown leather that made up in gloss what it lacked in quality, small neat shoes that came to a point too stylishly narrow for everyday use. (Schulberg 1993: 13)

As Sammy climbs the Hollywood ladder, every step is signalled by the acquisition of a new pair of shoes. When he sells his first (stolen) screenplay, his brown alligator shoes 'scream newness'. In his first office he sports *huaraches*, gifted to him by a director. Later, taking on the unions, he sports Cromwells. 'I've got a standing order for a couple of pairs a year,' he tells Manheim (Ibid.: 132). At the peak of his success, Manheim watches a man tracing the outline of Sammy's feet onto paper, to custom make the shoes that will continue to bear Sammy forward into his bright shiny future. Four bucks. Fifteen bucks. Fifty. Priceless. Sammy – the epitome of the American Dream – is the 'frantic marathoner' of life, 'sprinting out of his mother's womb, turning life into a race in which the only rules are fight for the rail, and elbow on the turn, and the only finish-line is death' (Ibid.: xvii). His shoes are emblematic not only of Hollywood, but of America as a whole. 'How do we slow Sammy down?' asks Schulberg. Perhaps the more important question is: 'How do we slow down the whole culture he threatens to run away with and that threatens to run away with us?' (Ibid.: xviii).

But Sammy – born in Brooklyn to Jewish parents – bespeaks other, more primal, urges to run: not towards, but away. In his memoir of Auschwitz, *The Truce*, Primo Levi writes that in war, 'the first thing is shoes, and second is eating', because 'if you have shoes, then you can run' (Levi 1991: 34). When Bernard Stiegler writes that 'everything begins with the feet' he is quoting the paleoanthropologist André Leroi-Gourhan, who developed the idea that human language and tool use – the features that separate us from other animals – are the result not of expanded brain use but of becoming upright. 'The brain was not the cause of locomotor adaption but the beneficiary' (Gere 2006: 16). As Charlie Gere explains, the achievement of upright posture frees the hands for tool use, which in turn frees the lower jaw for language. The upright posture also enables the spinal column to support a heavier braincase enabling the expansion of the cortex – the area of the brain that controls speech (Ibid.: 16). In short, to be shod is to be human. As a child, Sammy has no shoes of his own: he has to shuffle around in the too-large hand-me-downs passed on by his brother, Israel. The pervasiveness of the Cinderella story means we all know what it means when the shoe fits. But what if the shoe doesn't fit? In the Iraqi film *Children of Heaven* (Majid Majidi, 1997) a young girl loses her shoes and is forced to share her brother's worn tennis shoes. The ensuing narrative turns around their attempts to negotiate who wears the shoes when, so as best to survive their impoverished existence in Tehran. The brother longs for new trainers; the sister for party shoes. For both, the wearing of shoes is fraught with compromise.

As objects designed for the body, shoes also affirm the materiality of individual bodies and the endurance of the human body itself when physical presence has been progressively de-emphasised, first with the advent of technical reproducibility based on indexicality (printing, photography, cinema, radio and the like), and now with the rise of digital technology in the virtual era. The very materiality of shoes – the fact that they are things – is what makes them ripe for analysis. Things have at least as much to tell us about human society as humans have to tell us about things. As Arjun Appadurai puts it, 'even though from a theoretical point of view human actors encode things with significance, from a methodological point of view it is the things-in-motion that illuminate their human and social context' (Appadurai 1986: 5). Objects and subjects shed light on one another; they belong to the same ecosystem, the same semantic field. For Bruno Latour, 'the human, as we now understand, cannot be grasped and saved unless that other part of itself, the share of things, is restored to it' (Latour 1993: 136). Shoes are that other part – or at least *an* other part – of human beings. They humanise, setting people apart from non-human animals (with the exception of horses, who are often shod by humans), but, empty, they can also serve to dehumanise. Paula Rabinowitz points to '[t]he lone shoe lying in the middle of the street following the shooting of Red Army Faction leader Rudi Dutschke ... the catalogue of photographs of articles of clothing, mostly shoes, – remains of the slaughtered men of Srebenica' (Rabinowitz 2011a: 191). Shari Benstock and Suzanne Ferriss give other examples: the 1994 protest in Washington, DC, where 38,000 pairs of shoes stood in for victims of gun violence in the United States, and the demonstrations in Paris and other French cities in which empty shoes symbolised more than 600,000 civilians killed by landmines (Benstock & Ferriss 2001: 8). Most potently and most consistently, empty shoes have been used in photographs, paintings, poems and memorials, as in *Night and Fog* (*Nuit et brouillard*) (Alain Resnais, France, 1956), in which the iconic mountains of shoes retrieved from the victims of Nazi death camps are a stark reminder of the abasement that is the precondition for and product of genocide. The piles of shoes, jumbled up in an almost indistinct mass, figure the effacement of differentiation among individuals that heralds atrocity. In their excess, these shoes are, to a certain extent, the mirror image of hyper-consumption, the product of instrumental reason pushed to its logical conclusion. As Ellen Carol Jones puts it in an essay titled 'Empty Shoes', 'abject survivors of the abjection suffered by the men and women and children killed in the Shoah, the shoes – derelict, decaying – figure the abandonment of European Jewry by the West, the decomposition of a people under the Nazis' (Jones 2001: 197). When our shoes outlive us, they haunt those surviving with the spectre of death. Perhaps this explains the potency and the poignancy of the six-word story, apocryphally attributed to Ernest Hemingway: *For sale, Baby shoes, Never worn.*

The structural opposite of the empty shoe, it could be argued, is the unshod foot. Maureen Turim reads *Children of Heaven* as a 'celebration of [the children's] barefooted grit and determination', arguing that 'we trust bare feet ... more than fancy shoes' (Turim 2001: 85). The fashion theorist Janet Lyon paints a rather more ambivalent picture, however, when she contrasts a ballerina's shod feet with the exposed feet of the modern dancer. The modern dancer's feet represent 'freedom, sexuality, and abandon' – to be unshod is to be untethered from social positioning. But at the same time, critics associated bare feet with 'bestiality and moral degeneration' (Lyons 2001: 278). For these critics, the bare foot is somehow primal, less than human, abject: a position that elides a wealth of socio-cultural nuance, but that gestures towards the deeply embedded Western association of shoes with civilisation.

For Shahidha Bari, wearing shoes 'imparts a basic sense of dignity' (Bari 2019: 150). But questions of dignity are tied to shoes in other ways, too. We might think, say, of the profession of shoeshining, depicted (more or less

Figure I.1 The pile of empty shoes in *Nuit et brouillard*

accurately) in films of Golden Age Hollywood as a trade practiced predominantly by African Americans in service to white Americans. For example, Fred Astaire, a white dancer who excelled in a predominantly black dance form, seemed to acknowledge this tradition in films such as *The Band Wagon* (Vincente Minnelli, USA, 1953), in which he dances while getting his shoes shined by an African American man, and *Swing Time* (George Stevens, USA, 1936), in which he appears in black face before a set painted with an enormous caricature of an African face, which pulls apart to reveal two giant shoes. Shoes in these dance numbers are not only a prosthesis helping a dancer move his body rhythmically, but also decoration and metaphor. And yet – or perhaps because of this – both films have caused a certain measure of controversy, not least because Astaire appropriates the dance styles of both Bill Robinson and Lee Daniels, the figures to whom he is ostensibly paying tribute in these sequences. At the end of *The Band Wagon* Astaire tap-dances out of the shot, the metal plates of his shoes ringing on the soundtrack, while Daniels is left on his knees. For the philosopher Stanley Cavell, this final shot is a deliberate gesture towards the invisible labour (again!) of black dancers (Cavell 2006: 18). For Robert Gooding-Williams, on the other hand, Astaire is almost literally attempting to fill Daniels' shoes (Gooding-Williams 2006: 245).

Figure I.2 Lee Daniels and Fred Astaire in *The Band Wagon*'s shoeshine number

Shoes can be objects of abjection, appropriation and subjugation. But they an also be implicated in violence and rebellion. Rabinowitz gives the example of the Iraqi journalist Muntadhar al-Zaidi, who, on 14 December 2008, hurled his black leather Oxfords at then-US president George W. Bush during the latter's 'farewell' visit to the nation he had invaded five years before (Rabinowitz 2011b: 237). The act inspired a number of shoe-related demonstrations, including

> a Mexican student setting fire to his shoe at a demonstration in front of the United States Embassy in Mexico City protesting Israel's war on January 11, 2009 . . .; another student, Selcuk Ozbek of Anadolu University, flinging his shoe, a Nike sneaker this time, at Dominique Strauss-Kahn, director of the International Monetary Fund at a speech at Bilgi University in Turkey. (Ibid.)

We might think, too, of Richard Colvin Reid, who in 2001 attempted to detonate an explosive device packed into his shoes while on an American Airlines flight, or of Nikita Khrushchev denouncing capitalism by banging on the United Nations table with his shoe. The word sabotage comes from *sabot*, the French wooden clogs that eighteenth-century workers threw into the machinery of mills as an act of defiance. Stilettos are named after daggers.

If Carrie Bradshaw tells us that to understand the woman we need to walk in her shoes, for Martin Heidegger it is sufficient to *see* the shoes. In his famous interpretation of Vincent Van Gogh's painting *A Pair of Shoes* (Heidgger [1886] 2002), Heidegger argues that shoes tell us all we need to know about the world of the person who walks in them. In the case of Van Gogh's painting, we learn this not through a description of the pair of shoes, nor by a report on how to make shoes, but by *looking* at the shoes. Heidegger thus gestures towards the power of the visual arts to show us human truths through images of footwear and the feet they conceal or reveal, a power that finds its fullest expression in the cinema. From Chaplin's meal of boots (*The Gold Rush*, USA, 1925), through Powell and Pressburger's titular red shoes (UK, 1948) and Dorothy's ruby slippers (*The Wizard of Oz*, USA, 1939), to Julia Roberts's PVC thigh-highs (*Pretty Woman*, USA, 1990), Marty McFly's power-lacing Nikes (*Back to the Future*, USA, 1985) and the slim, spike-heeled stiletto that graces the poster for *The Devil Wears Prada* (David Frankel, USA, 2006), shoes are not only some of the cinema's most enduring icons but they also serve as tools of characterisation, plot devices, soundtracks, metaphors and philosophical touchpoints. The wearing of shoes tells us a great deal both about the wearer and about the time and place in which the shoes are worn. Forrest Gump put it succinctly when he said: 'You can tell a lot about a person by their shoes – where they goin', where they've been.'

Figure I.3 Chaplin eats his boots in *The Gold Rush*

For Maureen Turim, 'shoes are shown from the earliest films to be sites of inscription, a way of writing the body. They should be considered alongside such significant and far more recognised sites as the face, the eyes, the hat or the hair, and the hand' (Turim 2001: 61). In an essay entitled 'High Angles on Shoes: Cinema, Gender and Footwear', Turim describes, amongst other things, the capacity of shoes to shape the form of film. Shoes serve as metonomy, she states, as in the famous Odessa Steps sequence of *Battleship Potemkin* (Sergei Eisenstein, Soviet Union, 1925). In films from *The Gay Shoe Clerk* (Edwin Porter, USA, 1903), to *Double Indemnity* (Billy Wilder, USA, 1944), to *Clueless* (Amy Heckerling, USA, 1995) shoes call for close-ups; often – but not always – these close-ups are the opening shot in a familiar vertical pan that moves up the body and comes to rest on the face. In dance film – in the films of Rogers and Astaire, for example – shoes are very rarely shown. Yet the movement of feet across the dance floor, the rhythmic patter of ballroom shoes or the metallic strikes of tap shoes, which shape the *mise en scène*, are key to the aesthethic of these films (Ibid.: 73–4).

Shoes not only play a key role in the narrative and *mise en scène* of many historically significant films; they also pop up behind the scenes in the history of film production and exhibition. In the late nineteenth century, financial capital provided by Georges Méliès's family boot factory allowed him to finance his pioneering film studio, which lends a particular poignancy to the fact that during the First World War many of his films were burned in order to make army boots. At the end of the twentieth century, Daniel Day-Lewis famously took a hiatus from his acting career in order to learn the craft of shoemaking in Italy. In 2012, the Empire Cinema chain thought it necessary to publish guidelines urging viewers to keep their shoes on in the cinema. In 2015 'Flatgate' erupted at the Cannes Film Festival, as several women were barred from a screening for wearing flats, and in 2018 Kristen Stewart protested against the restrictive high-heels policy at Cannes by removing her shoes and walking down the red carpet barefoot while carrying her stilettos – mobilising, once more, those associations of bare feet with all that is primitive, abandoned, beyond.

Nowhere, perhaps, is the relationship to shoes more vexed than in questions of gender. Shoes are privileged sites of gender performance and identification (witness the cowboy boot, or the importance of stiletto heels in a drag queen's kit). It is therefore notable that in the film that is credited as the first in history to explicitly eroticise women's footwear, Porter's 1903 *The Gay Shoe Clerk*, the female customer whose foot and ankle so excite the eponymous clerk is actually played by a man. This scenario evokes a fetishist's vision of a woman as a castrated man and the subsequent disavowal of the imagined castration through a phantasmagoric replacement of the supposedly 'missing' member with a nearby object – in this case, a shoe.

Many readers will already be familiar with Freud's writing on fetishism, where he announces 'that the fetish is a substitute for the penis ... To put it more plainly: the fetish is a substitute for the woman's (the mother's) penis that the little boy once believed in and – for reasons familiar to us – does not want to give up' (Freud 1959: 52–3). The shoe is at once a reminder of an absent penis and a 'symbol of the *female* genitals' (Ibid.: 153, emphasis in original). In this construction, the shoe is thus a stand-in for both a phallus and vagina: a reminder of the threat (of castration), and a soothing disavowal of it. As Summer Brennan wryly puts it:

> this reading lends a startling cast to the classic fairy tales – to the piercing foot pain felt by the little mermaid when she steps into the world of men, or the young girl whose red shoes won't let her stop dancing even after she no longer consents, to what Cinderella may have *really* lost to the prince at the ball. (Brennan, 2019: 27)

Throughout the history of film, the high-heeled woman is presented as a threat to masculinity, most notably in film noir (Rabinowitz and Georcelli 2011), but also in 1990s erotic thrillers such as *Disclosure* (Barry Levinson, USA, 1994) and *Basic Instinct* (Paul Verhoeven, USA, 1992). Indeed Barbet Schroeder's 1992 *Single White Female* literalises this threat in the indelible image of Jennifer Jason Leigh stabbing her lover through the eye with the heel of her black patent stiletto. Of course, a woman can kill with her heel, but not run in it, as Naomi Wolf astutely points out in *The Beauty Myth* (Wolf 1990: 246). In ancient China and contemporary ballet companies alike, women bind their bleeding feet in the name of beauty. *Sex and the City*'s Carrie Bradshaw can't afford her apartment because she has spent all her money on shoes. The little mermaid is left in agony by the shoes into which she must force her newly sprung feet. Paula/Victoria Page in *The Red Shoes* (Michael Powell and Emeric Pressburger, UK, 1948) dances to her death. In more ways than one, shoes cripple women. No wonder they wield them as weapons.

Objects *par excellence* of hyper-consumption, shoes are situated at the crossroads of sexual fetishism and commodity fetishism. Whether they are practical or extravagant depends on cost, number and comfort. Beyond protecting part of the body from the elements and from rough ground, shoes have come to symbolise, among other things, creative expression, fun, seduction and frivolity, and commodity culture's worst excesses. They are implicated in violence and in mourning. They are mobilised as objects of celebration and commemoration. As such, they take on a quasi-spiritual quality. 'In the magical thinking of American advertising, shoes have acquired a talismanic significance' (Benstock and Ferriss 2001: 6).

Figure I.4 A stiletto heel drips blood in *Single White Female*

Shoes are clearly more than just good to wear, then: to paraphrase Claude Lévi-Strauss, they are also good to think. The essays in this collection think with shoes, and about shoes, through film's unique focus. *Shoe Reels* examines the special relationship between footwear and film, exploring images of shoes in cinema, what they mean in the context of narrative, aesthetics and symbolism, why they are so memorable and what their wider cultural resonance might be. Written by experts from a range of disciplines, including film and television studies, philosophy, history and fashion, this volume covers cinema from its origins to the present day. The first three chapters analyse silent films from France, Italy and the USA, the three biggest film-producing nations before the First World War. All the films discussed in these chapters focus on shoes as an expression and a tool of social mobility. Margaret C. Flinn's chapter examines a Max Linder film composed entirely of shots of shoes. She shows how the eponymous character in 'Max's Stylish Shoes' (France, 1912) manipulates sartorial convention by convincing his future in-laws that his worn-out working man's boots are the height of fashion, to which they, too, must aspire. Flinn refers to this confidence trick as a 'sleight-of-foot', which allows the sly Max to profit from his bumbling mismanagement of objects to turn misfortune into an advantage, while exposing the fragility of bourgeois pretensions. Similarly, Malgorzata Bugaj's chapter, 'A girl and a shoe: Marcel Fabre's *Amor Pedestre*' (Italy, 1914), discusses a subgenre of films in the silent era that focused entirely on shoe-clad feet, questioning the commonly held perception that silent film was dependent for its emotional force on shots of the face and hands. Bugaj shows that this film challenges convention and rewrites the grammar of cinema in the early days of its development in its emphasis on shoes as markers of gender and class. Likewise, Pamela Hutchinson's essay also focuses on the capacity of shoes to signify class and gender in two films that American director Lois Weber made in 1916 (*Shoes*) and 1921 (*The Blot*). Although these films show more than feet, they nonetheless give shoes a starring role in exposing wage inequality and provoking discussion of the rights of women, highlighting the function of these sartorial commodities as signifiers of social class in an era of burgeoning consumer culture.

The following chapters move into early decades of the sound era, exploring shoes as the stuff of fairy tales and fantasy, which can nonetheless tell us a lot about real-world concerns. In her chapter, Elizabeth Ezra explores the idea that there can be a 'right' shoe and a 'wrong' shoe, equating symbolically with people's positions in the social order. She argues that magic shoes in particular (such as Cinderella's glass slipper, or those worn by Dorothy in *The Wizard of Oz*), which have historically been used to represent monogamy, class and even sexual preference, may appear to offer fantasies of social mobility, but they ultimately reinforce traditional hierarchies and structures of exclusion. Dorothy's ruby slippers are also the subject of the chapter by Keith Lodwick, curator at the Victoria and Albert Museum in London who helped oversee the *Hollywood Costume* exhibition in 2012–13. In his account of the ruby slippers' journey to London, Lodwick details the extraordinary efforts made by the museum to get hold of a priceless piece of film history, and the role of storytelling in conveying the importance of these treasures to the public. An almost equally famous pair of red shoes is the focus of Ian Christie's chapter on the 1948 Powell and Pressburger *The Red Shoes*, which examines the production history of the classic film and analyses the ways in which it refigures the original Hans Christian Andersen fairy tale. Post-war audiences embraced the magic world of the film, often while ignoring the darker aspects of the narrative, notably its violence and its gender politics. Christie compares these red shoes with Dorothy's ruby slippers, arguing that while the latter serve as symbols of domesticity, the bloody ballet shoes of the Powell and Pressburger film ultimately reject domesticity, taking women, as he puts it, 'far from home'.

A number of chapters in this volume explore the function of shoes in Hollywood films from the classical era. Kelli Fuery's essay on *Sullivan's Travels* (Preston Sturges, USA, 1941) uses Derrida's analysis of the parergon (a supplement or embellishment in the context of a work of art) to show how shoes in the film allow characters to move between binary states such as inside/outside, wealth/poverty and guilt/innocence. Ana Salzberg performs a close reading of the fashion show sequence in *How to Marry a Millionaire* (Jean Negulesco, USA, 1953), in which the transparent lucite heels worn by Marilyn Monroe act as a metaphor for the luxury afforded by the film's use of CinemaScope, which also invites viewers to 'see through' the film's visual splendour in order to notice intertextual references to other films starring the principal actors. Christopher Holliday's chapter examines the role of shoes in cartoons from the Golden Age of Hollywood animation, the 1930s through the 1950s, suggesting that, in their material specificity, animated shoes show us how objects can both describe characters and be characters in their own right. Paying particular attention to the faceless African American housemaid referred to as 'Mammy Two-Shoes', visible only by her footwear in several *Tom and Jerry* short films, Holliday draws parallels between the labour of film animation and that involved not only in domestic service but also in the manufacturing of shoes.

In her essay, Eugenia Paulicelli explores the life's work of an actual shoemaker, Salvatore Ferragamo, whose creations appeared in many Hollywood films in the classical era. Once again, social mobility is at the heart of this story, but in real life rather than on screen, as Paulicelli traces Ferragamo's rise from humble origins to shoe designer of the stars, both male and female. In the following chapters, by contrast, Robert Rushing and Louise Wallenberg both focus exclusively on shoes that construct an image of hypermasculinity. Rushing shows how gladiators' sandals in peplum (largely Italian, low-budget) films of the 1950s and 1960s problematise the apparent invincibility of the masculine hero, rendering him vulnerable by exposing the wearer's feet to the elements and to the gaze of the viewer. Wallenberg focuses on men's leather boots in films that span half a century, as attire for cowboys and workmen, which enable the performance (or masquerade) of masculinity. Similarly, Lucy Bolton's chapter examines the deployment of shoes as a trope of gender identity in Alfred Hitchcock's 1964 film *Marnie*, which endows feminine artifice with a significance that exceeds the merely 'decorative'. In an exploration of the intersection between sex and crime, Bolton focuses on the material objects – notably, shoes – that give rise to feminine masquerade and the construction of multiple identities.

Shoes can both confer and express power not only in the construction of gender roles, but also in geopolitical contexts in which they can be used as tools of protest and resistance. In her chapter on shoes in three African films, Rachael Langford, noting that clothing is an expression of power, examines the ways in which the 'resistant charge of footwear' expresses the tension between agency and oppression in three films made in the periods of immediate post-Independence and later neo-imperial globalisation. In particular, shod and bare feet are structurally opposed, but even within this opposition there exists what Langford calls a 'hierarchy of the dispossessed', in which sandals trump bare feet, and 'the boots of authority' trump sandals. But although they may be used to convey larger political messages, shoes always carry personal meaning for the individual wearer. Tyler Parks's essay captures footwear's capacity to express intimacy in Wong Kar-wai's *In the Mood for Love* (2000), showing how different types of footwear – in this case, slippers and high-heeled shoes – create two distinctive temporal (and moral) visions, oscillating between past and present, and between the culturally specific and the universal. Kate Taylor-Jones also focuses on East Asian cinema, writing about the world of Korean corporate crime drama, in which footwear is used to highlight sexual, class and ethnic tensions. Focusing on two films by director Im Sang-soo, *The Taste of Money* (2012) and *The Housemaid* (2010), Taylor-Jones shows how 'all the women are potentially coded as both the site of corporate corruption and the means by which it may be undone.'

The following chapters in this volume show how shoes can exploit hegemonic discourses such as advertising and stardom to make subversive points about subcultures such as African American men and white teenage girls, both of whom use their knowledge of branding to navigate the complex world of consumer culture. Jeff Scheible discusses Spike Lee's relationship with Nike throughout his career. In the extra-cinematic universe of what Scheible calls the 'Spike-o-sphere', characters from Lee's films 'take on lives beyond film frames and narrative boundaries' in advertisements and branding across a range of media platforms, and Nike shoes are a central feature of this universe. Scheible considers both the benefits and the political contradictions that arise within this cosy corporate partnership, especially when it comes to 'doing the right thing' by the African American community in the United States. In a similar vein, Hannah Hamad, writing on (post-) racial discourse and the symbolic significance of footwear in the stardom of Will Smith, focuses on the ways in which shoes can be key signifiers of blackness and masculinity. Two films in which Smith starred, *I, Robot* (Alex Proyas, USA, 2004) and *The Pursuit of Happyness* (Gabriele Muccino, USA, 2006), feature shoes as markers of both race and its transcendence, in what Hamad calls the 'cultural logic of post-racial America' on the eve of the Obama era. In her analysis of consumer culture in Sofia Coppola's films, Fiona Handyside discusses the specialist knowledge of teenage girls who display considerable familiarity with the complex codes of celebrity and designer clothing gleaned from the world of fashion magazines and social media. Rather than read this familiarity as a sign of superficiality or a symptom of pathologised hyper-consumption, Handyside argues that this knowledge is a form of expertise that recognises the artistic qualities of the designer articles in question – most notably, shoes. Finally, Catherine Wheatley looks at the way in which actress and character meet in the shoes of French star Isabelle Huppert in order to challenge assumptions about female stardom and performance.

There is no better medium than film in which to convey the myriad qualities of shoes, which have the capacity to be both very special and very ordinary. According to Maureen Turim, film is a 'kinetic museum of footwear history' (Turim 2001: 58), and this collection attempts to provide a glimpse into just such a kinetic museum. At the same time, it aims to capture the fundamental capacity of shoes to be all things to all people, without denying the specificity of each individual pair. As Lucy Johnston and Linda Woolley put it: 'Sculptural, beautiful, high-performance, impractical, evocative and personal – every shoe has its own story to tell' (Johnston and Woolley 2017: 8). The following pages recount some of these stories, in what we believe to be the first collection of its kind – the first steps in what we hope will be a long and productive journey.

References

Appadurai, Arjun (1986), 'Introduction: commodities and the politics of value', in *The Social Life of Things: Commodities in Cultural Perspective*, Cambridge: Cambridge University Press, pp. 3–63.

Arnold, Rebecca (2009), *Fashion: A Very Short Introduction*, Oxford: Oxford University Press.

Bari, Shahidha (2019), *Dressed: The Secret Life of Clothes*, London: Jonathan Cape.

Baudrillard, Jean ([1970] 1998), *Consumer Society: Myths and Structures*, London: Sage Publications.

Benjamin, Walter (2008), 'The Work of Art in the Age of its Technological Reproducibility', in M. W. Jennings, B. Doherty and Y. L. Thomas (eds), *The Work of Art in the Age of its Technological Reproducibility and Other Writings on Media*, Cambridge, MA: Belknap Press of Harvard University Press.

Benjamin, Walter (1999), *The Arcades Project*, trans. H. Eiland and K. McLauglin, Cambridge, MA: Belknap Press of Harvard University Press.

Benstock, Shari and Ferriss, Suzanne (eds) (2001), *Footnotes: On Shoes*, New York: New York University Press.

Brennan, Summer (2019), *High Heel*, London: Bloomsbury.

Cavell, Stanley (2006), *Philosophy the Day After Tomorrow*, Cambridge, MA: Belknap Press of Harvard University Press.

Collins, Lauren (2011), 'Sole Mate', *The New Yorker*, 28 March.

Evans, Caroline (2003), *Fashion at the Edge: Spectacle, Modernity and Deathliness*, New Haven, CT and London: Yale University Press.

Freud, Sigmund (1959), *Standard Edition of the Complete Psychological Works of Sigmund Freud*, ed. and trans. J. Strachey, London: Hogarth Press.

Georcelli, Cristina and Rabinowitz, Paula (2011), *Accessorizing the Body*, Minneapolis, MN: University of Minnesota Press.

Gere, Charlie (2006), *Art, Time and Technology*, Oxford and New York: Berg.

Gooding-Williams, Robert (2006), 'Aesthetics and Receptivity: Kant, Nietzsche, Cavell and Astaire', in A. Norris (ed.), *The Claim to Community: Essays on Stanley Cavell and Political Philosophy*, Stanford, CA: Stanford University Press, pp. 236–62.

Heidegger, Martin ([1886] 2002), 'The Origin of the Work of Art', in J. Young and K. Haynes (eds), *Off the Beaten Track*, Cambridge: Cambridge University Press, pp. 1–56.

Hertz, Norman (1920), *Hides and Leather in France*, Washington, DC: Department of Commerce 'Special Agents Series', no. 200/Government Printing Office.

Johnston, Lucy and Woolley, Linda (2017), *Shoes*, London: Thames and Hudson/V&A.

Jones, Ellen Carol (2001), 'Empty Shoes', in S. Benstock and S. Ferriss (eds), *Footnotes: On Shoes*, New York: New York University Press, pp. 197–231.

Latour, Bruno (1993), *We Have Never Been Modern*, trans. C. Porter, Cambridge, MA: Harvard University Press.

Levi, Primo (1991), *The Truce/If This is A Man*, trans. S. Woolf, London: Abacus.

Lindner, Christoph (2015), 'The Oblique Art of Shoes: Popular Culture, Aesthetic Pleasure and the Humanities', *Journal for Cultural Research*, vol. 19, no. 3, pp. 233–47.

Lyon, Janet (2001), 'The Modern Foot', in S. Benstock and S. Ferriss (eds), *Footnotes: On Shoes*, New York: New York University Press, pp. 272–81.

Marx, Karl ([1867] 1990), *Capital*, trans. S. Moore and E. Aveling, New York: International Publishers.

Rabinowitz, Paula (2011a), 'Barbara Stanwyck's Anklet: The Other Shoe', in C. Georcelli and P. Rabinowitz (eds), *Accessorizing the Body*, Minneapolis, MN: University of Minnesota Press, pp. 185–205.

Rabinowitz, Paula (2011b), 'In Clothing/Close Clothing', in C. Georcelli and P. Rabinowitz (eds), *Accessorizing the Body*, Minneapolis, MN: University of Minnesota Press, pp. 237–44.

Rocamora, Agnès and Smelik, Anneke (eds) (2016), *Thinking Through Fashion: A Guide to Key Theorists*, London and New York: I. B. Tauris.

Schulberg, Budd [1941] (1993), *What Makes Sammy Run*, New York: Random House.

Stiegler, Bernard (1998), *Technics and Time*, trans. R. Beardsworth and G. Collins, Stanford, CA: Stanford University Press, p. 112.

Turim, Maureen (2001), 'High Angles on Shoes: Cinema, Gender, and Footwear', in S. Benstock and S. Ferriss (eds), *Footnotes: On Shoes*, New York: New York University Press, pp. 58–87

Wilson, Elizabeth (2004), 'Magic Fashion', *Fashion Theory: The Journal of Dress, Body and Culture*, vol. 8, no. 4, pp. 375–85.

Wilson, Elizabeth (2003), *Adorned in Dreams: Fashion and Modernity*, London: I. B. Tauris.

Wolf, Naomi (1990), *The Beauty Myth: How Images of Beauty Are Used Against Women*, London: Chatto & Windus.

Chapter 1

Max's stylish shoes

Margaret C. Flinn

Across his œuvre, Max Linder's character 'Max' consistently misuses objects to comic effect, with his awkwardness or clumsiness demonstrating his uncouthness or inability to manage the everyday world. That everyday world is bourgeois and materially rich, thus Max's inability to master the objects that are his 'due' makes him into a sort of class failure. Shoes for the most part play a role consistent with that of other objects in Linder's films: they are somehow beyond Max's ability to manage them, and thereby they function as a reliable source of audience laughter.

   In the 1912[1] film *Max lance la mode/Max Sets the Style*, however, Max's bumbling with objects leads not (or at least not only) to him appearing as a figure of ridicule, but rather it opens an avenue of social critique when Max gets the better of society. On the morning of his nuptials, Max becomes so absorbed in attempting to tie his bow tie that he burns the soles off his fancy dress shoes. En route to the wedding, he purchases a broken-down pair of old hobnail boots from a passing working man. His soon to be in-laws are horrified by Max's fashion faux pas. But by a sleight-of-foot, Max tricks his fiancée's father into believing the shoes are the height of fashion and, in the end, the entirety of the wedding party and guests have all procured broken down old shoes or boots for the occasion. While Max is no true class interloper, his incompetence at managing the material world (the enjoyment of which he is entitled to, under the logic of patriarchal capitalism) sets him at odds with society. Normally, he is himself the butt of the joke, but in *Max Sets the Style*, society at large falls victim to Max's incompetence, thereby exposing their gullibility and the emptiness of bourgeois conventions, making them the figures of fun. In this essay, I will consider how shoes allow Max to 'set the style', shifting the human-object paradigm in the film from one where objects act against Max to one where objects are something that he effectively deploys in order to keep his social standing and marital plans on track.

The dandy's shoes

Linder's slapstick comedy would famously influence Charlie Chaplin, among many other silent comedic greats, but would be at least semi-overlooked for a significant portion of early film history.[2] By the mid twentieth century, however, when film historians began to take serious stock of the medium's more than half century, French scholars were quick to point out Linder's pioneering status vis-à-vis his more famous American counterparts. In that literature, the nearly universally remarked upon characteristics of Max Linder's film persona are his dandyism and social class. Georges Sadoul describes Max as a 'the son of a good family, impeccably dressed', while for Henri Agel, Max embodies a 'somewhat showy and rather exterior dandyism' (Ford 1966: 127).[3] Charles Ford describes Max as:

> a gentleman correctly dressed in a jacket, striped trousers, top hat, patent leather shoes with spats and white gloves, holding in his hand a strangely winning and casual cane. It was often said that this was not a princely elegance but rather a bourgeois one, placed precisely at the level to be appreciated by the masses. (Ibid.: 23)

In this passage, Ford is in fact recycling language he originally used to detail the characteristics of Max's dandyism as well as its social ambiguities and ambivalence. Co-writing with René Jeanne, Ford previously published the following:

> But on the contrary, with that dignity, that conventional concern for being correct and respectable that since Louis-Philippe has characterized the French bourgeoisie, and with a certain elegance: a just a bit too snuggly tailored jacket, a top hat blinding like a fun house mirror, shiny patent leather shoes, white gloves, and casual cane. But note that this is not real elegance, it corresponds to nothing deep, it is only superficial, it's not that of a true gentleman, but rather that of a high-level shop clerk who has assembled all the elements from the catalogues of *prix fixe* tailors and department stores. By a miracle of composition – which is probably only the effect of chance – if it does not fool the truly stylish, it does correspond to the ideal that the little people who are ignorant of the sporting high life (as one was in that era), and are not all shop clerks. (Ibid.: 131)

What is striking in these characterisations of Max's 'subtly affected elegance' and 'pretensions' (Abel 1994: 235–7) is, as I have just mentioned, the insistence upon the dandyism as encoded in a very specific set of accessories: including the shiny, patent leather shoes (often with spats). The showiness of Max's vestments are a social *trompe l'œil*: a presumably unsophisticated, lower-class film-going public ('the little people who are ignorant of the sporting high life') is assumed not to be able to distinguish (or at least not consistently or reliably) that the Max character is not necessarily so at home in such a get-up (as opposed to the 'truly stylish' who are not fooled). These turns of phrase of course tell us as much or more about the types of class-based assumptions mid-century French film historians were making about early and silent film audiences as how the film in fact was read by or resonated with those audiences, but they are interesting nonetheless, because they give an indication of how important Max's dress, in particular the shoes, were in the development of his persona and his ongoing film legacy.

The class ambiguities of the Max character are further complicated by Max Linder's personal history. Born Gabriel-Maximillien Leuvielle to wealthy vine-yard-owning parents near Bordeaux, Linder initially aspired to act in 'serious' theatre, attending an arts conservatory. The young Leuvielle was forced by his disapproving father take a stage name, eventually settling on Max Linder, so as not to taint the family name by association with acting of any kind. I do not propose a reading of Linder's work that would make of it a psychodrama about his family origins, yet it nonetheless seems worth remarking how unsurprising it is, given his family background and parental hostility to his career choices, that Linder would make films haunted by ambivalence about social class and propriety. Leuvielle would certainly have had the wealth to be at home in 'Max's' social sphere and clothing, but as a provincial, would he have mastered codes dictated by the Parisian centre? Leuvielle's rocky road towards becoming Max Linder, his long struggle with depression (triggered by his experiences in the First World War) and his eventual suicide, as well as the inherent challenges faced by a wealthy provincial '*monté à Paris*' and ultimately finding international success in the new medium of cinema seem rich in biographical possibility, and further excavation of how Leuvielle's class history was deployed or occluded in fan magazines or trade magazines is in order.[4]

The importance of shoes for the Max character is evident not only in their evocation by film historians but indeed by the recurrence of shoes as a trope in Max Linder films. Varying dates are given for *Max Sets the Style* in different sources. This confusion is compounded by the fact that Linder, like so many productive and successful early silent era directors, producers and actors, frequently revisited themes, essentially duplicating his own work. In the 1951 edition of his *Histoire générale du cinéma*, Georges Sadoul, after a somewhat dismissive evaluation of *Max Sets the Style*'s lack of narrative coherence and clarity and over-reliance on long shots, adds a footnote to the effect that Linder must have agreed with Sadoul's negative evaluation, writing,

> Max Linder was himself aware of this [weakness of *Max Sets the Style*]. In 1913 he returned to the same script with *Les escarpins de Max/Max's Shoes*, where a systematic and felicitous use of the close up makes the story

comprehensible and the film excellent. When we are better acquainted with the entirety of Linder's œuvre, we will no doubt find analogous variations on the same theme. (Sadoul 1951: 146)

Today, we do know Linder's œuvre better than in the 1950s, but I have nonetheless found it difficult to ascertain with certainty exactly how many films Linder made with close to the same story and shoe-focused theme (probably two or three), and to what degree slippage in naming and haphazard conservation have made it appear that he did so more often than he had. With the generous help of archivists at the Cinémathèque française, the Gaumont Pathé archives and the George Eastman Museum, I have been able to determine that in addition to *Max lance la mode/Max Sets the Style*, there are catalogue references to films with the titles *Le Soulier trop petit* (also known as *Chaussure trop étroite/Escarpins de Max/The Joys of Tight Boots* or *Max's Feet are Pinched*) *Max et les escarpins* and *Max collectionne les chaussures* (or *Max collectionneur de chaussures*) with distinct (but currently unverifiable) dates ranging from 1907–16. Several of these titles are specifically designated as 'alternate' titles. These archived prints are on a variety of film formats, some nitrate, and none are currently visible by researchers due to their state of non-restoration or local limitations on viewing formats, except for an incomplete 35mm copy at the Eastman Museum. Nitrate prints at the Cinémathèque française could not even be taken from the vault to be examined by archivists because of the weather at the time I made my request – high temperatures made the risk of combustion even greater than usual. I relate this somewhat digressive panorama of 'film historian problems' not only for the sake of anecdote. Even with the obvious likelihood of inaccuracies in some catalogue and secondary source entries, it is clear that Max Linder did probably make multiple films explicitly about shoes. Titles in various filmographies also give evidence for films about hats – and, as I showed above, the top hat is a clearly class-marked accessory similarly important to Max's character. It seems we can safely take this as at least semi-concrete/suggestive evidence that certain accessories, and arguably shoes above all, provided Linder with fruitful possibilities for exploring the comedic possibilities of Max's dandyism.

Re-shod feet: no mean feat?

The main thrust of the study of objects and things in film has in recent years been towards trying to understand how objects act independently of human agency, how consumerism interfaces with representation, and how the film apparatus as an object itself problematises the consideration of diegetic objects.[5] I would here simply sidestep the problem of the filmic apparatus and instead look briefly at the way in which the represented, diegetic object relates to, acts upon or is acted upon by the main character in *Max Sets the Style*. Max's shoes begin by being one of the many objects that 'act up,' and whose independence from the will of the protagonist gives rise to humour at the expense of that character. However, Max turns the situation to his advantage by acting upon the shoes, and through them upon society at large.

Max Sets the Style opens with the bride and her parents awaiting the groom, who, after an insert of the father's hand holding his pocket watch, we see cheerfully waking up in bed in medium close-up. Another insert of a hand with a pocket watch (this time Max's, since there is a visible signet ring) emphasises that time is not on Max's side – he is definitely late. After another long shot of the family's impatient fussing about, we see Max in a profile medium close-up struggling with his collar in front of a mantlepiece mirror. The film cuts back and forth between Max's grimaces and contortions with the collar, including Max shaking his fist at his image and close-ups of Max's shiny dress shoes sitting dangerously close to and ultimately catching fire at the hearth. Once the shoes catch, we see (in long shot) Max jump up and stamp out the flames and, after a moment's pause recovering from the discomfort, he again consults his pocket watch, realises his increased lateness, hurriedly dons his top hat, tails and overcoat and rushes from the room. This scene of Max preparing is consistent with Linder's other films in that while Max wakes with a certain insouciance, he is shown to be the victim of the fashionable objects that he does not in fact totally control. When we typically see the Max character in other situations, he is already dressed and thus his vestments appear to be a relatively 'natural' part of his person. In this scene, however, the efforts involved in putting together that pretty package are revealed. And indeed, Max's inability to successfully manage both time and objects is what serves as the film's triggering event: the burning of the dress shoes.

Once in the street, Max finally manages to get his second arm fully into his jacket and overcoat, but realizes after a scant few steps that the soles of his shoes are hopelessly ruined. Because they are falling off the bottom of his feet, they bring Max to the verge of despair until he encounters the poor man whose heavy, worn-out boots he will purchase at the very doorstep of his fiancée's home. While the boots initially seem to save the day, Max momentarily loses all hope as he approaches the boots and takes in their decrepitude (and possibly, given his scrunched-up face, their smell). Max staggers back and launches into a performance where he sobs melodramatically while leaning against the apartment building, looks back at the boots, then sobs again. Again, the degree to which Max appears to be the victim of his inability to manage the objects surrounding him is the source of the film's humour – the more so when, in his gaucherie, Max accidentally stomps on his fiancée's ankle, thereby drawing her family's enraged attention to his inappropriate footwear. It is at this point that Max sets in motion the reversal upon which the film turns.

Prior to the stomping, Max had continued to signal to the audience that his footwear was unacceptable (the camera's frontal positioning in relationship to the shy/coy turn of the fiancée's body away from Max means that she does not herself see his gesticulations). However, once the fiancée's pained sobs bring her parents running back into the room, Max immediately transforms his gestures into a grand discourse on the superiority of his feet, indicating dismissively that the father's shoes are hopelessly passé. Once Max exits the room, though, he frets as to how to support this assertion, pantomiming a dramatic light bulb moment after which he hurries into the salon where the wedding guests are all gathered. Max crawls behind and below the chair of the most obviously wealthy and stylish female guest, pushing the unsightly boots through her voluminous skirts and agitating them in a pleasant, toe-tapping little dance. His father-in-law-to-be storms into the room, clearly ready to appeal to the matriarch to adjudicate the trespasses of his would-be son-in-law, but then draws up short as he catches sight of the hideous boots dancing under the grande dame's skirts, as Max laughs riotously behind the chair. Eventually the aggrieved father shrugs and sends his butler with a note recalling Max (who has by then rushed back to the entryway), while rounding up the other guests. Here indeed the editing is quite elliptical, as the next shot jumps to the wedding reception where all the guests are now dancing, somewhat clumsily in the ill-fitting, hard-worn, heavy, working-class footwear that the father-in-law apparently encouraged everyone to hastily procure. In the closing minutes, inelegant dancing goes on, more toes are stepped on, and the bride even loses a shoe, but all is well that ends well, as the close up of Max's hand replaces the bride's errant clodhopper and the film culminates in a studio shot of two naked children in an oversized old boot. Max's trickery has resulted not only in saving his wedding, but successful and repeated consummation and procreation.

Max has set the style, indeed – *le beau monde* has not only been taken in by his paradoxical combination of maladroitness and finesse, but the children in the boot suggest that through his adventures with shoes, Max has 'seeded', quite literally, himself within the social hierarchy that he initially appeared not to master. Max's initial relationship with the trappings of his wedding costume's heightened dandyism is not auspicious – his struggles with his collar, leading to the fire, and the subsequent efforts to get on his coats show collar, coats and timepieces all working against him. Max's success is not that of mastering the codes and requirements of fashion by becoming invisible or fitting in through doing the socially 'correct' thing – which would be to have the proper patent leather dress shoes on his feet. Instead, Max manages to change what everyone else has on their feet. Moreover, the image of the children suggests that Max's feat has been reproducible or, at least, has led to the reproduction of himself within a social hierarchy in which his place had seemed questionable due to his initial inability to make the fashion objects work for him. The apparent rapidity and ease with which the bride's father leads the guests towards radical fashion change is of course a somewhat toothless social critique insofar as it is embedded in the reassuring conventions of humour. It does however show the emptiness of social conventions: how can anything be meaningful if it can be so rapidly abandoned, without discussion? Whatever might be reassuring about the comedic potential in the dance scene is at least partially undercut by the punchy conclusion of the film with the epilogue showing the children. With that image, Max is shown to be like the cuckoo that lays its eggs in other birds' nests to hatch: his initial ineptitude is transformed into effective self-reproduction, thus the potential transformation of society is one not limited to a particular fashion moment, but could extend who knows how far, through the future behaviour of his offspring and even beyond.

Notes

1. *Max Sets the Style* is distributed on DVD in the United States on *Laugh with Max Linder (Seven Years Bad Luck; Four Short Sketches; Be My Wife)*. In secondary source filmographies, 1914 is sometimes also given as date for the film – I will address film historical confusion around Max Linder's shoe-themed films below.
2. Linder started making films in the mid-1900s and was a major international star by 1910–11. Working in both France and the United States until his death by suicide in 1925, Linder made well over one hundred films (mostly shorts) – exact numbers are hard to determine due to the number of lost/unavailable titles.
3. All translations are my own.
4. For a more extensive biography, see Linder 1992a, 1992b, 1992c, Ford 1966, and Vincendeau 2000.
5. As a select but rich and compelling bibliography see: Maurizia Boscagli, *Stuff Theory: Everyday Objects, Radical Materialism* (NY/London: Bloomsbury, 2014); Volker Pantenburg, ed., *Cinematographic Objects: Things and Operations* (Berlin: August Verlan/IKKM, 2015); Luka Arsenjuk, 'On the Impossibility of Object-Oriented Film Theory,' *Discourse* vol. 38, no. 2 (spring 2016), pp. 197–214; Elizabeth Ezra, *The Cinema of Things: Globalization and the Posthuman Object* (NY/London: Bloomsbury, 2018); Mackenzie Leadston, *Theorizing the Comic Object in Classical French Cinema*, Ph.D. Thesis, Ohio State University, 2019.

References

Abel, Richard (1994), *The Ciné Goes to Town: French Cinema 1896–1914* (updated and expanded edition), Berkeley, CA: University of California Press.

Ford, Charles (1966), *Max Linder*, Paris: Seghers.

Laugh with Max Linder: Seven Years Bad Luck; Four Short Sketches; Be My Wife, DVD collection, director David Shepherd, USA: Film Preservation Associates/Image Entertainment, Inc.

Linder, Maud (1992a), *Max Linder*, Paris: Atlas.

Linder, Maud (1992b), *Max Linder était mon père*, Paris: Flammarion.

Linder, Maud (1992c), *Max Linder par Maud Linder. Le cinéma de Max Linder*, Paris: Éditions Montparnasse.

Sadoul, Georges (1951), *Histoire générale du cinéma vol. 3, Le cinéma devient un art (l'avant-guerre) 1909–1920*, Paris: Denoël.

Tim (2012), 'Max Linder: The Overlooked Silent Movie Star from Saint-Loubès, http://invisiblebordeaux.blogspot.com/2012/12/max-linder-overlooked-silent-movie-star.html, accessed 19 November 2019.

Vincendeau, Ginette (2000), *Stars and Stardom in French Cinema,* London and New York: Continuum.

Chapter 2

A girl and a shoe: Marcel Fabre's *Amor pedestre*

Malgorzata Bugaj

In *Amor pedestre* (Italy, 1914), part of a series of silent comedy shorts directed by and starring Marcel Fabre, shoes take centre stage. This humorous Italian melodrama, a likely influence on Filippo Tommaso Marinetti's Futurist theatre play *Le Basi* (1915), features the familiar plotline of a love triangle, jealous husband and subsequent revenge. However, Fabre employs a formal experiment with the emerging medium of film: the actors are shot entirely from the waist down. By reducing the whole of the actor's body to a part and questioning the notion of the face as the essential element in silent film, *Amor pedestre* subverts established conventions and challenges traditional film grammar.

This chapter describes the origins of *Amor pedestre* and sets it amongst other similar productions released around the same time, films whose proliferation seems to suggest the existence of a subgenre based entirely on the concept of feet-focused synecdochic framing. It then traces the links of Fabre's film with Italian Futurism and considers it as an example of a 'proto-futurist film' (O'Pray 2003: 12), or 'unwitting avant-garde' (Montanaro 2002), demonstrating how popular entertainment influenced this artistic movement. The text also discusses gestures and costumes in *Amor pedestre*. While the details of the evolving story are conveyed solely through the expressive actions performed by the feet, it is through shoes that we come to recognise the characters, their role, gender and social class. At the heart of the film is the footwear of the female lead; as an object of fetishist fixation, her shoes set the narrative in motion.

Amor pedestre and its origins

The title *Amor pedestre* has been variously translated into English as *Foot Love* (Sorlin 1996: 41), *Pedestrian Love* (Kirby 1986: 58), *Playing Footsie*

(Gianetto 2000: 246) or *Love Afoot* (Massa 2015: 7; Grimaldi-Pizzorno 2018: 94). In terms of its plot, the film is a clichéd and simple urban melodrama with a love triangle in the centre. Its humour stems mainly from the subversion of social and filmmaking conventions. Set in a middle-class milieu, *Amor pedestre* mocks 'the codes and practices of bourgeois respectability' (Paulicelli 2016: 21), especially through its amoral, suggestive finale. Most importantly, the unconventional element is introduced by framing: characters, their interactions and gestures are represented entirely by their lower limbs. By introducing a flipped medium shot framing human figures from the waist down (rather than, conventionally, focusing on face and hands), the film subverts a young, but already well-established film grammar.

This silent production was made in 1914, during what Leprohon calls 'the Golden Age of Italian Cinema' (Leprohon 1972: 16). The second decade of the twentieth century saw the rapid development of the Italian movie industry and 'by 1914, the country was, together with Denmark, the third largest exporter of films in the world' (Sorlin 1996: 44). Originally tinted, *Amor pedestre* was produced by the Turin-based production company Ambrosio Studios, which specialised in historical epics. Alongside popular costume spectaculars, the company produced melodramas, documentaries and comedies.

Amor pedestre was directed by and starred Marcel Fabre whom Brunetta considers among the few stars of early Italian comedy (Brunetta 2011: 40); Sorlin one of the three best contemporary comedians (Sorlin 1996: 41); and Massa 'perhaps the best silent comedian who no-one's ever heard of' (Massa 2015: 1). At the time of the film's production, Fabre was a resident comic at Ambrosio Studios and was known mostly for a popular comedy series depicting the adventures of Robinet, 'a tall and clumsy type, a shameless libertine' (Blom 2005: 225), which he directed and played the lead in (much like his more famous equivalent, Charlie Chaplin). As a letter appearing halfway through *Amor pedestre* reveals, the film was actually a part of the aforementioned series. Although conflicting information was provided by the artist himself, Steve Massa in his biography establishes that the director of *Amor pedestre* was born Manuel Fernandez Perez, was of Spanish origin and, before turning to screen acting and filmmaking, worked as a clown in Paris. He frequently changed his names (Marcel Fabre, Fernandez Perez, Marcel Perez), screen personalities (Robinet, Tweedledum, Boungles, Twede-Dan and Tweedy) and residence, living in several European countries before ultimately relocating to the United States (Massa 2015: 3). He made more than 200 short comedies (Massa 2015: 1), but *Amor pedestre* remains his most discussed film.

Feet in early cinema: a subgenre

Responding to Mary Ann Doane's claim that in silent film 'the absent voice re-emerges in gestures and the contortions of the face – it is spread over the body of the actor' (Doane 1980: 33), Jane Gaines states that 'it is spread unevenly, with expressivity concentrated on the upper parts [...] favouring fingers, eyes, and lips' (Gaines 1990: 188). While the hands and face have been described as the focus of silent cinema, *Amor pedestre* eschews the traditional framing of the human figure. On the contrary, the fragments of the body that 'commonly served as a vehicle for emotions' (Tsilibaris 2006a) are here obscured. By moving beyond the traditional forms of representation, the film shifts the attention to the lower half of the body and, as a result, 'the viewer, confronted with an alternative cinematic grammar, is obliged to search for new ways to approach the characters' (Ibid.). Simultaneously, however, the structure of *Amor pedestre* is rooted in traditional storytelling: the film develops a logical opening, climax and resolution. The details of the narrative can be understood partially through changing props and settings, but primarily through costumes (shoes in particular[1]) and the gestures made by the actors' legs and feet. Despite its lack of intertitles (with the exception of the letter) and the absence of opening or closing credits identifying the roles of the characters, the film still manages to construct a coherent, logical narrative whole and demonstrates that the story in silent cinema can be understood without the facial performance of the actors.

Amor pedestre is not the first work to employ the experimental concept of focusing on actors' extremities. The production was preceded by a number of shorts in which the 'footage is all about feet' (Grimaldi-Pizzorno 2018: 95). An early example is a production by British film pioneer George Albert Smith, *A Photograph Taken from Our Area Window* (UK, 1901), filmed from the point of view of a basement window and showing a street and its passers-by in a range of footwear. Of note here is the catalogue description advertising the film: 'What do we see? Nothing but feet and legs, but oh! What a variety!' (Barnes 1997: 39). Barry Salt identifies the same idea appearing in three anonymously directed shorts by the American Vitagraph Studios: *The Story the Boots Told* (1908) using conventional framing with close-ups of shoes communicating key moments in the story; *Over the Chafing Dish* (1911) told entirely through gestures of hands and feet; and similarly, *Extremities* (1913), a love story featuring Clara Kimball Young, one of the brightest female stars of early cinema (Salt 2009: 99).

Other films in the same vein include the French *La journée d'une paire de jambes/A Day in the Life of a Pair of Legs,* an anonymously directed short production released by Gaumont in 1909, which depicts the comical adventures of a drunken man and his distinctive, intoxicated gait. A few scenes from this piece bear a striking resemblance to *Amor pedestre,* including the opening sequence in which a female character (here the wife rather than a maid) sends the protagonist to work, or an attempt to play footsie with a woman sitting next to him and the angry reaction of her male companion. The characters' faces are finally revealed in the film's finale to strengthen the comic effect. In contrast to *Amor pedestre,* the focus is on the working class, a fact signalled mainly by the protagonist's hard-wearing, slightly stained boots.

Giovanni Lista points to two similar Italian films produced prior to *Amor pedestre* (Lista 2013: 204). Created by the successful duo of Giovanni Vitrotti (as a cinematographer) and Arrigo Frusta (as a writer and a director), *La Storia di Lulù/The Story of Lulu Told by her Feet* (1910) is a social drama about the fall and rise of a young peasant girl (her social status is here indicated by her wooden clogs) mixing with high society. With a female protagonist in the spotlight, the film features innovative (for the time) use of stop-motion animated shoes (Montanaro 2002). Meanwhile, the 1910 *Storia di un paio di stivali/The Story of a Pair of Boots* – part of the Robinet series – is 'centered on an object, a pair of stolen boots, which triggers the classic chase ending in a tumble' (Lista 2013: 204). Written again by Arrigo Frusta, but starring Fabre in the main role, the film demonstrates that *Amor pedestre* is not simply an outlier in Fabre's body of work, but rather a refinement of a previously successful idea.

Slightly later *Des pieds et des mains/Feet and Hands* (France, 1915) was directed by accomplished silent film duo Gaston Ravel and Jacques Feyder and starred Kitty Hott and André Roanne (known better as Count Nicolas Osdorff in *Diary of a Lost Girl*). Released by French Gaumont, this 17-minute production is a love story of an infatuated man and the reluctant object of his desire. The details of the narrative are conveyed not only through gestures performed by the feet (with the by now obligatory game of footsie), but also those of hands, recalling the aforementioned *Over the Chafing Dish* and *Extremities.* The film features a wider variety of costumes and accessories than its predecessors, including a range of fashionable shoes and jewellery. In the final scene the faces of the protagonists are cleverly revealed as the couple picks up their baby, indicating the ultimate happy ending. Significantly, in its positive resolution the film reverts to the conventional medium shot, framing the protagonists from waist up and reversing the view previously restricted to their extremities; in this way, at its conclusion the film ultimately takes advantage of the expressive potential of the human face.

It is worth also mentioning fragments of René Clair's *Entr'acte* (France, 1924) with its teasing depiction of a dancing ballerina framed from the waist down and reduced to moving feet and legs. Echoing the aforementioned movies, these sequences play with the viewers' imagination of the off-screen presence (that is, the upper part of the performer's body) and draw on the erotic connotations of feet (with footwear removed). The scene is repeated several times throughout the film; however, here the final joke is on the audience – the barefoot dancer turns out to be a bearded man.

This range of early cinematic productions sharing the same traits suggests the existence of a subgenre focused on shoe-clad feet. Such fragmentation of the body recalls P. Adams Sitney's notion of 'synecdochic representation' (Sitney 2002: 10). Sitney refers to the rhetorical figure of synecdoche, which denotes a distinct part standing in for the whole, while discussing Maya Deren's *Meshes of the Afternoon* (USA, 1943). Its opening sequences introduce the protagonist through the elements of her body: feet and hands along with a shadow. Such synecdochic, or *pars pro toto,* framing limits the representation of the human form to its fragments. Correspondingly, in *Amor pedestre* the body parts – legs and shoe-clad feet – stand in for the whole figure. In addition, its second scene briefly features the silhouette of Robinet presented as a shadow play, the only time when the film presents a whole figure of any of its characters. While such synecdochic framing is deployed in *Meshes of the Afternoon* for the oneiric exploration of the protagonist's identity, in *Amor pedestre,* comprising part of a popular comedy series, it is used for providing amusement and entertainment by reversing conventions.

Amor pedestre and Italian Futurism

Amor pedestre is frequently associated with Italian Futurism, particularly Filippo Tommaso Marinetti's 1915 theatre play *Le Basi,* translated as *Feet* (Kirby 1986: 290–1) or *The Bases* (Rainey, Poggi and Wittman 2009: 494–5). *Le Basi*[2] is composed of seven unrelated episodes, each consisting of one or two lines of dialogue. During the original performance, only the actors' lower limbs and footwear were visible; as stage directions instruct: 'a curtain edged in black should be raised to about the height of a man's stomach. The public sees only legs in action. The actors must try to give the greatest expression to the attitudes and movements of their lower extremities' (Kirby 1986: 290). The brief scenes employ a variety of props (armchair, couch, desk, table, pedal-operated sewing machine), indications of activities performed with feet (working on a pedal-operated sewing machine, running away, giving a kick, walking), and background descriptions for characters that might be otherwise difficult to deduce (a bachelor, a married woman, an official, a father).

Amor pedestre was released before *The Futurist Synthetic Theatre* manifesto written by Filippo Tommaso Marinetti, Emilio Settimelli and Bruno Corra at the beginning of 1915 and Marinetti's *Le Basi* published later the same year.

As the chronology suggests, in this case popular cinema inspired an artistic avant-garde. Lista emphasises that 'within months, in referring not to the film, but to the Futurist poetics of his own "synthetic theatre", Marinetti explained that his choice to focus exclusively on performers' feet was meant to avoid any psychological interpretations of the characters' behaviour' (Lista 2013: 205). However, *Le Basi*'s similarity to *Amor pedestre,* and, indeed, also to the aforementioned films preceding it, exists solely in terms of the formal conceit: reducing the representation of the performers' bodies to the knees down. Whereas the on-screen works discussed in this chapter were intended to entertain and amuse, *Le Basi* reflected the directives of an artistic programme. While the cinematic productions based on the concept of foot-focused synecdochic framing employ a conventional three-act structure, Marinetti's discreet vignettes abandon causality and rational time, reflecting the manifesto's statement that 'the Futurist theatrical synthesis will not be subject to logic' and 'it will take elements from reality and combine them as its whim dictates' (Kirby 1986: 201). In contrast to the films – silent productions relying entirely on the visual aspects of the medium – Marinetti's piece incorporates dialogue. Additionally, *The Futurist Synthetic Theatre* manifesto praises the value of simultaneity, with more than one event taking place on stage at the same time: and indeed a surviving photograph from the 1915 production of *Le Basi* indicates that during a performance all of the actors were present in front of the audience concurrently (Ibid.: 57).

The early twentieth century avant-gardes absorbed a broad swathe of ideas from mainstream culture and Futurism was no exception. The emerging medium of film, with its rapid innovations, prompted calls for the redefinition of other art forms. As Lista states: 'with its direct and vital immediacy, the new art form of cinema embodied the same anti-bourgeois and anti-establishment expressivity extolled by the avant-garde manifestoes – without their consulted and apocalyptic theorizations' (Lista 2013: 204). *Amor pedestre* along with *La journée d'une paire de jambes, La Storia di Lulù* and *Storia di un paio di stivali* are examples of forms of expression that would later be associated with experimental artistic movements. These films chime with Futurist ideas in a variety of ways. Innovations from the emerging medium of cinema – its experiments with visual language and challenge to established conventions – fascinated the Italian avant-garde. Pointing to the Futurist synthetic theatre as the field in which the revolution began, the same Italian artists announced in *The Futurist Cinema* manifesto published in 1916 (two years after the release of *Amor pedestre* and a year after Marinetti's *Le Basi*): 'it is logical therefore to carry our quickening energies into a new theatrical zone: film'; their aim was to 'liberate film as an expressive medium' (Rainey, Poggi and Wittman 2009: 230). Lista highlights the productive exchanges between Futurism and mainstream entertainment: 'early popular cinema, when it did not attempt to duplicate bourgeois art, was unknowingly and instinctively Futuristic [...] Popular cinema and Futurism were direct competitors' (Lista 2013: 204).

Lista further states that 'the drama of objects' and the fragmentation of the human form were amongst the key Futurist themes (Lista 2018: 22–31). *The Futurist Cinema* manifesto formulated the need for the 'filmed drama of objects. Objects animated, humanised' (Rainey, Poggi and Wittman 2009: 232). *Amor pedestre*, whose actors' performance of wearable items – shoes – is a crucial element of the production, corresponded with this aesthetic proposal. In contrast to Fabre's film, but also linking to the same Futurist concept, the closing scene of *La Storia di Lulù* employs stop-motion animation of footwear freed from its human agent; the dramatised objects acquiring a life of their own. Furthermore, the films with feet-focused synecdochic framing echo the avant-garde call for the deconstruction of the human body. It is worth noting that in *Amor pedestre* the human body is shown not only as a fragment – the lower bodily extremities – but also as a shadow. In a brief fragment, Robinet's whole moving silhouette is visible; the performer himself remains hidden while the viewers' imagination is required to supply the missing details.

Noteworthy is the fact that although *Amor pedestre* cannot be classified as a Futurist work – its author did not identify it as such and its primary function was as a piece of popular entertainment – the film is often mentioned alongside such Futurist cinema classics as *Thaïs* (Anton Giulio Bragaglia, Italy, 1917) or *Velocità* (Tina Cordero, Guido Martina and Pippo Oriani, Italy, 1930). It has been shown at a number of experimental and avant-garde film festivals and exhibitions all over the world, examples of which include 'The Universe of Futurism: 1909–1936' in Buenos Aires (2008), the celebration of the one-hundredth anniversary of the Futurist Manifesto in San Francisco (2009), or the 'Italian Futurist Cinema' strand of the Italian Film Festival in Turkish Bursa (2014). Rather than describing *Amor pedestre* as a Futurist film, Marcello Seregni (Seregni 2018: 243–5) lists Fabre's production, along with the aforementioned shorts, among major cinematic works that 'were crucial – visually or in terms of content – for the formation of a Futurist cinema' (Ibid.: 241). Descriptions of the production also tend to emphasise *Amor pedestre*'s affinity with Futurism. For example, O'Pray proposes the term 'proto-futurist film' (O'Pray 2003: 12), which places Fabre's work as one of the direct precursors of the Italian avant-garde movement. Correspondingly, Montanaro uses the term 'unwitting avant-garde' (Montanaro 2002), suggesting that any influence popular entertainment might have had on the Futurists was unintentional.

Gestures and costumes in *Amor pedestre*

In silent cinema gestures and costumes are of paramount importance. With regard to the former, 'visible actions used as utterances' (Kendon 2004: 7) must compensate for the lack of spoken word, recalling again Mary Ann Doane: 'the absent voice re-emerges in gestures' (Doane 1980: 33). In *Amor pedestre* this is especially challenging since the most expressive parts of an actor's body – the hands and the face - are off-screen and it is left to the legs and feet to carry the narrative. Chare and Watkins see gestures in film as 'a key means by which an actor can establish the personality of a character' (Chare and Watkins 2017: 1). In *Amor pedestre* a range of expressive actions – nonchalantly swinging a cane or wiping his shoes with a white handkerchief – identify Robinet as a playful and frivolous individual, conscious of his appearance. Robinet's repeated gesture of tapping his feet – following his first encounter with the lady while he is deciding whether or not to pursue his prospective conquest; when his love interest departs after he has polished her shoes; and later while he is sitting in the chair and waiting for her visit – elicit an interpretation of this character as an impatient and indecisive individual. The visible utterances of the second male protagonist, especially his relaxed air in the presence of the female lead (he is sitting in the corner reading a newspaper while she enters and changes her footwear) suggests that the couple have achieved some level of familiarity, perhaps as in a marriage. His angry feet movements upon finding the letter – abruptly leaving the house, kicking his opponent or adopting a fencing stance – seem to hint at his explosive temper. A certain manner of walking imposed by a narrow dress and high heels – short but decisive steps and a gentle swaying motion of her hips – communicates the erotic allure of the female lead.

Likewise, changes in the orientation of the body, deftly communicated through the repositioning of lower limbs, articulate the intentions and attitudes of the characters. By walking around the lady, Robinet makes clear his fascination with her. Turning her back on the admirer – an action performed entirely through the female character's feet – suggests that she is not interested in flirting. Playing footsie is a straightforward signal of Robinet's desire. By moving her foot away during his attempts to touch her shoe with his, the woman decisively rebuffs the amorous intentions of her admirer. Kneeling in front of the lady during the shoe polishing scene and again in the final scene hints at Robinet's progress in his conquest.

Jane Gaines emphasises the pivotal role not only of gestures but also costumes in silent film: 'in the absence of sound it was seen as a substitute for speech [...] attending to costume and gesture was somewhat like listening' (Gaines 1990: 188). In *Amor pedestre* footwear, the only element of costume consistently present, must signify the role, gender and social status of each character. Gaines further argues that costume allows for ready identification of characters: 'if it "speaks", it is treated rather like the flat character who is never given more than one line to deliver' (Ibid.: 188). In Fabre's film this one-line description is limited even further by the use of synecdochic framing: it is provided almost entirely by shoes, with brief, fragmented glimpses of other items of costume. Robinet's attire (a coat, a cane and hat) and, crucially, his smart, narrow pointed and buttoned shoes, introduce him as an upper-class gentleman of taste, or someone aspiring to this profile. His counterpart is first shown in a lush apartment halfway through the film: his sturdy, but well-maintained shoes without any clearly discernible fashionable details, along with stripes on the sides of his trousers suggest a military man (Paulicelli 2016: 22). The same one-line, or even one-word, characterisation can be applied to the peripheral characters in the film. A tram passenger sporting men's shoes with buckles and a long black garment might be a priest. A shot of a child's shoes rocking on the lap of a plainly dressed woman in a scarf with buttoned footwear covering her ankle suggest 'either a nanny (she is dressed more modestly), or a mother who does not belong to the upper middle class' (Ibid.: 22). A man stopping briefly in front of the passengers wearing functional boots along with uniform trousers can be understood to be a ticket inspector. Earlier, in Robinet's apartment, the film shows a woman in plain leather shoes, white apron and long housedress – possibly a maid. Here the film offers an interesting insight into how costume (particularly shoes) defines lower social stations at the background of the story focused on the bourgeoisie.

At the centre of *Amor pedestre* is its female protagonist. She is introduced with an image of a seductive pair of legs clad in black stockings revealed almost to above the knee. A slit in her narrow, fur-trimmed dress opens as she walks, playing with fashion's eroticised dynamic of concealment. Paulicelli perceives her alluring attire as 'innovative for the film at this time' (Paulicelli 2016: 21); it is more readily associated with the later *femme fatale* trope of film noir and its lingering shots of long legs in obligatory high heels (Place 1980: 45). The illicit sexual thrill of a mere glimpse of exposed female legs dates from the late nineteenth century when the lower parts of women's bodies were hidden under long dresses (Steele 2006: 251). Even by the early twentieth century 'revealing legs was for the most part reserved for music hall entertainment' (Tsilibaris 2006b).

It is a woman's shoe that ignites passion and advances the plot. The female protagonist's footwear catches the attention of Robinet when he bends to retrieve her dropped purse. In a tram (where she is placed between a mother/nanny and a priest, symbolically guarded by church and motherhood), her shoes seductively peek out from under her dress, prompting the man to reveal his overtly erotic interest through a game of footsie. Kneeling in front of the lady under the pretext of polishing her shoes – an homage paid to her footwear – Robinet slips a note declaring 'your little feet have bewitched me'. Shoes are also used at another key moment when the woman swaps her high heels for more comfortable slippers in front of her husband; this change of footwear signals domesticity and ease. During an argument with the jealous spouse, the high-heeled shoes rest by the chair placed to the side; her slippers indicate a cosy home life, but the sensual desires represented by the heels are lurking on the edge of the frame. When her shoes appear amongst a small group of men (or rather a gathering of male shoes) following the duel, Robinet is miraculously revived. Finally, after removing her dress in front of her lover – a suggestive detail that establishes the consummation of the relationship – she leaves her high-heeled shoes on as the crucial element of her seductive powers.

The protagonist's shoes with shiny decorative buckles and a design that exposes the foot are key to her allure. Writing about the erotic currency of the high heel, Steele points out that such shoes are typically associated with 'a certain kind of fashionable and sexually sophisticated woman' (Steele 2006: 269), while Pine sees it 'as visual shorthand for "woman" and sex itself' (Pine 2006: 358). The footwear of *Amor pedestre*'s female lead is more ornamental than those of any other women presented in the film; what she wears and how she wears it indicates a desire to project her independence and erotic appeal. Moreover, her figure, reduced to her shoe-clad feet and stockinged legs, illustrates Laura Mulvey's discussion of the female body as a coded sexualised spectacle for the voyeuristic pleasure of the male spectator (Mulvey 1975). The male attention is here directed towards the woman's feet, and more precisely towards the shoes, recalling Mulvey's notion of fetish as a glittering object that attracts the gaze (Mulvey 1996: 6). However, *Amor pedestre* foregoes the lingering fetishist close-ups present in such earlier productions as *As Seen Through a Telescope* (George Albert Smith, UK, 1900) or *The Gay Shoe Clerk* (Edwin S. Porter, USA, 1903) in which male characters fondle the footwear of a female character.

Conclusion

Amor pedestre is an interesting illustration of how artistic avant-gardes, here Italian Futurism, appropriated ideas from the arena of popular entertainment. The film points to a peculiar trend in early cinema, a subgenre of stories told almost entirely through shoe-clad feet. Such synecdochic representation, reducing limiting an actor's means of expression to just their lower body, disproves the notion that the silent film was dependent on face and hands. Paraphrasing Jean-Luc Godard, all you need to make a movie is a girl and a shoe.

Notes

1. Interestingly, the film was featured as part of the 2006 Fashion Film Festival in London, and the 2007 Fashion in Film Festival in New York, both of which emphasised the importance of costumes, especially footwear, in this short production.
2. The companion piece to *Le Basi* was *Hands/Le Mani* (1915) written by Marinetti and Bruno Corra where the hands of the performers were seen above a curtain stretched across the stage (Kirby 1986: 58).

References

Barnes, John (1997), *The Beginnings of the Cinema in England, 1894–1901: Volume 5: 1900*, Exeter: University of Exeter Press.

Blom, Ivo (2005), 'Fabre, Marcel', in A. Richard (ed.), *Encyclopedia of Early Cinema*, London and New York: Routledge, p. 205.

Brunetta, Gian Piero (2011), *The History of Italian Cinema: A Guide to Italian Film from Its Origins To The Twenty-First Century*, Princeton, NJ and Oxford: Princeton University Press.

Chare, Nicholas and Watkins, Liz (2017), 'Introduction: Gesture in Film', in N. Chare and L. Watkins (eds), *Gesture and Film. Signalling New Perspectives*, New York and London: Routledge, pp. 1–8.

Doane, Mary Ann (1980), 'The Voice in the Cinema: The Articulation of Body and Space', *Yale French Studies*, vol. 60, pp. 33–50.

Gaines, Jane (1990), 'Costume and Narrative: How Dress Tells the Women's Story', in J. Gaines and C. Herzog (eds), *Fabrications. Costume and the Female Body*, New York and London: Routledge, pp. 180–211.

Gianetto, Claudia (2000), 'The Giant Ambrosio, or Italy's Most Prolific Silent Film Company', *Film History*, vol. 12, no. 3, pp. 240–9.

Grimaldi-Pizzorno, Patrizia (2018), 'Of ghosts and girls in "Ulysses 13"', in J. Owen and N. Segal (eds), *On Replacement: Cultural, Social and Psychological Representations*, Cham: Palgrave Macmillan, pp. 91–102.

Kendon, Adam (2004), *Gesture: Visible Action as Utterance*, New York: Cambridge University Press.

Kirby, Michael (1986), *Futurist Performance*, New York: PAH Publications.

Leprohon, Pierre (1972), *The Italian Cinema*, London: Secker and Warburg.

Lista, Giovanni (2018), 'The Poetics of Futurist Cinema', in R. Cantonese (ed.), *Futurist Cinema. Studies on Italian Avant-garde Film*, Amsterdam: Amsterdam University Press, pp. 19–32.

Lista, Giovanni (2013), 'Futurist Cinema: Ideas and Novelties', in G. Bertellini (ed.), *Italian Silent Cinema. A Reader*, Bloomington, IL: Indiana University Press, pp. 202–11.

Massa, Steve (2015), *Marcel Perez. The International Mirth-Maker*, New York: Undercrank Productions.

Montanaro, Carlo (2002), *21st Pordenone Silent Film Festival. Program Introduction*, <http://www.cinetecadelfriuli.org/gcm/ed_precedenti/edizione2002/edizione2002_frameset.html> (last accessed 23 June 2018).

Mulvey, Laura (1975), 'Visual Pleasure in Narrative Cinema', *Screen*, no. 16: autumn, pp. 6–18.

Mulvey, Laura (1966), *Fetishism and Curiosity,* London: BFI.

O'Pray, Michael (2003), *Avant-Garde Film: Forms, Themes, and Passions*, London: Wallflower Press.

Paulicelli, Eugenia (2016), *Italian Style: Fashion & Film from Early Cinema to the Digital Age*, New York: Bloomsbury Academic.

Pine, Julia (2006), 'Sole Representation: Shoe Imagery and Twentieth-Century Art', in G. Riello and P. McNeil (eds), *Shoes: A History from Sandals to Sneakers*, Oxford and New York: Berg, pp. 352–72.

Place, Janey (1980), 'Women in film noir', in A. Kaplan (ed.), *Women in Film Noir*, London: BFI, pp. 35–68.

Rainey, Lawrence, Poggi, Christine and Wittman, Laura (eds) (2009), *Futurism. An Anthology*, New Haven and London: Yale University Press.

Salt, Barry (2009), *Film Style and Technology: History and Analysis*, London: Starword.

Seregni, Marcello (2018), 'Filmography', in R. Cantonese (ed.), *Futurist Cinema. Studies on Italian Avant-garde Film*, Amsterdam: Amsterdam University Press, pp. 241–54.

Sitney, Adams P. (2002), *Visionary Film. The American Avant-garde 1943–2000*, Oxford and New York: Oxford University Press.

Sorlin, Pierre (1996), *Italian National Cinema. 1896–1996,* London and New York: Routledge.

Steele, Valerie (2006), 'Shoes and Erotic Imagination', in G. Riello and P. McNeil (eds), *Shoes: A History from Sandals to Sneakers*, Oxford and New York: Berg, pp. 250–71.

Tsilibaris, Christel (2006a), 'Marcel Fabre's Amor Pedestre', *Between Stigma and Enigma, Fashion in Film Festival*, <http://www.fashioninfilm.com/essay/marcel-fabres-amor-pedestre/> (last accessed 13 July 2018).

Tsilibaris, Christel (2006b), 'Shoes, Eroticism and Fetish', *Between Stigma and Enigma, Fashion in Film Festival*, <http://www.fashioninfilm.com/essay/shoes-eroticism-and-fetish> (last accessed 14 October 2018).

Chapter 3

'An intensive study of – *feet!*' in two films by Lois Weber: *Shoes* and *The Blot*

Pamela Hutchinson

'There is a fascinating and perhaps outrageous thesis to be developed on the subject of Lois Weber and the footwear in her films,' wrote Anthony Slide in his 1996 book-length study of the director (Slide 1996: 93). He wasn't the first writer to record that she had a 'fixation with shoes'. In the May 1918 issue of *Motion Picture Magazine*, a journalist called Fritzi Remont interviewed Lois Weber about the painstaking efforts she put into making her films. 'She cannot stand for slipshod work, but ever before her vision flickers an El Dorado which is to please as well as raise to a higher standard the human mind.' Following that giveaway word 'slipshod', Remont praises Weber's ability to 'work out each smallest difficulty of construction', singling out her skill at filming faces in the most flattering way, to hide a 'faulty profile' or avoid a 'crooked-mouth effect'. Which is perhaps why she may have misinterpreted Weber's perplexing boast: 'This famous woman producer and director also told me that she makes an intensive study of – *feet!*' (Remont 1918: 61).

Remont's interpretation is that Weber's interest in feet is the same as her interest in faces, and so she assumes the director's intention is photographic flattery: 'posing feet and so throwing shadows and lights that a tall woman may look as if she owned a 3-A boot' (Ibid.). Slide, in his far more in-depth study of Weber, developed that idea to its erotic endpoint, arguing that 'in fact, the director does have something of a foot fetishism' (Slide 1996: 91), which he concedes to be an unusual proclivity in a woman. 'Women love shoes, but they do not regard them as erotic. While a man may need to conceal his shoe fetish, a woman can openly indulge her fantasy' (Ibid.: 92). Slide provides evidence for Weber's sexual interest in footwear from films including *Hop – The Devil's Brew* (1916), *Too Wise Wives* (1921) and, of course, *Shoes* (1916). If a critic wanted to build on this theory and write that particular 'outrageous thesis', mentioned above, they might note that the sensual heroine of *The Dumb Girl Of Portici* (1916), played by the ballerina

Anna Pavlova, goes barefoot, a fact Slide doesn't mention in his discussion of the film.

There are directors who have incorporated their own foot fetishes into their films, including most famously perhaps, Quentin Tarantino, but also, say, Erich von Stroheim in *The Merry Widow* (USA, 1925)[1]. This essay seeks to explore other arguments for Weber's 'intensive study of – *feet!*', especially in two works in which footwear plays a crucial role: *Shoes* and *The Blot* (1921). Weber once compared her films to the opinion pages of a broadsheet newspaper; in her famously comprehensive *mise en scène*, visual details carry a great deal of narrative information, and also what we might call editorialising, or social comment. Both of these films are inspired by written work, by magazine reportage of social issues, and they both revolve around feet and footwear. If there is a moral message in these films, it may be found in the feet.

Shoes takes its story and situation from two texts. Social reformer Jane Addams's book on prostitution *A New Conscience and an Ancient Evil* (1912, also serialised in *McLure's Magazine*), inspired Stella Wynne Herron's short story, also called 'Shoes', first published in *Collier's Magazine* in January 1916. Herron took a quotation from Addams as her epigraph, which Weber then quotes in her introductory title card:

> When the shoes became too worn to endure a third soling and she possessed but 90 cents toward a new pair, she gave up the struggle; to use her own contemptuous phrase, she 'sold out for a new pair of shoes'. (Addams 1912: 76)

The story concerns a young woman, Eva Meyer (Mary MacLaren), who lives in a city tenement with her parents and younger sisters and works in a five-and-ten-cent store. Her wages largely support the family while her father is out of work (he is shown to be idling, resting in bed drinking beer and reading novels), so when her shoes, a pair of simple buttoned boots, wear out she can't afford to replace them. After falling sick because she has been walking to work in the rain with her soles patched by sodden cardboard, Eva prostitutes herself to earn the money she needs. The final sequence of the film contains two alternate fantasies of how her life might have been different: an upper-class life in which she attends a ball with her family and is admired by several suitors, and a rural middle-class existence in which a man returns from work to greet her at the gate of their home. The implication is that Eva has 'sold out' not just her body but any future happiness as a wife and mother, and possibly also her position within her family. The film is fairly faithful to the plot of Herron's story, although it places Eva as part of a family rather than a single girl living alone.

Crucially, Eva presents no sexual desire towards the man (Charlie) who attempts to lure her into prostitution. Her desire for the new shoes is pre-eminently presented as a matter of concrete need (hers are no longer viable), but that need is also slightly complicated by capitalism. The shoes are displayed elegantly in a shop window, in contrast to the cheap necessities piled high in the store where Eva works. If the shoes are fetishised in Weber's film it is not by Eva but by consumer culture – the capitalist drive to make essential goods seem more attractive in order to charge a higher price for them. Eva, who takes home a meagre wage, is excluded from that culture as a consumer – as a worker, she becomes part of a display of cheap goods. Charlie sees her behind the counter, and next to a shop window. Lil, Eva's colleague who succumbs to Charlie's persuasion before she does, displays expensive accessories such as a wristwatch as her ill-gotten gains. Weber's film hints that after earning her shoes, Eva may be drawn further into consumerism and the work (prostitution) necessary to fund her purchases. The fetishisation of footwear is achieved by the window display, not Weber's camera, which would by implication relate that fetishisation to Eva's perspective or Weber's authorial intent. Instead, Weber lingers longer over close-ups of Eva's distressed shoes and feet than the pristine new ones, leading reviewer Peter Milne to voice his disgust in *Motion Picture News*:

> Miss Weber has gone a step too far in showing a close-up of the girl extracting splinters from the sole of her foot. She has gone too far in showing the girl scraping mud from her feet with a pair of scissors. There is such a thing as being too realistic. (Milne 1916: 3927)

In Herron's story and Weber's film both, Eva jealously eyes the well-shod feet of other women – if the films reveal an obsession with feet, it is one shared by the heroine for the starkest economic reasons. Far from attempting to flatter or sexualise feet, Weber uses them to construct the argument of her film, which sits squarely in the contemporary genre of 'sociological' cinema, as outlined by Constance Balides (Balides 2017), and deals with an issue familiar from many contemporary titles such as *Traffic in Souls* (George Loane Tucker, USA, 1913), the so-called 'white slave trade'. Like Jennifer Parchesky, I would like to put forward 'a more materialist analysis' than Slide's. For Parchesky, shoes are the 'perfect commodity to represent deprivation, since they are both a necessary protection from the elements and, in their more fashionable forms, objects of consumer desire' (Parchesky 1999: 38). I would go further and say that Weber uses footwear to represent the limits of social mobility: in this film, for young working women, and in *The Blot*, for certain (male) middle-class professionals. From the popular instruction to pull oneself up by one's bootstraps, to Cinderella's glass slipper, footwear is linked to social mobility in language and literature, but Weber inverts this image to reveal shoes as a signifier of status that delineates class and economic boundaries rather than crossing them. If the right shoes will allow you to pursue the American dream, the wrong shoes will stop you in your tracks.

As Parchesky suggests, Eva's shoes are not just a commodity, and for her they are far from a fashion item. Instead they are her means of transport through the city and therefore essential for her to go to work. Without them, she would leave the workforce and lose her economic independence. They become a symbol of the deprivation she suffers as a member of the working poor – her wages cannot sustain a family – and of her precarious status as a young working woman. If the wages paid to women in a retail job are not high enough for them to buy new shoes, they are not enough for them to continue to function as a worker in the city. Further, said low wages also put women at risk of the extreme economic vulnerability that the sex trade thrives on, driving them out of respectable capitalist work into something morally unsavoury and illicit. As in *The Blot*, here shoes become a symbol of an inadequate wage that creates an unjust social inequality. Young, underpaid working women are forced into the sex trade, rather than entering a lucrative but respectable career, or taking the more traditional route of marriage and becoming the domestic head of a household sustained by a man's superior ability to command a high salary.

Eva's shoes also present something of a hidden problem, which the audience is uniquely privileged to view, especially in those excruciating close-ups of her sore feet. Charlie the predator is the only character in the film who really notices her shoes – as a marker of her economic vulnerability, they don't elicit his sympathy but present him with a recruitment opportunity. Eva's mother, who controls the household finances, tries to ignore the state of her shoes, while being more easily persuaded by the younger children's requests to buy meat with the money, and her father erroneously claims his pair is just as tattered (by contrast with the minor damage on his pair, the state of Eva's shoes also reveals the extent of her labour outside the home, the worn shoe leather of a worker). Eva's shoes are hidden from view behind the shop counter all day and when a group of fashionably shod women pass her in the park, she tucks her feet under the bench she is sitting on. When she dresses up for the nightclub where she will strike her deal with Charlie, she is able to change other aspects of her appearance – restyle her hair, wear a clean, smarter blouse – but her unsuitable shoes cannot be transformed and must instead be hidden, by dropping the waist of her skirt. Finally, her mother understands the depth of the crisis only when she sees Eva return from her night with Charlie wearing new shoes. Her sight of the problem, like her husband's job offer, comes too late.

Figure 3.1 Eva draws her tattered shoes out of sight in the park

Five years later, Weber made another film inspired by magazine texts, but one that explores instead a middle-class milieu. *The Blot* recycles part of the footwear plot of *Shoes* and features the lower extremities so prominently that on its re-release in 1982 critic Richard Combs called attention to its 'shoe fetish' in his review for *Monthly Film Bulletin*: 'characters are forever comparing their footwear . . . it is the *Los Olvidados* of the literally down-at-heel middle-class' (Combs 1982: 96). The comparison to Luis Buñuel is not intended to flatter Weber, for he finds her accumulation of material detail (chickens, threadbare upholstery, shoes) obsessive, rather than revealing of character or argument. I would argue the opposite. Not only do the material details of Weber's characters' lives take on vast narrative importance, the director is particularly interested in who notices them, and why.

The 30 April 1921 issue of *Literary Digest* magazine, a popular general interest weekly offering abridged versions of articles published elsewhere, contained at least two articles and an advert that contributed to the genesis of *The Blot*. The two articles, which are excerpted in the film itself, along with the title and date of the issue, concern first the unjustly low wages paid to educators, and second the equally skimpy remuneration given to members of the clergy. In its opening scene, the film shows the spoiled children of wealthy families ignoring their lecture. One of the boys, Phil West, is the son of the college trustee. The lecturer is: 'Professor Andrew Theodore Griggs whose reward for long and faithful service was less than a bare living wage.' Later, when a committee of local tradesmen convenes to give the vicar, Rev Gates, his wages, an intertitle contrasts the prosperity of a butcher and a tailor to 'the men who fed their souls and clothed their minds'. This wage inequality is the 'blot' on society referred to in the title. Weber's film tells this middle-class story from a female perspective, which feminist critics have isolated as 'a radical departure from Hollywood practice' (Parchesky 1999: 23). We witness the agonies suffered by Professor Griggs' wife, as she struggles both to run a household on a poverty wage and to afford certain genteel necessities such as tea, cake and cream to entertain Rev Gates, or Phil West, when he courts her daughter. She is reduced to requesting credit at the grocery store, and even stealing a chicken from her neighbour, although in her moral disgust she immediately replaces it.

A telling detail from *Shoes* is reintroduced and reworked in *The Blot*. In one scene in the earlier film, Eva passes a cat eating from a dustbin in the hallway of her tenement building. The Griggs family has a pet cat, her 'a luxury made possible only by night raids on the Olsen garbage can'. The Olsens are the Griggs family's prospering neighbours, immigrants who thrive because father Hans manufactures 'the high priced shoes that ruin the feet of the women who wear them'. Mrs Olsen senses that Mrs Griggs sneers at her, so she moves her dustbin out of reach of the cat and piles her food high in the kitchen window where her neighbour can see it. The Olsens buy a cheap Ford car without a starter, and their children run riot – the implication is that they have ascended from the working-class only in monetary terms, but have not become truly middle-class in manners or morals. An advertise-ment in the 30 April 1921 issue of *Literary Digest* provides another piece of scaffolding for *The Blot*. The advertisement for Cantilever Shoes asks what could be the cause of 65–85 per cent of women 'born with perfect feet and hands' having 'some form of foot trouble'?

> *Shoes*. There can be no other answer … Nature, in her infinite wisdom, designed the human foot to carry its load, to do its full duty in the life of every woman. Nature must have been thwarted and abused and restrained by the artificial footwear made by man. (Unknown 1921: 31)

With its illustration of a mother and baby and this choice of language, the ad-vertisement creates a division between woman/Nature on one hand and man/shoes on the other. Mr Olsen's shoes are the unnatural kind, damaging women's feet, and represent the cheap commodity culture that puts profit ahead of use. Early in the film, one of the children plays in the mud in satin slippers; later a close-up reveals Mrs Olsen's ankle twisting painfully in her high-heeled pump. These shoes are flimsy, consumer items with no intrinsic value, in contrast to

Figure 3.2 One of the Olsen children plays in the yard wearing $18 high heels

the intangible intellectual and spiritual goods offered by Professor Griggs and Rev Gates.

Parchesky has thoroughly described the middle-class setting of *The Blot* and identified it as reflective of Weber's intended audience for her work. The film has a rigorous class structure, with the Wests at the top, then the Griggs family and Rev Gates on an equal footing and the Olsens a notch below. Phil drives a Packard Twin-Six Town Car, around ten times as expensive as the Olsens' Ford, while the Griggses and Rev Gates travel on foot. When Amelia accepts a lift from Phil, she is at pains to hide her scuffed shoes from his view. Because Rev Gates's shoes are shabby and dull from his parish rounds in comparison to those of his rival Phil West, he slicks them with goose grease – a subterfuge that might have passed unnoticed if not for the Griggs family cat licking the fat from his feet[2]. While the upper and lower middle classes spend imprudently, the middle-middle is humble, frugal and self-denying. Cross-cutting between Olsen and Griggs family meals and Phil West's extravagant night at the country club emphasises the division – and it is at this moment that Phil West has the crucial revelation (which the audience is also guided towards by the pattern of cutting): 'I seem to be getting soft. It never mattered to me before that some people had too much to eat while others hadn't enough.'

Figure 3.3 The hungry cat gives away the secret of Rev Gates' goose-grease shoe polish

The romantic plot of *The Blot* concerns the Griggses' daughter Amelia (played by Weber protégée Claire Windsor), and recalls Eva's situation in some key particulars. While Eva's father wastes his money on cheap novels, Amelia's father's passion for 'rare old books' is presented indulgently as his 'one vice' and Phil West and Rev Gates share a passion for art books. Fittingly, Amelia works in a library, but behind a counter, as Eva did. Her shoes, too, are worn thin and she also patches the soles with cardboard and catches cold as a result. More delicate, or with more lenient employers than Eva, she stays home sick – and Phil West and Rev Gates, who are both in love with her, come to visit her. Mrs Griggs spends her last money on cakes and cream to impress Phil West ('her one big chance' at a good marriage), but he leaves and they are consumed by the vicar instead. Phil, noticing the poverty of the Griggs house, attempts to leave some money for the family, but it goes unnoticed. Later, he will see Mrs Griggs asking for credit at the store (because she spent her money on cakes to impress him) and send a basket of food to the family instead. At the conclusion of the film, Amelia accepts Phil West's proposal of marriage and the final shot is of Rev Gates walking despondently home. It's a rather bleak and perplexing conclusion, which encapsulates Weber's distrust of the Hollywood happy ending. For each loving couple created, there are others left alone, and as Shelley Stamp observes: 'many of the problems the film raises cannot be resolved with the tidy conclusion of a Hollywood marriage' (Stamp 2015: 212).

Phil West's encounters with the Griggs family and Rev Gates have inspired him to offer more than one-off gifts of charity. First he brings flowers, then money, then food – and finally he discusses their plight with his father the college trustee, using the *Literary Digest* articles as a reference, in order to help the professor make a permanent improvement in his situation, using his own labour. Morally, by this point, Phil is worthy of Amelia and they make a fitting couple, but there is a note of regret in the way that she breaks the news to Rev Gates, the morally and intellectually superior man, and Weber allows a suspicion to hover in the air: that her final decision was as financially motivated as Eva's in the earlier film. Faced with the choice between two suitors, Amelia has chosen the best 'match', on a purely financial basis. As the middle-class daughter of a college professor, she too feels that her social position is precarious. For Professor Griggs, the film concludes with the prospect of an advantageous marriage for his daughter and promises of a raise in his income. For Rev Gates, the promises are fainter and he is disappointed in love. Weber portrays American society as not just economically unjust but also un-Christian – with the church having fallen out of favour. This recalls earlier Weber films such as *Hypocrites* (1915), or her later film *Sensation Seekers* (1927), in which characters are shamed for their moral failings and brought back into the teachings of the church. The final scene of *The Blot* is clearly intended to create a similar impact.

There is a third admirer, in fact: the Olsens' eldest son, who can only love Amelia from afar but is inspired by these feelings to question his mother's misbehaviour. At the end of the film, Mrs Olsen has relented and chooses not to accuse Mrs Griggs of theft, but is still wearing those unsupportive shoes. Amelia, transformed from 'working girl' to future bride, wears shoes that are white – a practical colour only for women who spend their days at home rather than work – but not shown as detrimental to her feet. With a little spending power, she has chosen wisely. In both of Eva's fantasies she wears white shoes (dancing slippers at the ball, white boots in the rural setting) and Amelia's finale is perhaps just as far-fetched for many among *The Blot's* audience.

As cinematic technique developed from the theatrical, fixed-camera style of early cinema to transitional and feature films, with more edits and facial close-ups, feet were increasingly cropped out of the frame. Weber puts them back in, a choice as potentially radical as her decision to put female characters at the centre of her narratives. As stated previously, only damaged or damaging footwear is highlighted in these films. In neither the fantasy sequences of *Shoes* nor the closing scenes of *The Blot* are Eva and Amelia's perfectly adequate footwear given special attention in the form of close-ups. Weber's 'study of – *feet*' has been much misunderstood. Her films do not present shoes as something to aspire to, but as pointers towards understanding social problems.

It is intriguing, in light of the fact that certain critics have incorrectly ascribed an erotic fascination with feet to the prolonged emphasis on footwear in these films, that Weber clearly puts a lot of value in the way that shoes are looked at in these films, just as much as their intrinsic material condition. There is a moral danger in ignoring or misreading the shoe signals. Eva's immoral descent into sex work is prompted both by the fact that her parents turn a blind eye to her shoe problem and that conversely, the predatory Charlie has clocked her dilapidated boots instead. A rival for Phil West's affection identifies Amelia as a 'working girl' and then, with her shoes hidden behind the library counter, as 'the real thing – a gentlewoman'. In a godless world, no one but the cat notices the grease on Rev Gates's shoes. Instead of flattering feet, Weber is guiding us towards looking at them with compassion, with each film as an exercise in extending our sympathies in order to condemn inequality. Balides writes that 'sociological films as lessons about society also conformed to the more general pedagogy of educational film' (Balides 2017: 18), which is to say that, like teaching films, social problem films allow the audience to 'see for themselves' the issue, rather than reading about it – a method that recalls the mirror held up by Truth in *Hypocrites*. As Stamp has written, '*Shoes* invited civic-minded middle-class woman to reorient their gaze within retail space, away from the merchandise, and toward the young woman serving them behind the counter' (Stamp 2015: 117). Weber's social-issue films *Shoes* and *The Blot* transfer a narrative from magazine page to film screen and teach us the importance of looking, even at footwear, to the point of leading the audience into making an 'intensive study of – *feet!*'

Notes

1. A famous Hollywood anecdote runs thus: that when viewing the day's rushes Irving Thalberg questioned Baron Sodja's obsession with Mae Murray's feet. Stroheim replied: 'That is a foot fetish'. To which Thalberg is said to have reprimanded the famously extravagant director: 'You, Von, have a footage fetish!'
2. Goose grease was a well-known homespun alternative for boot polish. In the comedy *Grandma's Boy* (Fred C. Newmeyer, USA, 1922), released a year after *The Blot*, the goose grease on Harold Lloyd's shoes attracts a swarm of cats, to comic effect. In *The Big Show* (Robert F. McGowan, USA, 1923), an Our Gang short, a boy goose-greases his shoes in order to impersonate Lloyd.

References

Addams, Jane (1912), *A New Conscience and an Ancient Evil*, New York: The Macmillan Company.

Balides, Constance (2017), 'Sociological Film, Reform Publicity, and the Secular Spectator', *Feminist Media Histories*, vol. 3, no. 4, pp. 10–45.

Combs, Richard (1982), 'Retrospective: The Blot', *Monthly Film Bulletin*, vol. 49, no. 580, p. 96.

Milne, Peter (1916), 'Shoes', *Motion Picture News*, 24 June 1916, p. 3927.

Parchesky, Jennifer (1999), 'Lois Weber's *The Blot*: Rewriting Melodrama, Reproducing the Middle Class', *Cinema Journal*, vol. 39, no. 1, Fall 1999, pp. 23–53.

Remont, Fritizi (1918), 'The Lady Behind the Lens: Lois Weber, Photo-Genius, in Front of, or Back of, the Camera', *Motion Picture Magazine*, May 1918, pp. 59–61 and p. 126.

Slide, Anthony (1996), *Lois Weber: the Director who Lost her Way in History*, Westport, CT: Greenwood Press.

Stamp, Shelley (2015), *Lois Weber in Early Hollywood*, Oakland: University of California Press.

Unknown (1921), 'Your feet were like this' [advertisement for Cantilever Shoes], *Literary Digest*, 30 April 1921, p. 31.

Chapter 4

Magic shoes: Dorothy, Cinderella, Carrie

Elizabeth Ezra

The most famous shoes in film history, Dorothy Gale's ruby slippers in *The Wizard of Oz* (Victor Fleming, USA, 1939), are first shown on the feet of a witch. When the Wicked Witch of the East is killed, her stripy tights-clad legs protrude from beneath the house that has flattened her in the tornado. Red shoes sparkle momentarily on her feet before vanishing, and the witch's legs shrivel up and withdraw beneath the house. The shoes immediately appear on Dorothy's feet, where they stay until the end of the film. We don't know what happens to the shoes after Dorothy goes back to Kansas, but as long as she is in the Land of Oz, she wears the ruby slippers, despite attempts by the Wicked Witch of the West to take them from her. When the witch, having imprisoned Dorothy in her castle, reaches for her shoes, the slippers emit a kind of electric shock, prompting the witch to exclaim: 'Fool that I am! I should have remembered. Those slippers will never come off as long as you're alive!' The slippers appear to be made for Dorothy, not the witch, reinforcing the film's lasting message: not only are there right shoes and left shoes; there are also right shoes and wrong shoes.

This essay seeks to ask: What does it mean to find the *right* pair of shoes? Or perhaps the question should be: what does it mean for a pair of shoes to find the right wearer? Could it be that the witch who originally wears the ruby slippers was wearing the wrong shoes, and that Dorothy's appropriation of them restores the rightful order of things? Are the shoes 'wrong' in that they are too pretty, too sparkly, too alluring for the ageing, unattractive witch? Perhaps the house falls on the Wicked Witch of the East precisely because she is wearing the wrong shoes – maybe those shoes can only properly be worn by Dorothy, just as Cinderella's glass slippers only fit Cinderella.

It is worth noting the oddity to modern ears of the word 'slippers' used in English to describe both Dorothy's red shoes and Cinderella's glass footwear. The word 'slippers' sounds like Midwestern shorthand for slip-on shoes, but the footwear thus described would be called 'pumps' in the US and 'court shoes' in the UK. In the 1900 L. Frank Baum novel *The Wonderful Wizard of Oz*, Dorothy wears *shoes*, not slippers, a term introduced in the 1939 film. The shared term establishes a symbolic resonance between Dorothy's slippers and Cinderella's. In fact, Dorothy's ruby slippers are the direct descendants of Cinderella's glass slippers: both types of shoe are equally iconic and have much in common (as well as some notable differences). Both pairs of magic shoes have stories to tell, stories that have been recycled and refashioned from the earliest days of cinema to big-budget film franchises of the twenty-first century. Cinderella's glass slipper may lead to marriage, but Dorothy's ruby slippers have arguably more emotional resonance and trace the contours of an on-screen relationship that is all 'wrong'.

The fact that the shoes in these narratives – the films as well as Perrault's fairy tale – are coded as magic amplifies the metaphorical meaning of a 'good fit'. Well-fitting shoes are an indication of being in the 'right' place in the social order, a sign that wearers slot in to a role for which they are destined by virtue of their gender, age, social class and/or ethnicity. Magic may grant access to another realm but, at least in Dorothy's case, that access is temporary. Magic may also allow the beneficiary to accede to a higher social standing, as in the case of Cinderella, but it does not dismantle the social order in which some people attend balls and others scrub floors. Magic exaggerates the hierarchies that already exist, making the restrictions imposed by these hierarchies all the more visible.

If the shoe fits

The *Cinderella* story was mined for cinema audiences virtually from the beginnings of the medium. Film pioneer Georges Méliès made two different versions of Perrault's tale: one in 1899, and one in 1912, almost bookending a film career that lasted only about seventeen years. The 1899 production is the first of Méliès's films – and the first in the history of cinema – to use dissolves as transitions between scenes, which Méliès implemented in order to prevent exhibitors from changing the order of the scenes. The 1899 version of *Cinderella* thus stands out for its technical innovation, which was motivated by a proprietary desire to protect the artistic integrity of the work. It is notable that this film, which is ultimately about marital union and, therefore, filial succession, gave birth to the development of a mechanical means of narrative progression.

In the earlier film, the scenes involving the glass slipper are brief and perfunctory. However, Méliès's 1912 production of *Cinderella* (perhaps the earliest example of a cinematic reboot) places much more emphasis on the magic shoes, from the inclusion of the words '*la pantoufle merveilleuse*' (the marvellous slipper) in the title, to the extraordinary extended scene of shoe-fitting shot in medium close-up on the lower extremities, wherein ten women troop across a table and push one of their feet into the slipper. (There is a similar scene in a 1934 animated musical Betty Boop short entitled *Poor Cinderella* [dir. Dave Fleischer] which shows an endless line of women's legs trying on the glass slipper that has been placed on a footstool.) This scene is highly unusual in Méliès's œuvre, which contains few 'close-ups', conventional or otherwise. The extended scene in the 1912 film could reflect Méliès's experience working in his parents' boot factory for three years before becoming a filmmaker (or even an acknowledgement of his heritage as the grandson of the Official Bootmaker of the Dutch Court), but it can also be read as a nod to the silent-era tradition of 'feet films'.

The scene starts as a long shot, but then cuts to a shot of two men seated at the table over which the women walk, which can only be described as a kind of reverse ¾ shot: it cuts off the women at the knees, but instead of showing the body above the knee, the camera placement at table level captures the body below the knee. The two seated men are shown in medium shot, but the emphasis on the women's lower legs and feet hybridises the shot, making it a partial close-up. The scene ends with the appearance of two muddy feet clad in enormous clogs presenting themselves for the fitting, which turn out to belong to a drunken male labourer who has gatecrashed the occasion.

Méliès is here sending up assumptions about class and gender in the fairy tale, assumptions that can be immediately grasped at the sight of the large mud-and-hay-strewn peasant's *sabots*. The intrusion may also be a nod to the apparently apocryphal origins of the word sabotage in *sabot*, from when workers would throw their wooden shoes into machinery in order to destroy it. The word sabotage is certainly linked to workers' wooden shoes, though in all likelihood it is attributable to the disruptive clattering sound they make. Perhaps not coincidentally, the year before this version of *Cinderella* appeared, the anarchist trade unionist Émile Pouget published *Le Sabotage* (1911), which introduced the word in ordinary French usage. The labourer's appearance among the queue of aspiring princesses is a stark reminder of the rags-to-riches premise of the Cinderella story, as if daring the royal retinue to take the possibility of class mobility seriously. (The male candidate also makes plain the heteronormativity underlying the match: of course, the film jokes, the prince's mate *must* be a woman. Mustn't she?)

Unlike Cinderella's slipper, which spends more time off her foot than on, Dorothy's shoes are practically bolted to her feet, and don't even come off when she offers to give them to the Wicked Witch of the West in return for her dog Toto, who the witch has kidnapped. The sparks emitted by Dorothy's shoes when the witch tries to prise them from her feet are a sign that what the witch is attempting is wrong. The shoes' staying power, however, seems to be an innovation of the 1939 film. In Baum's novel, the shoes Dorothy inherits from the deceased witch (and which are silver, not red) can be separated from their wearer, however briefly. When the wicked witch dissolves after Dorothy throws a bucket of water on her, she leaves behind a puddle 'and Dorothy's silver shoe' (Swartz 2000: 247).

In the 1939 film, of course, no shoe is left behind. Whereas Baum's novel invokes a generic version of *Cinderella* in its abandonment of a single shoe, the film invites a contrast between Dorothy's slippers plural and Cinderella's slipper singular. For one thing, a glass slipper is practically invisible, or at least transparent, whereas ruby (or silver) slippers are highly visible, and draw attention to themselves. Moreover, Dorothy's shoes famously transport her back home to the world of familiar domesticity, whereas Cinderella's slippers get her out of the house and into an exotic new world of royal privilege. Dorothy's shoes are magic because they take her *out* of a magical place, while Cinderella's shoes are magic because they transport her *to* an enchanted realm. In Oz, Dorothy is a kind of queen, a position she relinquishes in order to return home to a life of curtailed freedom and childhood drudgery in the service of her aunt and uncle. In her family home, Cinderella waits on others and occupies the lowest position in the domestic hierarchy, but ends up being waited upon herself when she eventually becomes a princess.

Figure 4.1 All wrong for the witch

Both *The Wizard of Oz* and the Cinderella story emphasise the importance of wealth. Although in some versions of *Cinderella*, Cinderella's slippers were actually made of squirrel's fur (*vair*), by the time Perrault wrote down the tale, they had become glass (*verre*). Such a mistransmission, if that is what it was, can perhaps be explained by the fact that glass was a rare commodity in the Middle Ages and Early Modern era, giving Cinderella's transparent slippers a monetary value that far exceeded the economic means of most of those who heard the tale. The unusual nature of glass slippers is invoked in Perrault's tale when Cinderella's fairy godmother first presents her with them:

> '...the chief mark of a lady,' said her Godmother, eyeing her with approval, 'is to be well shod,' and so saying she pulled out a pair of glass slippers, into which Cinderella poked her toes doubtfully, for glass is not as a rule an accommodating material for slippers. You have to be measured very carefully for it. (Perrault [1697] 1998: 80)

This scene, in specifying the precision with which feet must be measured, emphasises the importance of fit and, by extension, validates the prince's chosen means of finding his perfect match. Cinderella's doubts about the comfort and practicality of glass slippers are echoed in the more recent live-action Disney version of the tale (Kenneth Branagh, USA, 2015), when the fairy godmother first conjures up shiny shoes for Cinderella and the young woman exclaims, 'They're made of glass!' to which the fairy godmother replies conspiratorially, 'And you'll find they're *really* comfortable'. This reassurance would not be necessary if glass were not such an unusual – and impractical – material for a shoe. As Alan Dundes explains, '... glass, copper, gold, silver, diamonds are the precious materials of which things in the fairy tale realm are made, things which in our real world are made of ordinary materials' (Dundes 1988: 113). Similarly, in both the book and film versions of *The Wizard of Oz*, the Emerald City is made of a precious material. According to Salman Rushdie, the silver shoes of Baum's novel, too, had an economic significance: 'Baum believed that America's stability required a switch from the gold to the silver standard, and the Shoes were a metaphor of the magical advantages of Silver' (Rushdie 2003: 8). In keeping with this emphasis on precious materials, when the silver shoes were changed to red in the MGM film to highlight the wonders of Technicolor, they were repeatedly referred to as 'ruby' slippers rather than red, the gemstone reinforcing the idea that Dorothy was headed to the Emerald City.

There were several silent-era precursors to the 1939 film (including Otis Turner 1910, J. Farrell MacDonald 1914 and Larry Semon 1925), but among all these cinematic versions of Baum's novel, only the MGM film gives pride of place to the magic shoes. The emphasis on the ruby slippers in this film both glamorises Dorothy and associates the idea of a portal to another world with a single (or rather, double) object. Dorothy's shoes are what the Wicked Witch of the West wants most in the world: as Glinda, the Good Witch of the North, tells Dorothy when they first meet, 'Keep tight inside of them. Their magic must be very powerful, or she wouldn't want them so badly.' The value of Dorothy's ruby slippers is in part determined by the Wicked Witch's desire to own them, and in part by the law of supply and demand.

The economics of magic shoes naturally exceeds the boundaries of a film that would contain it. According to Rushdie,

> A pair of ruby slippers, found in a bin in the MGM basement, was sold at auction in May 1970 for the amazing sum of $15,000. [...] It turned out, incidentally, that the $15,000 slippers were too large to have fitted Judy Garland's feet. They had in all probability been made for her double, Bobbie Koshay, whose feet were two sizes larger. Is it not fitting that the shoes made for the stand-in to stand in should have passed into the possession of another kind of surrogate: a film fan? (Rushdie 2012: 47–8)

It is also fitting – or ill-fitting, as the case may be – that this desire to own the ruby slippers resulted in the acquisition of the wrong shoes, as if the props themselves were obeying the film's narrative logic that there may be only one foot for every shoe.

The sexual economy of magic shoes

In both *The Wizard of Oz* and *Cinderella* shoes are a commodity that trades on power. In the MGM *Wizard of Oz* film the Wicked Witch of the West makes it very clear that she wants the power conferred by the ruby slippers Dorothy is wearing. In *Cinderella*, the woman who is able to wear the glass slipper the prince is offering (which, though it does not belong to him, has become his to barter for a marriage partner) will gain untold riches and the power that comes with royalty. These transactions do not involve the exchange of like for like: the power conferred on the wearer of the slippers in each case is both magical and symbolic.

In both the film and the fairy tale, the adolescent who wears the slippers undergoes a rite of passage, which leads to the power of maturity. In the case of *Cinderella*, this power is an explicitly sexual one, as the glass slipper allows the young girl to accede to matrimonial union. In *The Wizard of Oz*, Dorothy gains the ability not only to infuriate the Wicked Witch of the West but also to broker a brain for a scarecrow, a heart for a tin man and courage for a cowardly lion. Additionally, Dorothy possesses the power, while wearing the shoes, to expose and shame an influential imposter (the 'wizard' of the film's title) and, perhaps most important of all, to get back to the place that is unlike any other: home. Once back in Kansas, Dorothy might be missing her magic shoes but she has gained the capacity to recognise the kernel of truth behind the fantasy. As both symbols and instruments of this rite of passage, the ruby slippers point towards the future, to a level of maturity that the young Dorothy does not possess. The red sequined pump is a grown woman's shoe, at odds with Dorothy's plaits, blue-and-white gingham dress and otherwise childlike demeanour. (This tension is emblematised in a close-up of Dorothy's feet in the moment the red shoes appear on them: Dorothy's ankle socks emphasise her youth, but the deftness with which she 'models' the shoes, turning her feet this way and that in a 'Y' formation that would not be out of place on a catwalk, suggests an understanding of both fashion and seduction that is beyond her years.)

Similarly, Cinderella's glass slipper provides a titillating glimpse of the wearer's naked feet. Bruno Bettelheim argues that the brittleness of the glass not only ensures that the shoe ends up on the 'right' foot because it cannot be stretched to fit the 'wrong' one, but also 'reminds us of the hymen' (Bettelheim 1976: 265). Glass slippers, moreover, are begging to be broken. In Disney's classic 1950 animated version of *Cinderella* (Geronimi, Jackson and Luske), the prince's representative (no doubt his footman) drops the glass slipper in the climactic shoe-fitting scene and it shatters into multiple fragments. Cinderella then takes the broken slipper's mate from her pocket and allows the prince's aide to slip it on to her foot. Needless to say, the shoe fits.

All the myriad versions of the fairy tale discount the possibility of counterfeit-slipper fraud because becoming a princess is Cinderella's fate. Cinderella's mateless shoe is surely a metaphor for a mateless lover, one of a pair of sole-mates temporarily separated but destined to be reunited. Each shoe is the mirror image of the other: too much sameness would jar, but just enough difference makes for symmetry and perfect union, or so the story goes. (Of course, the shoe can be worn on the other foot, too. In the TerryTunes animated short *The Glass Slipper* [Paul Terry Studios, 1938], Cinderella dances to jazz music at the ball with a prince who resembles Harpo Marx, and when the prince later shows up to try the slipper on her, the fairy godmother, who bears a very strong visual and aural resemblance to Mae West, reappears and grabs the slipper from Cinderella, saying 'That slipper belongs to me', before carrying off the prince and commenting, 'I always get my man'. The shoe can also be worn on no foot at all, as in the case of Roald Dahl's 1982 *Revolting Rhymes*, in which Cinderella rejects the prince in favour of a jam-maker.)

The form of the shoe in each tale (*Cinderella* and *The Wizard of Oz*) is significant: its heel lifts the wearer off the ground, away from the humility (from *humus*, ground) of the life of a labourer, whether grounded in farm work (*The Wizard of Oz*) or domestic servitude (*Cinderella*). The fact that the shoes do not have straps means that they can be slipped on and off with ease (hence the term 'slippers'). In the case of *Cinderella*, this feature is crucial to the narrative: if the glass slippers were fastened securely on Cinderella's feet both of them would have stayed on her feet as she rushed from the ball. The ability to slip the shoes on and off also suggests the power of magical transformation, of the ability to slip into and out of a magical realm. In Dorothy's case, since the magic shoes *cannot* come off, their lack of a strap or buckle serves to underscore the strength of the magic that keeps them on. The shoes' heels, of course, fulfil the same function that high heels do in the non-magical world: they force the wearer to jut her posterior out as she walks, drawing attention to that part of the body in a sexualised way. The heels also hinder full mobility, hobbling their wearer and making her reliant on someone (usually a man) who is not wearing heels for tasks that require more active physical engagement. In Kansas and in ordinary flat-heeled lace-up Oxfords that are either brown or a scuffed-up black (the sepia tone of the film at this point making the shoes' colour difficult to identify), Dorothy climbs fences and runs around the farmyard. In Oz, her steps are generally more delicate, and though she skips down the Yellow Brick Road and stumbles across the poppy field, she generally comports herself in a more conventionally 'ladylike' manner than she does on the farm while wearing flat shoes. In all the versions of *Cinderella* examined here, the glass slipper falls off when Cinderella tries to run; that is, as soon as she does anything more active than waltzing.

In both narratives, the slippers accompany a cosmetic makeover. In the myriad versions of *Cinderella* the slippers are part and parcel of that makeover, part of the outfit given to the girl by her fairy godmother for her trip to the royal ball, which comes complete with an elegant dress, jewellery and new coiffure. In *The Wizard of Oz*, Dorothy and her companions submit to a makeover in the Emerald Castle, receiving a manicure, pedicure and hairstyling (even the cowardly lion ends up with a ribbon in his mane). In each case, the makeover is both the sign of and catalyst for sexual maturity, a rite of passage that is a central feature of the Hollywood canon, from *Cinderella* to *Pretty Woman* (Garry Marshall, USA, 1990), *Miss Congeniality* (Donald Petrie, USA, 2000), and beyond.

Sexuality, notably by way of the castration complex, has been a central feature of the *Cinderella* story from the very origins of the tale. Marina Warner notes that the earliest extant written version of Cinderella featuring a lost slipper dates from AD 850–60 in China, where '[t]he tiny, precious, golden shoe, a treasure among country people who would have gone barefoot or worn bark or straw pattens, also reverberates with the fetishism of bound feet' (Warner 1994: 203). Freud ([1927] 1961) established the significance of the foot or shoe as a reassuring substitute for the phallus the fetishist fears has been cut off. Indeed, in the Grimms' version of *Cinderella*, *Aschenputtel* (Grimm 1857), the wicked stepsisters cut off their toes and heels in an attempt to squeeze their large feet into the delicate slipper (a severance perhaps alluded to in Méliès's truncated view of women's feet). This graphic scene from the Grimms' story is depicted in Lotte Reiniger's 1922 animated silhouette-figure film *Aschenputtel* (*Cinderella*), when one of the stepsisters cuts off her heel to make her foot fit into the shoe and the prince only realises that he has chosen the wrong woman when her foot begins to haemorrhage, causing her body to shrivel up from the loss of blood. (The allusion to castration in the woman's severed foot is repeated in Nicolas Roeg's 1990 film *The Witches*, which, like Roald Dahl's 1983 book of the same name, shows squared, toeless feet as the distinguishing feature of witches.)

It is no accident that both the glass and ruby slippers, with their narrow and slightly pointed toes, are more phallic in shape than, say, clogs or hiking boots, making them less obviously feminine than Bettelheim's comparison between the glass slipper and the hymen, above, would suggest. Jack Zipes contends that Cinderella has much less sexual agency than Bettelheim claims she does, arguing that '[h]ow Bettelheim twists the meaning to see *Cinderella* as active is actually another one of his Freudian magic tricks' (Zipes 1979: 173). However, regardless of whether Cinderella's sexuality is 'active' or 'passive' (and regardless of the meaning that those terms may or may not have), and regardless, finally, of whether Cinderella is a feminist fairy tale icon or a compliant victim, it is clear that her shoe story, like Dorothy's, is a fetishist's dream.

'It's so kind of you to visit me in my loneliness'

Of course, women's shoes often convey sexual meaning in cinema and in fashion more broadly speaking. The film (and television) franchise that has done more to convey this meaning than perhaps any other is *Sex and the City*, the first television episode of which aired in 1998, with the first film appearing in 2008 (dir. Michael Patrick King). In the television shows and the films, four multiple-shoe-owning women frequently get together to discuss their purchases and contemplate buying yet more shoes. The main character, Carrie Bradshaw, has so many shoes that her consort builds a special walk-in closet for them in order to win her heart and, in the first film, he even proposes by slipping a sparkling shoe onto her foot in lieu of an engagement ring, suggesting that he is indeed Carrie's fairy tale prince. The film sequel, *Sex and the City 2* (Michael Patrick King, USA, 2010), also revolves around shoes, but this time moves to Abu Dhabi, where Carrie's shoe-purchasing is limited to buying a pair of leather slippers. The film contains many overt references to *The Wizard of Oz*, from the appearance of Liza Minnelli, Judy Garland's daughter, at a wedding at the beginning of the film, to a character's exclamation, upon seeing the swanky hotel they will be staying in, that 'we're not in Kansas anymore'. When shopping in a souk in the old part of Abu Dhabi, Carrie spies a shoemaker selling traditional leather shoes at a kiosk. She sets her sights on a particular pair, with a phallic protuberance jutting out from the toe; she is delighted to learn they are 'only' twenty dollars and tries them on. It goes without saying that they fit perfectly: she and the shoes were destined to be together.

When Carrie tries on the shoe in the souk, viewers might wonder, is she channelling Dorothy or Cinderella? Carrie might end up with the 'right' man and a black diamond engagement ring, but in return, she must promise 'never, ever' to kiss another man. This 'never, ever' is not the inverse of, but rather the precondition for, a 'happily ever after'. Carrie has travelled both to a magic life with her prince and away from a Technicolor world in which she was free to kiss whomever she wished. She is both Cinderella and Dorothy.

Both stories alluded to in *Sex and the City 2*, the 1939 film *The Wizard of Oz* and a generic version of the *Cinderella* tale, not only establish what is/are the 'right' shoe(s), they also show scenarios depicting the 'wrong' shoes: Carrie dates a lot of men over the course of the television and film franchise; the prince or his representative try the glass slipper on a number of women before finding the shoe's owner; and the ruby slippers are first worn by the Wicked Witch of the East before magically appearing on Dorothy's feet. The contrast is instructive: without the 'wrong' shoe, it would be hard to recognise the 'right' one. (It should be noted, though, that, despite Big's proposal to her with a shoe – her own shoe, in fact – that is just the right size, suggesting that their impending marriage is the right fit, Carrie continues to own a whole walk-in closet full of shoes, which leaves open the possibility of other relationships in future sequels.)

However, the scenario of the 'wrong' shoe also begs the question: what are the criteria for right and wrong here, since size and destiny are so clearly metaphors for something else? In *Cinderella*, the small size of the maiden's foot connotes daintiness, beauty and, by extension, purity and goodness. Cinderella's stepsisters struggle to squeeze their feet into the glass slipper not only because their feet are the wrong *size*, but also because the women themselves are not beautiful or delicate enough for the prince or, in the case of Perrault's tale, young enough: they are described as 'both somewhat past their prime' (Perrault [1697] 1998: 69). The stepsisters in *Cinderella* are usually described in popular culture using the epithet 'ugly', suggesting they are unlikely to be selected as marriage partners by a prince or anyone wealthy and powerful enough to be choosy. The witch in Oz is, as her moniker suggests, 'wicked', but the implication is that she is also past childbearing age. Dorothy's acquisition of the shoes signals a transfer of power from the East Witch, but the power conferred by the ruby slippers is not that of monarchy but of menarche. They make Dorothy seem 'old enough' to be a potential reproductive partner, while the Witch of the West appears to hope they will make *her* seem 'young enough'. Neither the Wicked Witch of the West nor the wicked stepsisters are presented as viable marriage partners. The Kansan version of the Wicked Witch, it will be recalled, is Miss Gulch, the dour bicycle-riding neighbour who complains about Toto. Gulch lives alone, and her title, 'Miss' implies that she is not and has probably never been married, therefore suggesting – in 1939, and in light of her apparent class and social standing – that she does not have children. Dorothy and Cinderella, by contrast, are both destined to marry and breed a new generation of, respectively, farmhands and princes. Dorothy's ruby slippers are the 'right' shoes precisely because they are not meant for a woman fated to remain single and childless.

As in the Cinderella story, the question of who should wear the magic shoes is central to the plot of *The Wizard of Oz*, but in the latter work the emotional transaction takes place not between a young woman and a male suitor but between a young woman and an older female antagonist who wants the shoes

Figure 4.2 Dorothy and her new friends

at all cost. But what will the shoes actually give her? The witch seems to believe that they will confer upon her a power of some sort, but the nature of this power is never disclosed. Is it the power of glamour, of sexual attraction, of the chance, ultimately, to marry and have children? The shoes certainly provide her with an excuse for companionship, a pretext for Dorothy to come and see her. When Dorothy is cornered by the Wicked Witch of the West in her castle, the witch says to her, 'It's so kind of you to visit me in my loneliness'. This line is delivered in a sarcastic tone of voice, but as Freud said, no one is ever 'just kidding'.

The ruby slippers, while marking out the differences between Dorothy and the witch, also remind us, on a certain level, of their similarities. Although the witch, like the other main Ozian characters, is the uncanny double of a Kansan, she finds a surrogate sister in Dorothy, someone who has stepped into the East Witch's shoes. The West Witch may threaten to kill Dorothy, but then she did profess rivalry with her sister, too. The witch both wants to be with Dorothy and to be her, but she can be neither. She cannot wear the slippers because she has no place in a world that privileges feminine fecundity and desirability above all else. The shoes do not fit because the Wicked Witch does not fit in.

References

Baum, L. Frank (1900), *The Wonderful Wizard of Oz*, Chicago: George M. Hill.

Bettelheim, Bruno (1976), *The Uses of Enchantment: The Meaning and Importance of Fairy Tales*, Harmondsworth: Penguin.

Dahl, Roald (1983), *The Witches*, London: Jonathan Cape.

Dahl, Roald (1982), *Revolting Rhymes*, London: Jonathan Cape.

Dundes, Alan (1988), *Cinderella, A Casebook*, Madison, WI: University of Wisconsin Press.

Freud, Sigmund [1927] (1961), 'Fetishism', *Standard Edition of the Complete Psychological Works of Sigmund Freud*, trans, and ed. J. Strachey, London: Hogarth Press, vol. 21, pp. 149–57.

Grimm, Jacob and Wilhelm (1857), 'Aschenputtel', *Kinder- und Hausmärchen [Children's and Household] Grimms' Fairy Tales*, 7th ed., Göttingen: Verlag der Dieterichschen Buchhandlung, no. 21, pp. 119–26.

Perrault, Charles [1697] (1998), 'Cinderella', trans. A. Quiller-Couch, *Perrault's Fairy Tales*, London: Folio Society.

Pouget, Émile (1911), *Le Sabotage*, Paris: Librairie des Sciences Politiques et Sociales Marcel Rivière.

Rushdie, Salman (2012), *The Wizard of Oz*, London: BFI.

Rushdie, Salman (2003), *Step Across the Line: Collected Nonfiction 1992-2002*, New York: Modern Library, p. 8.

Swartz, Mark Evan (2000), *Oz Before the Rainbow: L. Frank Baum's The Wonderful Wizard of Oz on Stage and Screen to 1939*, Baltimore: Johns Hopkins University Press.

Warner, Marina (1994), *From the Beast to the Blonde: On Fairy Tales and their Tellers*, London: Chatto and Windus.

Zipes, Jack (1979), *Breaking the Magic Spell: Radical Theories of Folk and Fairy Tales*, London: Heinemann.

Chapter 5

The ruby slippers at the V&A: an odyssey

Keith Lodwick

In January 2012 the V&A (Victoria and Albert Museum, London) announced its major autumn exhibition to the press. *Hollywood Costume* would feature more than one hundred costumes, celebrating the most remarkable characters in motion picture history. The exhibition was marketed as a 'once-in-a-lifetime experience' for the public to see their favourite characters up close ('Hollywood Costume Exhibition' Press Release 2012).

Guest curator Deborah Nadoolman Landis, an award-winning designer and academic, conceived a designer-led exhibition looking at all periods and genres of film; whilst fantasy or period pictures win awards, she argued that 'every picture is a costume picture' (Landis 2007: xxxiii). Costumes for the cowboys in *Brokeback Mountain* (Ang Lee, USA, 2005) were displayed alongside those of *Queen Christina* (Rouben Mamoulian, USA, 1933) and *Marie Antoinette* (W. S. Van Dyke, USA, 1938); suits from *Superman* (Richard Donner, USA, 1978) and from *Star Wars: Episode IV – A New Hope* (George Lucas, USA, 1977) were displayed alongside James Bond's iconic tuxedo. But it was two particular films that created the biggest reaction from the media, both released in 1939 and both directed by Victor Fleming: *Gone with the Wind* and *The Wizard of Oz*.

Guest co-curator Christopher Frayling argued in the book that accompanied the exhibition that *The Wizard of Oz* is an allegory of the filmmaking process itself, and many of its scenes and characters are still instantly recognisable:

> A depression farm-girl from Kansas, whose world is black and white, dreams of three-strip Technicolor land of Oz beyond a rainbow where the flora and fauna are larger than life, the costumes cartoonish and where the Emerald City resembles a Hollywood studio, complete with props and sound stage. The Wizard himself does not possess real magic powers, so like the fairground huckster he is, he gives a Scarecrow a degree certificate,

the Tin Man a heart shaped clock and the Lion, a medal, so they can feel
better about themselves. *The Wizard of Oz* is at the same time an exposé
and a celebration of the Hollywood dream factory. (Frayling 2012: 200)

At the heart of the exhibition was a scholarly premise: how does a costume
designer create authentic characters? The narrative aim of the exhibition
was to place the art of the costume designer at its centre, exploring their
creative process from script to screen and revealing the collaborative
dialogue between designers, actors and directors. The curatorial scope of the
exhibition had never been attempted before, as previous exhibitions on film
costume had focused on the images that Hollywood had created, including
Romantic and Glamorous Hollywood Design at the MET in New York (1974)
and *Hollywood and History: Costume Design in Film* at LACMA, Los Angeles
(1986).

There was never any doubt that the dress from *The Wizard of Oz* would
serve as a figurehead for the exhibition's marketing campaign. Judy Garland's
Dorothy Gale became the 'pin-up girl' of the show, and re-uniting the dress
and the iconic shoes became the ultimate goal.

Early in the 'treasure hunt', the curators had secured Dorothy's blue-and-
white gingham dress (Lodwick 2012: 203). The costume was offered on loan to
the V&A in a phone call from a private collector and was being held in a secure

Figure 5.1 The ruby slippers

bank vault in London's Fleet Street. In June 2010, Deborah Landis, a V&A textile conservator, and I were ushered through the depths of the bank past corridors with glass cases containing ledgers dating back to the seventeenth century. Once we were safely inside the large vault, two security men appeared carrying a huge box. As the lid was removed, we gathered around to watch Deborah remove reams of tissue paper to reveal one of the most iconic costumes in film history: Dorothy's blue-and-white pinafore dress. For the exhibitions team it was a 'holy grail' moment. One of the most enduring and cherished films of all time would now be part of the V&A exhibition.

Having secured the loan of the dress, it was felt by the curators that the exhibition would not be complete without a pair of the ruby slippers, arguably the most famous shoes in film history.

The ruby slippers were designed by Adrian (Adrian Adolph Greenberg 1903–59), MGM's premiere costume designer and one of the most significant designers in film history. However, they were not originally conceived as red: it was screenwriter Noel Langley who changed the slippers from the original colour of silver to 'ruby', which would look better in Technicolor film. The slippers were made for Adrian by the Western Costume Company (Los Angeles) in 1938 by veteran shoemaker Joe Napoli. They were created from original red satin shoes with a French heel of one-and-a-half inches. Covered in red sequins sewn onto fine chiffon, the large centre-bow is edged with red glass bugle beads, crystals and three emerald-shaped crystals. The actual colour of the original slippers is a deep garnet, which photographed a bright scarlet under the hot Technicolor lighting.

We were hopeful of borrowing a pair of the ruby slippers and knew there was more than one pair in existence. But what happened to the ruby slippers after filming was completed at MGM in 1939 is unknown. What is known is that every costume, prop and piece of furniture created by the world-famous studio was sold over a series of days in 1970. This event, described by Landis as 'the dissolution of the studio system' (Landis 2007: 247), marked the end of the studio that at its 1930s peak was the most successful in the world. Film assets, highly prized today by collectors, museums and historians, were sold off piece by piece and fifty years of film history was dismantled. The sale heralded the emergence of the modern memorabilia collector, and many items' provenance can be traced back to this sale.

Lot. W.1048 'Shoes, red sequined ruby slippers' were auctioned at 8pm on Sunday 17 May 1970. They were auctioned on stage twenty-seven, the same stage on which Judy Garland had followed the yellow brick road in 1939. It was assumed on the day that they were the only pair in existence.

Rhys Thomas's book *The Ruby Slippers of Oz* offers a fascinating account of what happened to the slippers post-sale and traces the other pairs as they began to surface over the 1970s and 1980s. Three of the four known pairs were discovered by costumier Kent Warner, who was hired by the David Weisz Company to identify costumes and organise the MGM sale. Knowing this, Landis and the V&A established contact with the known owners of the ruby slippers.

One pair belonged to Michael Shaw, who obtained them from Kent Warner around 1970. This pair was stolen in 2005 from the Judy Garland Museum in Grand Rapids, Minnesota. The theft prompted intense media speculation and the story became a 'whodunnit' in film memorabilia circles. *The Slippers*, a 2016 documentary by Morgan White which aimed to tell the story of the ruby slippers and their cultural iconography, also attempted to unravel the mystery of the theft. This case was resolved in 2018 – too late for the *Hollywood Costume* exhibition – when the FBI proudly announced on their Twitter account that the stolen pair had been discovered during an undercover operation in Minneapolis.

A second pair of slippers were won as a prize by Roberta Bauman in 1940 for a national 'Name the Ten Best Movies of 1939' competition. These slippers feature red painted leather soles with orange felt glued to the front foundation. Their condition is worn, with sequins missing. In black ink the word 'double' is handwritten on the white kid lining of each shoe, meaning these slippers were the second or third pair made for use in the production, as a spare in case the first pair was damaged. A common misconception is that 'double' suggests they were only worn by a stand-in – a different actress placed on set for testing lighting and camera angles rather than Judy Garland – but, according to several MGM costumiers this is not in accordance with the studio's practice for labelling wardrobe items. These slippers were sold at auction through Christie's East on 21 June 1988 for $165,000 and were later resold by Christie's East on 24 May 2000 for $666,000. This pair of shoes is owned jointly by collectors and is kept in a bank vault in Los Angeles. Landis met one of the owners and managed to persuade him to lend one of the slippers. The owner of the other slipper remained unmoved, so this loan fell through. At one point, we considered displaying one slipper with a mirror.

A third pair, owned by art collector Philip Samuels, were Kent Warner's 'prized' size 5B slippers. They are marked on the inside lining '#7 Judy Garland' and the leather soles are painted red on the bottom. The lack of felt, in addition to light, circular scuffs evident on the soles indicate their use in the extra close-up or 'insert' shots when Garland famously taps her heels together at the film's climax. The Academy of Motion Picture Arts and Sciences acquired these slippers, with a fundraising campaign led by Leonardo DiCaprio and Steven Spielberg, at an auction by Profiles in History on 16 December 2011. These were unavailable for loan as they were to be revealed at the new Academy Museum of Motion Pictures in Los Angeles.

The fourth pair of ruby slippers is the most well known as it is one of the most popular exhibits at the Smithsonian Museum in Washington. These slippers are the centrepiece of an exhibition called *Icons of American Culture*. *The Wizard of Oz* is a cultural signpost in American literature, film and popular culture. The text is also a cultural export and it is suggested that the film is the most watched in history. The carpet in front of the case has to be replaced on a regular basis due to the crush of people passing before it. Carl Scheele, former curator at the Smithsonian, has stated that around five million people visit per year to see the ruby slippers.

When the Smithsonian generously agreed to lend this pair of ruby slippers to the V&A, it was on the understanding that the shoes would have to be returned to the United States before the Thanksgiving holiday in late November. Securing the slippers for the exhibition warranted a major press release: 'Ruby Slippers to leave America for the first time in history' (Press Release 2012) headlined the V&A's announcement. For their journey from Washington to London, the slippers travelled with their own security guard and allocated seat on the plane. The box containing the slippers was handcuffed to the guard and they were accompanied by the Smithsonian's curator, Dwight Blocker Bowers. Their arrival at the V&A prompted a top-secret security operation. Once the slippers were securely installed inside the bulletproof case, they were positioned next to the gingham dress.

Landis commented on the importance of this moment in the exhibition narrative:

> The Ruby Slippers transcend Hollywood costume design and have the power to transport us to the limits of our imagination. These precious shoes exemplify the best of cinema storytelling because they evoke memory and emotion. ('Ruby Slippers' Press Release 2012)

Hollywood Costume opened in October 2012, and people queued to get a chance to see these iconic slippers. The exhibition remains one of the most successful in the V&A's history. Rhys Thomas, who has devoted a whole book to the subject of the ruby slippers, believes:

> The ruby slippers were much more than just a piece of Hollywood memorabilia, much more than a valuable piece of industry history. They have transcended Hollywood, to the point where they represented the powerful image of innocence to all America. (Thomas 1989: 168)

The Wizard of Oz continues to inspire filmmakers and theatremakers today, with re-tellings of the story in *The Wiz* (Sidney Lumet, USA, 1978) and in Stephen Schwartz's musical *Wicked*, which has run on Broadway and London's West End for more than fifteen years. Writers from fans to academics have tried to deconstruct its popularity and we chose the shoes as the high point on which to end the exhibition.

For the V&A and *Hollywood Costume*, re-uniting the dress and slippers was a vision realised. A fitting legacy of this popularity is that in an exhibition that featured a hundred iconic costumes, but only one pair of original shoes, it was these ruby slippers that were chosen as the front cover image on the exhibition book.

References

Frayling, Christopher (2012) *Hollywood Costume*, London: V&A Publishing.

'Hollywood Costume Exhibition' press release 2012, Victoria and Albert Museum, London.

Landis, Deborah Nadoolman (2007), *Dressed: A Century of Hollywood Costume Design*, New York: HarperCollins.

Lodwick, Keith (2012), *Hollywood Costume*, London: V&A Publishing.

'Ruby Slippers to Leave America for the First Time in History', press release 2012, Victoria and Albert Museum, London.

Thomas, Rhys (1989), *The Ruby Slippers of Oz*, Los Angeles: Tale Weaver Publishing.

Thomas, Rhys (2018), 'The Ruby Slippers of Oz', in *Icons of Hollywood, Profiles in History Auction Catalogue*, https://profilesinhistory.com/product/icons-legends-of-hollywood-hard-bound-catalog/

Chapter 6

Blood-red shoes?

Ian Christie

A decade separates the two most famous pairs of red shoes in film history: Dorothy's ruby slippers in *The Wizard of Oz* (Victor Fleming, USA, 1939) and Vicky's pointe shoes in the eponymous *The Red Shoes* (Michael Powell & Emeric Pressburger, UK, 1948). But the cultural arc associated with red shoes is much longer, stretching from their adoption as a motif by the pioneers of the modern folk and fairy tale, the Brothers Grimm and Hans Christian Andersen, up to multiple modern iterations, drawing upon and adding to the tradition. As Hilary Davidson concludes in her wide-ranging survey of 'the magic of red shoes', they have become 'complex and conflicting symbols' (Davidson 2011: 288). Between these two films came a world war, and it is certainly tempting to contrast Dorothy's innocent journey to and from Oz with Vicky's tragic fate in light of what had transformed the world in which Powell and Pressburger's film was made. What worried and even repelled some viewers of *The Red Shoes* was what they considered the unnecessarily 'gory' ending, showing Vicky's bloodstained shoes. No matter that Andersen's tale of the same name was even bloodier, with Karen having her feet amputated: many felt a film centred on a 'fairy tale' ballet should not even hint at mutilation.

Yet Michael Powell believed it essential that his 'haunting, insolent picture' would show art as 'something worth dying for' (Powell, 2000: 660). *The Red Shoes* may draw inspiration and 'cultural capital' from Andersen's fable but it is very much more than a cinematic expansion of it, in the way that *The Wizard of Oz* and Jean Cocteau's *La belle et la bête* (1946) were of their source material. And despite the careful avoidance of any markers of period, it is very much a film born of post-war Britain. Tracing the routes that led to its production in 1947–8 will reveal some of the complexity that Davidson finds in all re-tellings of 'The Red Shoes'.

Unique among all Powell and Pressburger's films, its origins lay in a project announced by Alexander Korda soon after his first major success in Britain with *The Private Life of Henry VIII* (1933). Kevin Macdonald's biography of his grandfather Emeric Pressburger records its meandering, profligate progress (Macdonald 1994: 274). First conceived in 1934 as a biopic of the dancer Vaslav Nijinsky, based on his widow's biography, with Paul Muni as Nijinsky and Charles Laughton as the impresario Sergei Diaghilev, it was announced with Korda as producer and director. By 1937, it had become a potential vehicle for Korda's discovery, Merle Oberon, with a new script about 'the life of a Russian dancer' by a prolific popular novelist of the era, G. B. Stern. Two years later, in 1939, it was back as 'the ballet film', re-conceived as a Technicolor production starring Oberon, now married to Korda, with Ludwig Berger potentially as director.

Macdonald records various attempts by well-known screenwriters of the era to create a credible script. Pressburger, now under contract to Korda, recalled: 'there was no story at all, except that Alex had the idea of basing it on the Hans [Christian] Andersen tale "The Red Shoes", which is a great favourite for children in Hungary' (Macdonald 1994: 275). He set to work, informed by intensive observation of the rehearsal process at Covent Garden for a new ballet being choreographed by Michel Fokine, *Variations on a Theme of Paganini*, which was set to Rachmaninov's piano concerto *Rhapsody on a Theme of Paganini*. This experience would play a vital part in informing the theatrical milieu of the script, which was especially important to Powell, after the effort to create a credible neurosurgical context for *A Matter of Life and Death* (UK, 1946). Pressburger may also have been influenced in his treatment of Lermontov by the 'demonic' aspect of the Paganini legend, which Rachmaninov had recommended to Fokine (Fischer 2010;Bertensson et al. 2001: 333). Indeed one image in the 1948 film's phantasmagoric ballet shows Lermontov assuming such a figure, as if drawing the girl towards her doom.

Other events in 1939 ensured that the ballet project made no further progress, as Pressburger began his partnership with Powell by working on *The Spy in Black*. The formation of The Archers partnership followed, supported by J. Arthur Rank's Independent Producers structure, which gave all its members extraordinary freedom during the war to operate within a secure production and distribution framework. However, the end of the war brought new challenges, not only due to Britain's virtual bankruptcy but also for filmmakers who had been focused on the needs and interests of a wartime audience. By 1947, Powell and Pressburger had struck out in a new direction with *Black Narcissus*, essentially a melodrama in which erotic obsession leads to tragedy in an exotic Himalayan setting, and had been encouraged by the warmth of public and critical response. *Black Narcissus* also confirmed the pattern that had been emerging in their later wartime films, increasingly centred on women facing existential choices: Joan in *I Know Where I'm Going!* (1945) and June in

A Matter of Life and Death are both challenged to change direction and follow their heart, at whatever risk.

When The Archers decided to resurrect Pressburger's ballet project, they had first to buy it from Korda, but more importantly to consider it afresh in the context of 1947, when planning got under way. An important part of that context was now Britain's dire post-war economic situation. The Labour government that had come to power in July 1945 was forced to negotiate a large loan from the United States and Canada in 1946. By August 1947, the deteriorating balance of payments encouraged a rash attempt to prevent American film earnings being repatriated by an exceptional 75 per cent tax on imported films.[1]

This provoked an immediate retaliatory embargo on sending new releases to Britain by the Hollywood majors, which lasted for eight months. Compromise led to lifting the boycott in April 1948, just three months before *The Red Shoes* appeared. But during that period both Rank and Korda had accelerated their production programmes to fill the void left by Hollywood and now found themselves heavily over-committed – which no doubt helps to explain the fury directed at Powell and Pressburger's overspend on a film that Rank's John Davis considered unlikely to prove popular.

Beyond these film industry issues, there was a much larger and more urgent set of problems afflicting Britain. Rationing, originally introduced during the war, became more stringent, making everyday life in 1948 a struggle for many to find adequate food, clothing and fuel. And much of the resulting strain was most acutely felt by women, endeavouring to provide for their families. Surveys also confirmed a majority feeling that women should put duty to home and family before the desire to work independently. And a majority of women would have been regular cinemagoers, with attendances at their all-time peak between 1946 and 1948. So it is perhaps not surprising that in his study of 'austerity Britain', the historian David Kynaston offers *The Red Shoes* as a prime example of 'the harsh home and/or work dilemma' faced by many British women in 1948 (Kynaston 2008 : 209).

After the canonisation and elaborate restorations of the film during recent decades, it requires some effort of research and imagination to discover what *The Red Shoes* may have meant for audiences in 1948. At the most basic level, it must have offered a welcome relief from the privations of life in 'austerity Britain'. Vicky (Moira Shearer) is first encountered in the privileged world of her aunt, Lady Neston (Irene Browne), in a box at the Royal Opera House and at a lavish after-party. But she is next seen dancing in a modest gramophone-accompanied production of *Swan Lake* for Ballet Rambert. The contrast between a first night at Covent Garden and a rainy afternoon at the Mercury Theatre in Notting Hill Gate would certainly have struck a chord with audiences in 1948.

So too would the film's magic-carpet progress to Paris and then to Monte Carlo, at a time when hard-pressed finances and currency restrictions meant that few could travel outside Britain. An important feature of the film's story-world is its careful avoidance of any specific dating. We appear to be in a 'present' that is neither identifiably pre- or post-war, but offers a luxurious world which must have seemed deeply attractive to the film's first audiences. From the novel that Powell and Pressburger later published, it is clear that the setting is essentially pre-war, influenced by Pressburger witnessing Fokine's rehearsals at Covent Garden (Powell and Pressburger 1978). But the film contrives to create a world without such markers, other than perhaps the visit to Jacques Fath's Paris fashion show – an episode that would have struck a chord with many female viewers after nearly a decade of restricted access to couture fashion.[2]

Vicky enters a magical world, signalled by her stately ascent of a spectacular staircase leading to the French Riviera villa where Boris Lermontov (Anton Walbrook) and his key creative staff are holding court. Yet what she finds on entering is not a fairy tale kermesse, but a business-like meeting about creating the work in which she will star: the ballet of 'The Red Shoes'. What Powell and Pressburger had been developing, since *I Know Where I'm Going!* and *A Matter of Life and Death*, was a sophisticated balance between emphasising the 'everyday' and creating what Andrew Moor aptly termed 'magic spaces' (Moor 2005). The ballet itself would be a full-scale phantasmagoria, a kind of film within a film, building on the climactic sequence of *Black Narcissus* but also showing the extent of Powell's enthusiasm for Disney and for the stylised world of Oz.[3]

How then does this version refigure Andersen's 'Red Shoes' tale? Davidson has traced the transformation of the tale across the twentieth century, before which it apparently had little currency outside Denmark. She notes what may well be the beginning of a tradition of *mise en abyme*, in which the story of a girl fascinated by dancing shoes becomes itself a ballet. In 1899, the Alhambra Theatre, one of London's premier music halls, famous for its dancing troupe and elaborate decor, presented a 'grand spectacular ballet' under this title, based on 'Hans Andersen's pretty story'. Here the story was set in Russia, with a village girl succumbing to the 'Spirit of Temptation' and stealing 'pretty scarlet shoes' from a church. As Davidson observes, this version is significant in that it 'foregrounds the element of dance, connecting all parts of the story through that medium' (Davidson 2011: 279). Indeed, it is not impossible that Emeric Pressburger may have been aware of it, in view of his commitment to research for scripts.[4]

The work that will bring Vicky fame will also seal her fate. In the ballet, the girl ('Karen', following Andersen) is tempted by a pair of red shoes prominently displayed in a shoemaker's shop window opposite a church. The shoemaker, danced by Léonide Massine as a veritable 'spirit of temptation', encourages her to follow her desire for the shoes, while her boyfriend tries vainly to restrain her. Once the shoes are on her feet, the boyfriend draws back and Karen is launched on an increasingly hectic and picaresque passage through a carnival, followed by a series of surrealistic scenes in which characters from Vicky's 'real' life appear. Her colleague in the ballet company, Ivan (Robert Helpmann), appears both as the spurned boyfriend and as one of the phantasms she meets, a figure wrapped in print. The composer, Julian (Marius Goring), who is conducting this premiere, and will become her husband, appears to dance across the footlights towards her. And the impresario, Lermontov, who has conceived the ballet as a vehicle for her, also appears as a threatening 'demonic' figure. In the end, Karen returns from the dreamscapes she has danced through to the town square where she first saw the red shoes. A procession of respectable couples is gathering to enter the church, as Karen begs her one-time boyfriend, now appearing priest-like, for salvation. The shoemaker offers her a knife to cut off the shoes, but it becomes a wooden branch in her hand. Tenderly, the boyfriend reaches down and unties the shoes, whereupon Karen slumps in his arms, while the shoemaker carries the shoes away with a sly smile, to replace them in his window.

This extraordinary sequence presents a complete ballet of fifteen minutes, not as the theatre audience would see it, but as a phantasmagoric 'waking dream' that is danced and lived by Vicky/Karen. Formally, it would influence a succession of 'fantasy ballets' in many subsequent films, starting with the extended dance sequence that ends Vincente Minnelli's *An American in Paris* (USA, 1951). But its relationship, both to Andersen's story and to the narrative of the film that contains it, remains thematically unique. The original tale has Karen neglect her duties and behave irreligiously due to her fascination with the red dancing shoes. As a result, she is cursed by an angel to dance forever, until an executioner cuts off her feet, leaving her to suffer rejection while she expiates her sins. Only then is she forgiven and taken to heaven on a sunbeam.

The Red Shoes' ballet shows Karen tempted by the diabolic shoes that effectively dance their wearer to death, while she cannot join the 'normal life' that continues around her. Subjectively, Vicky begins to experience the conflict between the two poles of her life: her romantic attraction towards Julian and the artistic fulfilment made possible by Lermontov. At first, in the triumph of the ballet's reception, these are fused, but when Vicky and Julian announce their intention to marry, Lermontov furiously expels both from the company. Their exile enables Julian to advance his own career, writing an opera based on the classical subject of Cupid and Psyche. But Vicky longs for the fulfilment she experienced when dancing *The Red Shoes* for Lermontov. In the film's literally 'melodramatic' climax, she is about to perform the role again, while Julian abandons the premiere of his opera in order to win her back. Torn by these conflicting desires, Vicky flees the theatre and – as if danced by the shoes – falls to her death before a train. The gesture of Julian removing her now bloodstained shoes echoes her partner's gesture at the end of the ballet. And when the theatre curtain rises on an empty stage, a traumatised Lermontov announces her death, declaring that the ballet will still be performed in tribute, although without her. A ghostly, yet secular equivalent to Andersen's ending, in which Karen achieves salvation in death.

What has brought Vicky to this grim apotheosis? In various writings and interviews, Powell lent currency to the phrase 'dying for art'. Having spent the war urging people to die for their country, he joked, The Archers were now urging them to die for art. Certainly, this might be how we could read the film's framing story, of how a young ballerina is taken up by a powerful impresario and put under intolerable pressure, leading to her suicide. For Powell and Pressburger, it was essential that their film should not follow the convention of previous dance films, in which the discipline and sacrifice of a dancer's vocation merely serves as the backdrop to a conventional romance. The *work* of mounting a new ballet, which Pressburger had witnessed in 1939, was replicated in the exceptionally elaborate 'backstage' production of the film, which involved creating a temporary ballet company, and staging for the camera, not only 'The Red Shoes' but a series of vignettes from other works in a variety of authentic theatre settings.

In the post-war austerity climate of 1948, a part of the intended message of *The Red Shoes* was clearly that art *mattered*; that it was demanding as well as rewarding and not to be considered mere entertainment. Contemporary responses to this challenge are revealing. For the film's producers, headed by Rank's John Davis, its extravagance in going over budget and its unapologetic commitment to presenting ballet was deplorable. As a result, it was denied a full circuit release in Britain, and Powell and Pressburger realised they were no longer welcome within Rank's production framework. A *Daily Telegraph* review by Campbell Dixon began by emphasising how remote the world of ballet was from 'the average man', before offering a qualified endorsement:

> Other films have given us ballet, but generally as an interlude in a normal sentimental world. Messrs Powell and Pressburger have bravely gone the whole hog. From start to finish the characters live for ballet and nothing but ballet; one of them dies for it, a trifle gorily and unnecessarily, in Technicolor. (*Daily Telegraph*, 26 July 1948)

Despite equivocal critical reaction in Britain, with distinctly negative comments in the specialised dance press and by a younger generation of cinephile critics, the film apparently proved popular with those audiences who could see it in Britain.

However, its fullest recognition came with the American release later in 1948, which elicited unqualified praise from the *New York Times* critic Bosley Crowther:

> ... there has never been a picture in which the ballet and its special, magic world have been so beautifully and dreamily presented as the new British film, The Red Shoes. Here, in this unrestricted romance ... is a visual and emotional comprehension of all the grace and rhythm and power of the ballet. (*New York Times*, 23 October 1948)

The film's long-term impact in the United States can be traced in its continuing influence on Hollywood musicals of the 1950s, notably Vincente Minnelli's *The Band Wagon* (USA, 1953), and on many future filmmakers who saw it when young, such as Martin Scorsese. More widely, it has been credited with turning many young people growing up in the 1950s towards an interest in ballet – as evidenced by one of the auditioning dancers in the musical *A Chorus Line* (Richard Attenborough, USA, 1985).

What is notable in the scale and longevity of the American response is that this seems almost exclusively focused on the film's presentation of the 'magic world' of ballet, largely ignoring the darker aspects of its narrative.[5] Not until *Black Swan* (Darren Aronofsky, USA, 2010) did an equivalently tormented view of the dancer's life appear in cinema, owing much to *The Red Shoes* in the 'doubling' of its heroine. In 2016, the British choreographer Matthew Bourne took up the challenge of making a stage adaptation of the film, despite the earlier failure of an American stage version, and his show proved highly successful.

Amid the modern outpouring of admiration for the original film and its successful remediation in Bourne's dance theatre, the dramatic crux is constantly restated as a fatal choice between 'love and art'. Indeed, long after 1948, critics would adduce evidence from the history of dance of impresarios taking their revenge on leading dancers who had broken faith by forming romantic relationships. Léonide Massine, famously, was ejected from the Ballets Russe by Diaghilev after he married, as Nijinsky had been before him. Both, however, had previously been sexual partners of Diaghilev's, which implies a more complex motivation than the mere issue of marriage. *The Red Shoes* apparently coalesces the complexity of sexual and artistic loyalties from the history of ballet into a stark choice, stripped of sexual demands: total dedication to dance, or dismissal.

But is this a sufficiently nuanced historical reading of the film? Modern audiences are unlikely to be aware of the strong cultural prohibition against married women working that existed in the post-war period, and which must have struck a chord with many early viewers. Coincidentally, the sociologist Pearl Jephcott published her study *Rising Twenty: Notes on Ordinary Girls* in 1948 and discovered, from her extensive interviews, that few women expected to continue working after marriage.[6] After Vicky and Julian are expelled from the Lermontov company we see them in an intriguing domestic interlude, which registers her sense of anticlimactic loss. As they lie in bed at night, Julian 'hears' a passage from his opera and goes to play it on the piano, while Vicky goes to her drawer of shoes and fondles, not the red ones we can partially see, but a 'normal' pair of pink ballet shoes. As Julian continues to play, they embrace, she sinking wordlessly to sit beneath the keyboard, subordinating herself to his vocation.

Significantly, Bourne's dance-theatre version recasts this poignantly ambivalent scene as their being forced to work in a music hall: the choice is recast as between 'high' art and mere entertainment, rather than between art and ordinary life. But in the wordless choreography of the film we understand the complexity and dynamic of feelings involved. Vicky has sacrificed her artistic fulfilment in dancing the ballet created for her, while Julian has achieved his ambition, to write a work in what he considers a superior art form. Ironically, and pointedly, his opera is the story of the frustrated lovers in Greek mythology, Cupid and Psyche. But while these reached a happy union, after many obstacles, Julian and Vicky will not. Stung by Lermontov's challenge, 'go and be a faithful housewife', Vicky closes the link between Andersen and The Archers, becoming the doomed Karen as her red shoes carry her down a spiral staircase towards an escape from her impossible choice.

For some British critics, the blood that stains Vicky's legs and shoes after her leap was 'unnecessary'. But for Powell, we realise, it was as vital as creating the whole life of the ballet company, and filming in Notting Hill as well as in Paris and Monte Carlo. Without Vicky's suicide becoming 'real', echoing the shocking climax of *Black Narcissus* when Sister Ruth plunges to her death after trying to kill Sister Clodagh, the *cost* of art would remain merely symbolic. As Donald Clarke aptly noted in a 2015 note on the film:

> Powell and Pressburger, whose work was characterised by lack of compromise, had an uncluttered understanding of the core metaphor. The urge to make art can drive the truly committed like a madness that poisons everyday concerns. (Clarke 2015)

The message of *The Red Shoes*, which Lermontov reminds us 'are never tired', was more provocative than we might imagine in 1948, and it cost its makers the security of their production base with Rank, condemning them to uncertainty and compromise in their subsequent films.[7] In translating Andersen's morbid, sentimental tale into a new era and medium, Powell and Pressburger created a tragic myth that continues to resonate.

Davidson's essay valuably explores this extension into recent times by discussing Kate Bush's 1993 album, entitled *The Red Shoes*, which she locates in a 'New Romantic videoscape', referring to the film that accompanied the album, *The Line, the Cross and the Curve*. Bush's project, she notes, 'drew ideas from the film, rather than directly from Andersen' (Davidson 2011: 281), with an image of red satin ballet shoes on the cover, adding:

> Within the lyrics, Bush uses the red shoe motif to trace a journey through feminine emotional experience, losing and regaining love, passion and a sense of self … Issues of individual women's agency or movement through a lifecycle match the theme of the physical journey and mobility of red shoes in Andersen's original model. (Ibid.)

Davidson concludes her survey of the red shoes motif across culture by observing that 'no response to it is neutral', claiming that it still has the power 'to incite passionate controversy, attachment and desire' (Davidson 2011: 288).

But even if red shoes have become a highly 'malleable' symbol, present in many new cultural arenas, such as queer culture and avant-garde fashion, we cannot ignore the seeming antinomy between Dorothy's and Vicky's wearing of them – which brought them to the screen as potent modern symbols. Davidson attempts a bridging definition: 'a symbol for women who deviate from conventional social behaviour' (Davidson 2011: 281). But this is surely too broad, or bland. Dorothy's ruby slippers enable her to allay her companions' anxieties, to discover the truth about the Wizard, and to embrace home. They are linked to 'positive and transformative values' (Davidson 2011: 288). Vicky's bloody shoes stand for the rejection of domesticity, especially in the context of post-war gender politics, aimed at sending women back home. They take her far from home, to be torn apart by the forces at war in her psyche, and to pay the price. Healing magic versus sacrificial magic – you still have to choose.

Notes

1. On the Anglo-American 'film trade war', see Ian Jarvie (1986).
2. On the interaction between 1940s British costume design and Paris fashion, see Pam Cook (1996), *Fashioning the Nation: Costume and Identity in British Cinema*, BFI, pp. 53.
3. Recalling his admiration for the actor Ralph Richardson, Powell lamented that he was never offered 'the parts he was ideally made to play, for instance the Wizard in *The Wizard of Oz*'. He mentioned Richardson's enthusiasm for 'the Disney-Stokowski masterpiece *Fantasia*', one of many admiring references to Disney throughout the memoirs (Powell 1986: 608–9).

4. An example of 'historical' *mise en abyme* in an earlier Archers' script is the play about Ulysses that Clive Candy goes to see in *The Life and Death of Colonel Blimp* (1943). This verse play by Stephen Phillips, underlining the theme of the warrior's search for home, was actually on the London stage at the appropriate date.
5. For an overview of the film's legacy in dance and in the United States, see Alistair Macauley, 'Love and Dance: Two Obsessions, One Classic Film', New York Times, 29 August 2008.
6. Jephcott had previously interviewed young women for her *Girls Growing Up* (1942) and returned to sample their views after the war, during which most would have been working, for *Rising Twenty*. She would later return to this issue in her *Married Women Working* (1962).
7. Returning to Alexander Korda as producer, amid the crisis affecting British cinema in 1948, led to them being 'loaned' by Korda to the American independent producers David O. Selznick and Samuel Goldwyn for *Gone to Earth* (1950) and *The Elusive Pimpernel* (1950, with drastically reduced autonomy compared with their previous position at Rank. See Christie 1994: 79–83.

References

Bertensson, Sergei, Leyda, Jay and Satina, Sophia (2001), *Sergei Rachmaninov: A Lifetime in Music*, Bloomington: Indiana University Press.

Christie, Ian (1994), *Arrows of Desire: the Films of Michael Powell and Emeric Pressburger*, London: Faber.

Clarke, Donald (2015), 'Film of the Week', *The Irish Times*, 15 December 2015.

Cook, Pam (1996), *Fashioning the Nation: Costume and Identity in British Cinema*, London: BFI.

Davidson, Hilary (2011), 'Sex and sin: The Magic of Red Shoes', in G. Riella and P. McNeil (eds), *Shoes: A History from Sandals to Sneakers*, Oxford: Berg.

Fischer, Thierry (2010), Utah Symphony Programme Note. Available at https://utahsymphony.org/explore/2010/10/rhapsody-on-a-theme-of-paganini-the-ballet/ (last accessed 1 July 2020).

Jarvie, Ian (1986), British Trade Policy *versus* Hollywood, 1947–1948: 'food before flicks', *Historical Journal of Film, Radio and Television*, vol. 6, no. 1, p. 19.

Jephcott, Pearl (1962), *Married Women Working*, London: Allen and Unwin.

Jephcott, Pearl (1948), *Rising Twenty: Notes on Ordinary Girls*, London: Faber.

Jephcott, Pearl (1942), *Girls Growing Up*, London: Allen and Unwin.

Kynaston, David (2008), *Austerity Britain, 1945–51*, London: Bloomsbury.

Macauley, Alistair (2008), 'Love and Dance: Two Obsessions, One Classic Film', *New York Times*, 29 August 2008.

Macdonald, Kevin (1994), *Emeric Pressburger: The Life and Death of a Scriptwriter*, London: Faber.

Moor, Andrew (2005), *Powell and Pressburger: A Cinema of Magic Spaces*, London: I. B. Tauris.

Powell, Michael (2000), *A Life in Movies*, London: Faber.

Powell, Michael and Pressburger, Emeric (1978), *The Red Shoes*, New York: Avon Books.

Chapter 7

The two textures of invisibility: shoes as liminal questionings in *Sullivan's Travels*

Kelli Fuery

Ludwig Wittgenstein wrote 'one of the most difficult of the philosopher's tasks is to find where the shoe pinches' ([1961] 1984: 60e), a statement not so dissimilar from Carl Jung's oft-cited: 'The shoe that fits one person pinches another; there is no recipe for living that suits all cases. Each of us carries his own life-form – an indeterminable form which cannot be superseded by any other' ([1933] 2005: 62). Preston Sturges's 1941 film *Sullivan's Travels* investigates the question of what it is to wear another person's shoes, not by looking at shoes that pinch, *per se*, but shoes that are *pinched* (stolen). This pinching of a pair of shoes signals to the audience a philosophical questioning of truth regarding the human condition, a questioning which transcends the footwear itself.

John Sullivan (Joel McCrea) is a Hollywood director fed up with making successful and popular comedic films, wanting instead to make a more socially conscious film about poverty, so that he might 'feel what it's like to be in trouble, without friends, without credit, without check book, without name, alone.' Sullivan, or Sully to his friends, believes that his films are frivolous, too focused on comedy, and by making a film that looks at the experiences of the poor he will expose a social reality. He states:

> I want this picture to be a commentary on modern conditions, stark realism, the problems that confront the average man . . . I want this picture to be a document, I want to hold a mirror up to life, I want this to be a picture of dignity, a true canvas of the suffering of humanity.

The truth that Sully so desperately wishes to tell is not the presiding truth that results from *Sullivan's Travels*. We do not receive any real truth on the problems that confront the average person via stark realism or otherwise. Instead, we are offered a layering of truthful intentions and commitments that evolve throughout the film's narrative. The truth that Sully seeks is a masquerade, an important and purposeful displacement for the truth that director Preston Sturges speaks through the production of his film.

In *The Truth in Painting* Jacques Derrida writes of the commitment to truth through the act of painting, stating that a painter commits to speaking, rather than painting, truth. This follows Martin Heidegger's claim in 'The Origin of the Work of Art', that truth emerges through the interpretation of the artwork, quite independently from the artist's intention. Truth can only emerge, or become, through the intersubjective relationship with the work. As Derrida puts it, the painter says: '"I owe you the truth in painting and I will tell it to you." If we understand him literally, he swears an oath to *speak*; he does not only speak, he promises to do so, he commits himself to speak' (Derrida 1987: 8).[1]

We find a similar zeal and promise for speaking truth in *Sullivan's Travels*, evident in Sully's desire to make a different type of film from comedy. If Sturges, like Derrida's painter, speaks a truth through *Sullivan's Travels*, it is to reaffirm a commitment to cinema as a powerful tool to affect its audiences. Even further, Sturges's intention to reveal a truth about social inequity highlights a preference for the feel-good over the feel-bad film. This is seen in the film's denouement where Sully finally confesses, 'I say it with some embarrassment, I want to make a comedy,' explaining that despite the ordeal he has experienced, he remains too happy and hasn't really suffered enough to make an authentic film about the tragedy of socio-economic disparity. At the close of the film, where we have quite literally spent time with Sully walking in a poorer man's shoes, there is an acknowledgement of poverty, its hardships and denials, as well as an argument for the significance of cinema as a distraction from the circumstances of poverty. Of course, there is another truth that emerges in spite of Sully's protests: his embarrassment is the affective response to his unconscious concession that too strong a focus on comedy avoids doing anything to alleviate the social-political causalities that contribute to the persistence of poverty.

Here, then, are the two competing truths that the audience is asked to contain, and which a pair of shoes signify and embody in *Sullivan's Travels*. This desire to speak truth that is shared between Sturges, Sully and Derrida's painter is not simply an intention; it is the force and reason for creativity in and of art and the audience's use of the artwork. Indeed this echoes Heidegger's ([1935] 2008) claim that the function of art is to facilitate the distinction between a work and a thing – something that *Sullivan's Travels* manages to achieve very well, most notably through the exchange of a pair of shoes. Given the green light from his producers to make a more serious and socially aware film, Sully disguises himself as a homeless man and sets out to live on the streets for a few weeks, during which time he meets an out-of-work actress (Veronica Lake) who ends up joining him (also assuming a disguise) in his quest. Both Sully and the Girl, as she is known, spend time in poorhouses, sleeping rough and eating in soup kitchens, during which time Sully's shoes are stolen by a homeless man and substituted with another, less robust pair. Sully continues to wear this other man's shoes before he is later knocked unconscious and robbed. We will return to this point.

Yet it isn't just *Sullivan's Travels* that expects a lot from the quotidian signifier of a pair of shoes. Indeed, shoes have been at the heart of another significant exchange on the hermeneutics of truth, specifically how we are to articulate and recognise it. Derrida's analysis occurs in the fourth and final section of *The Truth in Painting*, 'Restitutions' (1987: 257–382), where he rigorously questions the correspondence that occurred between Heidegger and art historian Meyer Schapiro on the ownership, meaning and interpretative truth of the shoes in Vincent van Gogh's *Old Shoes with Laces* (1886).[2] Schapiro's 1968 article takes issue with Heidegger's interpretation of Van Gogh's painting, where, despite agreeing with Heidegger that the illustration of 'the nature of art [is] a disclosure of truth' (Schapiro 1968: 203), he arrives at a different conclusion concerning what is disclosed. In Heidegger's view, the shoes in the painting belong to a peasant woman whereas Schapiro believes that Heidegger has projected too much of his own world-view onto the painting, resulting in a misinterpretation. For Schapiro, these are Van Gogh's own shoes. Schapiro marshals evidence from Van Gogh's letters and includes considerable comparative analysis with many of Van Gogh's other paintings of shoes in order to prove that the shoes in *Old Shoes with Laces* are the artist's own.

> Alas for him, the philosopher [Heidegger] has indeed deceived himself. He has retained from his encounter with van Gogh's canvas a moving set of associations with peasants and the soil, which are not sustained by the picture itself. They are grounded rather in his own social outlook . . . He has indeed 'imagined everything and projected it into the painting'. (Schapiro 1968: 138)

Derrida's return to this exchange is an attempt at restitution as he sees Schapiro's argument resting too much on a literal analysis of the content of the painting, which ignores Heidegger's larger philosophical argument, 'What does the work, as work, set up? Towering up within itself, the work opens up a *world* and keeps it abidingly in force' (Heidegger [1935] 2008: 169). Throughout his reflections, Derrida questions the correspondence itself, asking whether or not something else has emerged from the two differing perspectives on the ownership of the old shoes in the painting and, in doing so, returns the argument concerning the notion of truth to the context of Heidegger's original claim.

Shoes as visual signifiers of truth permit the becoming of a further invisible truth of the function of cinema within society, as seen in the ending of *Sullivan's Travels*. Read along these Heideggarian lines, the shoes permit the film to open up different worlds. Sully's worn-out shoes grant his invisibility in the marginalised world of the homeless. They are the very same signifiers that allow the audience to reflect on the invisible power of cinema, a blend of form and matter (Heidegger [1935] 2008: 154), which serve to illustrate how the formal aesthetics of film can work as social, visual equipment that engenders possible story worlds, and in turn, enable an hermeneutics of truth. The work of Sturges's film is not its story of a man in search of a 'document' that mirrors the deplorable conditions of the poor; rather *Sullivan's Travels* reveals the capacity of cinema, through the mechanics of masquerade and metaphor (such are the shoes), to uncover the nature of things as truth, what Derrida refers to as 'a double belonging, a double articulation' (1987: 297). Acknowledging that poverty is entirely outside his own lived experience, Sully begins to execute his intention by impersonating a homeless person in order to discover what it is to be poor, alone and isolated at the margins of society. We are privy to his 'dressing up', where Sully selects torn, dirty and used clothing to affect his disguise. In this same scene, Sully's butler, Burrows (Robert Grieg), speaks his own very direct truth referring to Sully's mission and 'fancy dress' as a vulgar 'caricaturing of the poor'. This early scene is instrumental for how we are to view Sully's entire enterprise and additionally note the foreshadowed importance of the shoes. Sturges wants us to see that Sully's undertaking is riddled with difficulties and conceit, hence Burrows and the valet's (Eric Blore) respective misgivings and protective measures. A close-up on the shoes (Figure 7.1) shows Sully's valet inserting a secret identity card containing and protecting John Sullivan's name and details in the sole of one of his shoes.

In such a short scene, *Sullivan's Travels* establishes the central and critical importance that clothing, and specifically the pair of shoes, will have throughout the film. They are the film's first clear exemplar of the parergonal identity that will be examined throughout the film. Derrida reminds us that 'clothing is for Kant an example of a *parergon*, in its aesthetic representation' (1987: 302), a consideration for his interrogation of the Heidegger-Schapiro debate regarding Van Gogh's shoe painting(s). Derrida uses the concept of the parergon to question both Heidegger's and Schapiro's critique of Van Gogh's painting and to restitute Heidegger's critique as most valid. He is not interested in a specific formal analysis of the painting, instead referring only to the denotative elements of lace, sole, nail and shoe as separate objects (in order to consider the pair – discussed below) so that he might think more

Figure 7.1 The valet presents Sully the shoes with the hidden identity card in the sole

critically about the function of the frame and its relationship to (and use of) a work of art:[3]

> A parergon comes against, beside, and in addition to the *ergon*, the work done [*fait*], the fact [*le fait*], the work, but it does not fall to one side, it touches and cooperates within the operation, from a certain outside. Neither simply outside nor simply inside. (Derrida 1987: 54)

For Derrida, the parergon, as frame or border, is literally considered as both part of a painting and part of a wall. As '*par-ergon*' ('equal'-'work') it runs alongside the work, touching, linking (lacing) the work to the wall, or to put it in Heideggarian terms, the parergon unites earth and world (Heidegger [1935] 2008: 170–5). The parergon equally divides and links inside and outside, and with regard to *Sullivan's Travels*, the pair of shoes as parergon link Sully to another world – they place him 'inside' the world of the homeless, but at the same time, the insurance of the identity card keeps him 'outside', separated from it. The parergonal logic of the shoes occupies a liminal space that drives the film. Sully's shoes, with the identity card, formally establish and separate aspects of Sully's character worlds – homeless impersonator and Hollywood director. As these shoes are neither entirely of Sully's true world, or the world of the homeless and poor, they occupy a parergonal logic of their own throughout the film even, or perhaps especially, when stolen.

The parergonal logic of Sully's shoes differs from his other impersonator clothing because they offer the audience a signifier that permits a questioning of the truth that Sully seeks. Clothing is said to function as an example of the parergon because it is neither inside the body, that is, an integral element that contributes to the total representation of the body (which Derrida says 'would be the naked and natural body' (Derrida 1987: 57)), nor is it completely separate from the body. Clothing and shoes therefore supplement the aesthetic representation of the body and further supplement interpretation of said body's identity but do not 'belong to the whole of the representation' (Ibid.). Whilst Derrida considers the place and limit of the parergon, asking where it starts and stops, he does not necessarily consider the hierarchy of logic of different types of clothing and how these are ordered visually in painting or otherwise. How are we to distinguish between Sully's torn and dirty blazer and the shoes in terms of their respective parergonal logics? In cinema, we have the formal practice of the close-up to establish narrative significance and audience retention of an object's importance. Sully's shoes are given this formal time and space in the film, an option that is not transferable to painting. It is an attention to form that produces a specific form of attention in the audience, telling us that despite clothing and shoes having the capacity to function as parerga, not *all* clothing or shoes share the same parergonal value based on their supplementarity. The Girl's clothing, although to a much lesser degree, possesses a similar parergonal logic to Sully's shoes. When Sully and the Girl fall ill on the road they are temporarily returned to the security and care of the mobile production trailer. Both are given white clothing to change into; the Girl a white robe and Sully white pyjamas. Here, the colour of the clothing signifies the purity of intention (perhaps naiveté is more accurate), and the growing relationship and connection between Sully and the Girl. Derrida specifies that in addition to the parergon's 'exteriority as a surplus', the supplementary and external position of clothing and shoes (to continue the example here), there must be an 'internal structural link which rivets them to the lack in the interior of the *ergon*' (Ibid.: 59). Put simply, Sully's shoes must fill a gap in the overall 'look', which is seemingly the concealment of his identity. For the audience however, the parergonal logic of the shoes is far more complex, as we shall see.

There is another example of the parergon within the film, illustrated through Burrows' remark.

BURROWS
I have never been sympathetic to the caricaturing of the poor and needy, sir.
SULLIVAN
(Indignantly)
Who's caricaturing…

> VALET
> Burrows doesn't know about the expedition sir.
> SULLIVAN
> I'm going out on the road to find out what it is <u>like</u> to be poor and needy
> … and then I'm going to make a picture about it.
> BURROWS
> If you'll permit me to say so, sir: The subject is not an interesting one. The
> poor know all about poverty and only the morbid rich would find the
> topic glamorous.
> SULLIVAN
> (Exasperated)
> But I'm doing it <u>for</u> the poor.
>
> (Sturges [1941] 1986: 552–3)[4]

As Derrida sees it, the concept of the remark also exemplifies a key characteristic of the parergon, as it determines what the subject of a conversation is without 'being a part of it and yet without being absolutely extrinsic to it'.[5] Sully's desire to tell the truth is insistent throughout the film and is eventually realised in its last third, beyond the narrative intentions of Sully himself. The truth in the work of *Sullivan's Travels* lies in its reflexive position about the function and value of comedy for society, rather than the specificity of exposing or voyeuristically portraying the lived experience of poverty and its political economic causalities (even if these too occur in the film).

The pair: inside/outside

Let us return to the textuality of the shoes. Outside the classic (and often highly feminised) narratives of the singular and lost shoe such as Cinderella's glass slipper, shoes are obviously paired in cinema. This is certainly the case with Sully's homeless shoes, a literal pair in themselves, that go on to figuratively pair his Hollywood identity with that of a homeless impersonator, and later pairing his true identity, via the card in the shoe, with the homeless man (Georges Renavent). Similarly, at first glance the old shoes in Van Gogh's painting are also immediately viewed as a pair. Why then does Derrida frame his inquiry through the question of 'the pair' over the symbolism of the shoes? In part, it reflects his long-held examination of the binary and the continuous rigorous consideration of the margin, but equally it allows him to assess the multiplicity of pairs that manifest in the Heidegger-Schapiro correspondence concerning the analysis of Van Gogh's painting and, further, the aesthetic experience Heidegger theorised in 'The Origin of the Work of Art'. For inasmuch as we are shown a literal pair of shoes by Van Gogh, Heidegger is much more interested in the pairing of world and earth, of thing and work, in order to argue that art creates the potential for truth to become (or leap forth – *ursprung*). Derrida turns to question his own response to the dissatisfaction he felt when reading Heidegger's analysis of Van Gogh's painting. While Derrida defends Heidegger's analysis against Schapiro's critique, addressing the key themes of attribution (ownership/responsibility), supplementarity, and lacing, it is this concept of the pair that he uses to investigate and deconstruct the notion of pairing itself: 'what proves that we're dealing with a pair?' (Derrida 1987: 282).

Ursula Franklin (1991) continues this questioning of pairing, noting the names of Heidegger and Schapiro themselves have become linked to the analysis of Van Gogh's painting and of the shoes, forming another (arbitrary) pair. She questions why such limited correspondence (two letters, one from each author) should constitute a pair worthy of Derridean deconstruction, particularly as the coupling of 'Heidegger-Schapiro' is *ex post facto*. Franklin determines that Derrida's pairing of Heidegger and Schapiro is intentional, stressing 'the notions of *returning* and *restituting*, the *inside* and the *outside*, not of the shoes so much as of the picture, which passing over its frame suggests the *parergon*' (Franklin 1991: 142). The shoes belong to the painting, more than they do to a peasant woman (Heidegger) or city dweller (Schapiro) as Derrida establishes, but what is of more interest relative to the current example of shoes in *Sullivan's Travels*, is that both Heidegger and Schapiro invest a great deal of their own identity into their respective interpretation of the shoes. Thereby, in questioning the pair, Derrida establishes a parergonal logic between work and audience, evidenced via the Heidegger-Schapiro debate, and this enables his own critique to return to questioning the truth in art (in this case, painting). In each of their respective analyses (Heidegger, Schapiro, Derrida), the shoes in Van Gogh's painting are objects *not in use*, that is they exist within the 'inside' of the painting, the shoes sit untouched, unmoving – they are 'put to one side' (Derrida 1987: 265). If these are still shoes in a still canvas, what of moving shoes in a moving canvas?

Sully's shoes do move, they are active, they pinch and are pinched (stolen/exchanged/re-appropriated/restituted, although not returned); they are not put to one side as are the shoes in Van Gogh's painting. The shoes are the equipment that establishes and grounds Sully's disguise, furthering the direction of the story. Through the shoes, we come to witness a multiplicity of pairings that occur within the film as much as they highlight the relation of value through the exchange of economic status (Sully as director/as homeless) and use (the mobility and agency of the two men). The invitation here then, via Derrida, is to consider the textural invisibility of each pair as they surface and transpire inside and outside the film's story world, via the signifier and traffic of Sully's shoes. The difference between Sully's shoes and the old shoes in Van Gogh's painting is the more one looks at Sully's shoes, the more one begins to note different types of pairs precisely due to their movement and exchange. This departs from Derrida's position, who argues that the more he looks at the pair of shoes in the painting, the less he is convinced that they are a pair:

> I find this pair, if I may say so, gauche. Through and through. Look at the details, the inside lateral surface: you'd think it was two left feet. Of different shoes. And the more I look at them, the more they look at me, the less they look like an old pair. More like an old couple. Is it the same thing? (Derrida 1987: 278)

The potentiality of pairs presented within *Sullivan's Travels* rotate around Sully himself; a symbolism that is facilitated (or perhaps dependent) on the exchange of shoes between the two men. There are paired relationships with people, such as Sully and the Girl, who are both lost in their 'real' lives. She is a failing actor and he is a disillusioned director. Further, Sully and the Girl are paired as impersonators of the homeless, and at the end of the film, as a romantic pair, or couple – an equivalence worth considering. If the pairing of Sully and the Girl affirm his identity and privilege through similarity, then the pairing of Sully and the homeless man highlights the vulgarity of his intention and impossibility of knowing the lived experience of poverty unless you are poor yourself. These pairings of people, some intentional and some happenstance, are bound within the frame of the film's diegesis. These pairs do not occupy the liminal spaces of parergonal logic in the same way that the pairs of shoes do. These sets of pairs of relationships with Sully are completely within the inside of the film's story world and do not migrate to an external world.

The pairs of shoes (Sully's and the homeless man's) through their parergonal logic become the essence of relatedness and reflexivity within the film. Through their emphasis on the margin, the pairs of shoes allow questioning of the work itself (Sturges's film and Sully's intention to make *his* film). These margins are not just of Sully's body, as impersonator in another's world, but more pertinently the marginalisation of the unnamed and poor in society. Sully's shoes are stolen and replaced with a pair of shoes that have holes in their toes. Once more, the use of the close-up frames Sully's bare feet and pans to the replacement pair of shoes. This shoe-exchange permits the audience to ask: what is being framed here in the film? While one set of shoes has been exchanged for another, the logic of their respective parerga has not. Sully's replacement shoes, if anything, reinforce the parergonal logic of shoes in the film and reestablish the truth Sturges has committed to speak through the art of his film.

Derrida writes, '[s]omething *happens*, something *takes place* when shoes are abandoned, empty, out of use for a while or forever, apparently detached from the feet', referring to the ontology both Heidegger and Schapiro assign the shoes in the painting. Derrida argues that both authors rush to make the shoes 'into a pair in order to reassure themselves' (Derrida 1987: 265). With his replaced shoes and without the insurance of the secret identity card, Sully is relegated to the world of the unnamed, those who are forgotten in society; his privilege is lost for as long as he remains impersonating the homeless. Forming part of his masquerade, the original shoes when first worn appeared unremarkable, only taking on serious narrative importance after they are pinched. We already know this information, when, via close-up, we were alerted to the significance of the identity card his valet put in the shoe for security (the security of Sully's identity and proper location as named, as wealthy, as not belonging to the margins). The marked absence of Sully's impersonator shoes concurrently marks their presence as narratively important.

The two pairs of shoes that Sully wears (those in order to impersonate and the exchanged homeless pair) become 'subject-shoes' (Ibid.: 266); literally (the impersonator shoes are Sully's property) and figuratively (they are the means that Sully uses to fulfil his intention to walk the subjectivity of the homeless, perversely at the start of the film). Sully says that he wishes to make a film that is 'a true canvas of the suffering of humanity', an 'O Brother, Where Art Thou' type of film. His actions lead him to become a double subject, both Hollywood director and homeless (although this truly only occurs in the latter third of the film, when one identity supersedes the other). As shoes that pair two subjectivities – they carry and contain Sully's identity and the masquerade of homelessness (unnameable identity) – they offer the audience the space to register both the perversion of what Sully is seeking and equally the marginality of the poor. They facilitate recognition of cinema's capacity to create worlds that shed light on the inadequacies of our own by framing subjects otherwise ignored or 'put to one side'. Here we see a further craft of Sturges's film, the pairing of its intentionalities, or rather its layered truths between diegesis, directorial intent and audience reception.

Laced between two statuses

As a double subject, what are the liminal spaces the shoes occupy within the film that permit their mobility and exchange – both as subject-objects within the film and as objects that allow audiences to exchange the layered truths the film presents? One answer is that as clothing parerga, the shoes are often at the edge of the screen. We are shown frames of feet walking and Sully's replacement shoes (Figure 7.2), with each shot fully framing the 'subject-shoes' of Sully and the homeless man. In a later sequence, we see shoes belonging to the nameless prisoners walking into the church; these shoes (and feet) are chained together, being identical in appearance. Such sequences in the film invite audiences to investigate the shoes' parergonal logic. Shoes, shown on feet and framed separately from any face for context, ask that we consider their border status. These close-ups remind us of the specific narrative importance of the shoes and the mistaken identities that have occurred, but they also restitute the metaphor of 'walking in another's shoes' precisely in order to challenge it, and therefore permit the commitment to speak truth to emerge through the film, the dual context for both Sturges and Sully in *Sullivan's Travels*. The close-up of shoes linked in chains, and of shoes following other shoes, draws attention to the interrelationship of pairs concerning 'inside' and 'outside' that occurs within the film. Here is the lacing of statuses between self and other, rich and poor, criminal and non-criminal.

For Derrida, laces are the painted textuality that facilitate the invisibility of attachment, of what links the inside to the outside of the shoe to the spectator through the imagined movement of the shoelace. 'This first line is already a tracing of coming and going between the outside and the inside, notably when it follows the movement of the lace' (Derrida 1987: 303). While we are not

Figure 7.2 The replacement shoes left to Sully by the homeless man

shown any cinematographic emphasis on laces *per se* in *Sullivan's Travels*, the aforementioned pairs present a lacing of sorts, between ownership, economic status and traces (of the identity card, of Sully's incarceration). Further, the shoes lace Sully (and for a time, the Girl) to another world, playing out Sully's desire to commit to speaking truth by appropriating another world view, subtly suggesting the naiveté of his aim. This is clear in the first half of the film; there are no insurmountable obstacles that prevent Sully or the Girl being able to return to the position of economic security and status. The identity card in his shoes support and ensure such return, and yet the film never lets go of the notion and importance of what it is to walk in another's shoes, so much so that the theft of the shoes marks a moment in the film where they begin to function as truth in form. The theft (another parergon that propels the *ergon* [work] of the film) supplements the lacing of Sully's privileged status with that of his genuine experience and temporary status of being unnamed and sentenced. When Sully loses the insurance of the identity card in the shoe, and when he and the Girl have had enough of being hungry and tired, they return to the security of their privilege (home, food, wealth). It is this point in the film's narrative where the audience is returned to the parergonal identity of homelessness, and where the film begins to focus more on shots of shoes separated from any face.

The shoes become the 'truthless truth of truth' (Derrida 1987: 271) as they reveal the security of Sully's identity as being lost as much as it has been stolen. The card in the shoes retains a temporal truth, insofar as it reveals the shoes *were* Sully's property, not that they *are* (or end up remaining) his. After Sully returns home, believing he has achieved his goal of learning what it is to be poor, forgotten and alone (not really achieved at all due to the companionship of the Girl), he sets out for what he thinks will be his last walk as a homeless person. His shoes however are not his own; Sully now wears the shoes of the unnamed homeless man. Sully wants to give his thanks to the homeless community by passing out five-dollar bills, and this sequence shows the movement of shoes walking the streets. We never see Sully's face.

The homeless man recognises Sully, and begins to follow and subsequently mug him. In a brief altercation, the homeless man knocks Sully unconscious and locks him in a train car. Sully is now truly on his way to experiencing what it is to be 'in trouble, without friends, without credit, without checkbook, without name, alone' as he no longer has a traveling companion (the Girl) or insurance (identity card). This pivotal fight scene redirects the tone of the film. The previous close-up sequence of shoes, where Sully is followed by the homeless man while he hands out five-dollar bills to the homeless, is followed by the skirmish and subsequent death of the homeless man (who, transfixed by Sully's money, is unable to get out of the way of a moving train and is killed). We are not shown the homeless man's face, and this inability to facially recognise the dead man eventually becomes Sully's salvation at the end of the film.

Due to the blow to his head, Sully ends up lost and disorientated, which leads to another fight with a stranger. This time Sully is at fault, striking the stranger in the head with a rock. Sully's concussion results in amnesia, unable to recall his name or position (his privilege cannot be exercised now), and he is sentenced to six years hard labour. It is safe to say that at this point in the film the shoes appear abandoned. However the shoes remain useful, if absented, objects in the film, or more specifically the original 'exchange' of shoes (the theft) between the two men remains significant and effects a lacing between their two economic statuses. Recalling that for Kant, clothing is parergonal, we can further consider that the shoes signify the link between the inside and outside of truth, as it is the value and meaning of the shoes that is held by the audience even when we find Sully in a hard labour camp, shoeless and shirtless. This is also the part of the film where Sully's memory is restituted; he remembers who he is and concurrently becomes aware of the folly of his initial expedition. The shoes, or rather the identity card within the shoes, having mistakenly named the homeless man as John Sullivan, provides Sully with his salvation. He is able to use a newspaper photograph to affirm and prove his identity.

In what is arguably the film's most significant sequence, prisoners are taken to the local African-American church to watch a movie (Walt Disney's 1934 *Playful Pluto*). The tone of *Sullivan's Travels* remains sombre, delivering a message about how to treat those less fortunate than oneself, respectfully conveyed by those who, at the time of the film's production in 1941, existed at the margins of society themselves. Here we see Sturges doing what Sullivan initially could not – documenting the 'problems that confront the average man . . . [making] a picture of dignity, a true canvas of the suffering of humanity'. The montage of prisoner silhouettes and close-ups of chained feet and shoes refuse any possibility of individual character identity; instead the framing establishes the collective marginality of criminal, homeless, and the poor, structuring their agencies as members of society accordingly. The audience is offered the:

> temptation, inscribed from that moment on the very object, to put it back, to put the shoes back on one's feet, to hand them over to the subject, to the authentic wearer or owner reestablished in his rights and reinstated in his being-upright. The structure of the thing and the trial obliges you, then, always, to keep adding to it. (Derrida 1987: 273)

The invisible lacings made possible via the exchanged pairs of shoes include the following points:

1) Sully's first pair of 'homeless' shoes are false investments, as is any venture to masquerade in another's identity without lived experience. The shoes are useful and reliable; we are given no indication they are anything but comfortable (compared with his jacket).

2) They conceal Sully's identity, safeguarded to prevent any real experience of another class. The identity card facilitates safe return home three times in the film.

3) The shoes obscure the identity of the homeless person. He, like the Girl, remains unnameable even in the moment of death. Only Sully's identity (real and false) is permitted, due to the card, allowing Sully to remain in the domain of the named.

Pointure/nails that hold

Such invisible or imagined lacing, as Derrida sees it 'pierces the canvas' (Derrida 1987: 304). As an action of *pointure*, the two worlds inside and outside the work of art are stitched together via the limit of the frame. Derrida asks 'how can we distinguish the two textures of invisibility from each other?' (Ibid.). *Pointure*, used in this Derridean sense, refers to the pointing of canvas onto the wooden frame. For him, it is through *pointure* that the inside and outside of a work are able to be distinguished. We can apply this same understanding to *Sullivan's Travels* in a number of ways.

Firstly, *pointure* is understood as fit or attachment, that is the fixing of canvas to its frame, but perhaps more relevant here is 'fit' as the significance of the story to its context, and 'fit' as something that is deemed suitable but invisible. Indeed, it is Sully's epiphany that he would much rather make comedies than tragedies, learning of his 'fit' as a Hollywood director in the world. Secondly, *pointure* is translated as shoe size in English, making clear the very 'limit-possibility' (Ibid.: 278–9) of how an inside and outside of a work (or foot to shoe) attaches and reattaches to one another. Sully's intention (and we can say the same of Sturges) is to speak truth through film, that is, he intends to use film to speak *his* truth. Yet, as discussed, this is not the truth that emerges through the film; rather the different truth that emerges is Sully's self-awareness and recognition of his folly. The *pointure* that pierces the film becomes the audience's reflexive gaze, with the shoes working as the signifiers that make possible the 'leaping forth' of truth in the work. Derrida writes of Van Gogh's painting, 'the shoes are shared, each party keeps one piece of the *symbolon*' (Ibid.: 283). Similarly, in *Sullivan's Travels*, the audience shares the truth of the shoes, of Sully's identity and predicament, and most significantly, what the work of the film is, what the work of cinema becomes. The audience is able to distinguish between the two textural invisibilities of inside and outside the film's diegesis and of the layered truths the film commits to.

In *Sullivan's Travels*, shoes have no index of value until Sully is mugged and put on a train; truth made possible via the exchange of shoes. There is, of course, something in the lack of recognition that occurs at this point in the film. The homeless man's recognition of Sully is also a statement of *pointure*. He sees through Sully's masquerade (indeed, he does it twice over the course of the film) and perceives wealth and the opportunity it brings, leading him to mirror Sully's action by walking in a (richer) man's shoes. The audience however does not know it is the same homeless man who has stolen Sully's shoes because this act occurred off-screen. He is unnamed and such information occurs after the fact of his death. Is the suggestion here that the homeless see through the charade of wealth, or is it more likely that the homeless see the vulgarity and exclusion of wealth at every turn? Is the hit on the head punishment for the perversion of Sully's project, the exploitation of the homeless for his career profit and personal fulfilment? In death the homeless man gifts Sully two key things. First, Sully gets the experience he so desperately set out to have (without being mugged, or the mistaken identity, he would never have had the experience genuinely. Here is a truth in truth!). Second, Sully is able to divorce his wife; Mrs Sullivan (Jan Buckingham), believing that Sully was dead, remarries her lover thereby making it possible for Sully and the Girl to marry. These gifts are the only means by which Sully gets anywhere near close enough to fulfil his original commitment to speak the truth of the conditions of the modern human. Sully eventually experiences, truthfully and painfully, the world of poverty but only due to being misidentified. Without these gift-exchanges – all made possible via the pinching (theft) of his shoes – Sully would not reach his epiphany (the truth in the work) that the film has been promising to speak, which is 'There's a lot to be said for making people laugh. Did you know that's all some people have?'.

Derrida reminds us of Heidegger's position, that unless we apprehend the 'underneath' of things by reflecting on their capacity for bringing forth truth, then 'the ground falls away' (Derrida 1987: 290). The shoes in *Sullivan's Travels* offer a doubling of identity, a binocular vision of the world that makes it possible to see one world but hold two perspectives concurrently (Bion 1961). The symbolism of the shoes further suggests our place within the world, restituting and returning to the appearance of becoming of truth in the work, stating that it only appears *with* the work, not via illustration or in reference to something else. At the start of the film, Sully's shoes are his illustration. It is only when he is robbed of these shoes and his security of privilege that the truth of the film begins to leap forth, and we, as the audience, are given the opportunity to apprehend the underneath of things. It will not go unnoticed that these are the precise narrative points in *Sullivan's Travels* where best use is made of the frame; the close-ups of the shoes walking behind each other help create literal links between earth and world. The shoes, as Sully's illustration, must be put to one side and in so doing, free Sully from the foolishness of his original intention. For the audience, however, the shoes remain the necessary *parerga* that enable the bringing forth of truth in the film work.

Notes

1. Derrida is referring to Paul Cézanne and attributes the title of his book to him, '[i]t is a saying of Cézanne's' (Derrida 1987: 2).
2. Derrida notes that the title of Van Gogh's painting that Heidegger analyses was 'given by the large catalog of the Tuileries exhibition (1971–72) (collection of the Vincent Van Gogh National Museum in Amsterdam)' as *Old Boots with Laces*. Schapiro refers to the painting as *Old Shoes*. (Derrida 1987: 276). However, Derrida has the title on p. 258 as *Old Shoes with Laces* and I have elected to use this title to refer to this specific Van Gogh shoe painting throughout the chapter for consistency with Derrida's work. See Schapiro (1968) for the discussion of shoe painting titles.
3. It is tempting to entertain the unconscious double pairings Derrida has established between himself and Heidegger, and subsequently Schapiro, in writing his defence of Heidegger's analysis of Van Gogh's painting. Derrida points out that Schapiro 'can have the shoes' at a cost, so to 'acquire them with a view to a restitution' (Ibid.: 313). Perhaps this is so that Derrida can have back/restitute his Heidegger.
4. Thanks to my colleague James Dutcher for helping me locate this reference.
5. Derrida makes this point in reference to Kant's own use of the term parergon, found in a 'very long note added to the second edition of *Religion within the Limits of Reasons Alone*' (Ibid.: 55). He argues that by placing this word in a note, in the margin of the work, it becomes a term of extreme importance to the work itself. The 'concept of the remark' therefore, illustrates the hermeneutic interstices of work and frame.

References

Bion, Wilfred (1961), *Experiences in Groups*, New York: Basic Books.

Derrida, Jacques (1987), *The Truth in Painting*, trans. G. Bennington and I. McLeod, Chicago and London: University of Chicago Press.

Franklin, Ursula (1991), 'A different quest for truth and shoes: Derrida on Heidegger and Schapiro on Van Gogh', *The Centennial Review*, vol. 35, no. 1 (winter), pp. 141–65.

Heidegger, Martin [1935] (2008), 'The Origin of the Work of Art', in D. F. Krell (ed.), *Basic Writings*, New York: Harper Perennial, pp. 143–212.

Jung, Carl [1933] (2005), *Modern Man in Search of a Soul*, trans. W. S. Dell and C. F. Baynes, London and New York: Routledge.

Schapiro, Meyer (1968), 'The Still Life as Personal Object', in M. L. Simmel (ed.), *The Reach of Mind: Essays in Memory of Kurt Goldstein*, Berlin, Heidelberg: Springer, pp. 203–9.

Sturges, Preston [1941] (1986), 'Sullivan's Travels', in B. Henderson (ed.), *Five Screenplays by Preston Sturges*, Berkeley, CA: University of California Press, pp. 511–683.

Wittgenstein, Ludwig [1961] (1984), *Notebooks 1914–1916*, eds. G. H. von Wright and G. E. M. Anscombe, 2nd ed., Chicago and London: University of Chicago Press.

Chapter 8

How to see through a shoe: the fashion show sequence in *How to Marry a Millionaire*

Ana Salzberg

At the conclusion of the fashion show sequence in *How to Marry a Millionaire* (Jean Negulesco, USA, 1953) the playboy for whom it has been staged shrugs off its impact: 'I don't see anything here that I want.' Uttered midway through the film, such a sentiment seems incongruous, unexpected; after all, for the past forty minutes or so, the audience has followed models Schatze Page (Lauren Bacall), Loco Dempsey (Betty Grable), and Pola Debevoise (Marilyn Monroe) across the vast CinemaScope screen as they strategise how to marry a millionaire and, indeed, possess the many things they desire. Yet in both diegetic and extra-diegetic terms, the line is a feint. On one level, it represents another of Tom Brookman's (Cameron Mitchell) attempts to get – for better or for worse – Schatze's attention, which he unequivocally wants. Moreover, the line effectively teases the viewer who has just seen so very much to admire in the fashion show. Not only do Schatze, Loco and Pola appear in ensembles that highlight their elegant figures, but a series of anonymous models parade past in the most à la mode designs while orchestral music plays on the soundtrack and a voice-over narrator describes the luxurious creations. If the fashion show is a pretext for Tom to consider Schatze at his leisure, then it is also a pretext for the spectator to contemplate a spectacle of sensory plenitude. As Catherine Johnson writes, it is the 'most blatant [. . .]' moment of self-reflexivity in a 'film that is rich' in itself (Johnson 1982: 73).

Those riches – or the pursuit thereof – characterise the narrative as well as the imagery. The film begins with the three models moving into a Manhattan penthouse they can barely afford so that they can best meet and marry millionaires. What Schatze, Loco and Pola share are beauty, style and a passion for luxury; yet as the story progresses and the women are courted by a series of men ranging from the wealthy to the humble, each finds that she actually values love above money. These noble conclusions come after the fashion show, however, which celebrates the excessive and expensive. On a widescreen saturated with colours and textures – mahogany furs, pastel organza, inky twill – there are, as Amanda Konkle notes, 'myriad pleasures in looking [...] through both fashion and beautiful women' (Konkle 2014: 374). One item in particular invites a second look, if only to confirm that it is really there: the pair of lucite heels worn by Pola/Monroe. As part of a bathing suit and cover-up ensemble, the shoes are designed to give the illusion of invisibility; only the criss-crossed red straps, which Pola/Monroe is seen fastening in the preceding scene, draw the eye to the translucent platform heels. That is, only the red straps – and the fact that, after posing with total self-possession, Pola/Monroe stumbles in the heels while trying to step up onto a platform. For Pola is, as she explains later, 'blind as a bat' and never wears glasses if there is a chance that she might be around an eligible man. To paraphrase Brookman's statement, Pola knows how she wants to be seen – even if it literally and figuratively trips her up.

Even as the shoes generate a moment of physical comedy within a sequence that otherwise exalts ideal forms both human and sartorial, they also give objective form to the film's overarching games of revelation. Kaja Silverman has noted that '[c]lothing and other kinds of ornamentation make the human body culturally visible' (Silverman 1986: 145), citing the metamorphic impact of costuming in works such as *Now, Voyager* (Irving Rapper, USA, 1942). In the latter, a change in wardrobe allows the audience to see, literally, Charlotte's (Bette Davis) near-instant evolution from 'unsightly spinster into a beautiful sophisticate' (Ibid.); by contrast, the fashion show in *How to Marry a Millionaire* highlights a continuum of female beauty. This parade of beautiful sophisticates, continually emerging from behind a curtain to pose on the platform, not only asserts their status as 'culturally visible' but identifies them as part of an entire culture *of* visibility – that is, Hollywood. *How to* is a work that flirts with the viewer's awareness of that extra-diegetic context through numerous intertextual references, related especially to stars Monroe, Bacall and Grable, and, as Lisa Cohen (1998) and Konkle (2014) have highlighted, also through the expansiveness of the CinemaScope process itself.

The following will argue that the shoes worn by Monroe are a luxurious gesture of reflexivity, a fashionable comment on the film's invitation to engage with its intertwining of the extra- and intra-diegetic – or, very simply, to see through it. Yet reflecting on *How to* more than fifty years after its release invites still other questions about its own contemplation of Hollywood's culture of visibility. How do we see through, and what do we see in, that shoe when considering it on any number of modern-day screens: laptops, mobile phones, tablets? Through a detailed close reading of the fashion show sequence, the analysis will conclude that the heels, with their versatility in function and meaning, also offer a means of thinking through the shifting parameters of the screens on which they are viewed today. In a film about love and longing, which is in return admired in both critical and popular terms, the shoes introduce an opportunity to consider *how* both the characters and the audience see what they want.

The Monroe film perhaps most associated with luxury and the pursuit thereof, even more than *Gentlemen Prefer Blondes* (Howard Hawks, USA, 1953), *How to Marry a Millionaire* alternately celebrates and challenges the pleasures of living in a material world. As Johnson points out, it 'identifies itself as a *moneyed* film' (Johnson 1982: 72). Scholars have long examined the implications of such excesses for spectatorship, stardom and popular culture in the 1950s. Cohen has argued that the CinemaScope screen 'allegorize[s] Monroe's relation to the questions of excess, containment, and visibility that shaped both her star persona and postwar domesticity' (Cohen 1998: 273); and Konkle reads the film as a dialogue between the conventions of 'the Cinderella narrative and the gold-digging narrative,' as well as a commentary on the 'instructional texts' circulating in post-war culture (Konkle 2014: 366). In his exploration of the development of Monroe's star image, Richard Dyer considers the famous *How to* publicity still of Pola/Monroe in front of a four-way mirror within the context of 1950s psychoanalytic discourse around female sexuality (Dyer [1986] 2004: 51). The shot signals, as he describes it, 'an orgy of delight in her own reflection' (Ibid.), and thus corresponds to greater questions of female narcissism and sexual availability. Building upon this analysis of the extra-diegetic context, it is clear that the publicity around the film offered a Janus-faced female figure: Monroe as the star who loved to look at herself, playing Pola who, in her myopia, can only be looked *at*.

Pola/Monroe's heels illuminate even more about the elemental extravagance of *How to Marry a Millionaire*. The heels easily denote the Cinderella paradigm referenced by Konkle, for example, with its accompanying questions of 'mobility' and 'class position' cited by Cohen (1998: 277). As these critics both point out, the heroines' eventual decisions to choose romance over commerce speak to what Cohen calls a '*horizontal* mobility' in keeping with the latitude of the widescreen frame (Konkle 2014: 374; Cohen 1998: 277). That is, the women (with the exception of Schatze) do not 'marry up', but rather within their class. From this line of argument, Pola's stumble in the heels when stepping onto the platform could be read as a moment gently parodying her and her friends' eagerness to move up in the world through marriage. In her modern-day version of the glass slippers, Pola does not lose a shoe but misses a step – hinting that she is not quite as comfortable in the heady world of high finance as she would want to be. Nor, indeed, as she would appear to be: not only does Pola model diamond-accented swimwear in the fashion show, but throughout the film she and her friends wear the chicest of ensembles. Even while furniture literally disappears from their penthouse and the refrigerator is all but empty, somehow 'all three [women] own fabulous wardrobes' (Johnson 1982: 72).

The translucency of the shoes, however, also signals the very transparency of the models' plan – materialising the point at which Cinderella shifts to ingenuous gold-digger, to build on Konkle's point above. As Pola observes in an earlier exchange with Schatze:

> The men these days [are] getting more and more nervous, especially the loaded ones […] It isn't always easy to find out right away how much they're worth, or if they're married or not. They're looking like [*sic*] you're prying into their private affairs.

Knowledge, then, becomes as valuable a commodity as any luxury item in the film: what men and women choose to share throughout the courtship ritual and whether the models can carry out their investigations discretely enough to avoid the detection of those skittish millionaires. A nightclub sequence highlights the contrasts between each heroine's approach to her date: Schatze is elegant in her enquiries, while Loco and Pola are progressively more direct. Like the heels that Pola/Monroe wears, these women are easier to see through; they are also, as it happens, less successful in marrying millionaires.

At the same time that the models and their suitors make a flirtatious art out of withholding information, the self-reflexive nature of the film calls upon the spectator's knowledge of the performers themselves. As Johnson notes, there are a number of 'moments [that] separate the (wealthy) star from the character she plays' (Johnson 1982: 72). In this way, the audience is invited to play along in the game of revelation and concealment throughout the film; to see through the diegesis to its extra-cinematic framework. Paralleling the exchanges between the cinematic world and its socio-historical context as identified by Cohen, Dyer and Konkle, it seems that the very fame of Bacall, Grable and Monroe cannot be contained within either the parameters of the screen or the constraints of characterisation. Though Monroe's phenomenal popularity means that the film is often interpreted in terms of her stardom, *How to* is itself more democratic in how it treats the actors.

Indeed, in 1953, Monroe herself was the least established of the three leads and in this way received less reflexive attention. Certainly the voice-over narrator of the fashion show introduces Pola/Monroe with, 'You know, of course, that diamonds are a girl's best friend' – thus acknowledging Monroe's recent turn in *Gentlemen Prefer Blondes*. Yet the film goes on to comment more extensively on facets of Grable and Bacall's public images. Grable re-enacts her legendary pin-up pose in the fashion show sequence, turning her back to the viewer and smiling over her shoulder; and when lured to a remote cabin in Maine with a married man, Loco/Grable pines for 'good old Harry James' playing on the radio. Similarly, in an effort to reassure her older paramour, Schatze/Bacall declares how much she loves 'that old fella what's-his-name in *African Queen*'. As viewers of the day would have easily known, both Bacall and Grable were married to the stars they reference; and in this way, the dialogue asserts the stability of those off-screen unions even as their on-screen love interests resist commitment.

These fragments of the star image are not the only part-for-the-whole exchange in play. Just as the shoes are a defining point of attraction within the fashion show – itself a spectacle in which the excesses of the film coalesce – the characters themselves relate to the world through a kind of synecdochal economy. Schatze tells Pola that they are setting up a 'bear trap' to catch millionaires, but that 'you don't need to catch a whole herd of them; all you need is one nice, big, fat one.' The penthouse rented by the models spatialises that 'bear trap', giving concrete dimensions to the overarching strategy of, in Schatze's words, 'get[ting] a little organisation into this marriage caper: class address, class background, class characters.' The four-way mirror in the nightclub powder room is a single, if multifaceted, site through which the models may assess the various angles of their appeal – while, as scholars have noted, exhibiting those angles for the pleasure of the viewer (Cohen 281; Konkle 377). Konkle also points out that 'clothing, as a class marker, is crucial in *Millionaire*', with Schatze rejecting Tom because he does not wear a necktie (373). And Pola's glasses gesture to a greater anxiety over her own desirability – 'Men aren't attentive to girls who wear glasses' – as well as extra-diegetic issues of female objectification and spectatorship (Cohen 279; Konkle 378).

The CinemaScope screen, Pola's glasses, the mirror in the nightclub powder room –each of these things has generated illuminating commentary on female stardom, spectatorship and film history (Cohen 1998; Dyer [1986] 2004; Johnson 1982; Konkle 2014). Pola/Monroe's heels also belong to this canon of *objets* that reveals so much about the film and its questions of beauty, femininity and reflexivity. Designed to be all but invisible – the *all but* drawing all the more attention to clothing's place in the culture of visibility, to paraphrase Silverman – the heels emerge as an unexpected clue hinting that there is still even more to see in this film.

Given the focus on the historicity of the film, with its post-war audiences and CinemaScope process, the statement above could be reframed as a question: what does that 'even more' look like *now*? Where the scholars discussed above examine the stakes of the film for period spectatorship, a next step is to consider how contemporary audiences might view its excesses – on television,

DVD/Blu-Ray players, laptops and mobile devices. In this way, a kind of before-and-after effect comes into play, through which established knowledge of historical film exhibition meets the variability of modern-day screens. Laura Mulvey (2006) has theorised the possessive spectatorship offered by the ability to control these screens by pausing on and fast-forwarding (or rewinding) to a favourite scene or shot.[1] And as Martine Beugnet has pointed out (2015), the fact that many of the screens are minute (compared to the expanse of CinemaScope, for example) introduces still other visual pleasures. Writing specifically about the experience of watching films on an iPhone, Beugnet argues that 'the reduction in scale induces a commensurate concentration of details' (204) and allows the viewer 'an immersion in a miniature universe whose gate opens in the palm of one's hand' (206). As if extending the characters' own part-for-the-whole perspective, the spatial excesses of the original *How to Marry a Millionaire* widescreen may scale down to another kind of excess: the extreme intimacy of holding a miniaturised iteration of that screen. To paraphrase Tom Brookman, the spectator can see anything that they want *here* – within their grasp.

Yet just as various readings of *How to* have examined the ways in which its meaning exceeds even the vastness of the CinemaScope screen, it is worth considering how the film and its fashion show elude, rather than submit to, their modern-day audience. Indeed, throughout the work, there is a thematic emphasis on the transience of possession. In a dream sequence, Pola and Schatze fantasise about being showered with jewels and the power to buy anything they want; but in reality, they need to sell their furniture to pay the rent on the gorgeous penthouse. The ownership of that penthouse is itself in question, as Freddy Denmark (David Wayne) rents the apartment to the models and goes on to fall in love with Pola but is technically on the lam from the IRS. Similarly, Loco's boyfriend (and future husband) inadvertently confuses her by gesturing to an expanse of wilderness and telling her, 'It's all mine' – meaning that it is under his watch as a forest ranger, not a land baron. In this way, many of the spectacular images in the film – the luxury of the penthouse, the vista of the Maine timberline – are framed within a context of impermanence and misunderstanding.

The arc of the fashion show, and specifically Pola/Monroe's heels within that display, allegorise this dialogue between the tangible and the elusive. The sequence begins with an establishing behind-the-scenes exchange, as the models prepare for the show by adjusting their accessories: Loco fixes her earrings, Schatze puts on her belt and Pola fastens the straps of her heels. Though CinemaScope privileges the latitude of the screen rather than its depth, there are points of attraction in the background as models walk around the dressing room and sketches of dress designs hang on the wall. For all of

Figure 8.1 Behind the scenes

the sheer prettiness of the imagery, however, the textures of the costumes come across as fairly dense. Across the screen there are bold colours, large skirts, sleeves, hats and capes, and rich fabrics. Somewhat incongruously, three seamstresses either move towards or sit near the middle of the frame, bisecting the shot with their sombre long-sleeved black dresses.

There is, then, a kind of stolid saturation of the screen, with the *mise en scène* emphasising the material with which the fashion house works. Pola/Monroe, however, lightens this density. Dressed in a bathing suit, she is literally wearing less than the other women; but it is the accents to her outfit that shimmer and catch the eye. The rhinestone frames of her glasses, the jewelled armband and details on her suit, and the translucent heels – each of these reflects the light and flickers continually as Pola/Monroe moves, introducing an ephemeral quality to the frame that is comparatively lacking elsewhere.

The interlude in which Pola/Monroe models the ensemble for Brookman heightens this sense of the elusive. In medium shot from the waist up, her earrings and the jewelled detail at her décolletage sparkle and shine; but it is in long shot that the shimmering effect is fully realised. As Pola pivots and sashays between poses in the midground of the shot, the almost invisible heels match the glass table at which Brookman sits in the foreground as well as the clear legs of the stools on the podium in the background. The sheen of the heels, then, simultaneously suggests ethereality – the approximation of a bare leg; a lightness of physical presence in the midst of heavy fabrics – and groundedness, inasmuch as it refracts light in the same way as those static objects. Indeed, immediately after Pola trips and thus makes the shoes not only visible but audible, she seeks stillness by sitting down, stretching out one leg and aligning the heel with the vertical structure of the stool. Pola remains in this pose for the rest of the show.

Such a sequence undoubtedly brings to mind Mulvey's concept of to-be-looked-at-ness, through which the woman is 'simultaneously looked at and

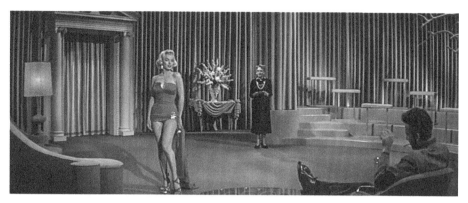

Figure 8.2 The fashion show

displayed' (Mulvey 2009: 19) in spectacles that 'freeze the flow of action in moments of erotic contemplation' (Ibid.: 19–20). Yet just as Pola/Monroe alternately glides and teeters on those heels it is clear that the film as a whole offers no solid ground for the viewer to consider the heroines as either objects only to-be-looked-at or total agents of their own destiny.[2] Silverman notes that '[d]ress is one of the most important cultural implements for [...] mapping [the body's] erotegenic zones and for affixing a sexual identity' (Silverman 1986: 146). What the heels offer, by contrast, are a means of exteriorising – making visible – the more mutable, even mobile, kind of desirability posited by the film. Pola, Schatze and Loco appear to be, alternately, high-society ingénues and canny Cinderellas (following Konkle); they long for luxury while acknowledging its transience, and they celebrate their own physical beauty in that four-way mirror even as they cannot always 'see' their suitors (figuratively and, in Pola's case, literally). To paraphrase Silverman, Pola's heels capture – synecdochally – the heroines' faltering but determined mapping out of their own happy endings.

This sense of variability refracts even further to include the very act of viewing the fashion show. Watching this sequence play out on a mobile phone or small tablet, the viewer of today would see, borrowing Beugnet's words, this 'intricate composition [...] and [its] variations' (Beugnet 2015: 196) emerge from the CinemaScope screen to flicker in the hand. But as the gaze in turn flickers to follow the shoes, it has a hard time keeping up. For the high heels continually shift, whether through their appearance in the play of light as Pola/Monroe moves, or in terms of their function as invisible accessory, impediment to action, or form of support. One may see *through* them without seeing *all* of them. Certainly the fashion show offers the sensory plenitude of various textured and coloured fabrics, as well as a number of beautiful models wearing the ensembles; these are sartorial vistas as impressive as the timberline or the penthouse. The dynamism of the high heels within the sequence, however, suggests that like these sites, the film itself eludes total possession. Just as Pola is utterly attentive to (the eligible men in) her surroundings while accepting the limitations of her vision, spectator and critic alike observe what they can of *How to Marry a Millionaire*. To revise the claim made earlier: there is always even more to see, and one can only hope to see it all.

Notes

1. See *Death 24X a Second*, chapter 9: 'The Possessive Spectator'.
2. Elsewhere, I have discussed the stakes of Monroe's own 'uniquely incandescent photographic presence' (Salzberg 2014: 128) for female stardom and audience identification.

References

Beugnet, Martine (2015), 'Miniature Pleasures: On Watching Films on an iPhone', in J. Geiger and K. Littau (eds), *Cinematicity in Media History*, Edinburgh: Edinburgh University Press, pp. 196–210.

Cohen, Lisa (1998), 'The Horizontal Walk: Marilyn Monroe, CinemaScope, and Sexuality', *The Yale Journal of Criticism*, vol. 11, no. 1, pp. 259–88.

Dyer, Richard [1986] (2004), *Heavenly Bodies: Film Stars and Society*, London: Routledge.

Johnson, Catherine (1982), 'Marriage and Money: *How to Marry a Millionaire*', *Film Reader* no. 5, pp. 67–75.

Konkle, Amanda (2014), 'How to (Marry a Woman who Wants to) Marry a Millionaire', *Quarterly Review of Film and Video* vol. 31, no. 4, pp. 364–83.

Mulvey, Laura (2009), *Visual and Other Pleasures*, London: Palgrave Macmillan.

Mulvey, Laura (2006), *Death 24X a Second*, London: Reaktion Books.

Salzberg, Ana (2014), *Beyond the Looking Glass: Narcissism and Female Stardom in Studio-Era Hollywood*, New York: Berghahn Books.

Silverman, Kaja (1986), 'Fragments of a Fashionable Discourse', in T. Modleski (ed.), *Studies in Entertainment: Critical Approaches to Mass Culture*, Bloomington: Indiana University Press, pp. 139–52.

Chapter 9

Frenetic footwear and lively lace-ups: the spectacle of shoes in Golden Age Hollywood animation

Christopher Holliday

One of the most enduring images of 1940s Hollywood animation is that of a pair of shoes. Appearing in nineteen *Tom and Jerry* shorts between 1940 and 1952 (and the only recurring human character across the series), the character known as 'Mammy Two-Shoes' was a faceless African American caricature of a housemaid who was one of only two 'well-known black stars' (Cohen 1997: 55) in animation popularised by the MGM studio (the other was Bosko, created by animators Hugh Harman and Rudolf Ising for Leon Schlesinger in 1929). A complex generalisation of black femininity and a stereotyped signifier for 'African American second-class citizenship in post-war United States' (Lehman 2007: 95), Mammy Two-Shoes, as the name implies, was visible largely by her imposing footwear, which stomped and scurried through absurd cat-and-mouse scenarios. Viewed only partially by spectators, the expressiveness of Mammy Two-Shoes was ultimately anchored to the symbolic function of her iconic feet and footwear. However, the character is one of a number of often playful, creative collisions during the Golden Age of North American cartooning between the rhetoric of animation as an expressive medium and the representation of shoes. This chapter concentrates on locating where studio-era animation turned to shoes and shoe production within its narratives, and then seeks to open up some possible lines of enquiry to explain such a pervasive and enduring presence.

The history of popular US animation certainly reveals a wide range of cartoon media that has explored the medium's 'illusion of life' credentials via the narratological possibilities of sentient and spectacular shoes. With animation studies coming to theorise what Paul Wells calls the 'scripted artefact' in which our 'phenomenological response' (Wells 2014: 9) to common objects is destabilised through metaphor, symbolism and animation's ability for transformation, the continual re-casting of footwear in animation can be used to examine the central role of objects and materiality within a cartoon context.

By interrogating animated shoes as sites of intrinsic dramaturgy and creativity rooted in their variant styles and designs, this chapter argues that the many kinds of 'animated' shoes on display bear out how objects can be acted *upon* and acted *with* through ulterior functionality, performance and the semblance of 'character'.

The sole of Golden Age animation

Adapted tales of Charles Perrault's Puss in Boots trickster; Cinderella's missing glass slipper in Walt Disney's 1950 cel-animated feature; Wile E. Coyote's purchase of 'Fleet Foot Jet Propelled Tennis Shoes' in his first appearance in *Fast and Furry-ous* (Chuck Jones, USA, 1949); Earth's last remaining plant stuffed inside a well-worn leather boot in *Wall-E* (Andrew Stanton, USA, 2008); the 52-episode UK television series *The Shoe People* (James Driscoll, UK, 1987–92); and the recurring 'Shoe Family' segment on HBO's *A Little Curious* (Steve Oakes, USA, 1998–2000) are just some examples of popular animation across twentieth-century film and television that displays a preoccupation with images of shoes. Indeed, to speak of the treatment of sneakers, sandals and slippers within animation is to identify certain key films and figures across the interstices of several national cinemas and filmmaking contexts. Animated characters eat shoes (as in Czech animator Jan Švankmajer's experimental stop-motion short *Food* [1992]), are able to live happily inside shoes (see *The Five* [Joy Batchelor, UK, 1970] produced for the British Medical Association), and are even overwhelmed by hundreds of sentient shoes cascading like water (in Nu Shooz's music video for 'Point Of No Return' [1986], animated by North American stop-motion animator Mark Sawicki) all due to the medium's creative multimedia repertoire. However, within the specific industry and artistry of the Golden Age of Hollywood animation (falling largely between the 1930s and 1960s), shoes can be understood as central and significant sites of meaning. Their presence, the analysis of which forms the basis of the first section of this chapter, can be aligned with the emerging dominance of the animated fairy tale adaptation and their own narrative creativity with shoes.

Since its inception during the last decade of the nineteenth century, the animated film has certainly been 'a ready bedfellow of the fairy tale, keen to exploit its rich symbolic and metaphoric principles' (Wells 2016: 48). The visibility of shoes in a number of studio-era shorts therefore emerges largely out of the conjunction between the arrival of the medium as an industry in America and the persistence of the fairy tale adaptation within animation's formative period. Shoes hold a strong symbolic or metaphoric function within a number of fairy tale stories, as Marilena Papachristophorou explains:

In the context of fairy tales and folktales, shoes may be moccasins, slippers, ballet shoes, boots, clogs, and sandals, marvelous or otherwise. Shoes in fairy tales contribute to the action by moving, and so by extension they may be involved, for example, in dancing, escape, flight, or wandering. They are also extremely desirable, either by virtue of their elegant appearance or their magical powers. (2008: 858)

The 'animation' of shoes through their powerful magical desirability across a number of folk and fairy tales (from Puss in Boots to Cinderella) can be allied to – and supported by – their 'symbolic qualities', which allows fairy tale footwear to be 'associated with social status, identity, female beauty, or sexuality' (Ibid.). The sudden movement of shoes into 'action' in these storytelling traditions finds a corollary in animation's own representational potential as a rhetorical form of communication. But if animation provides a creatively distinct mediation or 'working through' of the fairy tale as a mode of storytelling, then it was during the Golden Age of US cartooning – in which it solidified as an industrial art form – that the primacy of animation's subversive 'modern' vocabulary aligned most strongly with fairy tale archetypes to produce the 'fairy-tale cartoon' (Zipes 2011: 73).

Beyond the appealing narrative economy of 'pithy and direct' fairy tales and animal fables that could be told within the temporal limitations of theatrically exhibited animation (Barrier 1999: 99), seven-minute theatrical Hollywood cartoons also turned to fantasy adaptations as an extension of the fairy tale's own genealogy across a number of oral and literary storytelling traditions. Kristian Moen explains that in Hollywood animation of the 1920s and 1930s, 'fantasy and fairy-tale films navigated modernism and modernity,' and were part of a broader 'absorption' of fantasy within visual culture, which also pulled in 'theatrical spectacles, books, illustrations, facets of advertising and a host of other cultural and artistic manifestations' (Moen 2013: xv–xvi). With the formation of cinema closely tied to the 'imaginative and artistic potentials of this modern form of art, entertainment and technology' (Ibid.: xv), the animated medium was likewise figuratively drawn to the expressive and popular shapes of fantasy and fairy tale, which provided an outlet for new kinds of experiential and illustrative possibilities.

The early short *The Family Shoe* (John Foster and Mannie Davis, USA, 1931) shares with *The Kids in the Shoe* (Dave Fleischer, USA, 1935) a narrative adapted from the popular late eighteenth-century nursery rhyme 'There was an Old Woman Who Lived in a Shoe'. *The Family Shoe* was produced by the Van Beuren Studios (as one of their 'Aesop's Fables' film series of animated shorts created by American cartoonist Paul Terry, which had launched in May 1921) and combines the original fable with the storylines of both 'Jack and the Beanstalk' and 'The Golden Goose'. By comparison, *The Kids in the Shoe* was an entry in the Fleischer Studios' 'Color Classics' (1934–41) series, which was premised on the same basic plot as the Van Beuren short. The opening shots of both *The Family Shoe* and *The Kids in the Shoe* are certainly remarkably similar. Each depicts the energy of the shoe's youthful inhabitants, who scurry across and through its surface, before the film cuts to a close shot of the front door (situated on the boot's tongue and the instep, respectively) to confirm the shoe's status as a home. With their image of fantastical characters living entirely inside a tattered boot, each film places emphasis on the shifting possibilities of function, and the co-option of footwear into an alternative purpose. The shoe setting becomes largely rudimentary to the action in *The Family Shoe* and far from central to its narrative drama, though the cartoon's final scenes do depict the shoe's transformation from a well-worn leather boot to a sparkling diamond-encrusted stiletto. The 'double-edged' Cinderella narrative of individualism, imagination and subversion of patriarchy (Haase 2004: 20) within fantasy and fairy tale is, as *The Family Shoe* suggests, well served by animation's own creative capabilities for transfiguration, transformation and metamorphosis. The re-gendering of the shoe from male to female (cued by the financial security afforded by the Golden Goose in the film) through a visual superimposition is also reflected in the Old Lady's transformation. Her clothes rapidly metamorphose from an apron, bonnet and slippers to flowing dress, pearl necklace and high-heeled shoes. Dressed in her stylish new attire, the Old Lady looks down to take in her designer high heels before marching purposefully back to the family home (she now also carries fashionable lorgnette glasses, which replace the housework that had previously kept her hands busy). This makeover sequence equates newfound wealth with haute couture fashion and, ultimately, through the shift in footwear signals the character's improved social standing that comes with such an unexpected abundance of riches.

Throughout the 1930s, however, 'There was an Old Woman Who Lived in a Shoe' was not the only fairy tale to receive an animated reimagining. US cartoon *The Shoemaker and the Elves* (Art Davis, 1935) is a short animated adaptation of another fantasy story, the Brothers Grimm story originally titled '*Die Wichtelmänner*', or 'The Elves', and again owes a debt to animation's specific manifestation of fantasy. Produced the same year as *The Kids in the Shoe*, *The Shoemaker and the Elves* was the third entry in Columbia Pictures' 'Color Rhapsody' series. This was a run of cartoons (1934–9) that, like the Fleischers' 'Color Classics', was intended to follow in the slipstream of Disney's successful Silly Symphony series, which premiered with *Steamboat Willie* (Walt Disney, USA, 1928) and combined cel-animated visuals with musical accompaniment. As in the fairy tale source material, *The Shoemaker and the Elves* tells the story of a young child orphan, who, trudging through a ferocious snow storm, happens fortuitously upon a shoemaker's house.

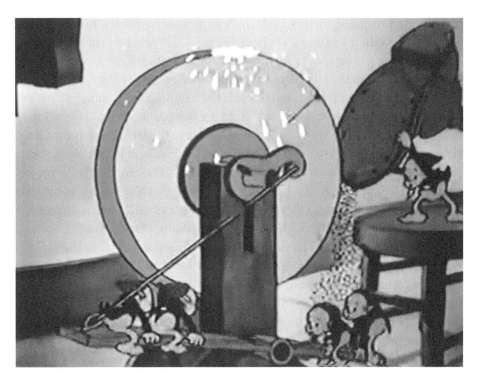

Figure 9.1 The spectacle and musicality of collective labour in *The Shoemaker and the Elves*

Taking in the shivering waif, the poor shoemaker provides food and warmth, putting to bed the stricken boy (who has now changed from pale skin to full rosy cheeks). As the duo sleep soundly by candlelight, however, a group of elves descend on the cottage to produce shoes (Figure 9.1), thereby helping the elderly shoemaker (a scroll explains that 'It is hereby proclaimed that ye all work this night and help ye old cobbler'). As the elves get to work, boxes labelled 'shoe leather' and 'tacks' are marched in from outside by the elves to music, while an array of hammers, mallets, brushes and leather cutters transform the cottage into a bustling shoe factory. Laces even become harp strings able to be plucked, while tacks hammered into the soles of shoes (here recoded as percussion instruments) provide melodic accents on many of the short's musical beats.

The Shoemaker and the Elves was one of a number of 'enchanted shoe' fairy tale shorts to emphasise the magical musicality of shoes. In *The Family Shoe*, for example, the action opens with a choral number sung by four characters in unison, which sets to music the Old Lady's difficulties in raising multiple children. *The Kids in the Shoe* likewise begins with a musical number, this time as the Old Lady character sings to entice her children to come in for dinner. This scoring of image to sound is in line with numerous Hollywood animations produced in this Golden Age period, in which 'musical scene setting was all there ever was' (Barrier 1999: 91). Writing on the scoring and compositional arrangement of cartoons through sound effects and music has certainly identified the paradigmatic importance of Golden Age animation as cartoons produced and exhibited towards the beginning of cinema's sound era (Goldmark 2005 & 2011). Not only did Disney's particular realist synchrony of animated action to music at this time give rise to the term 'mickey mousing', but the period's extensive use of classical and jazz music in hundreds of shorts produced a 'veritable cartoon canon' that reflected the central significance of musicality to animation (Goldmark 2002: 103). Such cartoons 'constantly played off the proponents of good and wholesome classical music against the evil forces of lasciviously dancing, morals-breaking, elders-ignoring, swing/jazz-loving kids' (Ibid.: 107). Given the contribution of sound to the Golden Age of US animation, *The Shoemaker and the Elves* is ultimately one of several fairy tale cartoons produced in the studio era that are complicit in showcasing the magic and musicality involved in the labour of shoe production. Columbia's film was released only a year after another musical version of the same European literary fairy tale, the first Walter Lantz two-strip colour *Jolly Little Elves* (Manuel Moreno and Bill Nolan, USA, 1934). Lantz's film was the first of six so-called 'Cartune Classics', his own response to the successful Silly Symphonies, and again reflects the expressive scope given to the animators by the industry, artistry and musicality of shoemaking. Lantz's musical includes scenes in which the elves dance around a sewing machine as if it were a maypole; ride the operating pedal like a see-saw; use a riveting machine to pneumatically compress tacks into the leather soles; and use head-mounted torches whilst sitting inside the shoes as if deep underground. This image of a well-oiled production is all animated in time to the musical score, a rhapsody sung as the elves gather to rejoice at their material abundance (the shoemaker's cottage has now, thanks to his successful business and the work of the elves, upgraded to a mansion house, thereby evoking the Old Lady's newfound wealth in *The Family Shoe*).

A similar approach is adopted in *Holiday for Shoestrings* (Friz Freleng, USA, 1946), another animated adaptation of the same Grimm fairy tale. Directed by Friz Freleng for the Warner Brothers studio and featuring no spoken dialogue, *Holiday for Shoestrings* accelerates the speed, skill and energy of bootmaking and shoe-heeling through its tight synchrony to music. *Holiday for Shoestrings* is a cartoon 'in which Romantic music makes up the majority of the soundtrack' (Goldmark 2002: 114). From buttoning to carving out insoles, the activity is frenetic as the elves again 'play' the shoes like instruments, while the soundtrack includes excerpts from classical arrangements by composers Chopin, Strauss, Liszt and Tchaikovsky. *Holiday for Shoestrings* therefore bears out Goldmark's claim that 'if cartoons have been associated over time with any one musical genre, it is classical music' (2005: 107), if not animation's wider ability to collapse distinctions between high and low cultures in just seven minutes. The film's use of classical refrains (from Tchaikovsky's 'The Nutcracker Suite' to Chopin's 'Grande Valse Brillante') is utilised to punctuate the effortless manufacture of shoes. In one scene, the upper surface of the fabric and toecap are embroidered with detail on the beat of each musical note in Strauss's 'Voices of Spring' waltz. In another, laces are charmed through eyelets and into position like snakes, apparently entranced by the sound of the pungi wind instrument. Many of the elves also take on the appearance of silent film stars as part of this process of manufacture. The parodic image of Stan Laurel and Oliver Hardy working together on a shoe (Figure 9.2) fits strongly Warners Brothers' pervasive culture of caricature that solidified their identity as 'jesting outside observers of Hollywood society' (Crafton 1993: 204), alongside the conspicuousness of celebrity exaggeration across the Golden Age cartoons more broadly (in *The Shoemaker and the Elves* too, a pair of oversized brown shoes is worn by an elf caricatured as Chaplin, complete with moustache, cane and hat).

What connects all these cartoon adaptations is the way in which multiple scenes of labour (hammering, sewing, threading, stitching, polishing) provide

Figure 9.2 Comedic performance and slapstick shoe production in *Holiday for Shoestrings*

the backdrop for a kind of comedy rooted in the tribulations of production. *The Shoemaker and the Elves, Jolly Little Elves* and *Holiday for Shoestrings* all delight in the joy and frivolity of shoe manufacture because of its many occupational hazards, as the elves work in unison to craft their creations but often do so by putting each other in danger (hammering is typically the cause of the elves' considerable physical pain). The struggle between characters in these shorts therefore emerges through the physical act of shoe creation and repair. The role of music within these largely dialogue-free shorts becomes central in this respect, accenting the elves' conflict and dramatising their playful rivalry as the 'carefully synchronized soundtrack' works to 'guide us on our journey through the cartoon universe' (Goldmark 2011: 270). More recent interpretations of the Grimms' '*Die Wichtelmänner*' story – such as the cel-animated *The Elves and the Shoemaker* (Carl Urbano, USA, 1990) produced for the 'Timeless Tales from Hallmark' series – have continued to mine the musicality of shoe labour. In this thirty-minute television version that premiered on 27 September 1990, the appearance of the elves to cobble the shoes becomes the episode's first musical number (lyrics include 'I'll stitch the tops all by myself' and 'Your heels will click, your toes will tap, and your feet will start-a-giggling'). The reappearance of the elves towards the end of the episode to fix a lone boot's loose thread is similarly matched to an uplifting melody, which celebrates the transformation of the cobbler's business into a 'successful shoe shop'.

The aural dimension to a kind of labour made musical – alongside the fascination with the auditory potential of shoemaking across these studio-era animated shorts more broadly – might expectedly be framed by wider industrial shifts, and the gradual arrival of synchronised sound (via 'sound-on-disc' systems) into international filmmaking practice. Within the complex and chaotic set of interactions between sound (listening) and image (viewing) during the birth of cinema's sound era, the sonic spectacle of shoes in many of these North American cartoons seems to carry the industrial, cultural and commercial impact of experimentations with sound effects, and attempts to approximate or correspond soundscape with visual representation. *The Shoemaker and the Elves, Jolly Little Elves* and *Holiday for Shoestrings* therefore mine the specific labour of shoe production and repair in ways that combined one kind of technology with the image of another. Furthermore, these shorts offered a playful extension of the role (and sounds) of feet that were so central to the identity of the Hollywood musical genre as a 'really significant' testing ground for sound systems in the late 1920s (Mundy 2012: 17), if not the spectatorial pleasure of hearing 'precision tap-dancing' on screen – the first feature to include 'tap dance to music on film' was *The Hollywood Revue of 1929* (Charles Reisner, USA, 1929) (Valis Hill 2010: 93). But as the next section of this chapter argues, the production of these sound cartoons in Hollywood was commensurate with another industrial paradigm in the US, namely the nascent shoemaking business of the 1920s and into the 1930s.

Cartoonal creativity and the 'scripted' shoe

In all these Hollywood cartoons the creative flurry of the elves set to music is intended to counterpoint the shoemaker's literal 'cottage' industry (for this is where it typically takes place), and his poverty and toil in fulfilling copious orders. In this way, the industrious procession of drawing, cutting and colouring that defines several adaptations of 'Die Wichtelmänner' might also reflexively evoke the creativity of the animated process. In a much later version of the fairy tale – The Peachy Cobbler (Tex Avery, USA, 1950) – the 'shoemaker elves' are actively seen threading, hammering, stitching, sculpting, polishing and building the shoes as part of their enchanted production line (even playfully firing a gun to create the embroidery on the shoes' surface). But as part of their processes, an elf dressed all in white uses the black dirt left on a shoe to effectively colour himself in, before transferring the ink back to the shoe's surface (in both Jolly Little Elves and The Shoemaker and the Elves the shoes are also coloured by paint, often applied with a brush). Director Tex Avery had himself worked on the 1934 Lantz version as an animator, which perhaps explains why several of the jokes are recycled between these cartoons, such as a waffle iron that burns an intricate pattern into the shoes' design. Many commentators even saw the irreverence of The Peachy Cobbler as a direct parody of Jolly Little Elves, as well as targeting Disney's popular 'sentimental excesses' (Rosenbaum 1975: 72). In this new Avery short, the elves are seen working perilously atop the upturned heels, their beating hammers perfectly synchronised with melodic chimes.

Each stage of shoe production in these cartoons is conducted with meticulous harmony, from initial drawings or sketches to completed boot, clog, roller skate or slipper. In Holiday for Shoestrings too, the elves gleefully cut out the rubber heels, crimp the fabric and even stencil intricate patterns and designs as part of their animated artistry. These sequences appear to combine the Fordian industrialisation of US animation as economically viable during the 1920s and 1930s – indeed, one scene from Holiday for Shoestrings involves a shoe jacked up as if it were a motor vehicle – with a perceptible nostalgic sentiment for the celebrated American shoe industry. Well into the 1920s, the rise in the number of animation studios in New York (the Bray and Fleischer studios, and another owned by Pat Sullivan, creator of Felix the Cat) created something of a centre for the US animation industry. The commercial popularity, cultural status and industrial growth of the medium would soon benefit from, and necessitate, a range of technological break-throughs in sound and colour (notably at Disney) that would refine its visual style, as the seven-minute format made the transition to feature-length. As Mark Langer states, the period between the 1920s and 1940s was structured by a chaotic and competitive 'pattern of innovation and production differ-entiation' (Langer 1992: 351). By comparison, shoe- and bootmaking in the US 'began as a specialized trade for cobblers who came [...] from Europe' (Bruemmer 2011). As David O. Whitten argues, 'between 1860 and World War II technological change aided mechanization in both tanning and shoe manufacture', leading to the expansion of foreign markets for US-produced shoes (Whitten 1990: 229–30). Despite economic 'fluctuations' in shoe and leather businesses thanks to the Great Depression and costly machinery, the shoe industry's 'recovery' in the middle of the 1930s (Ibid.: 230) coincides with the release of *Jolly Little Elves* in 1934 and *The Kids in the Shoe* and *The Shoemaker and the Elves* the following year. The industry and industrious-ness of the elves in these Hollywood cartoons might therefore, on the one hand, appear to embody a nostalgia for artisanal labour 'by hand', using their musical co-operation as a way of celebrating the shoe industry's returning economic success. On the other hand, and when situated alongside the ageing, singular 'cobbler' they replace, the elves' frenetic activity ultimately evokes the energy of the new factory floor, its organisation and division of labour, and the mechanisation of integrated processes, which would in reality implore 'wage movements and negotiations,' as well as trade unionisation (Ibid.). Interestingly, the parallel rise of labour unions across Hollywood during the late 1930s – including the animation industry's first major strike at the Fleischer studio in New York in 1937, followed by another at Disney in 1941 – further charges these animated scenes of collaborative labour with a rather different edge. The collective majesty of shoe production visible across several cartoons seems a stark, if unintended, counterpoint to low wages, worker dissatisfaction and mistreatment experienced by the army of animators no less 'fulfilling orders'.

The narrative framing of shoe production as a doubly magical and musical practice are revisited in Warner Brothers' Merrie Melodies short *Yankee Dood It* (Friz Freleng, USA, 1956), another fairy tale adaptation of 'Die Wichtelmänner' with a striking political agenda that folds in the gradual commercialisation of the shoe industry via the modern factory. The communal activity of Columbia's 'Color Rhapsody' or the later Avery cartoon is removed, here replaced by a cynical appreciation of outmoded technologies involved in shoe manufacture, as well as an altogether more positive capitalist image of mass production. The cartoon frames the shoemaker's business operations as 'primitive and backward' (Mastracci 2011: 594), with shots depicting the elves' frantic labour undertaken not at machines but at wooden desks, and far removed from the economy of modern production practices. The manufacturer runs his business out of a rural cottage, uses pen and ink to sign documents and even his telephone functions via an old-fashioned crank handle. As the shoemaker explains to an unseen caller, 'I'm not in the market for any machinery. My elves do all the work by hand.' It is only when Elmer Fudd (here taking on the role of King of Industrial Elves) appears that the elderly shoemaker understands the possibility of a new business model: 'A manufacturer who sticks to old equipment cannot compete and must fail. To survive he must persuade people to risk savings in his business. He can then buy new equipment, increase production and show a profit.' Fudd then proceeds to explain net profit, how the manufacturer 'must pay dividends to investors', and that 'profit must be put back into the business to fund newer and better machinery.' When the exasperated shoemaker asks 'Spend his profit on machinery? When does it all end?' Fudd replies:

> It never ends! Constant replacement with the latest machinery makes the industry more efficient, thus enabling it to pay higher wages and still make a profit. This efficient operation also results in more goods, a better quality, and produces them at a lower cost to everyone!

One of three cartoons funded by the Alfred P. Sloan Foundation, *Yankee Dood It* has been identified by Karl F. Cohen as an example of political cartooning in the 1950s that presented 'propaganda to the public', with its fairy tale narrative of bespoke shoe production used to veil 'heavy-handed economic messages' within 'normal-looking theatrical cartoons' (Cohen 1997: 194). *Yankee Dood It* is admittedly far less transparent, cutting from Fudd's explanation of economic prosperity directly to shots of middle-American modernity, including images of smoking and expanding factories, saving cheques of increasing value, motor cars and trucks, freeways and towering skyscrapers.

As the cartoon reaches its conclusion, the shoemaker's bespoke and 'by hand' industry has been enthusiastically replaced with the 'Elf Shoe Co.', no longer surrounded by provincial landmarks (market, church, farmhouses) but instead enveloped by encroaching urban sprawl (supermarket, high-rise buildings, factories). Even the shoemaker has traded in his brown apron for a smart blue suit, shirt and tie as befits his new role as successful CEO. Lantz's earlier 1934 version *Jolly Little Elves* had climaxed with a remarkably similar image. The elderly shoemaker's newfound economic prosperity means that he has 'money to burn', lighting his cigar with a flaming $100 bill whilst dressed in a black suit and bow tie. When placed alongside the similarly Sloan-underwritten *By Word of Mouse* (Friz Freleng, USA, 1954) and *Heir-Conditioned* (Friz Freleng, USA, 1955), *Yankee Dood It* presents 'a capitalist theory on how to run a profitable factory' (Cohen 1997: 194). The strong propagandist register within US theatrical animation that emerged in shorts produced during the Second World War and animation's co-option into an ideological vessel of patriotism, public information and policy is continued in *Yankee Dood It*'s transformation of the original fairy tale. However, the citation of shoes and shoe production in Freleng's cartoon reflects not only the narrative's fairy-tale roots, but also the politicising of the shoe industry. At the same time, many of these cartoons also use the image of the shoe in alternative ways, conferring on them other kinds of identities so that they might be able to perform in an altogether different register.

There is a climactic sequence in *The Peachy Cobbler*, for example, in which the labouring elves perform with the shoes they have diligently crafted. But as part of their celebration, they climb inside the shoes to engage in a set of culturally specific and highly gendered performances. Firstly, two 'clownish' elves jump into a pair of wooden clogs to perform a choreographed dance to a musical number, before a pair of red heels dance suggestively around a sombrero to Mariachi music. A similar joke about national identity appears in *Holiday for Shoestrings*, when two elves (dressed in furry black hats) manoeuvre brown boots as if participating in the Ukrainian folk-dance, the Hopak. But as *The Peachy Cobbler* progresses, the presence of the elves recedes and, instead, the shoes appear to take on a life of their own. We see five pairs of colourful high-heeled shoes high-kicking on a theatrical stage; pink ballet shoes gracefully holding a series of poses and pirouettes; and two pairs of hard leather cowboy boots (one blue, one brown) facing off against each other as if in a dancing duel. The characterisation of shoes in *The Peachy Cobbler* ultimately fits the charge of 'erotic mayhem' and rhetoric of desire often levelled at Avery's hyper-sexual brand of animated anarchy (Dillon 2015: 265). Jonathan Rosenbaum argues that the broader 'madhouse' of 'Averyland' where anything is possible is fully served in *The Peachy Cobbler*, because it becomes an innovative and highly creative space where 'disembodied shoes can perform a layer-peeling striptease à la Buñuel to an enthusiastic burlesque crowd' (Rosenbaum 1975: 70). Indeed, the final performance made by shoes in *The Peachy Cobbler* is undertaken by a pair of sumptuous knee-high boots, who perform a sexy routine across a vaudeville stage decorated with flowing red curtain, later unlacing themselves to saxophone music and the accompanying wolf-whistles of the watching (yet unseen and coded as strongly male) crowd.

What Avery's surreal and eroticised reframing of shoes in *The Peachy Cobbler* illuminates is the ability of animation to effortlessly transform footwear into characters. For Paul Wells, the 'visual dramaturgy made possible by objects and materials' can be connected not just to animation's creative history of anthropomorphism, but also to its preoccupation with the 'scripted artefact' (Wells 2014: 1). This is a process by which the animator 'invites the viewer into a pre-scripted narrative of an object, stimulated by knowledge, association and feeling, that in itself constitutes a necessarily new mode of perception' (Ibid.: 9). Although Wells is primarily concerned with three-dimensional object animation – rather than graphic cel-animation of the Golden Age in Hollywood – his conclusions drawn around 'stop-motion animation and its specific choreographies and meanings' (Ibid.: 2) can be usefully applied to the construction of animated shoes in several fairy tale cartoons, and specifically to their coercion as characters. The correspondence between the spectators' phenomenological response to the real-world object (shoe) and their understanding of its new situating (shoe-in-performance) creates an ulterior register of personhood, whether that person is a Ukrainian folk dancer or alluring cabaret performer. For Wells, '[a] scripted artefact, then, is an embodied object whose meaning and affect is revealed through its use and reuse, demonstrating an oscillation between its status as a design idiom, its functional purpose, and its associative and symbolic implications and interactions' (Wells 2014: 9). In the case of Avery's *The Peachy Cobbler*, Avery's symbolic or metaphorical interactions with the shoes allows the cartoon to *cast* an object, *work* with its physical dimensions and social/historical/cultural associations, and then engage in a move away from its status or 'functional purpose'. The outcome is that the film 'scripts' the performance of animated shoes through association as a way of inserting footwear into new narratives replete with high stakes and humorous drama.

For example, much like Avery's repeated attempts to 'stigmatise American puritanism' (Place-Verghnes 2016: 104) through the animated depiction of passionate erotic urges often expressed by his characters towards enticing sex symbols – exemplified by his short *Red Hot Riding Hood* (Tex Avery, USA, 1943) – the characterisation of shoes as a showgirl in *The Peachy Cobbler* functions as another instance of his provocative approach to the animated medium. Floriane Place-Verghnes cites the construction of a 'perfect home-made sexual bomb' across several of Avery's irreverent cartoons as central to his radical humour and treatment of sex and gender (Ibid. 2016: 107). Place-Verghnes explains the 'Averyan' sex symbol of the Golden Age is typically a 'composition of various norms of accepted beauty in the 1940s and 1950s', bringing Mata Hari (eyelashes), Rita Hayworth (red hair), Lauren Bacall (lips), Ruby Keeler (nose), Betty Grable (legs), Mae West (corseted waist) together with 'Judy Garland's tiny feet' (Ibid.). Indeed, Place-Verghnes continues to note in her discussion of Averyan beauty that whereas

> big feet have always been considered a disgrace [...] tiny feet are a timeless sign of feminine beauty because in the collective unconscious shoes are symbolic of the vagina: according to psychoanalyst and psychotherapist Bruno Bettelheim 'a small receptacle in which a part of the body is held tight'. (Ibid.: 107–8)

This perhaps explains why, during the cabaret performance in *The Peachy Cobbler* in which the shoes authoritatively patrol the stage as part of their tempting routine, the unlacing boots go through a series of transformations, getting smaller and smaller as they do. First, the boots kick off their leather attachments to reveal themselves as ankle-high black-and-white spats, which then become green high heels and, finally, smaller fluffy pink ones. As the wolf-whistles increase in frequency and volume, the shoes perform the equivalent of a striptease, enticing the increasingly exuberant audience through a sexualised personality that is reflected solely in the sensual, prowling movement of the shoes themselves. If the Avery temptress has 'disproportionately small feet and large everything else' (Ibid.: 108), then the use of shoes-in-performance in the climactic scenes of *The Peachy Cobbler* allows them to exude sexual energy at the same time – or perhaps in service of – the same kind of spectatorial desire. The burlesque activity of the boots as they gradually undress even goes as far as to culminate in their suspension in mid-air, a move that brings the exhibitionist performance to its high-kicking climax.

Unhappy feet

Along similarly 'symbolic' lines to that of Avery's creative shoe performances in *The Peachy Cobbler* are the 'scripted' representations of Mammy Two-Shoes in a number of *Tom and Jerry* shorts for MGM. Mammy's first appearance in the animated cartoon *Puss Gets the Boot* (William Hanna & Joseph Barbera, USA, 1940) – the first cartoon to feature the Tom and Jerry characters though the duo then went under the name Jasper and Jinx – establishes the template for how the Mammy character would operate. In her first 'appearance', for example, Mammy wears blue slippers to accompany her dress and apron and is voiced, as she was across the character's twelve years, by American actress and singer Lillian Randolph, who was known for portraying Mammy-type characters on the radio shows *The Great Guildersleeve* (1941–58) and *Amos 'n' Andy* (1928–60). Defined by her mobility and activity across the screen, the character Mammy Two-Shoes was exploited to establish the broader narrative jeopardy of the *Tom and Jerry* shorts, commonly appearing towards the beginning to threaten Tom with rules inevitably sabotaged almost immediately by his conflict with Jerry. Two minutes into *Puss Gets the Boot*, and as Tom crashes into a flower pot resting atop a pillar following a skirmish with Jerry, Mammy appears on screen below the knees marching left to right muttering 'that no good cat' (she had previously warned him about damaging her property).

As a character signified through her occlusion, Mammy Two-Shoes fully represents animation's propensity for 'condensation', defined as 'the maximum of suggestion implied in the minimum of imagery' (Wells 2014: 3). Her elliptical presence coerces the character into symbolism, while her metonymical visibility in no way destabilises her ability to contain narrational information. Indeed, she is a character that nonetheless 'appears' and performs as well defined and complete, which in turn permits her to bear out the rest of her unanimated, invisible body. Leonard Maltin argues that in this debut *Tom and Jerry* short 'the situations – funny enough in themselves – are enhanced by the persuasive animation of the leading characters' (Maltin 1987: 289). The development of 'personality animation' (Wells 1998) throughout the Golden Age was marked by the realisation of cel-animated characters as convincing individuals fully able to support the rolling storylines, or in this case the Sisyphean 'cat-and-mouse' narrative cycles at MGM. Such personality animation rapidly enabled Tom and Jerry to develop 'into full-bodied characters, with thoughts and feelings' (Maltin 1987: 298). Yet a similar construction of personality (attitudes, perspectives, signatures, behaviours) also marks the fragmented and far from 'full' body of Mammy Two-Shoes. Just as in Avery's shoe performances in *The Peachy Cobbler*, Mammy's feet and shoes – whether pacing from side to side, recoiling in horror at the presence of an agile mouse scurrying across her kitchen, or simply standing to attention while scolding Tom – effectively do the work of her entire body.

Throughout the character's screen appearances in these MGM cartoons Mammy's behaviour and domestic attire seldom deviated, and the effect of her personality was created largely off screen. Cohen explains that 'her face was never shown, her name was never mentioned, and in most of her appearances we see only her legs and shoes. [...] Her name comes from a description animators gave her' (Cohen 1997: 56). Her portrayal in *Puss Gets the Boot* is indicative of this image – a curiously hidden figure whose truncated and less than fully-formed appearance was central to the cartoon's armoury of gags. Henry T. Sampson explains that 'although Mammy Two-Shoes was only the maid, she exercised control over the house and held absolute authority over the two main characters. She also served as their foil, which generated most of the gags' (Sampson 1998: 55). Indeed, Mammy's quasi-parental authority continually surfaced so that it might be routinely undermined, thereby skewing her ability to command the increasingly anarchic and often destructively violent activity of the cat and mouse around her. Crucially, however, this authority was formally manifest in the visual dominance of Mammy's shoes. The perspective of the action from the ground up allowed them to fill the frame as Mammy walked across it, becoming an important shorthand that connoted the character's stern demeanour, fluctuating temper and no-nonsense personality (even if the cartoons themselves present such qualities in Mammy as fleeting or illusory).

The exchange between style and meaning central to the animated medium is accentuated in – and made pivotal by – Mammy Two-Shoes, whose invisibility places greater emphasis upon the ability of footwear to work alongside dialogue in lieu of visible facial expressions, and to craft what was ultimately a heavily racialised performance. The standard image of black femininity engendered by Mammy Two-Shoes that was a staple of MGM's *Tom and Jerry* series (until the early 1950s) gestures to the persistence of the stereotyping of race in popular cultural art forms. Donald Bogle argues that when placed alongside ulterior black types the tom, coon, tragic mulatto and buck, 'the mammy' figure is distinguished 'by her sex and her fierce independence. She is usually big, fat, and cantankerous' (Bogle 2001: 9). Dating back to the postbellum period, the middle-aged Mammy archetype 'came to dominate black characters' within histories of popular cinema from the early twentieth century to the 1960s, defining black presence in film to the extent that the success of the actors' performance came from their ability to counter such 'mythic' and durable types or eclipse or tower 'above' them (Ibid.: 3–4). In the period following the abolition of slavery the mammy archetype evidenced a potentially harmonious working relationship available between black and white society, partially reunified in the reconstruction era. In response to the black female's loyalty and commitment to the white family, they would in turn become 'the member of the black community most "honoured" by prominent white southerners' (Patton 1980: 149).

At the same time, the costuming of Mammy in these MGM shorts clearly works to enforce such an intersectional imaginary. Her traditional antebellum clothing denoting a 'lack of affluence' (Lehman 2007: 96) is evoked in several of the *Tom and Jerry* shorts – she regularly wears socks expertly repaired at the heels and a range of house slippers (she is often depicted inside), which are deliberately made to clash in colour. In *Puss Gets the Boot*, as well as in the character's second appearance in *The Midnight Snack* (William Hanna & Joseph Barbera, USA, 1941), Mammy wears ill-fitting blue slippers paired with red socks, just as she does in the later shorts *Dog Trouble* (William Hanna & Joseph Barbera, USA, 1942), *Puss N' Toots* (William Hanna & Joseph Barbera, USA, 1942) and *The Lonesome Mouse* (William Hanna & Joseph Barbera, USA, 1943). In *Fraidy Cat* (William Hanna & Joseph Barbera, USA, 1942), she wears no socks at all. *The Mouse Comes to Dinner* (William Hanna & Joseph Barbera, USA, 1945) opens with Mammy setting the table for a dinner party ('that's a beautiful table' she proudly proclaims as she exits the dining room), before a cut takes the action down to underneath the tablecloth. The gilded crockery and sparkling silver cutlery 'up top' are immediately matched to the reveal of Mammy's red socks – patched again at the heels – and bright yellow slippers 'down below', which in their droopy design augment her trudging pace and heavy steps. A similar effect is created in the first shot of *Mouse Cleaning* (William Hanna & Joseph Barbera, USA, 1948), as Mammy struggles against the size of her footwear (this time, red slippers contrasting with yellow patched socks) as she moves left to right mopping the floor, and then again in *A Mouse in the House* (William Hanna & Joseph Barbera, USA, 1947), which likewise opens with Mammy's heavy plodding across the kitchen in loping strides (Figure 9.3). This standardised visual repertoire of oversized slippers therefore achieves an exaggeration of movement appropriate to Mammy as a housekeeper or maid conventionally represented by 'carrying mops and pails or lifting pots and pans' (Bogle 2001: 36). The footwear enhances her often ungainly physicality as she undertakes these chores, while the visual clues built into the design of the well-worn slippers themselves presents a durable image of hard domestic labour and a character regularly 'on her feet'.

Despite the Mammy's iconography as a 'black, self-sacrificing (but feisty) caretaker', within the style of popular US animation there is evidence that the figure has 'changed shape and costume over time' (Bloomquist 2015: 745). For the cartoon short *Three Orphan Kittens* (David Hand, USA, 1935), for example, 'Walt Disney resurrected the hefty, de-sexualised, complaisantly servile "mammy" figure so often found in earlier animated films, but with a twist. In this case the mammy is also religiously devout' (Lehman 2007:

Figure 9.3 Mammy Two-Shoes' ill-fitting footwear, *A Mouse in the House*

49–50). For Christopher Lehman, 'MGM brought the mammy characteriza-tion back to its roots in slavery for the Harman-Ising film *The Old Plantation* (1935)' by giving her a more 'familial personality' and a more secure role as a mouthpiece for the slave community, while in *The Bookworm* (Friz Freleng, USA, 1939) the character would serve as the comedic site for 'puns based on racial and gender identification' (Ibid.: 50–1). However, *Three Orphan Kittens* does fall back on a problematic incarnation of the character that is once more rooted in her occluded, largely off-screen, presence. She is again introduced by her shoes, entering the screen from the right and stopping to pull up her oversize striped socks that fall down over her similarly ill-fitting brown shoes, an act she repeats a minute later albeit when moving in the other direction (in the Silly Symphony follow-up, *More Kittens* [David Hand and Wilfred Jackson, USA, 1936], the Mammy figure wears the same striped socks and shoes combination, chasing the felines through the garden). Mammy's position here in *Three Orphan Kittens* as subservient is further confirmed through the appearance of a set of shoes that are, this time, not her own. The film contrasts Mammy's large brown shoes with the black shoes and frilly socks worn by a child, presumably the daughter of her employers. This juxtaposition maintains Mammy's place in the domestic sphere, framing her outside the wealth of the children making her easily recognisable by her Southern accent and 'thick legs and ankles' that otherwise solidified her 'racial alterity' (Behnken and Smithers 2015: 93). But it was the repetition of her mismatched slippers or house shoes that became central to this portrayal of the Mammy image. The focus on shoes and feet helped 'to demarcate a subservient status' (Ibid.: 96) as much as it reinforced racist stereotyping.

The controlled picture of a happy and devoted black maid crystallised in the shoes of Mammy Two-Shoes in the *Tom and Jerry* cartoons is a signature of the MGM studio from the late 1930s onwards and is clearly intended to reprise the notion of skilled, domesticated labour embodied by the black servant. These were cartoons that explicitly co-opted the labour central to the Mammy figure in ways that traded her 'subhuman sexual characterization for a violent one' (Lehman 2007: 51), mining her characteristically short temper for comedy. The character's last appearance was in *Push-Button Kitty* (William Hanna & Joseph Barbera, USA, 1952), which opens on a familiar shot of Mammy's shoes as she sweeps the floor dressed in a blue dress, white apron, brown socks and dark brown slippers. Later in the cartoon, Mammy takes delivery of the 'Mechano' (subtitled 'The Cat of Tomorrow'), a robotic domestic pet that involves 'no feeding, no fussing and no fur,' as well as being 'clean, efficient and dependable'. This frames Mammy squarely as the home's faithful servant, if not identifying her relationship to post-war consumerist culture. As Lehman suggests, 'her purchase of the mechanical cat in order to keep her employer's home clean satirizes the post-war trend of white women hiring African American domestics to clean their homes with their new appliances' (Ibid.: 97). Yet despite her identification as a maid or housekeeper through her clothing, including her shoes, there is nonetheless evidence in several cartoons that she is the homeowner – in *Sleepy-Time Tom* (William Hanna & Joseph Barbera, USA, 1951) the implication is that Mammy resides at the house overnight.

The release of *Pet Peeve* (William Hanna & Joseph Barbera, USA, 1954) – as the first Tom and Jerry cartoon to be produced in CinemaScope – featured new owners to marshal the erratic behaviour of the eponymous cat and mouse. The death of actress Hattie McDaniel in October 1952, who had 'inspired' MGM's design of the Mammy character following McDaniel's appearance in *Gone with the Wind* (Victor Fleming, USA, 1939), has often been cited as the reason for why the character was retired (Bloomquist 2015: 747). As a tribute, the short replaced the heavy-set black maid who had served white households since the end of the American Civil War with a different kind of human presence, a white middle-class couple named Joan (voiced by June Foray) and George (Daws Butler). In *Pet Peeve*, the duo sit comfortably in armchairs rather than standing on their feet, discussing their finances while Joan knits, though both husband and wife (as with the previous occlusion of Mammy) remain faceless characters viewed only by their lower bodies.

When MGM created censored versions of its more racially insensitive cartoons featuring Mammy for broadcast on CBS television in the 1960s, the character was immediately replaced with this same kind of less contentious (and much younger) image of modern femininity. Cohen explains that animator Chuck Jones 'replaced her heavy, dark-skinned legs with thin white ones and removed her maid's apron. [...] Now, the only human in the cartoons was a white woman' (Cohen 1997: 57). Mammy's use of African American vernacular English was also changed, with Randolph's voice switched again for voice actress Foray. In the new version of cartoon *Saturday Evening Puss*, for example, the Mammy character is now removed with her place taken by a slim white female.[1] A key component of this alteration is a switch in costume, and in particular the shoes. Firstly, Mammy's blue dress, pink underskirt and green apron are replaced with a blue skirt and turquoise blouse. Mammy's vibrant red high heels – that accompany her jewellery, and are accented by red nail varnish she puts on to visit the Lucky Seven Saturday Night Bridge Club – are also omitted and replaced in the new version with smart white shoes belonging to the house's new resident to match her Caucasian skin and, by extension, to neutralise the character's prior racialised dimension.

Conclusion

The longstanding representational tradition of prescribing agency, authority and motion to footwear in animation (as part of their transformation into characters) provides the ideal place to explore some of the fundamentals of the medium's unique formal language and the cartoon's history within the Hollywood context. However, the vitality of animated shoes can not only be attributed to the representational traditions of human-like connotation, but can also be understood through their creative handling that permits footwear to trade in new performance pleasures, with shoes as sites of (diverse forms of) narrative, action and drama. The ongoing presence of shoes within a cross-section of studio-era US cartoons provides a 'way in' for thinking about this spectrum of animation's own entertaining shoe-business, from the emergence of the 'fairy tale cartoon' to the exaggerated fictional image of a black female servant that dominated classical animation's image repertoire. If the enchanted shoes of the Grimms are entirely appropriate to the modernity of animation's graphic stylings, then in Mammy's case, it is her animated shoes that play such a vital role in signposting traditions of racial caricaturing. The design of the shoes becomes significant in metonymically marking out such traditions, stabilising the 'mammification' of (Southern) American culture, and perpetuating the 'lexicon of antebellum mythology that continues to have a provocative and tenacious hold on the American psyche' (Wallace-Sanders 2011: 1–2). The expressivity of animation as both a creative intermediate and particular kind of aesthetic approach is therefore a good match to shoes and footwear as a medium of expression and identity. The oft-cited definition of animation provided by Norman McLaren is pertinent here. McLaren argues that 'what happens between each frame is much more important than what exists on each frame; animation is therefore the art of manipulating the invisible interstices that lie between frames' (in Lamarre 2009: xxiv). The impact of Mammy Two-Shoes is that she similarly functions as an 'invisible interstice', whose shoes suggest she is a character who is marginal and made central all at the same time. Mammy's power, like the animated medium giving her life but which simultaneously hides its laborious inner workings between the frames, becomes equally forceful in its constructed (if playful) invisibility.

Note

1. A similarly young (and, crucially, white) female Nanny character – again only pictured from the neck or waist down – appeared in both the original *Muppet Babies* (Jim Henson, USA, 1984–91) series (a sister, Aunt Fanny, was also shown in one episode), and again in

the recent 2018 computer-animated revival that aired on Disney Junior and the Disney Channel. Voiced by Barbara Billingsley and, later, Jenny Slate, the Nanny's signature costume of pink skirt, purple jumper, long green-and-white striped socks and purple shoes is more in line with the youthful white middle-class couple of the MGM shorts than with the original racialised Mammy image.

References

Aravind, Aju (2011), 'Mammy Two Shoes: Subversion and Reaffirmation of Racial Stereotypes in Tom and Jerry', *IUP Journal of History & Culture*, vol. 5, no. 3 (July), pp. 76–83.

Barrier, Michael (1999), *Hollywood Cartoons: American Animation in its Golden Age*, Oxford: Oxford University Press.

Behnken, Brian D. and Smithers, Gregory D. (2015), *Racism in American Popular Media: From Aunt Jemima to the Frito Bandito*, Santa Barbara, CA: Praeger.

Bloomquist, Jennifer (2015), 'The Construction of Ethnicity via Voicing: African American English in Children's Animated Film', in S. L. Lanehart (ed.), *The Oxford Handbook of African American Language*, Oxford: Oxford University Press, pp. 740–54.

Bogle, Donald (2001), *Toms, Coons, Mulattoes, Mammies, and Bucks: An Interpretive History of Blacks in American Films*, New York and London: Continuum.

Bruemmer, Claudia (2011), 'The History of Shoe Manufacturers in the United States', *TopTenWholesaleNews* (January), available at: https://www.toptenwholesale.com/news/the-history-of-shoe-manufacturers-in-the-united-states-3302.html

Cohen, Karl F. (1997), *Forbidden Animation: Censored Cartoons and Blacklisted Animators in America*, Jefferson, NC: McFarland & Company, Inc.

Crafton, Donald (1993), 'The View from Termite Terrace: Caricature and Parody in Warner Bros Animation', *Film History*, vol. 5, no. 2 (June), pp. 204–30.

Dillon, Stephen (2015), *Wolf-Women and Phantom Ladies: Female Desire in 1940s US Culture*, Albany, NY: State University of New York Press.

Goldmark, Daniel (2011), 'Sounds Funny/Funny Sounds: Theorizing Cartoon Music', in D. Goldmark and C. Keil (eds), *Funny Pictures: Animation and Comedy in Studio-Era Hollywood*, Berkeley, CA: University of California Press, pp. 257–71.

Goldmark, Daniel (2005), *Tunes for 'toons: Music and the Hollywood Cartoon*, Berkeley: University of California Press.

Goldmark, Daniel (2002), 'Classical Music and Hollywood Cartoons: A Primer on the Cartoon Canon', in D. Goldmark and Y. Taylor (eds), *The Cartoon Music Book*, Chicago: A Cappella Books, pp. 103–14.

Haase, Donald (2004), 'Feminist Fairy-Tale Scholarship', in D. Haase (ed.), *Fairy Tales and Feminism: New Approaches*, Detroit, MI: Wayne State University Press, pp. 1–36.

Lamarre, Thomas (2009), *The Anime Machine: A Media Theory of Animation*, Minneapolis: University of Minnesota Press.

Langer, Mark (1992), 'The Disney-Fleischer dilemma: product differentiation and technological innovation', *Screen*, vol. 33, no. 4 (December), pp. 343–60.

Lehman, Christopher P. (2007), *The Colored Cartoon: Black Representation in American Animated Short Films, 1907–1954*, Amherst: University of Massachusetts Press.

Maltin, Leonard (1987), *Of Mice and Magic: A History of American Animated Cartoons*, New York: McGraw-Hill.

Mastracci, Sharon H. (2011), 'The Conspicuous Absence of Government in a Looney Tunes Economy', *Administrative Theory & Praxis*, vol. 33, no. 4, pp. 592–8.

Moen, Kristian (2013), *Film and Fairy Tales: The Birth of Modern Fantasy*, London: I. B. Tauris.

Mundy, John (2012), 'Britain', in C. Creekmur and L. Y. Mokdad (eds), *The International Film Musical*, Edinburgh: Edinburgh University Press, pp. 15–28.

Papachristophorou, Marilena (2008), 'Shoe', in D. Haase (ed.), *The Greenwood Encyclopedia of Folktales and Fairy Tales – Volume 3: Q-Z*, Westport, CT: Greenwood Press, pp. 858–9.

Patton, Jo (1980), 'Moonlight and Magnolias in Southern Education: The Black Mammy Memorial Institute', *The Journal of Negro History*, vol. 65, no. 2, pp. 149–55.

Place-Verghnes, Floriane (2016), *Tex Avery: A Unique Legacy (1942–1955)*, New Barnet: John Libbey Publishing Ltd.

Rosenbuam, Jonathan (1975), 'Dream Masters II: Tex Avery', *Film Comment*, vol. 11, no. 1 (January/February), pp. 70–3.

Sampson, Henry T. (1998), *That's Enough, Folks: Black Images in Animated Cartoons, 1900–1960*, Lanham, MD: The Scarecrow Press.

Thomas, Bob (1991), *Disney's Art of Animation: from Mickey Mouse to Beauty and the Beast*, New York: Hyperion.

Valis Hill, Constance (2010), *Tap Dancing America: A Cultural History*, Oxford: Oxford University Press.

Wallace-Sanders, Kimberly (2011), *Mammy: A Century of Race, Gender, and Southern Memory*, Ann Arbor: University of Michigan.

Wells, Paul (2016), 'British Animation and the Fairy-Tale Tradition', in J. Zipes, P. Greenhill and K. Magnus-Johnston (eds), *Fairy-Tale Films Beyond Disney: International Perspectives*, London and New York: Routledge, pp. 48–63.

Wells, Paul (2014), 'Chairy Tales: Object and Materiality in Animation', *Alphaville: Journal of Film and Screen Media*, vol. 8 (Winter), pp. 1–18, available at: http://www.alphavillejournal.com/Issue8/PDFs/ArticleWells.pdf

Wells, Paul (1998), *Understanding Animation*, London: Routledge.

Whitten, David O. (1990), *Handbook of American Business History: Manufacturing*, Westport, CT: Greenwood Press.

Zipes, Jack (2011), *The Enchanted Screen: The Unknown History of Fairy-Tale Films*, New York and London: Routledge.

Chapter 10

Ferragamo's shoes: from silent cinema to the present[1]

Eugenia Paulicelli

> So many feet, hundreds of them, thousands of them, passing through my hands, talking to me: long feet and short feet, slim feet and broad feet, ruined feet, and, occasionally, like the feet of the Duchess of Windsor and Susan Hayward, perfect feet …
>
> Salvatore Ferragamo, *The Shoemaker of Dreams*

Salvatore Ferragamo's life and work is a compelling story that helps us understand several cultural contexts and threads that link different worlds and industries: shoes and cinema; Italy and America; cultural heritage and national identity. In the first decade of the twentieth century Ferragamo was a pioneer in the crafting of shoes as a foundational item in the elegant look of both men and women. During his time in Hollywood he designed and made shoes for many high-profile actors such as Rudolph Valentino, Douglas Fairbanks, John Barrymore and Mary and Lottie Pickford. Ferragamo, who defined himself as the 'shoemaker (an artisan) of the stars', established his business thanks to the synergy of two industries: film and fashion; his shoes were commissioned first by the former, and then later, by the latter, both to great acclaim.

A pair of cowboy boots

In his autobiography, *The Shoemaker of Dreams*, Ferragamo explains how he took pride in his identity as a 'shoemaker' and how shoemaking was his passion, a *mestiere* (craft) that he was able to pursue and perfect in the United States thanks to the link he established with the nascent film industry (Valleri 2018). His early life in Italy was one of great hardship but, having begun an apprenticeship with master cobbler Luigi Festa in Bonito at only nine years old, he moved first to Naples and then, aged seventeen, to the US, eventually settling in California.

Ferragamo was introduced to the world of cinema by his older brother Alfonso, who had found work in the wardrobe department of the Santa Barbara-based American Film Company (AFC). Salvatore was fascinated by this new world. Hollywood was just at the beginning of its development into what was to become arguably the most powerful dream factory in the world. It was here in California, amid the convergence of film and wardrobe production, including of course shoes, that Ferragamo's dream started to take shape. Alfonso thought that the AFC was in need of boots and shoes for its films, an opportunity that might serve his younger brother well, so arranged an appointment with the wardrobe director. In those early days of film production the professional figure of the costume designer did not yet exist – this was a role that would be established in the 1920s and the birth of the so-called studio system. As costume historian Deborah Nadoolman Landis has written (2018), the wardrobe director had an important role, similar to that of later costume designers, working with film directors and other professionals in order to achieve the desired aesthetic results. At this time, actors generally brought their own costumes to wear in the films set in contemporary times, while costumes for historical films were borrowed from theatres and adapted as required.

It was a pair of cowboy boots, the quintessential symbol of 'American-ness', that first attracted Salvatore's attention:

> Presently my eyes fell on a handsome pair of cowboy boots. I had never seen cowboy boots before and I picked them up, fondling the leather, examining the style. Emotion rose within me, the emotion I always feel when a challenge is placed before me. I saw at once that they were made of good leather but I also saw that the workmanship was not good – at least, it was not as good as my work. […] I turned the boots over and over, seeing at once in my mind the way I would make them: the heel could be changed, the lines of upper and mask could be changed – subtly, not to destroy but to enhance their appearance. (Ferragamo 1985: 47)

Ferragamo proposed to the wardrobe director that he remake the cowboy boots because he could do a better job. He added that, although the style of the boots was right for the film (and many Westerns were being produced at the time), there was always a problem with how the boots fitted the actor. Coincidentally, the wardrobe director had already complained about the boots because they were made in Eureka, in the northern part of the state and a long way from the studio, making alterations problematic. The wardrobe director decided to hire Ferragamo on the spot, saying: 'If you can make better boots than those you can have all the business I can give you. What's more, I'll pay you more than I pay them, just because I have the bootmaker under my eye' (Ferragamo 1985: 48).

Ferragamo went on to open a shoemaking and repair shop in Santa Barbara. At first he mainly worked on repairing the cowboy boots made in Eureka since Western films were the major productions. Later, as he says in his autobiography, he 'graduated to shoes for the actresses' (Ferragamo 1985: 48), and, as the company expanded, he became involved in making shoes for costume and historical films. In his autobiography he recalls that he not only made shoes for Douglas Fairbanks but also a pair of 'extremely flexible, padded riding boots to protect his legs during his athletic maneuvers' in the film *The Thief of Baghdad* (Raoul Walsh, USA, 1924) (Ferragamo 1985: 48).

Ferragamo's reputation gradually grew and actresses such as Mary and Lottie Pickford and Pola Negri turned to him for their shoes. In fact, Lottie Pickford was his first private customer. It was for her that he created his first model: 'a plain pair of court shoes in brown kidskin leather [...] with twin "ears" sticking up at the front' (Ibid.). After Lottie, her sister Mary became a customer, and so his reputation for making shoes for films and their stars was born. Ferragamo was keen to experiment with the design of women's shoes, most notably with sandals and exposed toes, but at a time when 'most of the stars of the period were intensely reluctant to bare any part of their feet, much preferring boots – greatly in vogue [...]' (Ibid.: 56–7) he was forced to resort to paying two extras to wear them in the streets of Santa Barbara to entice female customers. The strategy proved unsuccessful, but a chance arrived when he was commissioned by the AFC to make sandals for extras in a film about Roman slaves. An Indian princess saw the film and ordered a pair of the same sandals he had designed for the cast: in fact she liked them so much that she ordered them in five different colours. When she wore them in Santa Barbara she caused a sensation to the point that the *Los Angeles Times* wrote an article about Ferragamo's 'Roman sandals' (Ibid.: 57). He continued to make these sandals when he moved from Santa Barbara to Hollywood. Meanwhile, he had started to attend evening classes in both English language and human anatomy. He was interested in the construction and fit of the shoes and needed a scientific background to perfect his craft as a shoemaker.

From Santa Barbara to Hollywood

At the end of the First World War, on account of higher taxes, the American Film Company moved its business to Hollywood. Ferragamo moved with them and, in 1923, took over the Hollywood Boot Shop at the corner of Las Palmas Boulevard and Hollywood Boulevard right opposite Grauman's Egyptian Theatre. The position and the name of the shop were both strategic from a marketing point of view, something Ferragamo knew well as he launched his new designs to the general public as well as the industry. Just as importantly, the shop's opening loosely coincided with the founding of the Motion Picture Producers and Distributors of America (MPPDA) under the direction of the former minister of post and telecommunications, William Hays, who was in charge not only of censorship, but – crucially for Ferragamo – of publicising and promoting American products and culture through cinema. Costumes that appeared in films worn by famous actors and actresses were reproduced in department stores in the 1930s and were foundational in the promotion of a new American national identity and helped support fashion as a manufacturing industry (Eckert 1990). Ferragamo was thus a protagonist in a process characterised by the interconnections of manufacturing industries and the wider politics of promoting American culture to the world.

In the film *Show People* (King Vidor, USA, 1928) the protagonist, a young woman from Indiana (played by Marion Davies) marvels at the streets of Hollywood in the opening sequence. While she is sitting in a car driven by her father, who has taken her to Hollywood because she wants to become a movie star, there is a good shot of Salvatore Ferragamo's Hollywood Boot Shop along with other shops with attractive displays and signs. In awe, the young woman from Indiana exclaims: 'This must be Hollywood!' The film offers a fine glimpse of the Hollywood movie industry at the time, featuring cameo appearances by actors playing themselves, such as Charlie Chaplin, Douglas Fairbanks, John Gilbert, King Vidor himself and writer Elinor Glyn. We can just imagine how exciting this time was for Ferragamo – Marion Davies herself, who was a prolific and popular star also known for her relationship with the media mogul William Randolph Hearst, was one of his clients. Ferragamo soon remodelled the store, adding a series of colonnades that helped to maintain the privacy of the fitting as well as creating a more customised shopping experience for his clientele. The re-opening of the shop was attended by many of the movie stars with whom he had established friendly relations, including Pickford, Negri, Gloria Swanson and many more.

In the Hollywood film industry itself he worked on films such as Cecil B. DeMille's *The Ten Commandments* (USA, 1923) and *The King of Kings* (USA, 1927), where his shoe designs were made in conjunction with the costume designer Clare West. Meanwhile the Grauman Theatre, opposite the store, was not only where DeMille's films were projected but was an important musical theatre venue in Hollywood and Ferragamo supplied shoes for the dancers.

Ferragamo's work must also be seen, however, in relation to the establishment of large Italian communities and their contribution to work and business at that time. He not only met Italian actor Rudolph Valentino and many other Italian entertainers living in California, whose contribution to theatre, opera, film and entertainment was considerable (Muscio 2018; Bertellini 2019); it was also during his American experience and in the light of the friendships he struck up with Italians in California that Ferragamo came to know and appreciate an Italy he did not know when he was living in Bonito. This duality of language and culture cannot be underestimated: he came to know the beauty and the richness of Italian culture and it gave him a richer sensibility of his own Italian-ness.

The return to Italy

While in Hollywood, Salvatore's business expanded and he began to rethink and reorganise:

> Thus the demand for my shoes in Hollywood quickly fell into three categories: special shoes for film; shoes to order for individuals; and 'serial line', stage shows, and individuals, which could be carried in stock sizes and designs in the same way as in a normal retail store. (Ferragamo 1985: 86)

After gaining success, notoriety and wealth, Salvatore decided to go back to Italy in 1927. He opened a store and workshop in Florence, one of Italy's former capitals and the heart of a region where leather craftsmanship had long been established. It was in this cultural and economic centre that other brands had started to establish themselves and it was from here that the best of what would be called 'Made in Italy' would emerge. Earlier, in 1921, another Florentine artisanal leather and luggage company Guccio Gucci had opened a shop; even earlier, in 1913, in Milan, Mario Prada (the grandfather of Miuccia Prada) opened a bag and luggage accessory shop.

The return to Italy was not without its problems. The new store went through several transitions and reorganisations as Ferragamo chose and hired the skilled artisans he desired, but his American experience had established the foundations for his growing business and he continued to expand the export of his shoes. Italy, however, was a different country compared to the one the young Salvatore had left. He had returned during the consolidation of the fascist regime. Under fascism, film and fashion were both identified as powerful vehicles for shaping and projecting a national identity, a politics of style and to support economic growth and transformation. The propaganda the regime produced would later have a profound impact on the launch of Italian style and the 'Made in Italy' brand. This had happened previously in France, where Paris had succeeded in establishing itself as the capital of fashion and modernity. There are always several complex historical contingencies that explain why one country is able to establish cultural and economic hegemony.

One of these is the power the media has to shape a narrative that is consumed both domestically and abroad. In the 1930s, for instance, Hollywood films contributed to the launch of an American fashion industry and built a national aesthetic of glamour that was then sold to the world through cinema and its stars. However, despite the fascist aspirations, an Italian fashion system and organised industry was not yet in place and Italy would not develop a domestic or international reputation for its home-grown fashion industry until the end of the Second World War.

Nevertheless it was during this time that Ferragamo was selling his shoes in major international department stores. He created innovative designs, especially during the period of 'autarchy' (autocracy), a politics of self-sufficiency made necessary following Italy's invasion of Ethiopia in 1935 and the consequent economic sanctions emanated by the League of the Nations against Italy limiting its ability to import and export goods. Faced with the absence of the materials he needed, especially leather, Ferragamo created shoes with unusual materials such as cork, raffia and fabric. These shoes turned out to be a sensation in the history of design, as did his experiments with the different variations of wedge shoes and the sculpted heel, and can be considered the first attempts at what today we call ethical and sustainable design. This is, for instance, the theme of Ferragamo's 2019 exhibition 'Sustainable Thinking'. But there is also a timeless beauty and creativity in these shoes that we see recreated in many different ways in today's market.

Fascist Italy, despite the politics of self-sufficiency, turned out not to be completely immune – in line with other European countries – from a gradual process of Americanisation. Hollywood films played a key role in this process; so too did the several visits of Italian filmmakers and industrialists to the US. Ferragamo, who continued to rely on the American market, also played a part. Another Florentine designer who was to become very influential in the post-war period was Emilio Pucci, who went to study at an American college in 1935 and even designed the ski uniforms produced by the American company White Stag.

Ferragamo was quite an exception in the midst of nationalist policies on fashion dictated by the Ente Nazionale della Moda (ENM). In 1940 the ENM put together a four-hundred-page document to prepare for a National Congress of Clothing and Autarchy to which a vast number of people working in the fashion and handicraft industries contributed reports. The conference never took place because of the outbreak of the Second World War, but the document today exists in proof form. In this publication, Ferragamo is the author of a paper in which he states that, even faced with the economic sanctions against Italy, he had managed to sell his shoes to major department stores in the US, France and UK (Paulicelli 2004: 136–7). However, the war paralysed his business, he recalls: 'The war which broke in 1939 struck me hard. [...] There was nothing for the real *me* to do any more: no creating, no designing, no beautiful materials' (Ferragamo 1985: 175).

Walking in new shoes: Italy from the post-war years to the present

More than the empty and nationalistic fascist propaganda, it was the hands and minds of incredible artisans, artists and business people such as Ferragamo that contributed to constructing a more modern and appealing image of Italy and to launch Italian style to the world. In fact, it was in the Renaissance city par excellence, Florence, that in 1951, thanks to the astute PR expert Giovan Battista Giorgini, Italian fashion shows attracted major American buyers and journalists. Thus a new era and process of reconstruction began. In 1947 Ferragamo was awarded the prestigious Neiman Marcus 'Oscar of Fashion' for his services in the field of fashion, together with Christian Dior and Irene, the Hollywood costume designer. Before the presentation of the awards a fashion show was organised with models dressed in Dior clothes and wearing Ferragamo shoes. Ferragamo recalls that although he and Dior had not communicated before showing their collections, the two matched perfectly:

> One of my shoe styles was of satin, lined with satin, and the vamp was cut away to show the instep in precisely the same fashion as Dior's neckline. The second pair of shoes was made with two drapes only. Dior had designed a dress with two drapes. [...] Yet perhaps it was not so fantastic, after all. I had for many years believed that the fashion trend is not the exclusive prerogative of one designer but it is 'in the air' – a sort of manifestation of the world. (Ferragamo 1985: 218)

Old and new American stars, socialites and celebrities visited and spent time in Italy during this new season and, after Florence, the eternal city of Rome became the hub of fashion, film and glamour. 'Hollywood on the Tiber' came to see Rome and Italy as one of the most attractive places to visit and work for both actors and the American crews who spent time in the Cinecittà studios and enjoyed the Roman *dolce vita* (Paulicelli 2016). The name of Ferragamo will continue to be associated with cinema both in Italy and the US. The company thrived after the Second World War, with clients including major stars of the time such as Marilyn Monroe, Lauren Bacall and Audrey Hepburn, in whose honour Ferragamo named his ballerina shoe 'Audrey'. The Ferragamo museum has dedicated two exhibitions, one to Marilyn Monroe (2013–14) and the other to Audrey Hepburn (1999–2000), where their wardrobes, work

Figure 10.1 Décolleté, 1959–60, upper and heel covered by Swarovski crystals; designed for Marilyn Monroe

and personality were examined in detail. For Marilyn Monroe he created many versions of high-heeled pumps, especially the iconic red, with a very thin heel made out of metal and wood. Lana Turner, who played Cora, the femme fatale wife in the American remake of Luchino Visconti's *Ossessione* (Italy, 1943) entitled *The Postman Always Rings Twice* (Tay Garnett, USA, 1946), wore Ferragamo open toe white shoes to complement her white outfit as she first appears in the film. The actress liked the shoes so much that she ordered a pair for herself.

Ferragamo's shoes were worn by many different characters and featured many different styles, from the glamour of Marilyn Monroe in *The Seven Year Itch* (Billy Wilder, USA, 1955) to the simple, understated elegance of the English tourist in Italy played by Ingrid Bergman in *Journey to Italy/Viaggio in Italia* (Roberto Rossellini, Italy, 1954). Later the Ferragamo brand provided the shoes for Madonna in *Evita* (Alan Parker, USA, 1996) – the costume designer Penny Rose worked closely with the Ferragamo Archive to choose the shoes, including a red suede open toe sandal (Eva Perón herself had been a faithful customer of Ferragamo, for whom he made shoes to match her many outfits). In *Australia* (Baz Luhrmann, UK/Australia/USA, 2008) Nicole Kidman wears Ferragamo shoes and leather gloves (Ricci 2009). The costume designer for the film Catherine Martin worked with Ferragamo in order to create Kidman's 1930s and 1940s style and her red velvet and stingray

Figure 10.2 Salvatore Ferragamo, sandal, 1938, heel and platform covered by suede; created for Judy Garland

shoes were available to buy as a $950 tie-in, as were a pair of matching gloves (Laverty 2016: 184).

In 2018 the Salvatore Ferragamo Museum in Florence staged an exhibition entitled *Italy in Hollywood*, which tackled all manner of questions surrounding mass Italian immigration at the turn of the twentieth century, from stereotypes to inspiration, resentment to worship, tied together by the unique yet symbolic Italian migration story of Ferragamo himself. The intertwining of film and fashion is just a part of Ferragamo's story, then. But what I hope this essay has demonstrated is that, in its multifaceted dimensions and geography, that story sheds light on the crucial role played by fashion in the definition of Italian cultural heritage and the crucial role played by shoes in film.

Ferragamo's ongoing popularity as a brand is testament to the endurance of the mutual fascination of Hollywood and the footwear industry. To mark the occasion of the exhibition's opening, the company reproduced some of its most iconic designs from the past and made them available for sale. In this context, the past was revisited but lent a contemporary edge, in keeping with Hollywood's current concern with environmental matters. The rainbow sandal, created in 1938 for Judy Garland and described on Ferragamo's website as 'the most famous shoe ever made by Salvatore Ferragamo' was redesigned in sustainable materials: suede and cork replaced by crocheted organic cotton and a layered wooden heel. The name of the new model was 'Rainbow Future, 2018'. A reminder, should we need one, that Ferragamo's story, and by implication, that of shoes and film, is far from over.

Figure 10.3 Rainbow Future, Fall/Winter Collection 2018–19, handmade, crocheted sandal in organic cotton, heel and platform in wood covered with the same material

Note

1. I would like to thank Stefania Ricci and the staff at Ferragamo for their assistance and granting me permission to reproduce the illustrations accompanying my essay.

References

Bertellini, Giorgio (2019), *The Divo and the Duce: Promoting Film Stardom and Political Leadership in 1920s America*, Berkeley: University of California Press.

Eckert, Charles (1990), 'The Carol Lombard in Macy's Window', in J. Gaines and C. Herzog (eds), *Fabrications. Costume and the Female Body*, London and New York: Routledge, pp. 100–21.

Ferragamo, Salvatore (1985), *Shoemaker of Dreams: The Autobiography of Salvatore Ferragamo*, Florence: Giunti.

Laverty, Christophe (2016*), Fashion in Film*, London: Lawrence King Publishing.

Muscio, Giuliana (2018), *Napoli/New York/Hollywood. Film between Italy and the United States*, New York: Fordham University Press.

Nadoolman Landis, Deborah (2018), 'Hollywood 1908–1929: *Gli abiti, i costumi e la moda agli esordi del cinema*', in S. Ricci (ed.), *L'Italia a Hollywood*, Milan: Skira, pp. 411–35.

Paulicelli, Eugenia (2016), *Italian Style. Fashion & Film from Early Cinema to the Digital Age*, London and New York: Bloomsbury Academic.

Paulicelli, Eugenia (2004), *Fashion under Fascism. Beyond the Black Shirt*, Oxford and New York: Berg.

Ricci, Stefania (ed.) (2019), *Sustainable Thinking*, Milan: Skira.

Ricci, Stefania (ed.) (2018), *L'Italia a Hollywood*, Milan: Skira.

Valleri, Elvira (2018), '*Il 'Patto Autobiografico' di Salvatore Ferragamo*' in S. Ricci (ed.), *L'Italia a Hollywood*, Milan: Skira, pp. 339–79.

Chapter 11

Feet of strength: the sword-and-sandals film

Robert A. Rushing

The 'sword-and-sandals' film may be the only cinematic genre named after an article of footwear; called 'peplum' films in Europe, these largely Italian, low-budget films of the 1950s and 1960s starred American bodybuilders as iconic strongmen of mythological, Biblical and cinematic antiquity (Hercules, Samson and Goliath, as well as once-famous muscular characters from Italian silent film, such as Maciste and Ursus). For a brief period (less than a decade), such films enjoyed substantial popularity in Europe, India and the English-speaking world, and Italy produced or co-produced well over a hundred such films over the span of about seven years.[1] Cheaply made, repetitive and extremely simple, these films were almost completely devoid of nuance or artistic ambition. The sole purpose of almost every shot was to highlight the bodybuilder's amazing physique. Even for a genre that focuses on male bodies, the attention paid to the foot is slight – arms, shoulders and chest are the predominant focus of the camera's interest, and the bodybuilder's feet and footwear are shown, if at all, largely incidentally.

It is tempting, then, to dismiss the footwear in the genre's name as accidental or superficial: 'peplum', 'sword' and 'sandal' all point to the register of the 'merely' decorative or accessory, after all. The reference to footwear, however, is indeed accurate. I surveyed some fifty sword-and-sandals films and – apart from *Samson and the Sea Beast* (Tanio Boccia, Italy, 1963), a nautical peplum set in 1630, where the hero wears thigh boots for a good portion of the film – the bodybuilder almost always wears an open-toed, thin-soled variation of a Roman sandal, tied with laces that wrap around the calves (Figure 11.1).

As Galt (2011) has shown, the decorative register has been historically codified as feminine and is part of a general gender panic surrounding these films, primarily seen by adolescent boys: are they 'properly' masculine (sword) or ambiguous (sandal, peplum)? This clash between the strictly heteronormative gender types and the fluid or ambiguous is encoded within the

Figure 11.1 *Hercules* (Pietro Francisci, Italy/Spain, 1958)

diegesis of the film through the obvious (if perhaps excessive) masculinity of the bodybuilder, played off against one or more characters who are slight of build, younger, often explicitly adolescent, frequently moody, sullen or sulky. Their behaviour and unconventional performance of stereotypical masculinity is typically rectified by the end of the film, as they negotiate the apparently difficult and yet inevitable entry into manhood.

This essay looks at feet and footwear in the sword-and-sandals film along two coordinates. First, the foot occupies a central role psychoanalytically and sexually that is unusually clear in the genre, a largely *defensive* role (feet and footwear are the most iconic site of the Freudian fetish which is fundamentally a way of avoiding certain kinds of anxiety about the male body). Second, the foot has a certain *haptic* value within the genre, particularly when it is deprived of even the slender protection of the sandal, as it is from the mythological Hercules' fight with Antaeus, invincible while his feet touch the ground, to more recent films like *300* (Zack Snyder, USA, 2006), where the hero's bare feet suggest an intimate contact with the Earth. The slender sandal is indeed a fitting emblem for the genre, since it rejects a haptic openness to touching and being touched, while offering a 'defence' that leaves the foot as bare as possible for the viewer's gaze.

The film that began the sword-and-sandals craze, *Hercules* (originally *Le fatiche di Ercole* in Italian), follows two young men who accompany the eponymous hero: the explicitly teenage Ulysses and the more liminal figure of Jason, who is on the verge of manhood (Jason is almost fully grown and educated but has not yet come into of his rightful position, king of the city-state of Iolcus). The film recounts a number of Greek myths, but its central narrative is the quest for the Golden Fleece. This heroic quest is put into motion within the film (and in the original myths) by a sandal, however – and by the absence of a sandal. Jason's uncle has usurped the throne of Iolcus, murdering his own brother, but he has heard a prophecy that the true heir will return to the city wearing just one sandal. Indeed, with Hercules' help, this young man will be restored to his right place of masculine power (with both shoes on) by the end of the film.

The question of Jason's lost sandal has been the object of academic attention by classicists for some time, who have noted that there were a number of mythological characters who appear at least temporarily with one foot unshod. Brelich (1956) mentions Jason, Hermes, Perseus and Lycurgus – to which we might add the much more modern Cinderella – while others like Vidal-Naquet (1986) discuss Thucydides' account of fleeing Plataean soldiers, who adopted the odd custom of fighting while wearing only one shoe. While different scholars naturally take different approaches, a series of commonalities emerge in the many discussions of what became called 'monosandalism'. Firstly, the single sandal appears at a liminal moment, one related to danger or vulnerability. Secondly, the phenomenon seems related to the many other characters in mythology who display what Brelich calls 'claudication mythologique' (mythological limping) (Brelich 1956: 469), in which a character is marked out as special or significant by 'quelque anomalie ou défaut aux pieds, jambes ou genoux' ('some anomaly or defect in his feet, legs or knees') (Ibid.).[2] Thirdly, and finally, there is something potentially 'chthonic' in the gesture of wearing a single shoe, a desire to be in touch with the earth.

Perhaps the most notable characteristic of the one shoe trope is that it marks the subject as asymmetrical, and hence out of balance. Jason is, as it were, ready to topple from one state into another. Most critics particularly emphasise Jason as an 'ephebe', that is, an adolescent on the verge of manhood, a figure that the sword-and-sandals film has returned to again and again historically, and so his monosandalism functions precisely as a marker of the instability of his character. Vidal-Naquet relates Jason's liminal age to a liminal space as well (1986: 69–70); he loses his sandal in the movement from the countryside to the city. Vidal-Naquet underscores that monosandalism is typical of heroes who make a *safe* passage between the wilderness to the city, a transition that would have been dangerous in antiquity. (He doesn't say why the single sandal allows for safe passage, but one might imagine that it functions as a kind of sympathetic magic that guarantees safety – I traverse liminal space, but in footwear appropriately liminal, that is, half-shod, half-bare – or alternatively the single sandal is sacrificial magic: I sacrifice my one sandal to ensure my safe arrival.) Both the transition from boyhood to manhood and the transition between city and country were understood as perilous and fraught.

This is all true of Francisci's *Hercules*, which tells a version of the story of the quest for the Golden Fleece. In the film, Jason's comparative youth is marked both by his beardless face (compared to that of Hercules) and by his comparatively under-developed body. His transition to manhood is presented as potentially dangerous. In *Hercules* Jason's first encounter with adult female sexuality is on the island of the Amazons, and he finds himself particularly drawn to Antea, their queen. She asks him if he would 'be willing to risk death' to possess an Amazon woman; he looks concerned and begins to stammer – but Hercules arrives at that moment, having put to flight three Amazon warriors. Jason grins at Antea and says, 'with *him* here, I'm quite prepared to take that risk!' But there are other, less apparent risks to the young male subject in the sword-and-sandals film. When Jason first arrives at the court of Iolcus, Hercules pushes the young man into the centre of the floor, where his single sandal and bare foot are visible to the usurper, who has just suggested Jason might be an impostor, not the real heir. From a medium shot of Hercules and Jason that captures their bodies from mid-thigh to the top of the head, the camera tilts down and zooms in slightly as Jason is pushed forward, now capturing his legs from just above the knee down to his toes. We see a number of shocked and frightened reaction shots (and hear agitated whispering from the courtiers who are present). Jason is clearly embarrassed, although he does not understand what has happened – he knows nothing of the prophecy, unlike the rest of them. All of this configures him as typically adolescent, of course: the lack of adult knowledge, the embarrassment at being made visible, the way he is literally manhandled by Hercules.

But there is something more subtle here, too, which is that Jason's body (and potentially, male bodies more generally) can theoretically be made the object of the spectator's gaze, with the implied risk, following Laura Mulvey (1987), of a kind of symbolic castration that accompanies that position. One of the oddities of the sword-and-sandals film is that this is actually the *raison d'être* of the genre: look at this guy's amazing body! And yet, the hyperbolically masculine body of the bodybuilder actually functions as a kind of defence. Implicitly, all other (less hyperbolically developed) male bodies are concealed behind the massive bulk of Steve Reeves (Hercules), and it is, indeed, quite difficult to look at anyone else as he flexes and strains. Without his one bare foot, Jason would not be a spectacle, would be barely even visible, but instead he is out in the open, everyone looking at him, without the shield of Hercules that made him feel so confident on the island of the Amazons. If sandals are normally seen as a protection for the vulnerable foot, then Jason's partially unshod condition marks him as vulnerable to the spectator's gaze. 'Sword and sandals' can be read as offense and defence, the masculine subject that penetrates but cannot be penetrated.[3] To be barefoot, or to be wearing shoes – both conditions are normal, unmarked, although the former is generally associated with childhood, the latter with adulthood. The oddity of Jason's single sandal marks him as something to be looked at, a passive position that places both Hercules and Jason's uncle as those who will decide his fate. The (castration) anxiety Jason feels when he is exposed before an audience will have to be negotiated, and what follows in the rest of the film adheres quite closely to a Freudian notion of how that might be done. Jason learns to stand on his own two feet, as it were: he proves himself the heir, defeats the dragon guarding the Golden Fleece by himself (without the help of Hercules) and regains his throne. His symbolic promotion is registered formally within the film, as well: he is entrusted with the film's final voice-over.

Vivian Sobchack (1990) has a brilliant essay on the Hollywood epic in which she points out the way that spectators experience the film essentially encodes a lesson about history at the level of their body: 'history begins in our reflexive experience as embodied subjects. . .' for whom the extravagant length of the epic 'imprints the body with a brute sense of the possibility of transcending the present' (1990: 37). Although the peplum resembles the epic in some ways, it is in many other ways almost its opposite: cheaply made, mythological rather than historical, and barely qualifying as feature length (many peplum films just come to the seventy-minute mark). For Sobchack, the spectator's body is 'condemned' and 'tested' by the film, but the peplum does not allow the spectator to transcend the present; arguably, it instead maintains the viewer in a passive position in which the mythological register is unobtainable, just like the impossibly sculpted and massive body of the protagonist that belongs to that register. Peplum films were marketed to and primarily consumed by young adolescents, who were perhaps reassured to see that Jason could pass beyond his liminal position, and perhaps doubly reassured that the extravagant body of Hercules was relegated to mythic space, a brief and fleeting entertainment rather than the marathon-length struggle of the classic Hollywood epic. In short, both the peplum genre and its protagonist's muscular body encode a sense of anxiety about the future, but a double alleviation of those anxieties (I can be like Jason; I don't have to – and indeed, cannot – be like Hercules) in the present.

Chthonic/Haptic

The sequel to Francisci's *Hercules*, *Hercules Unchained* (*Ercole e la regina di Lidia*, or Hercules and the Queen of Lydia), appeared in 1959. One of the opening sequences is a comic one. Hercules has fallen asleep in the back of a covered wagon driven by Ulysses and Iole, Hercules' love interest (now wife) from the first film. The travellers are stopped by a giant who threatens them and Hercules initially refuses to wake up from his nap. When he does, however, he easily throws the giant, Antaeus, to the ground, but the fellow won't stay down until Ulysses explains to Hercules that Antaeus is the son of Gaia, the Earth, and derives his power from contact with her. Hercules, as in the myth, lifts Antaeus into the air to deprive him of this essential contact so that he may be defeated. The film here alludes (if only, perhaps, in passing) to the third function of monosandalism mentioned before: it represents a contact with the chthonic through the bare foot that actually touches the ground (although it is only a partial contact), the deep earth and the powers that lie below, an idea that will be touched on again a few scenes later, when Hercules and company descend into the underworld where they encounter Oedipus in person.[4]

Although it goes without saying in the myth that Antaeus fought barefoot, in the film he curiously wears fur slippers or booties, which would precisely *prevent* the direct contact with the ground and chthonic powers that would accompany such a contact. Virtually all artistic depictions of the struggle show *both* Hercules and Antaeus with bare feet, in fact. All this suggests that, while there may be a kind of strength in that direct contact with the earth, there may also be a vulnerability as well. To be barefoot is to be without protection, in direct contact with the natural world – a subject is also at risk, perhaps, of losing himself. To touch the ground directly is also to lose the mediation of culture. To return briefly to Jason, or to those Plataean soldiers in Thucydides, to wear one sandal is to be on the run, half in exile, between nature and culture, between wilderness and city. Tasker (1993), Hark (1993), Neale (1993), Dyer (1997) and other scholars of masculinity in film all noted that the male body is normally put on display only in scenes that are *marked* in some way as exceptions to the norm (in which the female body is put on display in ways that are not marked). For example, the male hero may be stripped naked if he is being tortured – and indeed, the only scenes in the mid-century sword-and-sandals films in which characters appear barefoot (and not even always, at that) are precisely in torture sequences. Such sequences invariably pose a risk to his upper body, and it is always the risk of being penetrated (one cannot complain that the sword-and-sandals film is too subtle about its sexual politics); he must lift an incredibly heavy weight, for example, to prevent a spear from piercing his heaving chest. Equally invariably, his immense strength breaks the entire torture machine before the blade can penetrate.

In only one instance that I know of, *The Fury of Hercules* (Gianfranco Parolini, Italy/France, 1962), is there a direct risk posed to the strongman's *feet*: Hercules and another strongman, Kaldos, must fight each other to the death in a public spectacle staged for the delight of the evil usurper Menistus. In a wooden cage, each is given a sword, but each has one arm chained to the cage. The true sadism is that the floor of the cage is covered in long metal spikes, so as the combatants manoeuvre, they risk being pierced in that part of the body that is so curiously calloused and subjected to constant wear and tear – and is still oddly sensitive (Figure 11.2). The rule is maintained, however, that the strongman's body is never more than scratched; both wear the usual leather sandals and, before either can take a wrong step, Hercules simply tears the cage apart. The sandal seems to represent that minimal amount of protection that the superheroic body of the peplum hero requires – or at least, that it required in its mid-century period.

The mid-century peplum vanished very quickly in 1965 in an oversaturated market and amidst flagging box office. The genre took a long hiatus before bursting back into activity in the 1980s with films like *Conan the Barbarian* (John Milius, USA, 1982), *Ironmaster* (Umberto Lenzi, Italy/France, 1983), *Barbarian Queen* (Héctor Olivera, USA/Argentina, 1985) and many others,

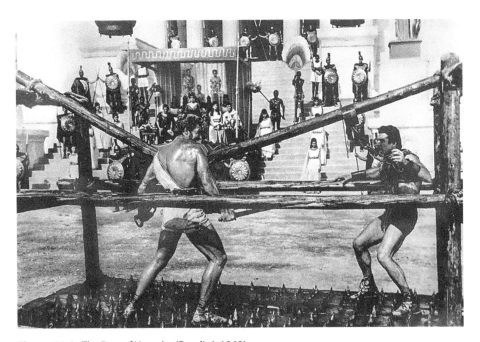

Figure 11.2 *The Fury of Hercules* (Parolini, 1962)

and it has remained largely active since – recent examples include *300* (Zack Snyder, USA, 2007), *Immortals* (Tarsem Singh, USA, 2011), the television series *Spartacus* (2010–13), and the 2014 *Hercules* (Brett Ratner, USA). Certainly the sandals have not gone away. *300, Amazons and Gladiators* (Zachary Weintraub, USA, 2001), the 2014 *Hercules, The Legend of Hercules* (Renny Harlin, USA, 2014), *Immortals* and more all feature sandal-clad heroes (the tight-fitting knee-high leather boot, with or without extensive straps, is making some inroads, however). What remains rare are scenes in which the hero appears with bare feet, in direct contact with the natural world. At times, this is in explicit opposition to the ideas expressed. For example, in the second episode of *Spartacus: Blood and Sand*, 'Sacramentum Gladiatorum' (Rick Jacobson, 2010) we witness the gaggle of new 'recruits' (most are slaves and captives) to the gladiatorial training school, including Spartacus, brought out on the training grounds for the first time, where they are mocked by the experienced gladiators. Unexpectedly, the camera cuts from a panorama of muscled torsos to show someone's feet coming to look at the new gladiators – he is wearing the usual sandals, but walks with a limping gait and, as he emerges, we see that he is wearing a leg brace. This is Ashur, and he tries to join in the trash talk. 'Not a cock among them,' he says knowingly to Crixus, the fiercest of the experienced gladiators. But Crixus snarls back, 'Well then, you should join them, you little cunt!' and Ashur looks away. As I suggested before with Francisci's films, the peplum revels in eliciting anxiety about adequate and inadequate masculinity and, with surprising frequency, that anxiety find its corporeal home in the feet. Indeed, immediately after Ashur looks uncomfortably away, the trainer, Oenomaus, appears –fierce, formidable, carrying a whip – and he has come to talk about feet.

> Oenomaus: What is beneath your feet? Answer!
> Recruit: [*After a long pause*] Sand.
> [*Crixus and the other experienced gladiators laugh*]
> Oenamaus: Crixus! What is beneath your feet?
> Crixus: [*Suddenly serious*] Sacred ground, Doctore.

Oenamaus and Crixus suggest that the source of the gladiator's masculinity is in their contact with a dark earth, soaked and sanctified by the blood of other 'real men' who have come before them. One cannot help but notice, however, that they are all, old hands and new recruits alike, wearing sandals, and so none of them is, properly speaking, in contact with that sacred ground. One might say that, as a general rule, the sword-and-sandals film has long been opposed to the entire *haptic* register of film. By haptic, I refer to the work of a number of film scholars from Vivian Sobchack (1992) to Laura Marks (2000) and Jennifer Barker (2009), who have argued that film is not a strictly audio-visual medium, but one that also activates our sense of touch. Images have visible texture, of course, but they may also activate a metaphorical sense of the tactile – movies can touch us and show us scenes of people being touched by the events around them. From this perspective, the sandals of 'sword-and-sandals' are a kind of protective insulation, a prophylactic against the vibrancy and immediacy of the world. Oenomaus gestures towards the ancient and awesome power of the chthonic when he suggests that his gladiators must put themselves in touch with 'sacred ground', but visually and materially, the recruits remain 'untouched' by that power, just as both Hercules and Antaeus are inexplicably separated from the power of the Earth, or as Hercules and Kaldos remain unthreatened by the spikes at their feet. The sword-and-sandals film refuses to be touched, and generally does a poor job of touching its audiences; the thick slab of its hero's muscles work like a barrier against any sort of emotion in the film or about the film. (Naturally, this anaesthetised numbness is itself part of the peplum's unique sense of touch, its particular 'feel'.)

There are a few moments in the contemporary sword-and-sandals film, however, that suggest something more like an openness to the haptic register (and along with it, the sacred and chthonic, as well). One might begin with *Gladiator* (Ridley Scott, USA, 2000), whose epic scope and big budget place it decidedly above the sword-and-sandals film, even though the relationship and influences are still clear. The film is framed by and shot through with a series of sequences that depict a haptic (both tactile and emotional) and chthonic contact with the Earth. Indeed, the film's opening shot is one of these sequences: we see Maximus' hand caressing the tops of the stalks of wheat that grow near his home, an image frequently repeated throughout the film, including at its end. Maximus does not resist a direct and unmediated contact with the power of the Earth, whether that is the burgeoning wheat stalks, the dead body of his wife (indeed, when he finds her dead, burned body hanging above the entrance to his home, we see him kiss her bare foot, the only part of her body that he can reach and that we can see), or the earth from the graves he has dug for his family. The film ends with one of these chthonic images as well, as Maximus' friend Juba digs a small hole in the ground and buries symbolic figures of Maximus' wife and son in the earth at the centre of the Coliseum.

More telling still is a moment from Zack Snyder's film *300* (USA, 2007), based on Frank Miller's graphic novel of the same name, which was in turn based on a mid-century peplum film – the film, unlike Miller's novel, also features numerous shots of golden wheatfields in a deliberate recall of *Gladiator*. The Spartans in the film are fearsome warriors, but notable especially for their impenetrable defence. In one telling sequence, the film's hero, King Leonidas, explains to a disabled character who wishes to join the Spartans that he cannot; his different body would place his shield out of alignment with the other soldiers and open up the collective body to a collective penetration (again, the film is quite clear about its sexual politics, from the 'perverse' sexuality that marks the Persian others to the Spartan fear of being 'taken from behind'). And yet there is a moment of defencelessness in the film that profoundly marks Leonidas' psyche. We see him on the verge of manhood, sent out into the wilderness with nothing in the middle of winter, when he confronts a terrifying wolf. In the moment of that confrontation that marks him as a man, he looks down for a moment and we see a shot of his bare feet in the snow, as the voice-over tells us that Leonidas experiences in this moment 'a heightened sense of things'. Both haptic and chthonic, then, because of this direct contact with the world around him (the voice-over cites the feel of the air in his lungs, the wind in the pines, and so on). As a result, 'his form is perfect' and his crudely fashioned spear pierces the wolf straight through the mouth and out the back of the head.

In Leonidas' final confrontation with the Persian emperor Xerxes, he returns to this moment, recalling that intensity of contact with the Earth and that 'heightened sense of things'. The confrontation emphasises more than ever the fundamentally defensive nature of Spartan masculinity: the soldiers behind Leonidas have formed a perfectly impenetrable dome of shields, with a handful of spears jutting out. But in this moment, Leonidas decides to remove his stifling helmet and drop his heavy shield. Leonidas then kneels, before placing his hands, too, on the ground (we then briefly cut to an image of Leonidas and his wife in the golden wheat from *Gladiator*). The gesture is, of course, suicidal – Leonidas is not surrendering but leading one last charge against Xerxes in which he and all his men will be killed, a charge in which he will fight all the better since he is unencumbered by his shield and helmet. His spear only grazes Xerxes' face, however, who is too stunned to even move as it approaches him. Why is Leonidas' youthful thrust against the wolf so perfect, while the seasoned warrior narrowly misses in his attempt to re-create that long-ago feat? Unlike that previous encounter, Leonidas has not divested himself of *all* his defensive measures; he still wears his sandals (Figure 11.3), and remains untouched by the dark and mysterious chthonic powers at his feet.

I have suggested that the sandal is indeed a fitting emblem of the genre, which manifests a certain anxiety about masculinity that perceives openness and direct contact to be full of risk. Jason's single bare foot marks him as both a passive subject, someone to be looked at, as well as someone in a liminal space between childhood and manhood. For Freud, the fetish is fundamentally an object that 'fills in' the castrated female body so the subject does not have to confront castration anxiety directly, 'a token of triumph over the threat of castration and a protection against it' (Freud 1961: 154) – indeed, Freud suggests the fetish is whatever was seen just before a direct encounter with genital sexual difference (Ibid.: 155), hence the frequency of the shoe as a fetish object. We might say something similar here, namely that the sandals of

Figure 11.3 *300* (Snyder 2007)

sword-and-sandals films are one of the ways that the genre alleviates anxieties for its putatively adolescent male spectators about their immature bodies and their masculinity. At the same time, the genre also occasionally flirts with a more haptic kind of openness, a different sort of strength that might emerge from lowering one's defences and touching the Earth directly – an openness that is almost invariably foreclosed in a genre of anxious and defensive masculinity.

Notes

1. There is no exact count, because definitions of what counts vary, but Wagstaff (1996) estimates about three hundred sword-and-sandals films were made; this is probably at the upper end of the estimates.
2. Bragg and others have discussed at length the common bond that Jason and his one exposed foot shares with other heroes with 'marked feet': 'As with Oedipus, Achilles, and Hephaestus, we have the anomalous foot as an identifying mark associated with ... paternity and patrimony, illegitimate attempts to divert the succession of the male line, and intergenerational transgression' (Bragg 2004: 36). For an extensive discussion of Oedipus and the sword-and-sandals film, see Rushing (2016: 60–92).
3. This, of course, is precisely the inheritance that King Aegeus leaves to Theseus: his sword and his sandals, which function not only as proof of his royal lineage but also as a kind of metonymy for manhood. It is not going too far to suggest that the foot really is a constant anxious site for epic masculinity, beginning with Oedipus, continuing through John

McClane's bare feet in *Die Hard* (John McTiernan, USA, 1988), and up to at least poor Theon Greyjoy, who spends much of season three of *Game of Thrones* (2013) having a sharp screw slowly driven through his big toe.

4. As Bragg (2004: 37) notes, Oedipus' line, the Labdacid line, comes from the *Spartoi*, or men who sprung up from the ground, sown by Cadmus, and all of the Labdacid line, as Lévi-Strauss observed, had names that referred to limping or leaning (implicit, perhaps, in the shape of the Greek letter lambda, λ, which gives them their name).

References

Barker, Jennifer (2009), *The Tactile Eye: Touch and the Cinematic Experience*, Berkeley: University of California.

Bragg, Lois (2004), *Oedipus Borealis: The Aberrant Body in Old Icelandic Myth and Saga*, Cranbury, NJ: Rosemont Publishing.

Brelich, Angelo (1956), 'Les Monosandales', *La nouvelle Clio*, vol. 9, pp. 469–84.

Dyer, Richard (1997), *White*, New York: Routledge.

Freud, Sigmund (1961), 'Fetishism', in J. Strachey (ed. & trans.), *The Standard Edition of the Complete Psychological Works of Sigmund Freud*, London: Hogarth Press, vol. 21, pp. 152–7.

Galt, Rosalind (2011), *Pretty: Film and the Decorative Image*, New York: Columbia University Press.

Hark, Ina Rae (1993), 'Animals or Romans: Looking at Masculinity in *Spartacus*', in S. Cohan and I. R. Hark (eds), *Screening the Male: Exploring Masculinities in Hollywood Cinema*, New York: Routledge, pp. 151–72.

Marks, Laura (2000), *The Skin of the Film: Intercultural Cinema, Embodiment, and the Senses*, Durham, NC: Duke University Press.

Mulvey, Laura (1987), 'Visual Pleasure and Narrative Cinema', in B. Rosen (ed.), *Narrative, Apparatus, Ideology: A Film Theory Reader*, New York: Columbia University Press, pp. 198–209.

Neale, Steve (1993), 'Masculinity as Spectacle: Reflections on Men and Mainstream Cinema', in S. Cohan and I. R. Hark (eds), *Screening the Male: Exploring Masculinities in Hollywood Cinema*, New York: Routledge, pp. 9–22.

Rushing, Robert (2016), *Descended from Hercules: Biopolitics and the Muscled Male Body on Screen*, Bloomington: Indiana University Press.

Sobchack, Vivian (1992), *The Address of the Eye: A Phenomenology of Film Experience*, Princeton, NJ: Princeton University Press.

Sobchack, Vivian (1990), '"Surge and Splendor": A Phenomenology of the Hollywood Historical Epic', *Representations*, vol. 29 (Winter), pp. 24–49.

Tasker, Yvonne (1993), 'Dumb Movies for Dumb People: Masculinity, the Body, and the Voice in Contemporary Cinema', in S. Cohan and I. R. Hark (eds), *Screening the Male: Exploring Masculinities in Hollywood Cinema*, New York: Routledge, pp. 230–44.

Vidal-Naquet, Pierre (1986), *The Black Hunter: Forms of Thought and Forms of Society in the Greek World*, Baltimore: Johns Hopkins University Press.

Wagstaff, Christopher (1996), 'Cinema', in D. Forgacs and R. Lumley (eds), *Italian Cultural Studies: An Introduction*, New York and Oxford: Oxford University Press, pp. 216–32.

Chapter 12

Men in boots: on spectacular masculinity and its desublimation

Louise Wallenberg

Focusing on one particular form of footwear – the male boot – this essay sets out to investigate how boots figure in a small selection of mainstream Hollywood films as conveyors of masculinity and heterosexuality. Few other pieces of garment visually articulate, promote and certify masculinity in film as much as a pair of boots does, and hence, boots are central in genres designated as 'masculine', such as the war film or the Western film. This is no coincidence: boots are part of the various uniforms that belong to certain male-connoted occupations such as the army, the police and the herding of cows.

At focus here are three films: *The Lives of a Bengal Lancer* (Henry Hathaway, USA, 1935); *Picnic* (Joshua Logan, USA, 1955); and *Midnight Cowboy* (John Schlesinger, USA, 1969), all of them telling the story of becoming Man. As such, they are examples of what Teresa de Lauretis has referred to as the 'Oedipal narrative' (de Lauretis 1984). Yet the three films are paradoxical and chafing in their *malestream* or male-centred narration and representation since they position their male lead in objectified and passive positions. Furthermore, they all tell of men's struggle in relation to that ideal and the active masculinity that society demands and expects from them. And in all of the films, the male boot figures as an important prop and symbol for both the masculinity they strive to acquire and for their very *struggle* to acquire this masculinity.

While the boot is a kind of footwear that is made to endure rough milieus and climates, and to protect the lower leg from injuries, it is may also, when more refined and slimmer in shape, connote a certain male elegance that can be read as feminised. Hence, the boot is a symbol of both rough, hard-working masculinity and of more refined, and possibly (ef-)feminised, masculinity. The boot can be understood as a kind of footwear that manages to occupy, and balance between, 'masculinity' and its 'other'. Here, the very material and shape of the boot is of importance: the working boot that is used for physical, outdoor labour – as in cow herding, farming, street and building construction – is often made out of thick, resistant and durable leather and has thick soles, whereas the uniform boot is made out of more refined, smooth leather and has thinner soles. The latter boot is connected to discipline, power and surveillance, but also to a well-kept and stringent silhouette. While both kinds of boots are symbols of both masculine work and identity, the slimmer boot has been given a more frivolous, feminine and erotic allure – even when worn in dominantly male contexts such as the police force, the artillery or the army. This kind of boot, largely because of the disciplinary (and often violent) context to which it belongs, has not surprisingly come to constitute an important piece of gear within S&M cultures.

In the three films discussed here, the boot belongs to both these strands: in *The Lives of a Bengal Lancer*, the more refined, feminised boot is at centre, while in the other two films it is the working boot or cowboy boot that takes centre stage. In the latter two, the boot figures as a functional, yet performative object: it is part of the work and the kind of life that its bearer wants the world to believe he is leading. In all films, however, the boot functions not only as a symbol of masculinity, but also as a symbol of what masculinity is supposed and expected to entail.

While the very phallocentrism of mainstream cinema constitutes a frame for this essay, earlier research on representations of masculinity focusing on spectacular male bodies, exaggerated physical masculinity and homoerotic bonding between men on screen is also of importance. A central notion within this research was that of masculinity always being in crisis, a notion found not only in cinema studies but in visual and cultural studies at large. Scrutinising masculinity through a feminist and queer lens, scholars such as Pam Cook (1982), Abigail Solomon-Godeau (1997) and Steven Cohan (1997) would pinpoint it as mere gender performance and as constantly failing, and so, proving that femininity and masculinity alike are constructions that are never natural, nor stable, in their constitution. Before taking on the films, let me shortly present the theoretical framework that will be used, starting with a presentation of what the Oedipal narrative may entail.

The Oedipal narrative and (its) troubled masculinities

Following Teresa de Lauretis's early treatise on how most Western narratives follow an Oedipal structure – emphasising a phallocentric, or even phallogo-centric, viewpoint and position – one can contend that mainstream cinema is about and for men and masculinity (de Lauretis 1984). The Oedipal story tells of a boy becoming Man, overcoming dangerous obstacles (most often constituted by other men), and conquering a Woman as the ultimate symbol for his heterosexuality and for his entrance into the Symbolic.[1] Within this narrative structure, women are left in the shadows. They are only allowed to act as erotic objects for an all-encompassing male gaze and subjugation, a subjugation that is both physical and psychological. This recalls Laura Mulvey's definition of mainstream cinema as inherently sadistic: 'Sadism demands a story, depends on making something happen, forcing a change in another person, a battle of will and strength, victory/defeat, all occurring in a linear time with a beginning and an end' (Mulvey 1975: 14). And as de Lauretis points out, this sounds like 'a common definition of [any] narrative' (de Lauretis 1984:103).

Yet, the supreme position of the male protagonist is in no way stable, nor is it constant. While the narrative structure may be one of phallocentrism and of phallogocentrism (Mulvey 1975; Derrida 1978; de Lauretis 1984, 1987), the phallic position is frail since the phallus (and its 'wearer') always risks being objectified. Film, as a visual economy that builds on and makes possible desires, poses a problem for the male subject: although he is in charge of the story, his very representation makes his position paradoxical. Represented visually, he is simultaneously made into an object since the cinematic apparatus inevitably positions him as an object for our all-consuming gaze: '[. . .] cinema satisfies a primordial wish for pleasurable looking, but it goes further, developing scopophilia in its narcissistic aspect' (Mulvey 1975: 9). In film, the male body is made into a site of pleasure and eroticism (but also, into a site of pain and torture, as we will see). As spectators, we are given the gaze so that we can read Man, judge him and own him – as we please.

The instabilities of the Oedipal hero were unpacked by feminist and queer film studies coming in the 1980s and 1990s, pinpointing how precarious cinematic representations of masculinity in fact are since they always run the risk of being read as possibly queer (Neale 1983; Tasker 1993a; Holmlund 1993; Cohan and Hark 1993; Cohan 1997). The instability points to the fact that masculinity is spectacle, masquerade and performance and that masculinity is hard, repetitive work – just like femininity.[2] A fundamental text for re-reading mainstream images of ideal masculinity was Steven Neale's 'Masculinity as Spectacle', published in 1983. Indebted to Mulvey's 'Visual Pleasure and Narrative Cinema' (1975), Neale focused on male 'the-to-be-looked-at-ness' as presented in various genres, including both male-oriented and female-oriented genres, such as the melodrama. Departing from Mulvey, Neale would investigate the instabilities in representing masculinity by looking at narcissism, narcissist phantasies and narcissistic identification, all of which the cinematic apparatus makes possible and builds upon (Neale 1983: 5).[3]

Most studies following Neale's work turned their gaze towards male-identified genres such as the Western or the action film, genres in which physical sovereignty and muscular strength are crucial ingredients. Here, we are often presented with heroes whose active, hyper-muscular (and scantily dressed) bodies seem to strive upwards, a movement that connotes muscle power and male sexual activity (Dyer 1982). The hero is thus made into an erotic spectacle and a sexual object. And while the super-muscular, gym-pumped body is meant to radiate immaculate masculinity and heterosexuality, it fails in doing so since it is so exaggerated: it looks like it is about to burst. Instead, this ideal lends itself to being read as a parody of heterosexual masculinity. There is nothing natural about this body: it is clearly the end product of persistent, narcissistic muscle-building activity, hour after hour in front of a mirror (Ibid.: 71). The erotic gaze that this body invites must be justified narratively to reject its homoerotic invitation: 'the male body cannot be marked explicitly as the erotic object of another male look: that look must be motivated in some other way, its erotic component repressed [. . .]' (Neale 1983: 8). This disqualification is often made through physical punishment and torment. And so, in mainstream cinema, the male body cannot be objectified without a consequence and therefore it has to be beaten bloody through physical destruction.

It is not only the objectifying spectacle of the male subject as desirable body that makes him unstable and queer. While some genres tell the story of one single hero, others instead focus on male relations, glorifying milieus that are inherently homosocial and embracing buddy relations. In these settings, focusing on the intimacy of male relations, the homosocial may easily lend itself to a homoerotic reading. As has been argued by Yvonne Tasker, among others, this intimacy proves a problem for the 'straight' text, and so, in order to keep the story and its male relations 'pure', a female character is thrown in (Tasker 1993b: 236). As a 'trophy' of straightness, the woman's role is to tone down the otherwise so overt queerness that tints the buddy relationship.[4]

Let me now turn to the films and focus on the meaning of the boot in relation to masculinity. The three films all visualise and bring to the fore a masculinity that is both spectacular and troubled. The characters all strive to be ideal in their masculinity, yet they are constantly positioned as feminised (and as possibly queer) through their very erotic 'spectacularisation' and through their intimate relationships with other men.

Picnic: posing as stud

[. . .] an anthropomorphised phallus, a phallus with muscles… they are simulacra of an exaggerated masculinity, the original completely lost to sight, a casualty of the failure of the paternal signifier and the current crisis in master narratives. (Creed 1987: 65)

Based on a William Inge's Pulitzer prize-winning Broadway play, Joshua Logan's romantic drama *Picnic* (1955) brings up questions of ideal masculinity and class in American society after the Second World War. At centre is its male protagonist Hal Carter, here played by the celebrated star William Holden.

Hal is a vagabond, travelling from town to town to find temporary work – if only for the day. He has limited means, and all that he owns he carries with and on him. Most dear to him are his leather boots, boots that he has inherited from his estranged and dead father. Once enrolled in college on a scholarship thanks to his athletic skills, with a possibly prosperous career awaiting him, he has played his cards badly, and is now outside of any kind of social and economic network. The film opens with his arrival in a small town and his coincidental entrance into an all-female community, an entrance that will change his life. The all-women milieu consists of Mrs Owens and her two daughters, their elderly neighbour Miss Potts, and the middle-aged schoolteacher Rosemary, all of whom – whether warmly (Miss Potts) or reluctantly (Mrs Owens) – invite him into their sphere. It is here that he meets his destiny: the oldest of the Owens daughters, Madge (Kim Novak). Hal upsets the status quo and in just a short time span, the lives of everyone involved will change forever. Yet, it is Madge's decision to go off with him and leave her all-female family that makes this change happen.

There is an iconic scene in *Picnic* in which Hal affectively talks about how much his well-worn leather boots mean to him. Having few material resources, these boots have both an emotional and an economic value for him: they are the only things he has inherited from his violent father, and – if cared for – they will serve him for yet some years to come. It becomes apparent that his identity is closely tied to these boots, and that he constructs his masculinity in relation to these boots, that is, his father. His talk is a sort of confession: opening up to his small audience, he 'undresses' himself as he tells of his humble background and current economically and socially low status. He is, however, in a safe position since his audience is infatuated with him: from Madge to Millie, Madge's younger sister, to their mother Mrs Owens and the elderly Miss Potts, to their lodger, Rosemary, and her beau, Howard.

While telling them his story, Hal is lankily leaning against a tree while most of his audience – except for Madge, who is seated on a swing on his right-hand side – is seated on blankets in the grass next to him. In silence, they look at him admiringly from below, while his eyes are mostly focused on his boots, as if he is too shy to look at the others. Yet, his expressive body language and assertive tone of voice give away his pride and self-assurance. He knows that Madge wants him, and he is also well aware of the fact that his erotic allure is quite remarkable in comparison with that of other (present or absent) men.

Figure 12.1 Hal's leather boots, inherited from his father, in *Picnic*

Hal is tall, muscular and good looking and the camera eye misses no opportunity to show him off to the three generations of desiring women within the narrative. There is no question about him being the erotic object within the visual and narrative economy of the film – as well as in relation to us, the spectators. Madge may be a 'pretty thing', for the occasion dressed in a pink chiffon dress, but it is Hal who gets all the attention. Building up to this scene, in fact, are a series of scenes in which he (as if by coincidence) appears half-naked. It is especially his well-shaved and muscular torso that is being flaunted, and in many of these scenes it is apparent that this exposure is against his will: being persuaded to work shirtless by Miss Potts when helping her in the garden on a hot summer day; swimming with Millie, Madge and his old fraternity friend Alan at the public swimming area (who admires and possibly also desires Hal); and then, having his shirt ripped off by Rosemary in an act of drunken jealousy and desire. As has been pointed out by Steven Cohan, this constant undressing coincides with the cultural obsession with the female *and* male breast in the 1950s (Cohan 1997). For male stars on the screen, the bigger and more muscular, the better. This last scene, in particular, serves to emphasise and augment his position as eroticised body. Yet, in all of the shirtless scenes, the boots play an important role: with the focus on Hal's naked upper body, making him into an object of desire, his boots serve to weaken his objectification. Dirty and worn, they anchor him to the earth and take away some of the 'feminised' upside, re-inscribing masculinity in his character from below so that we may never forget that Hal is, after all, all man.

In *Picnic* the Mulveyan scenario is turned on its head: Hal is positioned as problematic in terms of being both physically superior *and* socially excluded. He is a loner, a social outcast, yet, all women (and men) desire him. These two qualities make him a 'different' man, occupying a non-patriarchal position. For Madge he symbolises a way out of suffocating small-town life ruled by strict gender roles. Hal comes into a 'matriarchal' setting and becomes one of the women, yet, at the end of the film, he will disrupt this one-sex setting as he and Madge decide to run off together. In this way, *Picnic* is a heteronormative, Oedipal story with Man conquering Woman as its final outcome.

Like Neale, Cohan departs from Mulvey in his study of how male stars were displayed and represented on the screen in the 1950s (Cohan 1997). Studying the studs of that era, he concludes that men constituted spectacular erotic objects and, referring to humourist Richard Armour writing for *Playboy* magazine in 1958, he writes that this was the 'Age of the Chest' – and further, that '*Picnic* is an especially revealing (in all senses of the word) example of Hollywood's investment in the spectacle of the male body' (Cohan 1997: 167). While the then popular peplum film provided a way of displaying male bodies on screen without making them too questionable in terms of homoerotic looking, *Picnic* goes further in displaying male nudity. Holden was promoted as a hot hunk in the 1950s, appearing simultaneously as pumped beefcake and as sweet and homely poster boy, and flaunting his muscles on film and in fan magazines. Holden was far from alone: Kirk Douglas was building his early career on appearing in peplum films as a beefcake, and Cary Grant too appeared undressed in his 1950s films, for example in Alfred Hitchcock's *To Catch a Thief* (1955), and *North by Northwest* (1959).

It is interesting that gay culture at the same time starts cultivating a very similar ideal beefcake – that is, an ideal coming in the form of bodybuilders. While straight culture would flaunt beefcake spectacles on the silver screen, in fan magazines and in specific magazines dedicated to men's health, fitness and physics, gay culture adopted a similar masculine ideal. For example, the physics magazine *Physique Pictorial* clearly catered to a homosexual audience, although 'hiding' its queerness behind 'straight-looking' attractive, muscular young men in athletic poses. Using models such as Steve Reeves, who became Mr Universe in 1950, the magazine could display eroticised male bodies for a homosexual gaze without being accused of being a gay magazine – and yet, gayness was all there, in every photograph, blurring the border between homo and hetero.[5] It is interesting to note that as the magazine becomes more openly gay – in the mid 1960s – and its portraits more nude and sexually explicit, the one piece of garment that seems to be constant, is the boot: whether photographed or drawn, the two most recurrent 'types', the cowboys and the policeman, most often appear in the nude apart from a pair of leather boots. And while the boot clearly functions as a fetish object in this context, it also signals and flirts with 'proper', macho masculinity, but doing so in an all gay setting.

Discussing hyper-masculinity as a new ideal within the gay community, Richard Dyer points out how the gay macho man, via his excess of masculine traits and expressions, makes the straight man an unstable category (Dyer 1992). By embodying the hyper-masculine, the gay macho constructs himself as a parody, or travesty, of the straight construction of 'Man'. As such, he challenges the straight male's ownership of masculinity and disturbs the notion of gay men as effeminate, as *anima muliebris in corpore virile conclusa* (woman's soul in a man's body). Upsetting old notions about the relation between sex, gender and (homo)sexuality, and by flaunting his performance as performance, he unmasks all identity as drag.

Midnight Cowboy: 'one helluva stud!'

> In accordance with Lacanian motif, the male look is made to appear active, able to penetrate, and not passive, susceptible to penetration. It conveys the phallic function. Disavowing passivity, images of men are often images of men in action – playing sport, at work – or at least tightening the muscles ready for action. (Segal 1990: 75)

> 'Uh, well, sir, I ain't a f'real cowboy, but I am one helluva stud!' Joe Buck in *Midnight Cowboy*

Lynne Segal's description above refers to the popular action heroes of the 1980s and brings up the fear of feminisation and passivity as the unwelcome signs of possible homosexuality. Active men penetrate, passive men get penetrated: normative masculinity is connected with the activity of penetrating other bodies and queer masculinity is linked with being penetrated by other bodies. A gay man is always feminised, not 'because he is in love' – as Roland Barthes would have it – but because his bodily borders are open (Barthes 1978: 14).

In John Schlesinger's *Midnight Cowboy* (1969) the young Joe Buck, a Texan dish-washer dreaming of making money in New York City posing as a cowboy in full Western attire, including a pair of decorative cowboy boots made in black, shiny leather, is active enough. Yet his agency, as he roams the city to hustle up rich middle-aged women (thus making himself into an object to be bought and had), is far from enough to make him pass as masculine and straight. He fails to pass as a straight man, over and over, and his constant failing proves that the heteronormative cowboy ideal he is trying to incorporate is a construct impossible to become, impossible *to be.*

Figure 12.2 Joe Buck's decorative cowboy boots in *Midnight Cowboy*

Schlesinger's film documents a certain period in American history: the late 1960s is still severely affected by the Vietnam War, causing a crisis in US imperialism (Floyd 2001: 1), yet it is also a widely political time period characterised by the peace movement alongside various freedom movements such as the feminist movement, the civil rights movement and the gay liberation movement, the latter incited by the Stonewall riots in New York City in the summer of 1969.[6] This time period was in many ways a breaking point in terms of social, educational, cultural, political and economic change, and in the US, old Hollywood was giving way to what is often referred to as 'New Hollywood Cinema', a period in American film history that lasted from the mid-1960s to the early 1980s, breaking with the old in terms of narration, aesthetics, themes and subject matter and involving a clearly social awareness. *Midnight Cowboy* inscribes itself in this new filmmaking, outing social and economic injustices, while also problematising the most manly of all-American ideals.

The film's two main characters, Joe Buck (Jon Voight) and Enrico Rizzo/ Ratso (Dustin Hoffman), who is limp and who suffers from pneumonia, are both, due to their low-standing social class and/or ethnicity, excluded from most homosocial networks. Being outsiders, their very exclusion is what brings them together, and the film depicts one of the most sensitive and intimate male relations in film history. Following Solomon-Godeau, the film is a good example of how masculinity, through male intimacy, is being *desublimised*, that is, de-centred and liberated (Solomon-Godeau 1997).

Midnight Cowboy is also interesting in the way it 'outs' one of the most American and masculine film genres, the Western, as a clearly *queer* genre. Cowboys on screen have a long history and the first film to refer to the West, the new Frontier, was Edwin S. Porter's *The Great Train Robbery* from 1903. Most Western films serve to advocate a certain kind of ideal and heroic (white) hyper-masculinity – one that is free, sovereign, single, controlled and supreme. Supreme in relation to wild nature and animals, as well as in relation to women and to men of other ethnicities. *Midnight Cowboy* breaks with this representation and 'heroification': deconstructing the idealised American Man as a man of freedom, control and hyper-masculinity, the film must be understood not only as queer, but as inherently feminist.

The film presents gender identity as performative through protagonist Joe's efforts to pose as a stud. Dressing up as a cowboy, he performs straight masculinity to make himself attractive to women – but fails. In the opening of the film, Joe is shown getting out of the shower to step into his new self: he puts on a new embroidered cowboy shirt, a brand new cowboy hat and, most important, a new pair of black shiny leather boots with ornate golden embroidery. As he steps out from the motel, the camera focuses on these boots as he walks over to the diner to collect his pay and to say goodbye to his friend. Later, the camera again lingers on them as Joe tries to hustle up women on Fifth Avenue in New York: his boots somewhat hesitantly approach self-confident and busy women's pumps, only to be rejected by them. At one point, he thinks he strikes lucky, and as he gets into bed he keeps his boots on. This is an indication of his later impotence with women – and a clear manifestation of his masquerading. As the story progresses, and Joe ends up starving and with no place of his own, the boots will lose their shine, and they will become worn out, like the rest of his appearance.

By the 1960s, the cowboy ideal was becoming old-fashioned (and its weakened position is pointed out by both Rico and the female clients in the film), yet Joe hangs on to it as he fashions himself after his childhood idols Gary Cooper and John Wayne. As has been stressed by Kevin Floyd, *Midnight Cowboy* offers a narrative *deterritorialisation* of the cowboy, both as in the cowboy's geographical moving from Texas to New York (from the rural to the urban), and in his moving from a traditional straight masculinity to a gay one (Floyd 2001: 102). Floyd describes the film as mystifying in its making visible the socioeconomic contradiction that is a fundamental determinant of imperialism, but also, as

> a reifying narrative, a narrative that reifies the cowboy, resituating that figure in an allegorically incommensurate filmic environment, formally disarticulating that figure from the frontier myth that has traditionally provided its meaning: [...] the cowboy is transformed 'into an element which by definition has no content or territory'. (Ibid.: 120)

In fact, the early cowboy of the nineteenth century was queer, as has been discussed by Chris Packard in *Queer Cowboys* (2005). Refusing civilisation, he would embrace male, interracial and intimate relations while advocating hyper-masculinity. To be masculine was to be gay, and vice versa – hence cowboy culture created its own homosexual ideal 'identification', one that was clearly at odds with the more effeminate (and inverted) one created by nineteenth-century sexologists.[7] With the *cinematic* construction of the cowboy this homoerotic ideal becomes translated and transformed into a straight ideal. Mainstream Hollywood cinema implements a different cowboy than the one appearing in the literary Western genre of the previous century. This transformation has most probably to do with the 'discovery' of the homosexual, that is 'when it was transposed from the practice of sodomy onto a kind of interior androgyny, a hermaphroditism of the soul. The sodomite had been a temporary aberration; the homosexual was now a species' (Foucault 1978: 43).

When cowboy culture is translated onto film, it is a different kind of male ideal that we see: he is more of a loner, and if he has male friendships there most certainly is also a woman to make him heterosexual. In a way, this cinematic icon is made into a *hom(m)o-sexual*: he now desires difference, but he still prefers sameness (Irigaray [1977] 1985). *Midnight Cowboy*, however, bravely refutes any real desires of difference, and instead fully embraces sameness. As Joe and Rico leave New York to try their luck in Florida, Joe gets rid of his cowboy gear and instead buys them some casual clothes in light pastel colours. The camera follows him as he throws his now worn-out cowboy boots into a dustbin. He now refuses to perform as a stud and instead embraces his queer and caring self in relation to Rico. Of course, it is too late, and Rico will die from his advanced pneumonia before they even reach Miami.

The Lives of a Bengal Lancer: a queer family

> Masculinity, however defined is, like capitalism, always in crisis. And the real question is how both manage to restructure, refurbish, and resurrect themselves for the next historical turn. (Solomon-Godeau, 1997: 70)

My last example is a war film, depicting male friendship and camaraderie during rebellions carried out by native Indians during the British Raj. At centre are three cavalrymen who together come to form their own intimate unit that functions in many ways as a family. To withstand the queer connotations of this all-male family, the film makes sure to emphasise that all three of them desire difference: hence, there is one (single) woman in the story whose only function is to secure their heterosexuality. Yet, the film makes no effort to disguise that what they really prefer, as cavalrymen, is sameness.

The film stars Gary Cooper as Lieutenant Alan McGregor who, at the opening of the film, is in charge of two newcomers, or replacements: Lieutenant John Forsythe (Franchot Tone) and young, inexperienced Lieutenant Donald Stone (Richard Cromwell). While the film belongs to the more 'male' war genre, it is clearly made to cater to a female (and queer) audience: Cooper, Tone and Cromwell are prettier than most male stars and their prettiness serves to 'desublimise' normative and ideal masculinity through sublimising male femininity. Dressed up in tight-fitting uniforms emphasising their slim waists and shapely legs and wearing shiny, tight-fitting, knee-high boots, as well as filmed through soft-focus, the three men are presented as desirable objects, not only to us, the spectators, but also to one another.

The three men becoming family not only lays bare the homosocial bonding that they willingly create between them, but also the very queer bonding that this all-male setting, the army context, entails. Homosocial bonding is what is required of them as professional cavalrymen: after all, the military has long been just one single large male network. And this is one that valuates *sameness* over difference, relying on valuation and love for the same – no matter how forbidden in theory. Hence, the film reminds us of Eve Kosofsky Sedgwick's understanding of the homosocial as an oxymoron because of being both a social and a homophobic bond between men. This bond is characterised by intense homophobia, fear and hatred of homosexuality – while privileging sameness and relationships between men over those with women (Kosofsky Sedgwick 1985: 1).

Figure 12.3 Cooper, Tone and Cromwell desublimising normative masculinity in *The Lives of a Bengal Lancer*

In *The Lives of a Bengal Lancer*, the homosocial slides into the overtly homoerotic: in a six-minute-long scene McGregor (Cooper) appears in cavalry trousers and boots with his chest naked as he is about to shave – and he is positioned at the very centre of attention. His younger colleague Stone is placed stark naked in a bathtub next to him and he looks up admiringly at his superior. Forsythe is lolling on a couch just outside of the bathroom, playing a flute in order to get McGregor's attention. As the scene progresses, the flute playing is becoming desperate: it turns out that Forsthye has managed to attract a poisonous snake into the room. As the snake raises in an erect position to attack, McGregor appears from the bathroom and kills it with his gun. This scene clearly has a certain affinity with Hal's (Holden's) widely exposed naked torso in *Picnic*, which was made exactly twenty years later. Yet, there is a clear difference between the two films and their concentration on the male, uncovered body: within the narrative universe of *Picnic*, Hal's naked chest is constantly being put on display – often seemingly against his will – for the enjoyment of the female characters, whereas McGregor's naked torso is exposed and within an all-male (and between desiring men) setting. Further, there is a difference in bodily ideals: the 1930s male body is lean and refined, whereas the 1950s male body – as exemplified by Holden – is muscular and pumped-up.

In *The Lives of a Bengal Lancer*, the three stars are positioned as objects (to-be-looked-at) *and* as subjects (as active, upward-striving characters). Occupying a position ascribed by classical cinema to the feminine, their gender becomes fluid – and the otherwise natural visual order and symmetry between the sexes is altered. Through the use of well-fitting uniforms and elegant, slim boots, they are also being fetishised. For Cooper, who had come to fame in Victor Fleming's Western picture *The Virginian* (1929), strategic visual fetishisation was part of his stardom. Just think of him in Josef von Sternberg's *Morocco* (1930), in which he is as fetishised as his co-star Marlene Dietrich. Stella Bruzzi has pointed out the androgynous eroticism embodied by Dietrich, but a similar eroticised blurring of difference must be attributed to Cooper's appearance (Bruzzi 1997: xx; Cavell 2005: 131–2).

While being fetishised and feminised, Cooper would pass as straight because of playing traditionally masculine parts, such as cowboys or war heroes. When discovered in the late 1920s, he was soon referred to as a 'cow-punchin'' Cinderella man (Brown 1995: 196), but incorporating American ideal types, Cooper could pass as a male ideal. And so, although unquestioningly inviting homoerotic identifications and desires as McGregor in *The Lives of a Bengal Lancer*, Cooper's image as a masculine ideal was so ingrained that it could resist outright implications of homoeroticism.

The narrative structure of *The Lives of a Bengal Lancer* is indeed relying on the Oedipal narrative: the film is clearly about young lieutenant Stone becoming a man and for this to happen the homosocial bonding between the men, as a family, must be destroyed, and the beloved 'mother' – McGregor – must die. The killing of him serves two purposes: it positions Stone as Man while destroying the visual and narrative (homo)erotification of Cooper. It is interesting to note that at the end of the film, while being incarcerated, the men are stripped of their military attire: they are now clad in shirts and loose trousers and McGregor and Forsythe are wearing soft *slippers*. And it is at his most naked, with his masculine shield put aside, that McGregor will break out of prison, start a riot and sacrifice his life for his family.

As the film ends, the queer family, the gay threesome, is being refused and destroyed. And, again, one is reminded of Neale's treatise: '[. . .] male homosexuality is constantly present as an undercurrent, as a potentially troubling aspect of many films and genres [. . .] and that has to be repressed' (Neale 1983: 15). The seductive and appealing homoerotic bonding between the three men that has structured *The Lives of a Bengal Lancer* up until its closure is partly being denied us. Up until that moment of destruction, however, it is there in plain sight, making queer desires and identifications possible. For, as Neale writes, 'Cinema draws on and involves many desires, many forms of desire. And desire itself is mobile, fluid, constantly transgressing identities, positions, and roles. Identifications are multiple, fluid, at points even contradictory' (Neale 1983: 4).

Conclusion

Relying on earlier scholarship on masculinity as spectacle and focusing on the role that the male boot plays within three films coming out of twentieth-century Hollywood film production, I have tried to show how women are not '[the only] problem, [and] source of anxiety' (Neale 1983: 16). Men – and representations of men and masculinity – are just as problematic. If not more so, given that mainstream cinema still struggles with representations of an ideal and desirable masculinity that is not based in, or tainted by, homoeroticism, as well as with narcissism and masochism. While shying away from homosexuality to emphasize heterosexuality, most representations of masculinity still rely on narrating stories of sameness. The Irigarayan notion of a structurally dominant *hom(m)o-sexualité* is useful here: this is a structure of sameness that serves to exclude women from all areas of publicly social, cultural, political and economic life while refuting intimacy between men (Irigaray [1975] 1985). This refutation is expressed and kept in line through a required and violent homophobia. And, as Gayle Rubin once stated, homophobia is intimately connected with misogyny and the oppression of women, as these oppressive 'rules' are both products of the same patriarchal system (Rubin 1975).

While the reading of hyper-masculine representations as spectacle serves to deconstruct (and destruct) the dominant imagery of male sovereignty, it is important to note that this kind of representation may still be oppressive to women and gay men – and since these representations to a large extent are white, to people of colour. As Sally Robinson, following film scholars Tania Modleski and Yvonne Tasker, puts it: 'Self-consciousness does not, in itself, guarantee subversion of dominant representations or, more importantly, any change in existing power relations' (Robinson 2000: 198–9). Yet, as Eve Kosofsky Sedgwick has taught us, any understanding of modern Western culture and society is incomplete unless it incorporates a critical analysis of the modern hetero/homo definition and opposition (Kosofsky Sedgwick 1990: 1). This means that any analysis of male and female (and of feminine and masculine) must also include an analysis of homo and hetero. This latter opposition structures society as forcefully as does the former: in fact, the opposition between male and female may very well be understood as a difference that is built or based on the homo/hetero divide. Yet, as Diana Fuss reminds us: '[. . .] borders are notoriously unstable, and sexual identities rarely secure' (Fuss 1991: 3).

As I have tried to show here, even the most male-centred and heteronormative Oedipal narrative may in fact be a story that tells us about masculine precarity and (homo)sexual fluidity. In the chosen films, the male boot plays a very special role within this queer story: it is initially used as proof of 'true' and straight masculinity, but as the as the story progresses and the male ideal is deconstructed, the boot will lose its masculine connotation and meaning. Hal literally overcomes his painful and dependent relation to his father (his boots) as he wins the girl; Joe throws his ornate boots in the trash as he decides to scale off his cowboy armour and accept his gay self; and McGregor, now in unisex slippers, sacrifices his life to save the young Stone, his 'child'.

Notes

1. A prime example of the Oedipal story portraying how a boy becomes Man, would be Alfred Hitchcock's *North by Northwest* (USA, 1959) with Cary Grant starring as the (reluctant) mummy's boy – as analysed and discussed by Raymond Bellour (1975).
2. Surely, masculinity is as constructed, and as problematic, as is femininity, and both genders have always been troubled and troubling, from the Greeks onwards. Yet,

it is with the entrance of humanism and modernity and their emphasis on sexual difference as something natural and desirable that the two genders start trembling. Made, or forced, into two incommensurable and binary genders, any deviance (however miniscule) from the ideal norm makes visible how fragile and constructed both genders in fact are.

3. In 'Visual Pleasure and Narrative Cinema', Laura Mulvey writes: 'According to the principles of the ruling ideology and the physical structures that back it up, the male figure cannot bear the burden of sexual objectification' (1975, *Screen*, 16:3, p. 12). This is to some extent a contradiction to an earlier statement in that same text: 'A recent tendency in narrative film has been to dispose with the problem [woman] altogether; hence the development of what Molly Haskell has called the "buddy movie", in which the active homosexual eroticism of the central male figures can carry the story without distraction' (p. 11).

4. A prime example, in length discussed by both Tasker and Holmlund (Tasker 1993; Holmlund 1993), would be buddy cop action comedy *Tango & Cash* (Andrey Konchalovskiy, USA, 1989).

5. Because of the conservative and homophobic social culture of the era, and because of censorship laws, gay pornography could not be sold openly. Gay men turned to beefcake magazines, which were sold in newspaper stands, bookstores and pharmacies. By 1951, model agent Bob Mizer had created a large catalogue of bodybuilding men as models, and he began to collect his photos and sell them in a magazine format, *Physique Pictorial*.

6. The riots took place less than a month after *Midnight Cowboy* had premiered. The riots were a series of spontaneous demonstrations by the gay community in New York City against a police raid that took place on 28 June at the Stonewall Inn in Greenwich Village. These riots are considered the most important event leading to the gay liberation movement in the US.

7. Chris Packard writes: 'Particularly in Westerns produced before 1900, references to lusty passions appear regularly, when the cowboy is on the trail with his partners, if one knows how to look for them. In fact, in the often all-male world of the literary West, homoerotic affection holds a favoured position ... [I]n other words, the cowboy is queer' (Packard 2005: 3).

References

Barthes, Roland (1978), *A Lover's Discourse* (*Fragments d'un discours amoureux*), trans. R. Howard, New York: Hill and Wang.

Bellour, Raymond (2000), 'Symbolic Blockage (on *North by Northwest*)' in C. Penley (ed.), *The Analysis of Film*, Bloomington: Indiana University Press.

Brown, Jeffrey (1995), '"Putting on the Ritz": Masculinity and the Young Gary Cooper', *Screen*, vol. 36, no. 3, pp. 6–18.

Bruzzi, Stella (1997), *Undressing Cinema*, London and New York: Routledge.

Cavell, Stanley (2005), *Cavell on Film*, W. Rothman (ed.), New York: State University of New York Press.

Cohan, Steven (1997), *Masked Men: Masculinity and the Movies in the Fifties*, Bloomington: Indiana University Press.

Cohan, Steven and Hark, Ina Rae (1993), *Screening Masculinity: Exploring Masculinites in Hollywood Cinema*, London and New York: Routledge.

Cook, Pam (1982), 'Masculinity in Crisis?', *Screen*, vol. 23, nos. 3–4, pp. 39–46.

Creed, Barbara (1987), 'From here to Modernity: Feminism and Postmodernism', *Screen*, vol. 28, no. 2, pp. 47–68.

de Lauretis, Teresa (1987), *Technologies of Gender: Essays on Theory, Film, and Fiction*, Bloomington: Indiana University Press.

de Lauretis, Teresa (1984), *Alice doesn't: Feminism, Semiotics, Cinema*, Bloomington: Indiana University Press.

Derrida, Jacques (1978), *Writing on Difference*, Chicago: University of Chicago Press.

Dyer, Richard (1992), 'Getting over the Rainbow: Identity and Pleasure in Gay Cultural Politics', *Only Entertainment*, London and New York: Routledge, pp. 159–72.

Dyer, Richard (1982), 'Don't look now', *Screen*, vol. 23, nos. 3–4, pp. 61–73.

Dyer, Richard (1977), *Gays and Film*, London: BFI.

Floyd, Kevin (2001), 'Closing the (Heterosexual) Frontier: "Midnight Cowboy" as National Allegory', *Science & Society*, vol. 65, no. 1, pp. 99–130.

Foucault, Michel (1978), *The History of Sexuality: The Will to Knowledge* (*L'histoire de la sexualité. La volonté de savoir*), trans. R. Hurley, New York: Pantheon Books.

Fuss, Diana (ed.) (1991), *Inside/out: Lesbian Theories, Gay Theories*, London and New York: Routledge.

Holmlund, Chris (1993), 'Masculinity as Multiple Masquerade', in S. Cohan and I. R. Hark (eds), *Screening Masculinity: Exploring Masculinities in Hollywood Cinema*, London and New York: Routledge,

Irigaray, Luce (1985), *This Sex Which Is Not One* (*Ce sexe quin'est pas une*), trans. C. Porter, Ithaca: Cornell University Press.

Kosofsky Sedgwick, Eve (1990), *Epistemology of the Closet*, Los Angeles: University of California Press.

Kosofsky Sedgwick, Eve (1985), *Between Men: English Literature and Male Homosocial Desire*, New York: Columbia University Press.

Manners, Dorothy (1927), 'That Cow-punchin' Cinderella man', *Motion Picture Classic*, vol. 25.

Mulvey, Laura (1975), 'Visual Pleasure and Narrative Cinema', *Screen*, vol. 16, no. 3, pp: 6–18.

Neale, Steven (1983), 'Masculinity as Spectacle: Reflections on Men and Mainstream Cinema', *Screen*, vol. 24, no. 6, pp. 2–17.

Packard, Chris (2005), *Queer Cowboys: And Other Erotic Male Friendships in 19th-Century American Literature*, London and New York: Palgrave Macmillan.

Robinson, Sally (2000), *Marked Men: White Masculinity in Crisis*, New York: Columbia University Press.

Rubin, Gayle (1975), 'The Traffic in Women', in R. R. Reiter (ed.), *Toward an Anthropology of Women*, Monthly Review Press, pp. 157–210.

Segal, Lynne (1990), *Slow Motion: Changing Masculinities, Changing Men*, London: Virago Press.

Solomon-Godeau, Abigail (1997), *Male Trouble: A Crisis in Representation*, New York: Thames and Hudson.

Tasker, Yvonne (1993a), *Spectacular Bodies: Gender, Genre, and the Action Cinema*, London and New York: Routledge.

Tasker, Yvonne (1993b), 'Dumb Movies for Dumb People: Masculinity, the Body, and Voice in Contemporary Action Cinema', in S. Cohan and I. R. Hark (eds), *Screening Masculinity: Exploring Masculinities in Hollywood Cinema*, London and New York: Routledge, pp. 230–44.

Chapter 13

'The brunette with the legs': the significance of footwear in *Marnie*

Lucy Bolton

Marnie (Alfred Hitchcock, USA, 1964) is a film about sex and crime; in particular, about 'the sexual aberrations of the criminal female', according to the title of the book Mark Rutland (Sean Connery) reads in order to try to understand his new wife, Marnie (Tippi Hedren). These themes make a suitably salacious tagline for the film, described on posters at the time as a 'suspenseful sex mystery' (Nourmand and Wolff 1999: 84). But the film is actually the story of the woman who Mark first describes as 'the brunette with the legs', namely Margaret Edgar, or Marion Holland, or just plain Marnie, and her performance of feminine masquerade using what Michèle Montrelay might have called 'dotty objects' (Montrelay 1970, in Studlar 1988: 70): gloves, purses, handbags, nail files, hair combs, stockings and – most significantly – shoes. In three pivotal scenes, Marnie's footwear plays a major role in conveying her state of mind. In one, it enables her to lose her earlier identity, as her toe pushes the key to a railway station locker containing the accoutrements of Marion Holland down a grating. In another, Marnie's court shoe holds her exposure as a thief in the balance, sidling from her coat pocket as she tiptoes across the floor of Rutland's offices. And in a third, as her riding boots buckle and contort, they demonstrate how her resolve and spirit are being broken by her domineering husband, hell bent on behavioural analysis and psychiatric recuperation.

In this chapter I will demonstrate the film's deployment of shoes as a trope of Marnie's identity, and indeed of Hedren's star image more generally, and explore how they function as different sides to Marnie at stages in her story, speaking for her when she is unable to do so herself. In so doing, and drawing on Iris Murdoch's thoughts about the way cinema can show us 'dramatically significant objects' (Murdoch 1956: 98), I will argue that the film unusually imbues feminine footwear with significance and meaning, enabling Marnie's identity to be explored by elements of the *mise en scène* that might ordinarily be considered simply decorative.

When, in 1956, Iris Murdoch wrote about the specific abilities of cinema, she asked,

> Now what can the movie camera do which nothing else can do, and what should it therefore busy itself doing? It can present to us human drama and feeling in the form of momentary awareness. [...] It should resemble, not a vague detached awareness of things going forward, but a tense heightened awareness, such as we have in dreams or moments of emotional vision. After all, this is a form of Art. Therefore, objects in films ought never to look normal, since objects do not do this in ordinary life in our moments of most acute observation. A film should show us a strange and startling world, disintegrated and distorted, and full of dramatically significant objects. (Murdoch 1956: 98)

Murdoch's ideas about 'acute observation' and 'tense heightened awareness' relate to how shoes in *Marnie* attract our attention and also contribute to the construction of anxiety and suspense. Shoes highlight Marnie's 'strange and startling world', as parts of her meticulously constructed identities, and Murdoch's insights enable us to understand how they function to make meaning in the film.

Dressing Marnie and Tippi

Tippi Hedren as Marnie wears thirty-two costumes in the film. As Moral says, 'clothes play a crucial role in the plot of shifting identities, camouflage, gender relations, and class distinction' (Moral 2002: 68). There are sequences that look like the work of a meticulous fashion magazine stylist, such as when Marnie swaps her clothes and accessories, discarding the colour palette of a black-haired woman into a grey satin-lined suitcase and packing the new look of a brunette into a rose-lined one, before emerging as a blonde, in the classic Hitchcock blonde eau de Nil suit. In conversation with Deborah Nadoolman-Landis, co-curator of the *Hollywood Costume* exhibition at the Victoria and Albert Museum in 2012, Hedren said that Edith Head created and named the 'eau de Nil Green' for the suit worn by her character Melanie Daniels in *The Birds* (Hitchcock, USA, 1963). She also describes how much she had to move around wearing that suit, including climbing into and out of the motor boat that she drives to the Brenner house across Bodega Bay. She says that she could do all that in the green suit, 'but the shoes had to have a little more stability . . . than the spikes that I wore with the black suit at the very beginning'.[1] In that opening scene of *The Birds*, Hedren wears towering high heels, and walks somewhat gingerly across the road and into the pet shop, as somebody wolf whistles at her. This immediately draws attention to her glamour and fashionable clothing, but also shows her as having a somewhat precarious mobility. Unlike the shoes that Roland Barthes describes in *The Fashion System*, these shoes are *not* made for walking (Barthes 2010: 23). It is interesting to note that the brown courts that she wears with the green suit for the rest of *The Birds* have lower, thicker heels and are clearly more stable. They also function to emphasise Melanie Daniels' walk and the wobble in her heels. As the camera follows Melanie walking down corridors, along roads, and around Bodega Bay, her walk is quick-paced, deliberate and confident, but the wobble in her heels conveys her precarity, just as her confident smile and cheery mood is invaded by the attack of the seagull when she is sitting in the boat, smiling cheekily at Mitch Brenner. As she is attacked by birds in the telephone booth, or the upstairs room of the Brenner house, her confidence and composure are undermined by her physical vulnerability to attack, which is signalled as a possibility from the outset by the wobble in her walk.

This wobble is even more emphatic in *Marnie*. The opening shot of the film is of a woman walking away from the camera. The striking image of the yellow handbag nestled under the arm of the raven-haired, black tweed-suited Marnie walking down the train station platform highlights the significance of costume and accessories in the film. The fascinations, problems and pleasures offered to women by Hitchcock's films have attracted critical attention from the most eminent feminist film scholars, including Tania Modleski, Kaja Silverman and Laura Mulvey, and also attracted analysis in light of some of the foundational approaches of feminist film studies, such as masquerade, fetishistic scopophilia, and the medical discourse (Kapsis 1988: 54–9). Criticism and commentary of *Marnie* tends to focus on fetishism: the labial nature of the folds of the handbag (Figlerowitz 2012: 54), Smith (2016: 52); the womb-like function of handbags in the film as a whole (Bhari 2019: 264–6); Hitchcock's obsession with Hedren (Brody 2016; Fawell 2000: 275; Spoto 2009: 167–78); and Marnie's preference for her horse over men (Modleski; Figlerowitz; Columpar 1999–2000). But it is not just Hedren and her handbags that are the objects of fascination in the Marnie story. Accessories of all kinds feature heavily in the 1961 novel by Winston Graham on which the film adaptation is based (Graham 1997), and the opera which was staged in London and New York (Marfil 2017: 15). In the novel, as Marnie prepares for a new identity, her dressing is detailed minutely:

> Everything I put on was new: brassiere, panties, shoes, nylons, frock. It wasn't just taking care; it was the way I'd come to like it. I suppose I have a funny mind or something, but everything has to be just as it should be; and I like it to be that way with people too. (Graham,1997: 3)

This makes clear that in the novel it is Marnie's way to be precise and meticulous about assembling her identity through the process of dressing. Street notes how Marnie is referred to as 'the brunette with the legs' (Street 2002: 152), and how 'she must exploit her knowledge of how to masquerade in order to maintain that independence' (Ibid.:153). This fastidious devotion to image is conveyed in the film through the close-ups on clothing and accessories and the array of garments and outfits that Marnie works her way through, as well as Hedren's physically assured gestures that convey efficiency and confidence. And it is her shoes that participate in some of the more fundamental stages of her journey.

The legs and the feet

Marnie's footwear is a more significant accessory than the handbag in the trajectory of her character throughout this film. Shoes not only serve to facilitate Marnie's changing identities and masquerades, but also play integral roles in her criminal and 'civilian' lives, and indeed her psychic journey. As she walks down the railway platform in the film's opening shot, her firmly planted feet are undermined by the distinct wavering of the heels of her black court shoes. Her first victim in the film, Strutt, recalls with bitterness how she 'was always pulling her skirt down over her knees as if they were a national treasure'. His comment seems to surprise Mark Rutland at the time, and it is this gesture of Marnie's that contributes to his recognition of her when she later comes to be interviewed for a job at Rutland's. As Mark walks past her seated in the waiting area, she looks up at him, their eyes meet, and then she looks down, bashfully, and adjusts her skirt hem down over her knees. This pretence of modesty of course draws attention to the very feature she is ostensibly trying to conceal. One's eyes are drawn to the gloved hands, adjusting the hem of her beautifully coordinated outfit. And this in turn draws attention downwards to her legs.

Marnie focuses on legs as an element of Marnie's character. As Anne Hollander writes, 'exposing a woman's legs lays stress on her means of locomotion' (Hollander 1993: 339); the film shows Marnie frequently in motion, walking briskly through life on those legs. Learning about how Marnie pulls her skirt down over her knees suggests that her faux attempts to hide her legs is intended to send a message to those looking that she will be sedentary and submissive and will be no threat.

It is as the accessories adorning these legs that the shoes in the film come into their own. Paula Rabinowitz describes how 'shoes facilitate women's social mobility' (Rabinowitz 2011: 200), which indicates why shoes feature so meaningfully in Marnie's carefully orchestrated social passing. From the opening shot, so visually dominated by the yellow handbag, Marnie's shoes convey that wobbling walk, drawing attention to the movement of her hips and her outfit, but also focusing on her determined steps. As 'the brunette with the legs', her walk conveys efficiency and a relentless forward drive. In due course we discover that it was a severe injury to her mother's (Louise Latham) leg during an assault that drove Marnie to kill the predatory sailor (Bruce Dern), thereby traumatising her and creating her fear of the colour red, thunderstorms and men. It is therefore unsurprising that legs, mobility and footwear feature so prominently in Marnie's armoury of masquerade.

In the novel Marnie describes her mother's footwear lying in the hall, next to her walking stick, saying 'her shoes are very narrow and pointed: she'd always had narrow feet and wore pointed shoes long before they were the fashion' (Graham 1997: 336). Describing kicking off her shoes, or sliding on her shoes, forms a part of her accounts of each of her thefts. This serves to convey the level of detail with which Marnie executes her crimes, and also presents them in a feminine language, describing objects as we might think of them in these circumstances, rather than as they simply look in the ordinary course of events.

Iris Murdoch, objects and cinema

Returning to Murdoch about the 'tense heightened awareness' presented to us in a movie, there are certainly moments of heady excess in *Marnie*, which meet Murdoch's requirements of disintegration and distortion, such as the first time Mark kisses Marnie (Bolton, 2011: 140; Columpar, 1999–2000: 59), and the hyperbolic red drenching of the screen whenever Marnie sees the colour red (Bolton, 2011: 136–7). Florence Jacobowitz describes how the narrative is 'interrupted by moments that have a dreamlike emphasis exceeding narrative explanation', such as the anxiety caused when the shoe drops out of Marnie's pocket or the unspoken violence of the spilt pecan nuts in Marnie's mother's kitchen (Jacobowitz 2015: 17). When Marnie's gloved fingertip scans the newspaper columns looking for a job, we are compelled to follow the fingertip as closely as we would our own doing the same action, at a moment of 'acute observation'; and when the tree branch crashes into Mark's office, or the huge ship looms at the end of Bernice's street, we are certainly being shown a 'strange and startling' world. Murdoch's description of objects in film, in particular, unlocks the peculiar focalisation of the footwear in this film. In *Marnie* shoes are integral to the 'tense heightened awareness' that the film creates, and also are 'dramatically significant objects'.

Murdoch also writes that she is 'tempted to say that the cinema is an art of indoors' (Murdoch 1956: 98). Here she is referring to the way that outdoor shots do not linger in her memory, 'except as reminders of other landscapes'; rather she sees indoor spaces as more able to show the 'dramatically significant objects' that cinema can display. It seems appropriate to consider *Marnie* as a film that exhibits the art of the indoors in several key sequences, as offices, houses, rooms and beds become the loci of Marnie's actions and experiences. Through showcasing Hedren in multiple outfits, immaculately accessorised, one of the main themes of the film becomes the matter of being well dressed. In her work outfits she looks how her mother always wanted her to be, which is 'decent'; but her shoes point to her less decent behaviour. Her feet are where the action is, as the following close analysis of key scenes will demonstrate. Although Marnie's walking feet feature so consistently throughout the film, there are three scenes in which footwear plays a central role and is actively foregrounded in order to emphasise what Marnie is thinking, planning and going through.

The key down the grating

The identity of Marion Holland is discarded into one suitcase and the preparation of Margaret Edgar's new wardrobe in another. The camera focuses on two beautifully lined cases, with neatly folded grey and brown clothes and a pair of green satin slippers trimmed with silver in one, with two new pairs of different coloured gloves and tights, and the more casually discarded silks of paler colours in the other, including a discarded brassiere. Marnie opens her compact with a nail file, and an extreme close-up on her coral fingernails shows her thumbing through a selection of social security cards, before selecting Margaret Edgar as her next identity. She washes out her black hair dye, transforms into a blonde, and is next seen carrying both suitcases through a railway station. She wears an eau de Nil suede suit, her hair is neatly coiffed, and she wears pale cream driving gloves, a cream turtle neck sweater and a darker sage green floral scarf. She also wears pale eau de Nil court shoes, with a studded detail around the top edge of the upper. We see Marnie notice a grating on the floor and smile to herself. In noticeably slower steps than she usually takes, Marnie approaches the grating and drops the key to the locker where she has just consigned the suitcase containing the identity of Marion Holland. The key lands flat, highlighted by its bright yellow cap cover, and Marnie uses the toe of her shoe to delicately and precisely poke the key through the grating until it drops, ensuring the accoutrements of her previous identity will not easily be discovered.

Figure 13.1 The shoe as tool, disposing of Marion Holland's key

Shoe in pocket

In the sequence where Marnie steals from the safe at Rutland's, her shoes are the source of suspense that Hitchcock was such a master at creating. The establishing shot is of the interior of the office floor and the screen is divided down the middle by an office partition wall. On the right hand of the screen, Marnie conducts her theft from the safe. On the left, the cleaner (Edith Evanson) enters the room with her mop and bucket. Marnie completes her removal of the money from the safe and needs to make her escape by crossing the floor of the office. She notices the cleaner mopping the floor and removes her chocolate brown court shoes, placing one shoe in each pocket of her forest green coat. Following the formula Hitchcock describes to Truffaut of showing the audience the bomb under the table (suspense) rather than simply exploding the bomb (shock) (Truffaut 1986: 91), we are able to see Marnie's shoe slipping out of her coat pocket with each of her steps, as she tiptoes across the floor away from the safe, trying to avoid attracting the attention of the cleaner.

The shoe works its way further and further out of the pocket, before falling out and landing on the floor with a loud thud. Marnie's eyes are drawn to the shoe, as she freezes; her eyes then move up slowly towards the cleaner, as she realises that – for some reason – the cleaner has not heard the sound. Marnie picks up her shoe and moves swiftly to the stairs, disappearing down

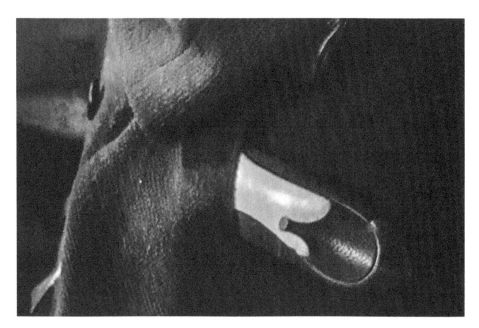

Figure 13. 2 The shoe as traitor, threatening to expose Marnie's crime

them on the right of the screen as the security guard emerges on the left. The guard approaches the cleaner and speaks to her loudly and close to her ear, revealing that Rita the cleaner is hard of hearing. In this sequence, with its heart-stopping tension created purely by the sight of the shoe's impending fall, the shoe is certainly 'dramatically significant' as Murdoch describes, and also a startling and distorted object, demanding a specific and heightened attention. Marnie's removal of the shoe, its falling, and her reactions, also serve to align us with her subjective experience, activating our own fears and emotions (Bolton 2011: 142).

Contorted riding boots

The third piece of footwear, the riding boots, are significant as a piece of costume in that they show how Marnie is outwardly changed by marriage to Mark and life as a member of the Rutland household. When Marnie first rides Forio at Garrod's stables she wears a simple cream blouse and jodhpurs with plain riding boots. When Mark brings Forio to be with Marnie at the Rutland home, Marnie kicks off her shoes and mounts the horse without a saddle, gripping his mane and riding away with him barefoot in an expression of pure joy and freedom. Once Marnie has been spotted by Strutt at the house party, however, after jealous sister-in-law Lil has invited him, Mark insists Marnie takes part in the fox hunt to defy Strutt's suspicion. Marnie is costumed in formal hunting wear: a riding hat, jacket, cravat, and stiff, long riding boots. Marnie witness the capture and mauling of the fox, and the repulsive guffaws of the hunters, and is compelled to ride away on Forio, who misjudges a stone wall while leaping over it and is injured. Devastated, Marnie gets a gun from a nearby resident and shoots the wounded horse. She is traumatised and propelled into a catatonic state of criminal behaviour, and heads to the Rutland offices, suggesting that she plans to steal from the safe and take off again, following her usual pattern of behaviour. Mark finds her at the safe, however, still armed with the gun she used to kill Forio, and challenges her over her desire to steal. Mark tries to force her to take the money but she resists. He shouts, 'you want the money, take it; I said take it!'; and, with a sardonically cruel smirk, he forces her hand towards the wads of cash in the Rutland safe. As Marnie is unable to take it, she resists Mark's force, and, struggling to break free, she twists and squirms under his pressure. A close-up of their feet conveys the battle and depicts their respective status through their feet: his, solidly square and firmly planted, in well-worn brogues with polished toes, and hers in twisting, squirming hunting boots that she is unaccustomed to wearing, looking like her legs themselves are buckling under the battle.

As Mark lets her go, Marnie crashes into the safe, and his smile confirms his feeling that he has beaten her and won this particular battle. This is a significant stage in his breaking her down before the final showdown at

Figure 13.3 The boot as surrender, buckling in the grip of Rutland patriarchy

Bernice's house. Another battle between Mark and Marnie includes the notorious rape scene, where Mark has sex with a catatonic Marnie on their honeymoon, having ripped off her housecoat, which lies in folds at her feet. Here, Marnie's naked, static legs convey that she is frozen to the spot. There can be no suggestion that Mark believes he has consent: the look in his eyes as he descends on Marnie, shown in looming close-up, is one of lascivious domination. Marnie and he return home early from the honeymoon and his project of getting to understand her and ostensibly to rescue her continues to play out through various verbal battles, including a game of word association, which ends with Marnie pleading for somebody to help her. Seen in the trajectory of his assertion of ownership of Marnie, which she herself identifies as his project, the shot of their feet in front of the safe, as Marnie buckles and crumbles, is a visual depiction of the final breaking of her resistance.

The not-so-neat ending

I have considered in depth elsewhere how the film has been analysed by various waves of scholarship: as exemplary of the male gaze, critiqued and also recuperated by feminist scholarship, and as queered and problematised by more recent scholars (Bolton 2011: 129–32). The ending of the film is a pat Freudian exposition, as mother is honest with daughter about the role sex has played in her life. When Bernice expresses her intention for Marnie to be decent, her daughter replies, 'oh Momma, well you surely realised your ambition – I'm a cheat and a liar and a thief but I am decent'. Mark supplies the neat psychiatric explanation for her thieving, as a child deprived of love taking whatever it can from wherever it can, and her mother still rejects her, as Marnie lying on Bernice is 'aching her leg': the leg that is a constant reminder of the damage a man can do to a woman's mobility and freedom. Mark can provide all reassurance of police, legal system and hospital, in one figure as her husband: she won't go to jail, he reassures, after what he has to tell them. As Columpar describes, 'Mark becomes a condensation of a variety of masculinised figures, including employer, observer, doctor and lover' (Columpar 1999: 58). We are invited to accept his authoritative reassurance as much as Marnie is. Marnie's final words, 'I don't want to go to jail, I'd rather stay with you', are hardly reassuring, although Mark looks pretty happy with the outcome of his project (Bolton 2011: 146). With his arm around Marnie, as he guides her to his car, he now seems to be in control of the previously resistant, independent woman and guiding her movements.

Shoes, Marnie and Tippi

The focus on shoes, feet and legs in *Marnie* is an illustration of how cinema can do more than simply involve an object in the narrative of a film, but rather it can utilise objects to create affective tension, to convey a character's state of mind and to represent a fundamental theme of the film. The three scenes I have analysed in this chapter use footwear to indicate Marnie's desire to bury her identity, to evoke tension and suspense during her theft from Rutland's and to demonstrate Mark overcoming her will to finally break her. When compared to the work that has been done to analyse the static female chamber of the handbag in this film, the focus on the shoes enables a greater understanding of the centrality of Marnie's mobility and independence. Yes, the handbag is significant for carrying and storing, but it is the feet and the legs that carry the handbag around. And for Marnie, whose mother's leg was broken so badly by a sexually aggressive man that she now walks with a stick, the significance of movement and freedom is abundantly clear. The very dynamic by which she conducts her life – stealing then fleeing – demands fleetness of foot and unencumbered movement. It is through capturing Marnie, holding her and keeping her, that Mark is able to finally bring her under control. As Mark, the amateur zoologist, says, 'I've caught something really wild this time'.

Looking at Tippi Hedren in *Marnie* and *The Birds*, which are by far her most high-profile and memorable film performances, it is striking how strongly her shoes, feet and walk feature in the construction of her characters, Marnie and Melanie Daniels respectively. This is entirely consistent with the confidence that both characters exude in the earlier stages of the films, as their nimble, adept movements are so fundamental to their stories. Both social adventuress and prankster Melanie and serial thief Marnie need to be physically unencumbered and agile. But, as both films trap and attack these characters, either in Bodega Bay or the Rutland empire, their mobility decreases and the physical assault on them increases until they are broken. The early smiles of self-satisfaction that Melanie and Marnie display are replaced with traumatised catatonia. The endings of both films are bleak and ambiguous, with a chance of a future but no guarantees as to how those futures will pan out. This double-edged facet to Hedren's unique screen image is summed up by Florence Jacobowitz's description of how 'she manifests vulnerability beneath the veneer of the competent, assured young woman as well as a façade that is more private and inscrutable' (Jacobowitz 2015: 16). I propose that the wobble in the heel of her court shoes, as both Melanie and Marnie, is the visual signal of this vulnerability and ambiguity.

Allegations about Hitchcock's obsession with Hedren have been made widely, and Hedren herself has recounted that the director sexually assaulted her (Fawell 2000: 275; Robinson 2000: 59; Hedren 2016: 72). This extra-textual information adds a sinister slant to the abuse that the on-screen Hedren has to go through in her films, and undoubtedly the allegations have damaged Hitchcock's reputation in the eyes of many (Brody 2016). It is also consistent with Hedren's on-screen image that, having captured and imprisoned her, Hitchcock curtailed her acting career and prevented her from accepting or even being told about offers from other directors (Hedren 2016: 74). MJ Robinson assesses *Marnie* as being 'an incongruous and ambiguous conflation of the star, actor, and director, barely held in check by levels of artifice and a dark camp humour' (2000: 63). Whilst this type of commentary may be inevitable given the prominence of Hedren's revelations, and their take-up by critics and indeed other filmmakers such as in *The Girl* (Julian Jarrold, UK, 2012), detailed analysis of the costume and accessories in the film still affords the character of Marnie a degree of subjectivity, personality and independence.

Although Street suggests some of the opportunities to read Marnie's subjectivity might not be deliberate on Hitchcock's part (2002: 155), he does certainly use footwear in this film to speak for Marnie. As John Fawell observes, 'Hitchcock had a fascination with femininity, and you can feel it in certain small but precisely etched moments in his films: in the way Marion clutches her purse in *Psycho*, in the close-up of Marnie's feet as she slips out of her pumps before going bareback riding in *Marnie*' (2001: 6). These close-ups on accessories, detailing the textures and structure of how Marnie orders her life, are powerful, affective indicators of her behaviour and feelings, including her battles with the patriarchal structures that seek to contain her. As such, they demonstrate cinema's capacity to show such objects as shoes, boots and bare feet, in ways that answer Iris Murdoch's prescription for what cinema should 'busy itself doing': showing us 'a strange and startling world . . . full of dramatically significant objects' (Murdoch 1956: 98).

Note

1. I am grateful to Keith Lodwick, co-curator of the *Hollywood Costume* exhibition at the V&A Museum, for sharing this interview with me.

References

Barthes, Roland [1967] (2010), *The Fashion System*, London: Vintage Books.
Bhari, Shahidha (2019), *Dress, The Secret Life of Clothes*, London: Jonathan Cape.

Bolton, Lucy [2011] (2015), *Film and Female Consciousness: Irigaray, Cinema and Thinking Women*, Basingstoke: Palgrave Macmillan.

Brody, Richard (2016), '*Marnie* is the cure for Hitchcock Mania', *The New Yorker*, 17 August.

Columpar, Corinn (1999–2000), '*Marnie*: a site/sight for the convergence of gazes', *Hitchcock Annual*, vol. 8.

Fawell, John (2001), *Hitchcock's Rear Window: the Well-Made Film,* Carbondale and Edwardsville: Southern Illinois University Press.

Fawell, John (2000), 'Fashion Dreams: Hitchcock, women, and Lisa Fremont', *Literature/Film Quarterly*, vol. 28, no. 4, pp. 274–83.

Figlerowicz, Marta (2012), 'Timing and vulnerability in three Hitchcock films', *Film Quarterly*, vol. 65, no. 3, pp. 49–58.

Graham, Winston [1961] (1997), *Marnie*, London: Pan Books.

Hedren, Tippi (2016), *Tippi, A Memoir*, New York: HarperCollins.

Jacobowitz, Florence (2015), 'A Feminist Reading of Hitchcock's *Marnie*', *Cineaction*, no. 96.

Hollander, Anne (1993), *Seeing Through Clothes*, Berkeley: University of California Press.

Kapsis, Robert E. (1988), 'The Historical Reception of Hitchcock's *Marnie*', *Journal of Film and Video*, vol. 40, no. 3. pp. 46–63.

Marfil, Lorelei (2017), 'Arianne Phillips says accessories play key role in "Marnie" opera', *Women's Wear Daily (WWD)*, 16 November 2017, https://wwd.com/eye/people/accessories-play-a-key-role-english-national-operas-marnie-says-arianne-phillips-11050512/ (last accessed 18 February 2019).

Modleski, Tania (1988), *The Women Who Knew Too Much*, London and New York: Routledge.

Montrelay, Michèle (1970) 'Recherches sur la féminité', *Critique*, no. 26, pp. 654–74.

Moral, Tony Lee (2002). *Hitchcock and the Making of Marnie*, Lanham, MD and Oxford: The Scarecrow Press, Inc.

Mulvey, Laura (1975) 'Visual Pleasure and Narrative Cinema', *Screen*, vol. 16, no. 3, pp. 6–18.

Murdoch, Iris (1956), 'On the Cinema', *Vogue*, pp. 98–9.

Nadoolman Landis, Deborah (ed.) (2012), *Hollywood Costume*, London: V&A Publishing.

Nourmand, Tony and Wolff, Mark H. (1999), *Hitchcock Poster Art*, London: Aurum Press.

Rabinowitz, Paula (2011), 'Barbara Stanwyck's Anklet: The Other Shoe', in C. Giorcelli and P. Rabinowitz (eds), *Accessorising the Body*, Minneapolis and London: University of Minnesota Press.

Robinson, MJ (2000), 'The poetics of Camp in the films of Alfred Hitchcock', *Rocky Mountain Review of Language and Literature*, vol. 54, no. 1, pp. 53–65.

Silverman, Kaja (1988), *The Acoustic Mirror: the Female Voice in Psychoanalysis*, Bloomington and Indianapolis: Indiana University Press.

Smith, Nathan (2016), 'The Blonde who Knew Too Much', *Screen Education*, no. 81. pp. 50–7.

Spoto, Donald (2009), *Spellbound by Beauty: Alfred Hitchcock and his Leading Ladies*, London: Arrow Books.

Street, Sarah (2002), 'Hitchcockian Haberdashery', in S. Gottlieb and C. Brookhouse (eds), *Framing Hitchcock*, Detroit, MI: Wayne State University Press.

Studlar, Gaylyn (1988), *In the Realm of Pleasure: Von Sternberg, Dietrich and the Masochistic Aesthetic*, Urbana, IL: University of Illinois Press.

Truffaut, François and Scott, Helen G. (1986), *Hitchcock*, London: Paladin.

Chapter 14

The sole of Africa: shoes in three African films

Rachael Langford

Introduction

Focusing on footwear in African films affords the possibility of understanding more about film and material culture and about the representation of agency, power and politics in post-Independence African cultural production. This chapter will begin by exploring the major critical approaches to clothing practices in Africa, outlining how these approaches underplay the specific ontological status of footwear. The chapter then examines how the anti-colonial writings of Bernard Dadié (1916–2019) and Frantz Fanon (1925–61) mobilise the ontological status of footwear for resistant purposes, arguing that these works set up representational paradigms grounding the debates with which post-Independence African filmmaking dialogues. The discussion then explores the depiction of footwear and bare-footedness in two African films from the immediate post-Independence era and one from the 1990s, tracing how these films engage the critical reach of images of footwear as oppression and agency.

   Until the late twentieth century academic research on African garment practices was grounded in colonial epistemologies that measured, described and naturalised hierarchised notions of difference. In the post-colonial era historical cultural studies have increasingly dialogued with ethnography, and scholarship has turned to explore clothing as material culture, examining its practical uses and symbolic representations, its role in meaning-making, and the body's surface as a uniquely important site in the construction of social identities (Hay 1996; Küchler and Miller 2005; Kisiang'ani 2011). This focus on clothing practice as meaning-making at the body's surface has allowed the exploration of 'one of the frontiers upon which individual and social identities are simultaneously created' (Hendrickson 1996: 2), and 'the symbolic stage upon which the drama of socialisation is enacted' (Turner [1980] 2007: 12).

However, these approaches are problematic for their Eurocentric belief that there is an '*inevitable* presence of the body in various discrete moments in diverse African cultures' (Burke 1996: 191), assuming 'the salience of the body as a subject in all societies' in contexts where Western colonisation invented that body as an imagined subject and then defined, controlled and 'improved' it (Ibid.), hiding the reality that clothing in Africa is involved on specifically African terms in issues of power, identity and representation.

Clothing in African societies has always signified in complex ways. For centuries before the arrival of colonial invaders, African dress 'was little associated with utilitarian needs [. . .] Rather, clothing and personal ornamentation conveyed identity, status, values and the significance of the occasion' (Martin 1995: 155), constituting simultaneously a form of communication and a social object' (Ngong 2012: 88–9, my translation). Contestations of the way that African bodies were clothed and presented 'were a crucial site in the [. . .] dialectic of means and ends that shaped the encounter between Europeans and Africans' (Comaroff and Comaroff 1997: 222). In the post-Independence era, 'dress and fashion have been centrally implicated in the forging of a distinct African modernity' (Allman 2004: 5); and in the contemporary period, clothing exercises power through networks of meaning that interconnect pre-colonial, colonial and post-colonial significations. This is particularly the case where protocols of power performed through dress solidified customs performing power and domination. By transferring expressions of power that were central in the preceding colonial era to transactions between coloniser and colonised, dress in post-colonial Africa became 'one of the covert sources of violence and an unforeseen locus of power-play in the postcolony [. . .;] clothing in postcolonial Africa can be analysed through the lens of domination [. . .;] clothing can be the instrument of command, threat, and even intimidation' (Ngong 2012: 89, my translation).

Post-colonial African elites bought titles and associated forms of dress denoting social status based on moral capital, using wealth rather than socially positive activity to gain these forms. This hijacking of forms of dress previously accessible only to those whose acts instanced the required moral values replaces social value with monetary value. This has led in the post-colony to a situation where traditional garments no longer reliably denote the moral values with which they were associated. Instead, such garments are acquired and worn precisely because at each moment when they perform the former moral value they also visibly perform the ability of power and wealth to buy out these values (Tcheuyap 1999: 7; Mbemebe 2001: 131–2). Thus where changes can be identified between colonial and pre-colonial, and pre-colonial and post-colonial clothing practices in African contexts, these should not be approached as the functional versus the symbolic, or the traditional versus the 'modern' (i.e. Western). Clothing practices in Africa are far better understood as active fashioning that has always engaged individuals and groups dynamically with meaning-making, time, place and power.

Footwear: ontology and post-colonial critique

Within the longstanding scholarship on clothing practices in Africa little attention has been paid to the specificities of footwear. Phyllis Martin's fascinating study of the challenges to colonial power expressed through a 1936 disagreement between African football players and Brazzaville authorities over 'native' players wearing boots (Martin 1995: 1–2; 99–125) makes a strong step in this direction. Nonetheless Martin reads the disagreement as part of the wider ways in which clothing has been a contested social symbol in African contexts; she does not emphasise anything *sui generis* about footwear in the debate. Yet while footwear's status clearly does intersect with that of all clothing as part of the flows of power mediated through the symbolic realm, treating footwear as merely the same as all other garments ignores the ways in which footwear constitutes, ontologically and phenomenologically, a category apart. Margot DeMello notes that 'feet, and [...] shoes [...] operate in the liminal spaces between the body and the physical space that surrounds it. Feet connect us to the world and allow us to move through the world' (De Mello 2009: xx). Footwear disrupts some tenets of the epistemological category of 'body coverings' while yet emphasising others; footwear is a protective covering and a tool for effective movement, but it is much more besides, constituting a threshold object that mediates the subject, its contexts and its perception of those contexts. The human's upright stance places the foot at the forefront of the production of knowledge and culture and enables locomotion and encounter. Footwear's enabling of the upright stance contributes to liberating the human hand to make and create, the prerequisite of the crafting of complex group cultures.

Further, footwear is unique amongst garments because it is the one item of clothing that, in the process of mediating the outside world, moulds itself to the wearer's body's individual contours. Footwear is created only by humans and it expresses certain inherent features of being human. Through its complex relations with the human body and the contextual grounds of human life, footwear is ontologically separate from other categories of garment. For these reasons the shoe has resonated as more than merely an item of clothing in human culture, from American folk shoe trees, to mediaeval European practices of walling up shoes to ward off evil, to faith injunctions about the shoes of the dead or the unholy uncleanliness of footwear (DeMello 2009: 33–8). And, in another parallel, footwear can be read to act as a synecdoche for all cultural products in its mediation between the tangible world, the human body and human perception: shoes can be concrete, literal, merely utilitarian; but they can also be fantastically embellished art objects, culturally high or low end, commercial or artistic. Footwear may be individual, artisanal and geographically specific, but it may also be mass, generic and ubiquitous. Footwear, therefore, provides a privileged perspective for exploring how material culture mediates power and agency in colonial, post-colonial and globalised contexts.

Given the complexity of the mediations that footwear as material culture affords, it is not surprising that the shoe emerges as an important motif in a range of cultural works that critique racialised encounters. With its evident play of visibility and occlusion and its intimate ontological connection with the state of being human, the shoe provides the perfect motif to critique historical reality and its symbolic expression in culture and representation. Footwear is powerfully resonant in cultural products grounded in contexts of racialised oppression, subjugation and marginalisation, where the denial of footwear is mobilised to express the denial of humanity (Angelou 1986; Butake 1993; Treviño 1999; Gutberlet and Snyman 2012). That this deployment of images of footwear to resist oppression is no coincidence is particularly well illustrated by two influential anti-colonial narratives, Bernard Dadié's novel *Un nègre à Paris/An African in Paris* (1959) and Frantz Fanon's *Les Damnés de la terre/The Wretched of the Earth* (1961).

In Dadié's novel the first-person narrator expresses multiple anxieties over temporal, geographical and personal boundaries, and the unease of inhabiting, on the Dakar-Paris flight, an in-between space where such boundaries dissolve (Dadié 1959: 21–2). The culmination of these anxieties focuses on footwear: the narrator realises that having removed his shoes earlier in the flight, he cannot find them; and once he does, his feet are so swollen he cannot get the shoes on again, his colonised body rendered monstrously excessive by the airborne dissolution of the boundaries that had defined it on the ground. Horrified by the idea of landing barefoot in Paris, he battles against the shoes with a pencil remodelled as a shoehorn, which snaps in the struggle (Ibid.: 21–3). This episode of bathos is also an important episode of ironic connection hinting at the barriers, customs and perceptions that make even a highly educated African man anxious when faced with the barefoot state. The internalised Western correlation of barefootedness with uncivilised status is shown to have a pyscho-affective power (Coulthard 2014: 26) so strong that even his status as highly educated cannot allay the fear of performing the West's Primitive.

As such, Dadié's narrator's acute concerns projected onto footwear bear all the hallmarks of Du Boisian double consciousness: footwear is so crucial because it constitutes a material sign located at the body's surface that can either mask or reveal the colonisers' phantasmagoric *nègre*. For whilst appropriate apparel worn in suitable ways can disguise or attenuate colonial constructions of blackness, the inappropriate deployment of clothing serves instead to compound and intensify otherness and stereotyping. Clothing acts as a proxy for the colonised body by its closeness to it. This can render individual items anomalous even when worn normatively. But clothing also acts as an extension of the colonised body when not worn normatively, such that garments and the black body can, in racialised contexts, become othered by white norms even when, as discreet items, they objectively inhabit those norms. Thus clothing can render difference both visible and invisible; it can both accentuate and mask black skin in white territory. So Dadié's narrator possesses shoes, but they are mislaid, or ill-fitting, or impossible to put on. His footwear may bridge the geographical and personal boundaries of colonial space, allowing him as an African to 'pass' with sufficient legitimacy to cross; but the footwear is also the source of paralysing anxiety, a tenuous disguise that may at any moment fall away and 'out' the African as colonialism's Primitive.

Dadié's narrator rehearses in microcosm the psychological complexes of domination that are central to Fanon's analyses of the structures of colony and postcolony in Africa. In *Les Damnés de la terre/The Wretched of the Earth* (Fanon 1961/1963), the barefoot state in Fanon's text communicates a strength of feeling far from the state of comic dissonance that Dadié evokes through mockery of the anxieties of both the colonised and the coloniser. Here, shoes are present as an arresting motif that indexes oppression by the colonial settlers:

> The settler's feet are never visible, except perhaps in the sea; but there you're never close enough to see them. His feet are protected by strong shoes although the streets of his town are clean and even, with no holes or stones [...] The native town is a hungry town, starved of bread, of meat, of shoes, of coal, of light. The native town is a crouching village, a town on its knees, a town wallowing in the mire. (Fanon trans. Farrington 1963: 38)

This polemical image of the colonisers' feet hidden in needlessly sturdy shoes is a powerful synecdoche that contrasts the 'bare life' existence imposed on the colonised with the 'sovereign' existence of the settler (Agamben 1998). The barefoot colonised of Fanon's description is the abject product of a regime that has enforced deprivations that simultaneously create and confirm the essentialised status of the colonised as Other. Fanon's oppressor's shoes represent the historical reality of the imposed economic indigence of *les damnés de la terre* and the economic sufficiency of their oppressors; and their use as textual motif also shows how expressing this oppression in the symbolic realm though footwear draws attention to the reliance of power on a dialectic of visibility and invisibility.

Dadié and Fanon textualise footwear as a socially charged material object, using images of shoes to explore the colonial Manicheanism that pits barefoot savagery against shod civilisation. These images of footwear articulate topoi of oppression, agency and resistance central to the discursive background of the immediate post-Independence period as well as the later period of neo-imperial globalisation, the periods from which the three films studied here derive. Film, as a visual medium, is particularly able to explore this dynamic tension between agency and oppression. In the next section, I will explore how *Borom Sarret, La Noire de . . .* and *Hyènes* achieve this through an exploration of the resistant charge of footwear via the films' visual and narrative motifs.

Footwear on film in Africa

Borom Sarret (1963)

Ousmane Sembene was the pioneering figure of African-directed cinema in Africa and in his early films, *Borom Sarret* (1963) and *La Noire de . . .* (1966), a range of images of footwear is used to examine the visibility and invisibility of power, opposing shod and barefoot states, 'high' and 'low' shoe types (heeled shoes or boots versus sandals and flip-flops), and closed versus open footwear (the enclosed shoe or boot versus the open sandal). Thus, from the very beginning of filmmaking by Africans in Africa, footwear occurs on screen with strategic intentionality.

Borom Sarret screens a day in the life of an indigent carter, a *borom sarret*. The carter's livelihood depends on his being mobile in the post-colonial city of Dakar. The film shows this mobility as a diegetic reality for the protagonist; however, it also acts as a metaphor for social power, with barriers to mobility connected visually to poverty and powerlessness. The carter is already a trans- portation anachronism (Green-Simms 2017: Chapter 3; Saul 2018) and the film charts his difficult day in Dakar as it worsens. The linear, chronological narrative of the film shows the carter providing transport for helpless, tragic or unscrupulous clients, and making, or failing to make, the right decisions in the context of post-colonial urban modernity. In the film's denouement, Borom Sarret agrees to take a client to an area of the city from which lowly carters are banned. His cart is confiscated by the police, his war medal too, and he returns home without the means to make a living. The final sequences show his wife leaving to search for work.

From the outset, the film installs visual tropes of movement as a human necessity. As the opening credits roll up, fixed-camera images of humans travelling along Dakar highways show motor vehicles, pedestrians and bicycles passing through the field of vision, before the film focuses down onto the carter's day, itself inherently responsive to the movements of others. Within this framework, two scenes further into the film are crucial for their visually striking and diegetically significant emphasis on footwear. In the first scene of interest, Borom Sarret is shown napping in his cart during a pause in work. The camera takes up a striking first-person narrative viewpoint, showing the carter's legs extended and his sandaled feet projecting over the side of the cart. Heard before he is seen, a disabled beggar, barefoot and with no function in his legs, drags himself along the street on his hands and knees, asking for alms. Sharp cuts change the camera angle to frame the beggar's movement from behind and place his dragging bare feet centrally in view. Borom Sarret lies across his cart and the beggar approaches perpendicularly so that the two bodies, one still and shod, the other barefoot and in movement, are in marked visual contrast. Borom Sarret ignores the beggar, commenting in voice-over that there are so many of them that there is nothing to be done and so better not to give money at all. Diegetically the episode is one of realism, emphasising the harsh realities for post-colonial Dakar's poor in the immediate post-Independence years. Visually however, a different dynamic is at work, with footwear signalling a hierarchy of the dispossessed: the carter's sandals physically occupy a space above the barefoot beggar, illustrating the city's socio-economic stratification through clear spatial relations. The flip-flop sandal, the coloniser's idea of primitive footwear, is contrasted in this episode against the barefoot state of 'bare humanity' to symbolise Borom Sarret's relative economic superiority, while the striking framing of feet and footwear in filmed space provides a visual illustration of this hierarchy.

The second episode of interest forms a corollary to this first scene in its use of a first-person viewpoint and visual rehearsal of spatial power relations mediated through contrasting images of footwear. Borom Sarret has travelled with an insistent customer to the off-limits 'Plateau' ['The Heights'], the district's name itself implying a vertical spatial relationship between different socio-economic groups. Here Borom Sarret encounters the forces that control movement in the city, in the person of a policeman who stops them. The smartly dressed customer and Borom Sarret descend from the cart to the ground, but while the customer quickly moves away into a waiting car, Borom Sarret is held up and required to account for his presence in the district. At the point of highest tension between the helpless carter and state authority personified by the policeman, the camera adopts a first-person narrative angle to show the encounter from the carter's point of view. The viewer looks down with Borom Sarret at his war medal crushed under the boot of authority; and looks up with him at the towering policeman making notes to impound the cart. At the very moment where state authority deprives Borom Sarret of his mobility and livelihood, the earlier spatial relationship between Borom Sarret and the beggar is recreated in the shot composition as well as the narrative of impassivity and resignation, this time with Borom Sarret on the lowest social and economic rung. In both these scenes the camera angles place the viewer as an observer of the events and also as a participant in domination, for the viewer is structured along with the carter to dominate the beggar but to be dominated by the forces of state authority.

These episodes draw a contrast between abject barefootedness and sandal-wearing, and between sandals and the boots of authority. This contrast exemplifies how forms of clothing mediate power transfers between the colonial and post-colonial orders in Africa, as identified by critics such as Mbembe, Ngong, Tcheuyap and Martin. In *Borrom Sarret* colonial commandment is depicted continuing seamlessly within the new post-colonial society. The carter's fatalistic acceptance of the hierarchy that places him well above the beggar is portrayed as a complicity with this continuity, for ultimately it is his acceptance of this status quo of power that leads to the film's denouement, from which stasis and increased indigence result. If in the post-colony, as *Borom Sarret* illustrates, 'the masses join in the madness and clothe themselves in cheap imitations of power to reproduce its epistemology [...] the practices of those who command and those who are assumed to obey are so entangled as to render both powerless' (Mbembe 2001: 133). For the viewer nonetheless, the unusual images of footwear that are foregrounded force an awareness of the post-colony's structural power relations through their revelation of the hidden continuities of power; and through their presentation of power's invisible naturalisation of social hierarchies as starkly unnatural.

La Noire de . . . / Black Girl . . . (1966)

La Noire de . . . (1966) was Sembene's second film. An adaptation of his short story of the same name published in *Presence Africaine* in 1961, it charts the story of Diouana, who takes up work as a children's maid for a French family in post-Independence Dakar and who is enticed to move to France to work for the family on the meretricious promise of a better life in *la belle France*. The film emphasises the tensions between legacies of colonialism, post-Independence African nationalism and burgeoning consumer society. The recurring motif of

Diouana's shoes and feet crystallises issues of power and race that are the central narrative and aesthetic features of the film; and its 'vocal cinema' (Wang 2017) uses voice-over to express Diouana's contestatory thoughts, censored from open expression by the power relations depicted in the narrative. Diouana's narrative viewpoint is also given prominence visually. There are avoidances of shot/reverse-shot conventions for dialogue that highlight the maid's lack of genuine right of reply: an early tracking shot is clearly situated on Diouana's passenger side of the car on the drive from Marseilles to Antibes, but she says very little; the view out from the Antibes apartment's high-rise window replicates Diouana's worldview, with oppressive, anonymous darkness across the Riviera filling the screen in evident pathetic fallacy. The *mise en scène* alternates this emphasis on the perspective of the oppressed maid with shots staging the characters' relationships from a third-person point of view. Crucially, however, the third person point-of-view does not coincide with that of the white *colons*; instead, their complexes of superiority and paternalism are acutely exposed through the alternate foregrounding of Diouana's viewpoint and white colonial privilege viewed from the outside.

Within this *mise en scène*, *La Noire de …* dramatises clothing as a highly charged object of desire that can both oppress and contest. At one point on a quiet street of the *Plateau*, Diouana admires two well-dressed African women passing in their stylish clothes and heels; and during their leisure time in Dakar, Diouana and her politically aware student boyfriend (he is pictured in his room against the backdrop of fabric bearing the Swahili word *Uhuru* [freedom], celebrating Lumumba and Congo Independence) pore over a French magazine's fashion spread, absorbing the lifestyle promises implicit in it. In France, Diouana speculates that the reward for a lunch well cooked for guests will be a shopping trip for stylish clothes, only to realise later in the film that she has been deceived: Madame's gifts of cast-off clothes, like so much else, were nothing more than a lure. Most of all, there is ongoing conflict between Madame's expectations of appropriate dress for a maid and Diouana's expectations of dress for an immigrant worker who has made it to France.

Madame employs several domestic staff in her large residence, where Diouana's role is restricted to looking after the children. In contrast, in Antibes Madame is reduced to one all-purpose maid in a small apartment, a significant drop in status. Diouana's comment that 'Madame wasn't like that in Dakar, nor was Sir', beyond commenting on their harsher behaviour towards her now in France, invites this more general interpretation of their straightened circumstances. Diouana's importance for Madame therefore lies as much in confirming Madame's non-labouring 'overclass' status, a status threatened by decolonisation and the return to France (Curran 2003: 123; Oscherwitz 2014: 57), as it does in the actual domestic labour that Diouana provides. In the French apartment, Diouana insistently dresses in Western dresses and heels, jewellery and smart wigs for her domestic work. Diouana's pride in and care over her appearance belies the demeaning work that she is doing, and marks her agency and aspirations. Confronted with this disruptive mimicry (Bhabha 1994: 86), Madame harangues Diouana for how unsuitably smartly she is dressed, disciplining the maid's body symbolically as she fastens her into an apron. These initial arguments about clothing in the film nuance the drama of racial oppression through a gendered presentation of the power struggle depicted, providing the context for the film's rehearsal of a gendered dialectical relationship between shod and barefoot states.

Diouana's footwear is the first aspect of her that the viewer perceives, the clack of her high heels against the hard floor of the port terminal heard before either she is seen or any of her thoughts communicated on voice-over. High heels are thus indexical of Diouana's presence even in her absence. Moreover, this sound of high heels follows immediately on from the mournful warning horn blasts of the docking *Ancerville* that punctuate the opening credits. Through the soundscape alone in the first few minutes of the film therefore, an African's arrival in France is predicated as isolation and danger but counterposed with quickening hope for the future; Diouana's high heels enter the frame as over-determined objects channelling this tension. Her footwear is later at the centre of two specific scenes of conflict in the film.

The first of these occurs between Diouana and her mistress, and is an intensification of Madame's frustration with Diouana's stylish dressing. On a day when Diouana has slept in and taken her time in the bathroom and dressing, Madame must prepare breakfast and clear away. As Diouana prepares to start the day's work, the camera lingers on her changing out of sandals into her high-heeled shoes, with a close focus on her feet crossing the bedroom floor to the living room in these shoes. Immediately Diouana reaches the living room, Madame orders her to take off these heels. In an act of mute rebellion, Diouana takes them off but leaves them in the middle of the floor and goes barefoot into the kitchen. Madame is obliged to stoop down to pick the shoes up and carry them to Diouana, extending the role reversal between maid and mistress. The camera pauses on a shot of Diouana's bare feet pressed against each other under the kitchen table and then on the heeled shoes thrown down next to her feet by Madame. Madame tells Diouana that if she does not work, she will not be fed. Diouana pushes her breakfast away and her voice-over informs the audience that if she is not fed, she will not work. Her passive resistance to colonial oppression through bodily non-compliance begins fully at this point, focalised through this dispute over footwear.

The second episode in which shoes figure prominently is presented in flashback as Diouana dozes in her room. The episode is triggered by the preceding argument over footwear that generates Diouana's resistance to Madame's orders. In the flashback, Diouana is walking with her new boyfriend on, significantly, Dakar's Place de l'Indépendance. She tells him that she is going to work in France for her employer, noting that he disapproves of her job and deriving satisfaction from having irritated him in this way. Taking off her heels, she skips barefoot along the war memorial commemorating the sacrifice of Senegalese soldiers in the Second World War, chanting 'I'm going to France, I'm going to France'. Her boyfriend is outraged by this disrespectful behaviour, and at this point there is a telling break in the realist diegesis of the film with intercut documentary footage of Senegalese dignitaries in European suits laying wreaths at the inauguration of the monument. This footage signals the contested narrative of the contribution of colonial troops to the Allies' triumph in the Second World War, for while this monument honours the war dead it does so by borrowing from the memorial discourse and architecture of the colonial power, and it does not hint at any memory of the colonial drafting, exploitation and post-war discrimination against African soldiers who fought for the French. It is telling that this documentary sequence, breaking the realist diegesis, is presented as springing from the boyfriend's thoughts; Diouana, caught up in her fantasies of *la belle France*, is oblivious to the monument's seriousness, while her boyfriend tries to defend the monument's values against her frivolity, shouting at her that she is committing sacrilege. Diouana is screened here crossing gendered and racial boundaries that others, in this case a masculine, nationalist other, police for her.

The scene depicts Diouana willingly choosing the barefoot state as an expression of her freedom from expectation and constraint, contrasting the past with her present of being ordered to go barefoot in the French household to emphasise her lowly status. Diouana's barefootedness in Dakar does not imply performance of the West's Primitive, but instead parallels aspects of the well known Democratic Republic of Congo dandy or 'sapeur' practices (Thomas 2003: 956; 958–9) by adopting of forms of dress and self-fashioning that disrupt the etiquettes of the post-colonial *cadres*, challenging the ways in which post-colonial power magnified colonial power by re-inscribing colonial-era clothing norms as dominant in the new nation (Mbembe 2001: 131–2). Diouana's modernity thus relegates her to an in-between space: she challenges the political consciousness of the post-colony through her rejection of masculine nationalist solemnities in favour of feminine consumer culture, but her embrace of consumer culture places her in opposition to the colonial complexes of white superiority in which such culture was embedded (Curran 2003: 123) because she refuses to accept the white disciplining of her body and the suppression of her subjectivity by white discourse. Diouana's double marginalisation from both white power and masculinist, nationalist post-colonial power demonstrates the extent to which such power is neither race- nor gender-neutral, and it is tropes of footwear and barefootedness that rehearse this in detail in the film.

To sum up, motifs of footwear in Sembene's early films comment on transfers of power between colony and post-colony, and on the desire to, and challenge of, contesting both new and established orders of power when these past and present formations are inherently entangled. In both *Borom Sarret* and *La Noire de . . .* film tropes of footwear and the barefoot state rehearse how, in the aftermath of African independence, the challenges of decolonisation compel individuals to re-fashion both appearance and mentality, chiming with Gayatri Spivak's insight that decolonisation 'involves a re-fashioning of the structures that we inherit from colonial days' and a 'change of mind' (Yegenoglu and Mutman 2001–2: 10).

Hyènes/Hyenas (1992)

Three decades later, in the 'sober era of globalised capital with pockets completely emptied by corrupt black leaders and debts to Western banks' (Mudede 2015: 4), Djibril Diop Mambéty's film *Hyènes* highlights the dialectic of barefootedness to footwear, and hierarchies in types of footwear, as part of its exploration of power and moral responsibility. *Hyènes/Hyenas* adapts Friedrich Dürrenmatt's play *Der Besuch der Alten Dame/The Visit* (1956) from its post-war European context to Africa in the wake of late twentieth-century IMF structural adjustment programmes. Through repetition that is nonetheless a highly original re-writing of the Swiss play (Gabor-Peirce 2011: 195), the film forms a recursive sequence with it and plays satirically with time-bound dichotomies between the original and the fake, and the essential and the contingent.

In the dilapidated Dakar arrondissement of Colobane news spreads of the return to town of an elderly lady 'richer than the World Bank'. Linguère Ramatou had left the town decades earlier, a disgraced teenager pregnant with the child of Draman Drameh. The latter refused to accept paternity and, rather than marry her, bribed two others to swear in court that they had slept with her. Ramatou now promises billions in riches to the Colobane townsfolk in return for justice: Draman Drameh must die and the townsfolk must make this happen. Gradually the power of money to undermine the townsfolk's loyal stance towards their well-liked prominent elder citizen Draman makes itself felt. While Draman comes to accept that justice must be done for his past behaviour, the townsfolk who conspire to bring about his death are left with no moral superiority; the final images of the film symbolise this through bulldozers, waste ground and high-rise flats where the town once was.

In spite of the increasingly claustrophobic atmosphere of *Hyènes'* narrative action, images of movement abound in the film, as they did also in *Borom Sarret* and *La Noire de . . .* In *Hyènes* however, human movement is limited from the outset. The train timetable is implacable, the rickety checkpoint barrier on the dusty town road impedes progress, and the shimmering expanse of the Atlantic Ocean is set against a concrete bunker; for all of the characters except Ramatou, mobility is trammelled by power's organisation of time and space through poverty (poor townsfolk can only travel as far as their feet can carry them) and power (trains cannot be made to stop at Colobane since there is no timetable for this as there is no station there; the town cannot be entered or left without its only road's barrier being raised by the sentinel). Only Ramatou's billions can re-order time and space: for she alone is able to buy train-stop-ping rights, the judicial process, religion's spiritual underpinning of temporal morality, and to 'abolish time' through Draman's death; while her riches allow the previously static, barefoot townspeople to whirl through the air in the funfair and escape from Colobane in their new 2CV cars.

Yet the film does not equate the mobility achieved to freedom and the extra-diegetic footage of animals cut into the narrative underscores this. First elephants, then vultures, hyenas and an owl wander, prowl, fly and observe, their freedom highlighting the circumscription of freedom taking place diegetically as Ramatou's billions wreak moral havoc. Where once the townsfolk's choice was limited by poverty, now it is limited by the promise of incoming wealth. In *Hyènes* the power of money is so great as to be totalitarian: there is no choice possible except the one that money dictates and no life possible outside the command of money.

Mambéty's conception of cinema as tracing imaginative worlds that can present the measure of human possibilities both aesthetically and in the realms of action aligns with Dürrenmatt's theatrical *mise en scène* where physical objects render visible the limits of the characters' agency via non-verbal connections and conceptions (Diller 1966: 198). In *Hyènes* it is clothing that is especially resonant with symbolic meaning: wealth's corrupting power is made visible as a contagion spreading throughout Colobane, the sickness manifesting visibly and bodily in clothing. With Ramatou's descent from the train dressed in a golden dress, boots and shawl, a vision intensified by her gold prosthetic arm and leg, a plague of golden items seeps into the town. From the police-chief's new gold tooth, to the mayor's increasingly Wild West garb (Oscherwitz 2008: 231), to Draman Drameh's wife's wholly gold outfit at the mass auction of white goods, down to the poor townsfolk's newly acquired gold neckscarves, pith helmets and brand new yellow shoes, this metaphor of sickness makes itself felt in all social classes. Even where clothes are not actually golden, the townswomen's dresses become either patterned increasingly with yellow mimicking gold or with black foretelling death, the latter echoing Ramatou's own hieratical clothing as she awaits the outcome of her plan. It is striking to note, however, that – as with structural adjustment – the new wealth signalled by golden and yellow garments remains concentrated in the hands of the already powerful: while the poor gain short scarves, helmets and footwear, they remain dressed in sackcloth, whereas whole suits of new clothes are the preserve of those with civic standing, for example the mayor and his wife. In addition, it is not the town's poor who are seen to buy up the vast quantities of electric fans, fridges and television sets that pour into the town, but instead those who are already relatively well off, such as the mayor's wife and Draman Drameh's.

Amplifying the impact in *Hyènes* of clothing as a visual symbol of wealth's corrupting power and power's oppressive stratification of society, images of shoes and barefootedness are a key focal point. The film's opening close-up sequences of a herd of elephants young and old walking together emphasises the ponderous movement of their feet. The scene then cuts to an extended fixed-angle shot as a mass of townsmen walks from the distance towards the camera. As they approach, the camera focuses in on their bare or sandalled feet, only showing their upper bodies from behind once they have passed the camera. In retrospect the audience understands these two sequences as a poignant juxtaposition of the communal society of elephants on the move protected by their matriarchs, against the splintered and individualistic society that Colobane will become once its own matriarch moves in.

Specific images of footwear occur at a high point of tension in the film. After there is a price announced on Draman Drameh's life, poor townsmen come to Draman's shop and intone ominously, 'Solidarity! To life and to death Draman! Solidarity!' before seeking credit for items they cannot afford. As they turn away from the counter, Draman notices their new yellow shoes and boots, which he identifies as imports from Burkina Faso. Later Draman notices others with new yellow shoes and the yellow footwear becomes part of the spreading plague of golden clothing. In Dürrenmatt's play this yellow footwear 'that flower[s] like daffodils' as the townsfolk's loyalties are slowly bought by the old lady are already powerfully material as well as semiotically and phe-nomenologically dense (Garner 1998: 55–6), but *Hyènes* screenplay makes yet more of them. *Hyènes*' yellow shoes intensify the effects already in play through golden costuming, but they also extend the film's symbolism in a specifically African direction. Amongst the many references to consumption and consumer products in *Hyènes*, brands are paraded both visually in the bottles, jars and bowls that line the shelves of Draman's shop, and aurally through the brand name-dropping that occurs in Draman's shop once the villagers give free rein to expensive tastes. The brands mentioned are all Francophone, such as

Calvados Simon, or associated with the Americas, such as Camel cigarettes, Prince Albert tobacco, the mayor's Remington typewriter and Havana cigars. Thus, the yellow shoes and boots that take the town by storm are notably the only items specifically referred to as coming from within Africa.

The identification of a provenance in Burkina Faso is not a coincidence. A country like many others in West Africa with centuries of history of trading including slave-trading, it was uniquely renamed in 1984 when Thomas Sankara changed the colonial-era Haute Volta/Upper Volta to the hybrid Mòoré-Dioula title of 'Land of Honest People'. Yellow footwear and boots therefore channel an Afrocentric irony that is additional to the symbolism of other yellow and golden garments in the film, since the aspiration of Sankara's nomenclature is evidently disappointed through the film's vision of boots from the Land of the Honest worn by those whose loyalty is easily sold out. In addition, Burkina Faso's post-1987 history of Blaise Compaoré's murder of Sankara and abuse of presidential power shows the country's ruling elites to be far from embodying the values of the country's name. Indeed, at the time of *Hyènes*' release, while Burkina Faso was the West's poster nation for the success of rapid economic liberalisation in Africa, 'behind such facile external perceptions [. . .] an impoverished populace [was] ill-disposed to the traumatic imposition of market dominance' (Harsch 1998: 625). The yellowness of the footwear in *Hyènes* coupled with its Burkina Faso origins combines layers of symbolic, historical and ironic meaning to point openly to the complicity of African elites in the depredations of World Bank and IMF loan regimes. It is significant in this regard that when Draman sees the newly purchased yellow shoes of his customers, this is not the first time that the audience has seen such shoes on screen: early in the film the rich women of Colobane dress in their finery to take up their seats on sofas lining the road that Ramatou will take to enter Colobane and they too wear yellow shoes from Burkina Faso. While Ramatou's billions therefore accelerate cupidity in the film, Mambéty's early images of yellow shoes alert the audience to moral dubiousness and African complicity in the post-colony's structures of inequality even before the influx of external wealth and excess borrowing triggered by Ramatou's fateful return.

Conclusion

The specific ontological status of footwear and its discursive mobilisation by anti-colonial authors forms the ground from which post-Independence African screen images of footwear and barefootedness reflect on colonial and post-colonial states of being. This reflection is articulated in screen images that signal the lived black experience of apparel as oppression, an experience born of colonialism but with strong ramifications in post-Independence debates over dress, belonging and identity, and in contemporary global Western cultural and economic imperialism. The films discussed here use the mediating power of footwear images to render such oppression visible while also highlighting possibilities for agency and refashioning even within contexts of oppression. African directors thus frame clothing practices as meaningful beyond ethnographic constructions of dress as tribal or formulaic, foregrounding the dynamics of individual and group agency in creating style, and highlighting style's value as resistance to 'a mainstream culture whose principle defining characteristic [. . .] is to masquerade as nature' (Schoss 1996: 189), whether that culture be colonial or post-colonial. Through the dialectic established in the films analysed here between images of footwear and barefootedness as oppression, and images of footwear and barefootedness as agency, clothing as style takes shape as a form of expression that plays knowingly with colonial and post-colonial norms. Within this, footwear assumes a significance through its specifically human dimensions as both extension of, and limit to, the wearer's body. The persistent juxtaposition in each film of tropes of footwear as agency and tropes of footwear as oppression communicates against the unitary discourse of apparel as oppression that is articulated in Dadié and Fanon's anti-colonial texts, and show African filmmakers marking out through their creative vision moments in the interstices of dominant cultures where style resists and agency can be returned to the subject.

References

Agamben, Giorgio (1998), *Homo Sacer: Sovereign Power and Bare Life*, trans. D. Heller-Roazen, Stanford: Stanford University Press.

Allman, Jean (ed.) (2004), *Fashioning Africa: Power and the Politics of Dress*, Bloomington: Indiana University Press.

Angelou, Maya (1986), *All God's Children Need Travelling Shoes*, London: Virago Press.

Bhabha, Homi (1994), *The Location of Culture*, London: Routledge.

Bloom, Livia (2015), 'Interview with Mbissine Thérèse Diop', *Film Comment*, 5 October 2015, https://www.filmcomment.com/blog/interview-mbissine-therese-diop/ (last accessed 14 January 2019).

Burke, Timothy (1996), '"Sunlight Soap has Changed my Life"': Hygiene, Commodification and the Body in Colonial Zimbabwe', in H. Hendrikson (ed.), *Clothing and Difference: Embodied Identities in Colonial and Postcolonial Africa*, Durham, NC and London: Duke University Press.

Butake, Bole (1993; 2013), 'Shoes and Four Men in Arms', in *Dance of the Vampire and Six Other Plays*, Mankon: Langaa RPCIG, pp. 331–79.

Comraoff, Jean and Comaroff, John (1997), *Of Revelation and Revolution: Dialectics of Modernity on a South African Frontier*, Chicago: University of Chicago Press.

Coulthard, Glen S. (2014), *Red Skin White Masks: Rejecting the Colonial Politics of Recognition*, Minneapolis: University of Minnesota Press.

Curran, Cynthia (2003), 'Class', in M. E. Page and P. M. Sonnenburg (eds), *Colonialism: An International, Social, Cultural and Political Encyclopedia*, vol. 1., ABC-Clio.

Dadié, Bernard (1959), *Un nègre à Paris*, Paris: Présence Africaine.

Dadié, Bernard (1994), *An African in Paris*, trans. K. C. Hatch, Urbana, IL: University of Illinois Press.

DeMello, Margot (2009), *Feet and Footwear: A Cultural Encyclopedia*, Westport, CT: Greenwood Press.

Diller, Edward (1966), 'Dürrenmatt's Use of the Stage as a Dramatic Element', *Symposium: A Quarterly Journal in Modern Literatures*, vol. 20, no. 3, pp. 197–208.

Fanon, Frantz (1952), *Peau noire, masques blancs*, Paris: Seuil.

Fanon, Frantz (1961), *Les Damnés de la terre*, Paris: Maspero.

Fanon, Frantz (1963), *The Wretched of the Earth*, trans. C. Farrington, New York: Grove Weidenfeld.

Gabor-Peirce, Olivia (2011), 'Returning Home: Djbril Diop Mambéty's *Hyènes*', *Journal of African Cultural Studies*, vol. 23, no. 2, pp. 189–203.

Garner, Stanton B. Jr (1998), 'Staging "Things": Realism and the Theatrical Object in Shepard's Theatre', *Contemporary Theatre Review*, vol. 8, no. 3, pp. 55–66.

Green-Simms, Lindsey B. (2017), *Postcolonial Automotobility: Car Culture in West Africa*, Minneapolis: University of Minnesota Press (ebook).

Gutberlet, Marie-Hélène and Snyman, Cara (2012), *Shoe Shop*, Auckland Park: Jacana Media.

Harsch, Ernest (1998), 'Burkina Faso in the Winds of Liberalisation', *Review of African Political Economy*, vol. 25, no. 78.

Hay, Jean (1996), 'Hoes and Clothes in a Luo Household: changing consumption in a colonial economy', in M. J. Arnoldi, C. M. Geary and K. L. Hardin (eds), *African Material Culture*, Bloomington: Indiana University Press, pp. 243–61.

Hendrickson, Hildi (ed.) (1996), *Clothing and Difference:Embodied Identities in Colonial and Postcolonial Africa*, Durham and London: Duke University Press.

Kisiang'ani, Edward (2011), '"Celebrating" the female body in global trade: fashion, media and music in Kenya', in J.-B. Ouedraogo and R. Achieng (eds), *Global Exchanges and Gender Perspectives in Africa*, Dakar: Council for the Development of Social Science Research in Africa.

Küchler, Susanne and Miller, Daniel (2005), *Clothing as Material Culture*, Oxford: Berg.

Lupton, Mary J. (1998), *Maya Angelou, a Critical Companion*, Westport, CT: Greenwood Press.

Martin, Phyllis (1995), *Leisure and Society in Colonial Brazzaville*, Cambridge: Cambridge University Press.

Mudede, Charles T. (2015), 'Neoliberalism and the New Afro-Pessimism: Djibril Diop Mambéty's *Hyènes*', *e-flux journal*, no. 67 (November 2015) (last accessed 12 January 2019).

Mbembe, Achille (2001), *On the Postcolony*, Berkeley: University of California Press.

Ngong, Benjamin (2012), '*Costume et pouvoir: la fonction comminatoire du vêtement dans la politique post-coloniale en Afrique*', in A. Mazuet (ed.), *Imaginary Spaces of Power in Sub-Saharan Literatures and Films*, Cambridge: Cambridge Scholars Publishing.

Oscherwitz, Dana (2014), 'A Twice-told Tale: the Postcolonial Allegory of *La Noire de . . .* and *Faat Kiné*', in L. J. Vitinde and A. T. Fofana (eds), *Ousmane Sembene and the Politics of Culture*, Lanham: Lexington Books, pp. 51–62.

Oscherwitz, Dana (2008), 'Of Cowboys and Elephants: Africa, Globalization and the Nouveau Western in Djibril Diop Mambety's *Hyenas*', *Research in African Literature*, vol. 39, no. 1, pp. 223–38.

Şaul, Mahir (2018), 'Film and Video as Historical Sources', *Oxford Research Encyclopaedia of African History*, http://oxfordre.com/africanhistory/view/10.1093/acrefore/9780190277734.001.0001/acrefore-9780190277734-e-247 (last accessed 17 December 2018).

Schoss, Johanna (1996), '"Dressed to Shine": Work, Leisure and Style in Malindi, Kenya', in H. Hendrickson (ed.), *Clothing and Difference*, Durham, NC: Duke University Press, pp. 157–88.

Swann, June M. (1996), 'Shoes Concealed in Buildings', *Northampton Museum and Art Gallery Journal 6*, http://witleysoralhistory.org/wp-content/uploads/2015/09/Eastgrove-Cottage_Little-Witley_Shoes-Concealed-In-Buildings.pdf (last accessed 12 October 2018).

Tcheuyap, Alexie (1999), '*Le moine habillé. Réflexes vestimentaires et mythologiques identitaires en Afrique*', *Mots pluriels* no. 10, http://motspluriels.arts.uwa.edu.au/MP1099at.html#fn4 (last accessed 10 October 2018).

Treviño Hart, Elva (1999), *Barefoot Heart, Stories of a Migrant Child*, Tempe: Bilingual Press/Editorial Bilingüe.

Thomas, Dominic (2003), 'Fashion Matters: "La Sape" and Vestimentary Codes in Transnational Contexts and Urban Diasporas', *Modern Language Notes*, vol. 118, no. 4, pp. 947–73.

Turner, Terence S. ([1980] 2007), 'The Social Skin', in M. M. Lock and J. Farquhar, *Beyond the Body Proper: Reading the Anthropology of Material Life*, Durham, NC and London: Duke University Press, pp. 83–03.

Wang, Benjamin (2017), '*Black Girl* (1966): Vocal Cinema', *Film Inquiry*, https://www.filminquiry.com/black-girl-1966-review/ (last accessed 20 November 2018).

Yegenoglu, M. and Mutman, M. (2001–2), 'Mapping the Present: Interview with Gayatri Spivak', in 'The Rendez-Vous of Conquest: Rethinking Race and Nation', *New Formations* no. 45; pp. 9–23.

Chapter 15

Slippers and heels: *In the Mood for Love* and sartorial investigation

Tyler Parks

In an oft-remarked-upon sequence early in Wong Kar-wai's *In the Mood for Love* (*Far yeung nin wah,* Hong Kong, 2000), one of the film's protagonists, Mrs Chan (Maggie Cheung), picks up some noodles from a local restaurant to take back home. The entire scene is in slow motion and accompanied by the intoxicating atmosphere of Umebayashi Shigeru's waltz, 'Yumeji's Theme'. As Mrs Chan climbs a set of stairs to leave the restaurant, she passes her neighbour, Mr Chow (Tony Leung), who is descending. We then see him eating in the restaurant, before there is a cut to a scene of the two passing on the stairs again, at normal speed now, on a different day. As the music fades, the rhythmic clicking of Mrs Chan's heels on the stone steps comes to dominate the soundtrack. Steady and mundane, this clicking breaks the spell of the trance-inducing atmosphere produced by music and slowed movement in the earlier incarnation of the noodle shop visit. There is, in the sound of the shoes on the steps, resignation and malaise, but there is also an orderliness. That is, the sound suggests the outward appearance of normality maintained – however lethargically – by Mrs Chan, which masks the intense inner turmoil she is experiencing as she comes to suspect her husband is having an affair. It is unlikely, of course, that the sound of the heels in the noodle shop sequence will be consciously understood by spectators, at least initially, as expressive of the predicament in which Mrs Chan finds herself. However, such a reading becomes more plausible and tempting retrospectively, after we have come to see how both clothing in general and shoes in particular are endowed with considerable significance throughout *In the Mood for Love.*

Shoes are not the only garments to carry symbolic and narrative significance in the film. Not long after the noodle shop sequence, Mrs Chan again bumps into her neighbour, this time as he exits the flat in which she and her husband rent a room. During their brief exchange, we see Mr Chow take note of the pink handbag Mrs Chan is carrying and see her slightly startle at the tie he wears. However, it is quite difficult on a first viewing to grasp what the attention of each has been attracted by. It is only in the following scene, during which the two talk at a restaurant, that it becomes clear what each has noticed and why their discoveries have led them to grudgingly admit that their spouses are almost certainly having an affair. Chow has noticed that Mrs Chan has the same handbag his wife bought while out of the country. Mrs Chan has noticed that Chow is wearing the same tie that her husband wears every day to work, claiming it was a gift from his boss. They both recognise that this 'coincidence' is nothing of the sort, that in all likelihood their spouses were together while out of the country 'on business' buying them gifts. Mrs Chan is particularly well placed to recognise the significance of these duplications since, as we have earlier learned, part of her job as a secretary is to purchase gifts for the wife and mistress of her boss, a task she generally deals with by purchasing two of the same item.

The strategy of investigation each has put to work in confirming the suspected affair – paying attention to clothing and accessories – immediately becomes pertinent to our comprehension of the film. That is, the sorts of details that serve as clues, tipping the characters off to the affair of their spouses, are of the same sort as some clues that the film demands spectators attend to – at least any spectators motivated to remain oriented in relation to the muted temporal shifts of the film and the boundary between 'objective reality' and the 'subjective worlds' of one or both characters. At the end of the sequence in the restaurant, Nat King Cole's version of 'Te quiero dijiste (Magic Is the Moonlight)' begins to play, ostensibly from a diegetic source. As the screen fades to black though the volume of the music increases slightly and it becomes non-diegetic, accompanying the following image of the two characters walking away from the camera in slow motion down a nocturnal street. In the next shot, we then see them as they begin to tentatively imagine and act out the first moments of their spouses' affair. Under cover of the music, two temporal gaps have been muted, and, as Giuliana Bruno notes generally about the film, Mrs Chan's 'changes of dress are the only way we know time is actually going by' (Bruno 2010: 227). She wears different *cheongsams*[1] in the restaurant, in the image of the two walking away from the camera and in that where they begin to act as their spouses. Images that, at first, give the impression of belonging to the same night as the revelations in the restaurant actually convey that the two have begun to meet regularly, conversing and investigating the spouses' affair as they traverse the streets of Hong Kong. Such clues then sometimes signal to the audience that undisclosed amounts of time have passed between apparently 'contiguous' images. Elsewhere though, they put into question whether certain images and events belong to diegetic reality or the fantasy or memory of a character.

In this chapter, my aim is to put this investigative strategy to work in relation to two types of footwear that are the objects of marked attention in *In the Mood for Love* – the high-heel pumps and lived-in pink house slippers worn by Mrs Chan. Directing the practice of sartorial investigation prompted by the film towards these items of footwear guides us towards a number of moments with the potential to further unsettle our sense of where fictional reality ends and the mental life of one or both of the characters begins. Consideration of both the material properties and symbolic resonances of these slippers and heels can also deepen our understanding of how the film attends to and evokes the disorientations occasioned by rapid modernisation and the influx of 'foreign' customs and cultural artefacts that accompanied it in Hong Kong, as elsewhere. Finally, the foregrounding of footwear can help us take stock of the multivocality of the film, which has opened it to compelling and competing interpretations that situate it in relation to the colonial 1960s Hong Kong it depicts, the global Hong Kong in which it was produced and the persistent philosophical preoccupations of Wong Kar-wai.

Footwear, modernity, intimacy

While I assume that most people who read this chapter will have already seen the film, I think it is worth briefly presenting the seemingly simple story it tells, with a certain emphasis for the purposes of my own arguments. Mr Chow and Mrs Chan move with their respective spouses to rooms in neighbouring flats on the same day in 1962. Eventually each learns that their spouses have begun an affair together, a fact that they confirm during the clandestine restaurant meeting mentioned above. Chow and Mrs Chan then repeatedly meet up and try to understand how that affair began, sometimes through play-acting as those spouses. Chow begins writing a martial arts serial and Mrs Chan, also an enthusiast of the form, collaborates with him, eventually in a hotel room he rents to avoid further becoming the subject of disapproving gossip. Chow eventually confesses he has fallen in love with Mrs Chan and asks her to move with him to Singapore. She declines. He goes. We later see her visit Singapore in 1963, where she steals back a pair of her slippers Chow has held onto, before leaving without contacting him. Time passes. They do not meet again, despite the possibility arising when Chow returns to Hong Kong. More time passes. Chow, a reporter, travels to Cambodia, apparently in order to cover Charles de Gaulle's historic 1966 visit, during which he advocated decolonisation and the sovereignty of formerly colonised nations. Chow then visits the ancient grounds of Angkor Wat where he appears to try to deliver himself from his secret passion for Mrs Chan by whispering it into the hollow of a stone wall and then burying it beneath dirt and grass.

Despite the simplicity of the story, its narration creates numerous possibilities for misunderstanding and uncertainty. Many of these possibilities revolve around changes in clothing that alert us either to the fact that events that seem initially to belong to a single day do not, on the one hand, or to the difficulty of separating out dream, memory or fantasy from diegetic reality on the other. The slippers and heels worn by Mrs Chan do not on their own play a marked role as signals that disturb or reorient understanding of temporal relations between images or the boundary between objective and subjective 'events'. However, in the light of more overt disturbances of spectatorial orientation, they appear potentially as clues that, scrutinised, might lead us to question the 'reality' status of certain events that initially appear to transparently further the story. That is, once we are aware of how things are often otherwise than they initially appear, we may feel prompted to bring the sartorial reading strategies elicited by the film to bear on the scenes that foreground footwear.

The slippers and heels can also, however, be read in a symbolic register as emblematic of, respectively, the private and public personas of Mrs Chan. She can be seen wearing her slippers several times during the first half of the film, for the most part in Mrs Suen's (Rebecca Pan) flat, where she and her husband rent a room. We also though see her wearing them in the neighbouring flat where Chow lives, once the two of them begin collaborating on the martial arts serial together. While she must remain aware of how the other residents see her within the space of her shared flat, the stark contrast between the worn, pink slippers and the sleek, black high-heeled pumps she favours outside the home can nevertheless be seen as reflective of the film's exploration of the conflict between private desire and social obligation, with the twist being that the former is tied to unglamorous house slippers. The fact that she visits her neighbour in her slippers, without putting on proper shoes, is a subtle mark of their growing intimacy, and the fact that he holds onto them as a symbol of their apparently unconsummated affair – after she leaves them in his room – further attests to their significance within the economy of the couple's unrequited affections.

We don't get a good look at the slippers until Mrs Chan finds herself trapped in Chow's room just over halfway through the film, after their landlords unexpectedly return from a night out. In the scene just before, Chow and Mrs Chan are presented collaborating on the martial arts serial, and while this takes place on a different day – as signalled by a change in *cheongsam* – it nevertheless prompts us to imagine they have been doing the same during the night on which they're interrupted. Upon arriving home, the landlords and their friends launch into a lengthy game of mah-jongg, which stretches deep into the following day. Mrs Chan is thus forced to take refuge in Chow's room in order to avoid provoking censure for being alone with him there (in her slippers no less!). When the game has broken off and Mrs Chan is finally able to return home she wears the high heels of Chow's wife, which fit her badly, in order to fool the servant at her flat, Amah (Chin Tsi-ang), into believing she has simply been out all day after leaving early in the morning.

After the initial commotion of the neighbours arriving home is presented, the film communicates the nature of the situation through dialogue between Chow and Mrs Chan. Importantly, this dialogue appears over an image of Mrs Chan's bare legs captured from the knees down, the hem of her dress just visible at the top of the frame. The slippers are foregrounded for the first time here, and we can see the once colourful, now faded flowers embroidered on the toe, the lavender trim circling her ankle, the open backs that bare her heels. When Chow steps into the frame in slacks and black loafers, her 'nakedness' – being caught in a situation in which she is vulnerable to the judgments of others – is further emphasised, as is an aura of everyday intimacy emanating from the slippers.

This aura is further amplified by one of the images of her escape the next day, after the mah-jongg players have gone to sleep. From a camera position beneath the bed, we see the slippers lying on the floor below the fringe of a blanket that hangs down. In the space between slippers and blanket Mrs Chan pivots briefly beside the bed in a pair of black pumps, before swiftly heading out the door and back to her own flat. For just a moment, the image registers the contrast between the footwear; the homely slippers, flattened on the ground without feet to fill them and the dark, angular heels behind them, pointed brusquely in the opposite direction (Figure 15.1). These heels, as mentioned, belong to Mrs Chow, but despite their bad fit they resemble the type of shoes favoured by Mrs Chan as well. However slightly, there is the suggestion of interchangeability here, a sense that both women play into the same kind of roles – as both women and residents in a largely Shanghainese neighbourhood in Hong Kong – outside of the home, even if Chow's wife is fully willing to flaunt such constraints and embrace more modern identity options in her private life.

The possible confusion between the two women – and their husbands – has already been played on earlier in the film when, during another mah-jongg game, we are prompted to mistake Mrs Chan's husband for Mr Chow and Mr Chow's wife for Mrs Chan. Seen from behind, the spouses resemble the film's central couple roughly through build and hairstyle, but above all through clothing. The slippers on the other hand are individualising, suggesting a reserve of personality beneath the various social roles one might feel pressed to play. They are not though particularly 'Eastern', not, that is, played off against

Figure 15.1 Homely pink slippers are contrasted with dark angular heels

the high heels as an emblem of modernisation or Western cultural influence, although heels had been associated with the adoption or appropriation of Western styles since the 1920s.[2]

Whatever the claims made for the centrality of nostalgia in *In the Mood for Love*, it portrays, as Gary Bettinson (2015) has argued, older Confucian mores in a negative light, as unnecessarily constraining the ability of individuals to act in accordance with their personal feelings and desires (or to act authentically, in the existentialist language Bettinson adopts). I would also argue, however, that the film does not hold up the more 'modern' behaviour of the cheating spouses as a positive alternative, as Bettinson sometimes seems to suggest it does. The characters are caught between two unpleasant options: restrictive traditions and a version of modernity associated with deception and selfishness. Wong's film is then quintessentially modernist in guardedly embracing the possibility for new forms of identity that offer an escape from repressive tradition, registering both anxiously and enthusiastically the forces of social disintegration released by rapid modernisation and the influx of new 'foreign' influences. In this context, the slippers might be seen as imbued with the hopes for a somewhat more quotidian modern identity, neither shaped by older, repressive social values, on the one hand, nor the artificiality and immorality of a too eagerly inhabited 'Western' model of identity on the other. The viability of this perspective, however, rests on understanding how both heels and slippers are employed elsewhere in the film.

Heels in Hong Kong

I contended at the outset of this chapter that we can understand the sound of Mrs Chan's heels on the noodle shop steps as expressive of her 'predicament', that it seems to attest to both her resignation at the thought of her husband's potential affair and her will to maintain the outward appearance of decorum. This interpretation is particularly appealing when the sequence is considered alongside another scene in which the chaotic clatter of heels on wood and linoleum serves to communicate a sense of rupture, of emotional turbulence that has broken out of its constraints to become externalised. In this later sequence (the 'hesitation sequence' hereafter), we see Mrs Chan visit Mr Chow for the first time in the hotel room he has taken so that they can work together on their martial arts serial without attracting the attention of disapproving neighbours. At first glance, the sequence seems to transparently convey Mrs Chan's emotional state at this particular moment, her hesitation at the idea of meeting Chow in a private space. It has also though been taken more broadly as expressive of this juncture in the relationship between the two characters, for instance by Mark Betz, who argues that her 'way into and exit from the hotel, via a riot of jump cuts and hesitant *longeurs*, underscores the emotional turmoil, the societal weight, and the indeterminate outcome of this moment in their relationship' (Betz 2010: 42). Crucially though, the film quite clearly positions us to understand the scene in these terms, and it is important to establish the relation of the scene to those leading up to it in accounting for its significance.

In the brief series of scenes just before her visit to the hotel, the film firmly establishes the chain of events that concludes with Mrs Chan's visit. Mr Chow proposes getting a room for them to write in; she dismisses the idea; he rents the room anyway; she doesn't see him for a time and tries to get hold of him at work; he calls her back at the office where she works (probably because he has checked in at work and been told a woman called for him) and asks her to come to the hotel. We then see her in a taxi, in the same dress that she wore while talking to him on the phone, visibly tense and pensive. The clear continuity established between the events leading up to the sequence of Mrs Chan entering the hotel gives us a good sense of her emotions as she does so. The film thus frames this visit in a way that prepares us to interpret the chaotic montage of images and sounds – in which the clatter of the shoes plays a crucial role – as reflecting her state of mind. Unlike so much of what we see in the film, this moment initially seems clearly situated when it appears and the potential for their relationship to 'become real' during this rendezvous is made fairly explicit.

Situated in this way, the scene seems initially to convey the hesitation and moral disorientation of Mrs Chan through a montage of brief images that are largely accompanied by the sound of her footsteps as she moves resolutely towards and away from Room 2046, where Chow awaits. Amidst the 'riot of jump cuts' (Betz 2010) we see her climb and descend – and climb and descend again – the stairs. We catch a longer glimpse of her leaning over the rail at the top, unnerved, then see her rise from a sofa, stride down the hall towards the room, away from it, and finally down the stairs again. At this point, as she descends, seeming to have firmly decided to turn back from the encounter, there is a cut to a dishevelled Mr Chow, impassive in close-up, in shirtsleeves, apparently waiting on the threshold of the room as three knocks sound on the door off-screen.

Throughout her journey to the door, the stuttered noise of the heels on linoleum deepens the sense of her indecisiveness, of abrupt shifts in a battle between desire and propriety. At a few points, the shoes are the focus of the images as well, particularly in the corridor, where a low camera height brings us down to their level as she strides away from the camera. However, the heels also serve as the focal point in a more distant shot in which the camera tracks upwards, holding them at the centre of the frame as Mrs Chan ascends the stairs. In each instance these foot-focused images tend to convey the speed of her movement, whether directed towards or away from Room 2046. While the film gives us no time to dwell visually on the materiality of the pumps, the collage of brief glimpses of them, in conjunction with the sound Mrs Chan's steps produce, makes these heels central to the expression of her uncertainty at this point. As I argued earlier though, however modern they might appear, the heels are associated with her social identity, with her adherence to the norms for women that prevail in the Shanghainese enclave in which she lives. The film constitutes the struggle with the restrictions of this identity as a key event, and the chaotic clustering of images and sounds of the heels are central to this construction. In the earlier scene at the noodle shop, the sound of her clicking heels seems – particularly in retrospect after this 'hesitation scene' – to express a certain resignation at the limits of her ability to act within a sphere bounded by traditional social mores. Here, on the other hand, the disorderly cacophony they produce seems linked to the spectre of her capacity to transgress such mores, to the uncomfortable acknowledgment that she harbours desires that incline her towards a break with the moral law she has internalised.

But is that actually what we are seeing (and hearing) during this sequence? Initially, this would seem to be the point at which the stylistic evocation of character subjectivity most clearly aligns us with Mrs Chan rather than Chow. But it is also true that we can interpret the cut from this sequence to the dishevelled Chow as establishing a link between the event of her indecision and the workings of his imagination at this moment. That is, it is perfectly tenable to argue that the 'hesitation sequence' conveys what he imagines Mrs Chan to be doing and experiencing as he waits for her. This could be read as an instance of recapitulative narration, a strategy that has already been put to use by this point in the film.[3] Through such narration, events are presented that we cannot initially determine the significance or meaning of; only in a later scene or scenes do we come to know what we have seen and/or heard. For instance, in the scene where Mrs Chan and Mr Chow have their suspicions about their spouses confirmed when they notice particular items of clothing, we cannot grasp their revelations until afterwards, when they go to the restaurant and talk. With the 'hesitation scene', on the other hand, what seems initially to be the case – we are being presented with a scene expressive of Mrs Chan's emotional state – becomes potentially something else, in being linked to the pensive face of Chow as he waits. Spectators may thus feel pressed to revise earlier assumptions or interpretations.

From this vantage, we would be 'set up' to incorrectly comprehend this sequence, both by the clear continuity between story scenes leading up to it and the linking of it to the unsettled demeanour of Mrs Chan as she is driven in the taxi, just before we see her on the stairs. The scene can be seen, in the final instance, as potentially an exteriorisation of Mrs Chan's own state of unrest in the taxi, as an 'actual' occurrence that the film presents in a way that concentrates and amplifies what she is feeling on entering the hotel, *and* as Chow's fantasy of what she is doing and feeling as he waits for her.

Yet things get even more complex if we accept the view that the entire film might potentially be read as Chow's remembrances from an undisclosed point in the future, like the film's quasi-sequel, *2046* (Wong Kar-wai, Hong Kong, 2004). The 'hesitation sequence' would then be an affectively charged recollection of what he was thinking and feeling as he waited for Mrs Chow, perhaps coloured or altered by what then actually took place. Even though the film elides her visit, transferring us directly from Chow waiting to Mrs Chan leaving, it does not suggest that it has screened us from anything momentous, contrary to Betz's assertion that the visit remains an 'unsaid mystery' (Betz 2010: 42). At the door, maintaining her formal if friendly deportment, Mrs Chan reiterates that they 'will not be like them', the adulterous spouses, freely acting upon personal desire. The event is the waiting, the indecisiveness, the 'could-be'. This would seem to be in line with Chow's recollection of the relationship in the future (and in *2046*), where he is uncertain still of what Mrs Chan felt for him, of what actually took place between them. What maintains an aura of unsaid mystery is the clatter of the heels, real and unreal, potentially both his and her fantasy, potentially both of these within his memory – not the fact that we are not shown what happens in Room 2046 on this occasion.

It has often been remarked that the film seems to evoke the workings of memory stylistically. As Paul Arthur contended, in a review upon the film's initial release, 'although never explicitly bracketed as someone's remembered images, the story emanates as if from the coils of a dream or a trance-state' (Arthur 2001:40). There is not space here to give a detailed account to support this perspective, but we can think of a number of formal tactics that suggest the workings of memory. There are the slow-motion sequences conjoined to music (above all 'Yumeji's Theme'), suffused with nostalgia or longing, as well as numerous images captured in mirrors and from behind objects, walls and gauzy curtains that obstruct vision and make our access to the story seem mediated by a consciousness. Then there are the moments perhaps most suggestive of the film as a collage of memories. There is, first of all, the strange fact that images of the couple in Room 2046 appear about fifteen minutes of film time before Chow rents the room. The other important case here is the repetition of the moment of farewell that the two act out in preparation for Chow's departure to Singapore. We see twice, in slow motion, the moment at which he unclasps his hand from hers and walks away. The second time, it is as if the incident has been played back as a particularly resonant memory, often returned to.

Taking into account the use of formal tactics that suggest the workings of memory, I want to finish by arguing that we also have good (enough) reason to puzzle over the status of one last scene that foregrounds footwear. It is perfectly plausible, that is, to see Mrs Chan's retrieval of her never-returned slippers from Chow's room in Singapore as entirely a product of Chow's imagination.

Slippers in Singapore

According to what we see, Mrs Chan shows up in Singapore after Chow has moved there, visits his room while he is at work, smokes one of his cigarettes and lingers wearing the worn pink slippers she has discovered there. Eventually, she calls him at work but does not speak and then, from beneath the bed – in an image that recalls her earlier exit from Chow's room in his wife's heels – we glimpse her hand as she leans down to pick up the slippers before leaving. The motion of her hand halts before the slippers are grasped though, leaving the outcome of the action momentarily in doubt (figure 15.2). This image, like its double, juxtaposes the heels worn by Mrs Chan to the slippers. This time, however, the woven-toed pumps she wears seem to suggest a relaxation of the rigid boundaries of her identity (as she imagines it) earlier in the film. This time, too, the toes face in the same direction, creating no stark sense of opposition between the varied identities she harbours, inhabits and performs.

Figure 15.2 Mrs Chan's woven-toed pumps suggest a relaxation of the rigid boundaries of her identity

Is Mrs Chan, we might ask on the basis of comparing the two images, more prepared now for a break with convention?

In any case, these slippers are of course the same that she had left in Chow's room earlier in the film, and this is the moment at which we – as well as Mrs Chan, it seems – learn that he has held on to them since the night she was forced to stay in his room overnight. However, we learn that he has lost something before we see her there and before we know exactly what he is looking for. The film presents him searching his room frantically, agitatedly questioning the manager of the hotel he lives in as to whether someone has been in his room. The manager insists no one has been there, although just moments before, at the beginning of this sequence, we see this same manager answer the phone and tell someone that Chow is at work. This call and a lipstick-smeared cigarette butt left in the ashtray are the major clues that seem to signal that Mrs Chan's visit to his room, which we then see – after an interlude where Chow eats with his friend Ah Ping (Siu Ping-Lam) – is the real story behind the disappearance of the slippers. But this ordering – showing the absence of the slippers and then the story of her visit – already suggests the possibility that this account of what took place has been constructed after the fact.

The setting of Chow's room, with its subaquatic hues and oneiric lighting, meshes well with a view that would see this scene as taking place in some kind of mental space. An image of Mrs Chan lounging in a wooden chair beside Chow's bed, the slippers dangling on her feet as she flexes her toes, in particular seems like a fantasy image. Shot from behind some sort of obstruction, both the top and bottom of the frame are blurred; in combination with minimal available lighting, this makes the image of Mrs Chan seem distant and on the point of dissolution. Given the indiscernible boundary already established between some objective situations and subjective events (like the 'hesitation' sequence and the scene of Room 2046 before Chow checks into it), it is plausible to see the style of this 'explanation scene' as suggesting it takes place in a future Chow's mind. However, the repetition of the slippers glimpsed from the same angle between two different beds is perhaps the most forceful visual evocation of the workings of memory – in this case, its power to 're-image' particular events to tie them together in ways that load them with latent meaning. This seems, at any rate, a more compelling explanation of this repetition than the argument that it is simply reflective of the 'aesthetic vision' of Wong, his attraction to images that repeat earlier ones, with a slight difference.

Still, there are potentially other objections to this reading. The cigarette could be taken, for instance, as putting it into question, but it could equally well be seen as the source of the fantasy. The discovery of the cigarette leads Chow to the imagined vision of the one who could have – who Chow would most like to have – smoked it. The alternatives to seeing this scene as imagined also seem somewhat questionable. Is it not, for instance, stranger that Mrs Chan should find the will to travel all the way to Singapore and then give up her mission of reuniting with Chow? Is there anything else in the film to suggest she is capable of this sort of behaviour? The hesitation sequence suggests a similar sort of conflict within Mrs Chan that might be linked to this later moment of indecision, but my point isn't that the film *ought* to be read in this way, as conveying that Mrs Chan's visit to Singapore *is* imagined. On the contrary, that it can be read as imagined, but not definitively, creates an experience of potentially losing hold on reality by fixating on details within it. And this experience is, in my estimation, crucial to conceiving the powers of *In the Mood for Love* to inspire reflection on the world depicted within it, the place and time of its production and the philosophical preoccupations of its director: time, ephemerality, chance and memory.

Conclusion

Some objects, settings and music in *In the Mood for Love* can to an extent be read in terms of modernising and globalising processes, such as the Western dress of the men, the restaurant, the gifts from Japan and the Spanish-language Nat King Cole songs (apparently popular with the sizeable Filipino population living then, as now, in Hong Kong). However, many films throughout the course of the medium's history have focused on objects and settings to reference changes being wrought in the real world, and it has been argued that such practices were already prevalent and decisive in East Asia by the late 1920s.[4] While the slippers and heels do not align with tradition and modernity, or the local and the foreign, they do seem to suggest a distinction between the social and the personal self, or performance and authenticity. The solidity of the latter distinction is, however, put into question by the function and effects of play acting in the film, which despite being 'unreal' produces 'real' effects – the tears and anger of Mrs Chan and feelings of affection between the two characters. From this perspective, the chance for a more grounded break with tradition lies not in authenticity, in that reserve of personality I associated earlier with the quotidian intimacy of the slippers, but in trying out new roles without being able to predict the outcome. The disorientation that can be read from – and experienced through – the 'hesitation sequence' and the scene supposedly explaining the disappearance of the slippers is closely related to this experience of needing to act without fully grasping a situation, such that the appropriate response would become evident. This is the case insofar as spectators feel pressed to interpret events in order to identify the nature of a situation without being granted a space 'outside' of the film from which to decisively evaluate their conclusions. We experience a disorientation that might be read as symptomatic in various ways.

However, what exactly this experience is symptomatic of is a conundrum facing those who attempt to address the social and political valences of Wong Kar-wai's 1960s films, as is clear from some of the most astute commentary on the films. Is the disorientation they explore and provoke symptomatic, as Bettinson (2015) has argued, of the crisis of Hong Kong in the film, of a Shanghainese enclave in a colonial hub where the dominance of a Confucian ethic is giving way as new foreign customs, beliefs, artworks and technologies breach the already precarious sense of identity within this diasporic community? Or is it, as Ackbar Abbas and others who have followed his lead have argued, primarily indicative of social disturbance in turn-of-the-century Hong Kong, of political transformations (the 1997 reversion of Hong Kong to Chinese rule), intensified globalisation and 'technologies that increase the speed of reproduction and information', which together produce a sense of 'proximity without reciprocity' (Abbas 2013: 187)[5]? Or, lastly, is the instability conveyed by the film attributable, above all, to Wong's philosophical 'worldview'? Is it, as Rey Chow contends, 'an index of the capricious (that is impermanent) nature of the human universe' (Chow 2007: 77)?

There is a good deal of merit to each of these propositions, but one problem with Rey Chow's argument, however astute her diagnosis of the predicament encountered by interpreters of the film, is that she holds on to the logic of the excluded middle. The film is about the everyday in early 1960s Hong Kong, or the attention to detail is just artifice that allows for Wong's self-expression, his assertion of ephemerality and loss as characteristic of the nature of both human life and the universe itself. In a Deleuzian spirit,[6] I would advocate rather the linking of the various reading options outlined above by the AND, and emphasise the way in which the potential, or virtuality, retained by the film allows for different spectators to read it in varied ways in relation to their own diverse experiences of social dislocation, or their own habits of negotiating fate, existential choice and the events of history.

Ultimately, footwear in *In the Mood for Love* functions both as expressive of the conflict between desire and decorum experienced by Mrs Chan and, in the case of the slippers, as an emblem of a relationship that never quite materialises, unable as the characters are to chart a 'hybrid' course between repressive traditions and modern identities that seem to undo such repression only at the cost of a radical break with (or prolonged absence from, in the spouses' case) one's community. But homing in on footwear also reveals how unstable our grasp of the challenges posed by the film to spectatorial orientation is. The more we notice, the more uncertain we may become about what items of clothing or other objects might lead us to question anew what actually takes place in the reality of the diegetic world, and what has been imagined or remembered differently by Chow. 'If you pay attention, you notice things,' Mrs Chan tells her boss early in the film, and *In the Mood for Love* provides a particularly resonant example of how this adage might pay off if applied to the investigation of footwear in film.

Notes

1. The *cheongsam*, also commonly known as the *qipao*, is a form-fitting dress with tradition-ally Chinese features. It appeared originally in the 1920s, adapted from men's garments that women had begun wearing to reflect 'their desire for equal rights and respect for their individuality'. *Cheongsams* served as symbols of Chinese Nationalism in the 1920s and 1930s, but, according to Wessie Ling, also offered, through subtle stylistic variations, a site of 'women's resistance to the Nationalist agenda for their bodies and appearance' by 'challenging dominant Western aesthetic standards' (Ling 2012: 83–4). It is worth keeping this history in mind when thinking about them as a figure of both constraint and expres-siveness, as for instance Bruno (2010) has.
2. High heels are mentioned a number of times, for instance in Ling 2012.
3. I have taken this term from David Bordwell's consideration of the work of Hou Hsiao-hsien in *Figures Traced in Light* (2005).
4. See for instance Miriam Hansen (2010) and Mitsuyo Wada-Marciano (2008), particularly Chapter One, 'The Creation of Modern Space'.
5. 'Proximity without reciprocity' for Abbas designates 'how we can be physically close to a situation or person without there being intimacy or knowledge.' He contends that Wong

more than any other Hong Kong filmmaker conveys a sense of the period after 1997, when Hong Kong reverted to Chinese control, as defined by this experience, which is referenced to 'some elusive and ambivalent cultural space that lies always just beyond our grasp, or just beneath our articulations' (Abbas 2013: 187).

6. In relation to cinema, the main points Deleuze makes about the powers of a logic of the included middle, predicated on the AND, can be found in the last section of Chapter Seven of *The Time-Image* (2005), 'Thought and Cinema', which elaborate on strategies of free indirect discourse in the films of Jean-Luc Godard, and how they counter a cinema (and philosophy) grounded in the formula 'Being=Is'.

References

Abbas, Ackbar (2013), 'The Erotics of Disappointment', in C. Berry (ed.), *Chinese Cinema: Critical Concepts in Media and Cultural Studies*, vol. 4, London: Routledge, pp. 216–32.

Arthur, Paul (2001), 'Review of *In the Mood for Love*', *Cinéaste*, vol. 26, no. 3, pp. 40–1.

Bettinson, Gary (2015), *The Sensuous Cinema of Wong Kar-wai: Film Poetics and the Aesthetics of Disturbance*, Hong Kong: Hong Kong University Press.

Betz, Mark (2010), 'Beyond Europe: On Parametric Transcendence', in R. Galt and K. Schoonover (eds), *Global Art Cinema: New Theories and Histories*, Oxford: Oxford University Press, pp. 32–47.

Bordwell, David (2005), *Figures Traced in Light: On Cinematic Staging*, Berkeley: University of California Press.

Bruno, Giuliana (2010), 'Pleats of Matter, Folds of the Soul', in D. N. Rodowick (ed.), *Afterimages of Gilles Deleuze's Film Philosophy*, Minneapolis: University of Minnesota Press, pp. 213–33.

Chow, Rey (2007), *Sentimental Fabulations, Contemporary Chinese Films: Attachment in the Age of Global Visibility*, New York: Columbia University Press.

Deleuze, Gilles (2005), *Cinema 2: The Time Image*, trans. H. Tomlinson and R. Galeta, London: Continuum.

Hansen, Miriam (2010), 'Vernacular Modernism: Tracking Cinema on a Global Scale', in N. Ďurovičová and K. Newman (eds), *World Cinemas, Transnational Perspectives*, New York: Routledge, pp. 287–314.

Ling, Wessie (2012), 'Chinese Modernity, Identity, and Nationalism: The Qipao in Republican China', in J. L. Foltyn, *Fashions: Exploring Fashion Through Culture*, Oxford: Inter-Disciplinary Press, pp. 83–93.

Wada-Marciano, Mitsuyo (2008), *Nippon Modern: Japanese Cinema of the 1920s and 1930s*, Honolulu: University of Hawai'i Press.

Chapter 16

Sex, corruption and killer heels: footwear in the Korean corporate crime drama

Kate Taylor-Jones

Whilst crime film has always been a dominant genre in Korean cinema, in the last decade the corporate crime film has been notable for bringing high-end visuals, star casts and a more political slant to the usual tales of murder and revenge. Key examples include *Inside Men* (Woo Min-ho, 2015), *The Taste of Money* (Im Sang-soo, 2012), *Intimate Enemies* (Im Sang-soo, 2015) and *Whistle-Blower* (Yim Soon-rye, 2014) and the films have seen box office and, in some cases, critical success with South Korean audiences and beyond. Focusing on a key example from this canon, Im Sang-soo's *The Taste of Money*, this chapter explores the interplay between gender, corporate corruption, age, nationhood and footwear.

Set in the luxury home of a fictionalised wealthy family, *The Taste of Money* follows the sexual, political and financial machinations of company president Yoon (Baek Yoon-sik), his wife Baek Geum-ok (Youn Yuh-jung) and their adult children Nami (Kim Hyo-jin) and Chul (On Joo-wan). Seen through the eyes of a lowly assistant Joo Young-jak (Kim Kang-woo) who aspires to the lifestyle of his employer, *The Taste of Money* offers an erotic but highly political exploration of the role that power and privilege play in contemporary South Korea.

Focusing primarily on the female characters via an examination of their footwear, this chapter will illustrate how *The Taste of Money* and another linked film, *The Housemaid* (Im Sang-soo 2010), utilises women as the site of both corporate greed and the potential site of its undoing. This chapter is based around three key elements. Firstly, I will discuss the role that footwear plays in constructing female sexuality on the screen. I will explore both how female sexuality is articulated and presented on the screen and how fashion is utilised as a marker of age, social standing and sexual availability. Secondly, this chapter will debate how *The Taste of Money* references South Korea's role in the global economy with the interplay between the Baek family and their Filipina maid, Eva (Maui Taylor), who becomes Yoon's lover and is eventually murdered on Geum-ok's orders. The South Korean economy has grown exponentially since the 1980s and it is now a common destination for Southeast Asian women and men seeking work, sometimes with tragic outcomes as this film melodramatically renders. Finally, this chapter will conclude with a consideration of how, via their footwear, all the women are potentially coded as both the site of corporate corruption and the means by which it may be undone.

The reason for the choice of *The Taste of Money* needs a short explanation. *The Taste of Money* is not Im's best film or indeed even the most successful example of the corporate crime drama. However, the corporate crime films are not notable for a focus on women. They are, for the most part, heavily male-dominated with women playing very limited or stereotypical roles. In contrast, with the heavily female-dominated cast and narrative, *The Taste of Money* opens up a relationship between the female characters' footwear and their social and cultural position. Whilst the male characters in these films sport the obligatory plain shoes (or, on rare occasion, trainers), which the camera glides over, female footwear is both more varied and is often the focal point of the shot. A good example in *Taste of Money* is when Young-jak first meets Na-mi as she putting on a pair of strappy designer shoes or when we first meet Eva as she totters by on her high heels carrying bottles of champagne.

South Korea, like most nations, has a long and complex national economic history that is, rather unsurprisingly, heavily intertwined with political, cultural and social changes. I will chart this history here in very broad strokes to give some background to this article but encourage those interested to explore some more detailed works (Oh 1999; Eichengreen et al. 2015; Chiang 2007). The destruction of the Korean War meant that South Korea was one of the poorest countries in the world in the decade following the armistice of 1953. The enforced rapid modernisation of the 1970s and 1980s, under the Fourth and Fifth Republics, saw South Korea enter a period of financial prosperity based on export-led manufacturing. Government control *pace* Michel Foucault was also demonstrated as the economic development took place alongside a dramatic decline in personal freedom, civil rights and political repression (Nilsson and Wallenstein 2013; Glenn 2018; Inda 2008). This decline would culminate in the Gwangju massacre in 1980 when government troops fired on pro-democracy demonstrators. The transition to democracy in the late 1980s and early 1990s saw the Korean economy develop rapidly and in 1996, South Korea became a member of the Organisation of Economic Cooperation and Development

(OECD), indicating that it was one of the thirty highly developed nations of the world. However, the 1997 financial crisis saw the South Korean state requiring an IMF bailout. Despite this setback, the South Korean economy dramatically bounced back with unprecedented growth between 1999 and 2000 and post-IMF South Korea is currently a nation that operates one of the most concentrated forms of free market capitalism and, as a result, contains one of the most stratified class systems (Wagner 2016).

Key in the development of a modern and indeed postmodern neo-liberal South Korea is the *chaebŏl*. Since the 1960s South Korean governments have chosen to work closely with selected businesses to achieve their economic goals; these businesses were or developed into large family-owned conglomerates, commonly known as *chaebŏls*. From initial manufacturing, most quickly diversified into multiple areas of the economy, including transport, media and electronics. The *chaebŏls* that flourished, first under the military push for development and then later those who survived the 1997 financial crisis, are now, in many ways, unassailable in their position. A series of high profile cases in the 1990s and 2000s, including the jailings of former presidents Lee Myung-bak and Park Geun-hye for corruption and the revilement of extreme narratives of entitlement (such as Cho Hyun-ah, who grounded a Korean Air flight over her desire for nuts on a plate rather than in a bag[1]), meant that public criticism turned towards the *chaebŏls*. As a result, a series of attempts have been made to both control and reform the political and financial elite, but in reality the status quo has not significantly changed. There are still unprecedented levels of wealth and political influence in the hands of a few private individuals leading to a dramatic poverty gap. A 2016 report by the International Monetary Fund (IMF) states that income inequality in Korea is the worst in the Asia-Pacific region[2]. In South Korea, the most negatively affected have tended to be the elderly lower class or anyone who does not have a family support network (Hwang 2016). The rise of the corporate crime drama has therefore found resonance with wider cultural debate.

The Taste of Money is the seventh feature film by Im Sang-soo, one of the most high-profile directors working in Korean cinema today. His films are usually imbued with sex and violence and take an often critical slant on contemporary South Korean culture. *The Taste of Money* is intricately intertwined with two other films, Kim Ki-young's famous 1960 film *The Housemaid* and Im's own remake with the same name released in 2010. Both these films engage with ideas of class, consumption and inequality. The original 1960 film focused on the experiences of a middle-class writer whose relationship with a maid takes a dark and disturbing turn and Im's 2010 adaptation moved the tale of lust and betrayal into the upper-class

Korean uber-wealthy elite. The basic story of the 2012 film, echoing the 1960 version, involves a maid, Eun-yi, who is first seduced by the husband and then attacked, poisoned and eventually forced into an abortion by the wife and her mother. The film ends as Eun-yi immolates herself as the family, including the small daughter Na-mi, watch in horror.

In *The Taste of Money* both the original and the remake of *The Housemaid* are screened in the private cinema the family have in their house. Cast-wise the films have several other links. Both films share one of the most notable and long-standing actresses in South Korea, Youn Yuh-jung (Geum-Ok in *The Taste of Money*), as one of the main leads. In the case of *The Housemaid*, Youn is the emotionally complex housekeeper Mrs Cho, who despises the family for whom she has worked for more than twenty years. Character actress Hwang Jeong-min also appears in both films – in *The Housemaid* as Eun-yi's best friend and then later, in *The Taste of Money*, as the wheelchair-bound patriarch's personal assistant.

The linkage between film and genre as a critique of the social agenda is something that has been seen in various global and national settings. In the South Korean context, melodramas throughout the 1960s to 1980s sought to present the debate on the role that women were playing in the process of modernity (Abelman and McHugh 2005). Exploring the 1990s, Chi-yun Shin posits a clear link between the gangster film genre and the IMF crisis, suggesting that 1990s Korean gangster films operated as a means via which disenfranchised Korean men could, vicariously, regain a sense of empowered entitlement that had been removed by the economic crash (Shin 2005: 123). In a similar approach, Keith B. Wagner (2016) and Graeme Gillespie (2016) have both written on the contemporary Korean crime film as a response to the post-IMF neo-liberalism.

So where does fashion, and specifically footwear, come into this debate? South Korean citizens spend a vast amount of money on fashion, make-up and, increasingly, plastic surgery. Body image and self-esteem are hot topics in South Korea as the nation contemplates the number of young men and women taking drastic measures to achieve the 'ideal image' (Park and Choi 2008; Lee and Park 2013). Female idol bands such as Red Velvet, Mamamoo, GFriend and Girls Generation are defined by youth, slimness, pale skin, flowing hair and the wearing of branded clothing. In terms of footwear, South Korean brands such as Suecomma Bonnie, Reike Nen and Yuul Yie have gained international distribution and recognition alongside Western designer brands that continue to hold a large market share in South Korea.

This background of class stratification and consumerism is strongly addressed in *The Taste of Money* and *The Housemaid*. Naomi Wolf makes the observation that 'the beauty myth is always actually prescribing behaviour' under the pretext of prescribing mere 'appearance' (Wolf 1992: 14). This idea is heavily referenced in *The Taste of Money* via the clear physical demarcating that clothing provides in the household. The men, both the family and their workers, wear a variety of suits. All the women wear heels, including the various maids and assistants who are present in the family home. The maids all wear a stereotypical black maids' uniform with a white apron, whilst the female assistants (we are uncertain of their jobs but they are always present) sport black skirt suits. All the employed women wear black, closed-toed high heel shoes. This is also the case in *The Housemaid*, where Eun-yi is given her uniform and told she must never be seen without it. The women of both families have access to a much wider range of shoe types. In *The Housemaid*, the wife and mistress of the household Hae-rae wears towering heels and tight-fitting clothing despite her advanced pregnancy with twins as she seeks to spark desire in her ever-straying husband. Na-mi in *The Taste of Money* favours high-heeled strappy sandals traditionally associated with designers such as Jimmy Choo, Christian Louboutin and Manolo Blahnik. These types of shoe, made popular in American television shows such as *Sex in the City* and promoted by the South Korean focus on designer goods, represent Na-mi's high-end fashion style and access to expensive global designer goods.

Figure 16.1 Na-mi's strappy designer footwear contrasts with the basic black stilettos the maids wear

As Bartky Lee notes 'in the regime of institutionalized hetero[patriarchal] sexuality woman must make herself "object and prey" for the man' (Bartky Lee 2003: 34). This is all too clearly the case in Im's film. High heels, together with the boundaries and ethics of social class, both passivise and limit the women (and men in the case of Young-jak), leading to a disempowered and, key for the neo-liberal agenda, controlled body. Morris et al. (2013), Smith (1999), Guéguen (2011, 2015) and Smith and Helm (1999) all report that high heels increase women's sexual attractiveness to men and the work of Guéguen and Stephan (2015) report that high heels increase the likelihood of men approaching women in a variety of settings. The fact that the maids are instructed to wear high heels speaks volumes about their perceived roles. The less-affluent employees in the film are utilised as disposable bodies for the richer employer's desires. Yoon has had a series of affairs with staff; Eva is his latest conquest. Chul and his friends (and, implied in the past, his father) are regular users of sex workers and we learn that Geum-ok has also abused a series of younger male employees. At one point Young-jak goes to collect Yoon where he has been partying with shady American businessman Robert Altman.[3] As Young-jak goes to depart (after placing a camera on Geum-ok's order to later blackmail Robert with) one of the scantily-clad women asks him if 'he wants to party'. In response Young-jak replies that he is not senior enough in the company to have sex with her. Class and money are therefore directly linked to the ability to have sex and, alongside this, to control others in their sexual activities. The evening that Young-jak tells the woman he is not able to have sex with her, he himself is raped by Geum-ok. As she notes, she is his boss and it is his job to obey her in all activities. At the film's end, the dying Yoon notes that his wife has maintained her position for so long by providing her ageing father with attractive younger women to abuse. We learn that in the past another of Yoon's conquests, Na-mi's nursemaid, died under mysterious and tragic circumstances. In another nod to the *The Housemaid*'s tragic ending, Na-mi is the only family member to show some sympathy for those they abuse when she comments, 'remember the maid that burned her mother? We shouldn't treat people like that.'

Comaroff and Comaroff note that in the neo-liberal present, 'the poor are no longer at the gates; bosses live in enclaved communities a world away, beyond political or legal reach (2001:13), and this certainly runs true in Im's film worlds. In both *The Housemaid* and *The Taste of Money* domestic spaces and the working world are intertwined and removed from the mainstream hustle and bustle of life. In *The Housemaid* the family home is a vast luxury mansion, kilometres from the city; in *The Taste of Money* both business and pleasure are conducted on the vast secluded opulent family estate. The family make business deals in a series of liminal spaces: the bedroom, a car park and at an elite massage parlour. We only see Yoon, and then later Young-jak, approach the formal site of the company business, a high-end tower block, to remove large sums of cash from a locked vault.

Even the shared spaces of the house are not coded as either relaxed or informal, and footwear is a dominant marker of the occupants inside it. The maids must always wear their formal shoes despite having to do a number of physical activities – in the case of *The Housemaid* Eun-yi chases after the child, washes clothes, serves meals and cleans, all in shoes clearly unsuitable for the task. When Young-jak first sees Na-mi she is putting on heeled shoes to attend a family dinner party. In both films, a lack of shoes is rare and implies both sexual activity and a private space as opposed to public space. The characters only remove their shoes in a space that can be designated as private – a bedroom or a bathroom. In *The Housemaid*, Eun-yi removes her shoes to clean the bathroom and it is whilst she is crouched over the bath that she first becomes aware of the husband's desirous glances. Later, once she is pregnant and slowly being poisoned by the family, she luxuriates in the bath herself. This visual statement of equality with Hae-rae (the wife), who had previously been seen in the bath, is quickly ended when she begins to bleed from the drugs Hae-rae has been secretly feeding her. Her bare feet, removed from her work shoes, are a symbol of the merging of the business and the personal and she will pay a heavy price for it.

In *The Taste of Money* Geum-ok is only shown barefooted in her bedroom. The only time we see her in the main house shoeless is when she has left her room in anger after seeing Yoon cavorting with Eva on a video camera (more on that later). Her bare feet in this context operate as a sign of her emotional upset and are in direct contrast to her usual controlled matter. In short, a lack of shoes symbolises a lack of control. However, in Geum-ok's case, unlike Eun-yi, she has the power to secure her revenge. Therefore, clothing in this context is both a marker of repression and potential empowerment. For those in power, their ability to control and enforce what those below them do is a key marker of their class status and is represented by the freedom they have to choose their own clothing and to adapt their footwear to better suit their needs. For those below them, their bodies are bounded and controlled by those who employ them. The servants live on the property with their employees with their uniforms operating as an endless reminder that they are accessible night and day to the whims of others.

The process of liberal feminism that many scholars (Fraser 2009; Negra 2009; Scharff 2016) have written about in the Western context has resonance in South Korea, where individualistic success and self-transformation are found in countless narratives promoted to women. Films such as *200 Pounds Beauty* (2006) and *Project Makeover* (2007), and TV shows such as *Let Me*

In, emphasise the need for women to work at their physical appearance as a means to improve their social and cultural value (Elfving-Hwang 2013). In South Korea this narrative also resides inside a space where a focus on family values and traditional gender roles continues alongside a popular misapprehension that the structural inequalities that women face have been removed (Kim 2018: 808), which is also combined with an open cultural misogyny that many women experience on a daily basis (Chung 2016). In 2010, the Global Gender Gap Report ranked South Korea 104th in gender equality among 134 countries surveyed (Haussmann, Tyson and Zahidi 2010: 9), and whilst some improvements have been made since then there are still many issues facing women. We are therefore in the territory of what Rosalind Gill calls 'post-feminist sensibility' (Gill 2008: 440–1), where the combination of post-feminism and neo-liberalism produce female subjects who are required 'to work on and transform the self, to regulate every aspect of their conduct, and to present all their actions as freely chosen' (Ibid.: 443).

Women are therefore trapped between the neo-liberal agenda of defining the self and the desire/need to maintain a more traditional female narrative. In her 2002 work anthropologist Haejeong Cho defined the new societal ideal of South Korean femininity, and allied power and status, as one no longer based on wife/motherhood (as it had been for generations prior), but instead on youth and attractiveness. She states that 'only young and attractive girls can have power so women find new ways to be powerful' (Cho 2002: 185) – in short, power was directly linked to attractiveness and hence, reading her argument some twenty years later, the rise in surgery and other allied acts of self-care and improvement continues in the name of empowerment. Jong-mi Kim (2011) describes this experience as the 'Missy syndrome', where older women engage in an endless search for youth and desirability (with suitable fashionable footwear as an important marker) as a means to maintaining some form of social status and standing and, in short, power.

The double standard of gendered ageing is unquestioned in *The Taste of Money*. Yoon's relationship with a much younger woman (we learn there is about a thirty-year age gap) is seen as almost natural, whilst Geum-ok's desire for sex is seen as simultaneously both ridiculous and offensive. The sequence when she forces Young-jak to have sex is constructed as humiliating for both, albeit in different ways. Traditional ideas about passive women and aggressive men are turned on their head as Geum-ok strips Young-jak and rubs herself against him. Scholars have noted that high heels help to put in place sexually gendered binaries by reinforcing a 'sex object role' for women on the one hand and the so-called 'sexual actor role' for men on the other (Graff, Murnen and Smolak, 2012: 773), however, in *The Taste of Money*, shoes represent both the object and actor. Geum-ok keeps her heels on for much of the encounter and

Young-jak is objectified as she continues to remove his clothing and kiss and touch him despite his protests. Her towering designer heels bring her closer to his height and symbolise her status as an affluent and powerful boss. Her ability to coerce him into unwanted sex is allowed due to her social and economic status but ultimately she is left humiliated by the encounter. When the wider family find out, she is ridiculed and it is this act that finally drives Na-mi away. Therefore, the boundaries of female desirability and power remain undisturbed as it is implied that the only way an older woman can gain sexual satisfaction is via coercion and abuse. Embracing a vision of the older woman as a sexual subject in her own right who could spark consensual sexual relations with a younger man would seem impossible in this background that insists on the desirability of youth. Her heels simultaneously act as a sign of her power and her powerlessness. She demonstrates many of the tropes of desirability (she is slim, wears close-fitting clothing and expensive designer heels) but her age means they are rendered abject in the moment of her attempt to assert her sexual self.

After the assault Young-jak tries to resign but is convinced by Geum-ok to stay on via a promise she will not assault him again and they will pretend it never happened. However, Young-jak is still beholden to her and she then entrusts him to act as her spy. Geum-ok reveals she has wired up her whole house to a hidden room in her bedroom. From here she can see all the activities taking place in the household. This local panopticon of surveillance, and therefore control, means that Geum-ok is able to maintain her position inside the family business. Is it perhaps no surprise that the hidden room is found in her wardrobe. Her shoes and clothing in this respect operate as they do on her body – as the outer layer – the symbolic indicators of her power and position that allow her to control and manipulate the bodies under her. When Eva's body is discovered in the pool, Geum-ok is seated in the lifeguard's chair, wearing her dress and heels. Her outfit may be incongruous as the naked body of Eva floats under her but it serves as another visual marker of her power. She may no longer have the power of youth on her side, but her economic weight means that she still has the power of life and death over those literally beneath her.

So what about Eva? Eva is both one of the more interesting characters in the film and, arguably, one of the least developed. She resides in South Korea but speaks English not Korean. A divorced woman herself, she is unrepentantly having an affair with a married man and yet we see her sobbing in the local Filipino Catholic church over her situation. She is a devoted mother who makes the tragic choice to remain in South Korea with her lover rather than return to the Philippines with her children when Yoon's passport is cancelled by Geum-ok.

The Taste of Money directly references a cultural and economic trend that has taken place in South Korea in the last couple of decades. The influx of cheap Southeast Asian labour, notably from the Philippines, has resulted in a group that resides in a precarious situation in South Korea. South Korea operates almost in a nod to Lauren Berlant's ideas in *Cruel Optimism* (2011). A site of potential development, success and economic freedom, the results are frequently negative for Filipino residents that relocate to the nation (Lee 2006: 160). Films such as *The Bacchus Lady* (Je-Yong Lee, 2016), *Punch* (Han Lee, 2011), *He's on Duty* (Sang-Hyo Yook, 2010) *Sea Fog* (Sung-bo Shim, 2014) and *Bandhobi* (Dong-il Shin, 2009) all reference the precarious position that immigrants to South Korea, specifically women, can find themselves in. Eva is no exception in this respect. She may work in a wealthy household, and Yoon may be open in his declaration of love and fidelity towards her, but she is also financially dependent on him for her family's welfare. We learn she was previously married to an abusive man and has left her children in care back in Manila. She, as millions of workers do globally, sends her money back home and hopes to return and live a successful life in her home nation.

Na-mi and Eva are friends who bond over being separated from their children (Na-mi's live with her ex-husband) and previous abusive marital relationships but Na-mi has social and consumer capital that Eva, as a poor female immigrant, lacks. Whilst Na-mi is able to control, to an extent, the world around her, Eva is unable to find even a physical space that she can control. When Young-jak first sees them together, Yoon is taking photos of her as she undresses for him (leaving only her work shoes on, a further visual reminder of her status in the household). Young-jak watches for some time before Eva spots him and it is only then he removes himself from the room. Her privacy is violated first by Young-jak and later by Geum-ok when she spies on the couple using a hidden camera in Yoon's office. When Eva collects her children from the airport, Young-jak is watching from above in the airport arrivals lounge. Eva goes to church, the site of a supposed sanctuary, but even here she is followed and spied upon by Young-jak and Baek family minions.

Eva is always situated as 'at risk'. When Geum-ok finds out about the affair she grabs Eva by the neck. Tottering on the shoes she is forced to wear for work, Eva is unable to fight back as Geum-ok pins her against the wall in rage (Figure 16.2). Yoon is even in the same room as his lover and estranged wife but is apparently unable to see or hear the assault taking place. Eva is later dragged off the street and brutally murdered on Geum-ok's and her father's orders. Eva may try to assert herself as an equal and independent woman but she is unable to escape the codes that define her as both poor and female and therefore, in the world of the film, exposed to the whims of the globalised economy and those who most benefit from it.

The last insult to her is offered when she is found half naked in the pool, her breasts exposed as more than a dozen people stand around and stare at her dead body. Eva is both a symbol and a reflection of the treatment of Southeast Asian women in South Korea. She is shown as loving, loyal and kind but at risk due to her sexual activity – in short, a stereotypical image of a migrant woman worker in South Korea (Brooks 2016; Yea 2015). Rather than an empowered subject in her own right, she becomes the sacrificial victim that allows Na-mi and Young-jak a chance at redemption. On her death Young-jak places all the money he has accrued during his time with the family in her casket as a clear indication of his desire to begin a new wholesome life and Na-mi rejects her family and puts in motion a criminal investigation into her grandfather and brother.

The final scene is somewhat bizarre given the tone of the rest of the film but clearly aims to make a much firmer link between the abuse of others and the neo-liberal state that South Korea has wholeheartedly embraced. Na-mi and Young-jak head to Manila to take Eva's body back to her children. The children, understandably upset, ask to see their mother and, as they cry over the casket, the camera shifts to inside the coffin where we see a deathly white Eva scream silently. This is not 'real' inside the film world – Eva is still dead – but it is designed to unsettle the audience as the film ends on Na-mi, Young-jak and the children crying in the rain. In this way *The Taste of Money* avoids a happy ending, as the film seems to tell us that the eternal state of global economic

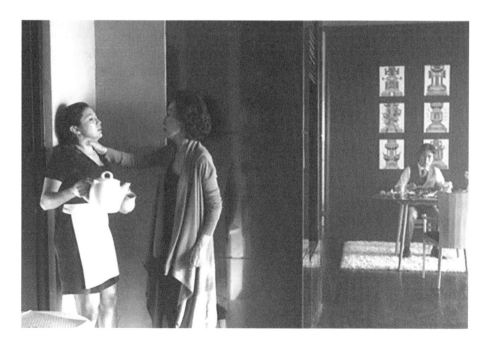

Figure 16.2 Eva is unable to fight back against the vengeful Geum-ok

abuse will continue. There are, we are shown, many more Evas who will travel to South Korea in search of their fortunes.

Conclusion, or not?

With a film such as *The Taste of Money*, a conclusion is hard to reach. As stated above, we have both a narrative of redemption but also a nod to a future, where the story is doomed to repeat itself. Neo-liberalism, as McGuigan notes, is bound up in the articulation and reproduction of a very specific vision of the self, one that combines 'freewheeling consumer sovereignty with enterprising business acumen' (McGuigan 2014). This self, as McGuigan continues, is not unattractive and, as Young-jak is shown by the Baek family, has the ability to control and affect the world around them and will always be an attractive narrative. The family can organise and structure the world according to their own desires – any political or criminal inconvenience is sorted by a payment of money and the bodies of the staff that surround them are endlessly utilised for their sexual and emotional pleasure with, until Eva's death, no repercussions. The other is therefore reduced to a non-entity that holds no long-term or meaningful role in the endless project of the neo-liberal self. The attitude that Geum-ok, Robert and Chun take towards the casual plundering of pension funds to enlarge their own expansive coffers is representative of a lack of concern for the wider social matrix.

The ending of *The Taste of Money* offers a new vision, the self that has also embraced the other as part of an intertwined globalised community. Na-mi and Young-jak come face to face with the reality of the events as they stand in Manila with Eva's children. Yoon is dead, Geum-ok is a broken and repudiated figure, Chun is facing jail and Na-mi has ostensibly walked away from her family and everything that they stand for and has been reunited with Young-jak. She may have worn the shoes of a corporate manager but we are shown that Na-mi no longer desires to conduct her business in the same fashion as her wider family. In this sense, the female figure has become the undoing of the corporate moment. Firstly, via the now dead Eva and her romance and love for Yoon and then later by Na-mi leaving, the Baek family has come to ruin. Women therefore have been potentially coded as both in opposition to neo-liberalism and in alliance with it (Geum-ok).

However, does the film really offer an alternative ending to an endless cycle of economic and social abuse via Na-mi? I wish to end on a discussion of the final sex scene between Na-mi and Young-jak. We see them consummate their relationship in a plane toilet as they fly to Manila to deliver Eva's body to her children. Na-mi gets on the plane without Young-jak's knowledge and manages to secure a seat next to him by offering a woman her first class seat in lieu. They meet, kiss and then have sex in the toilet. The sex scene is strange to watch for a variety of reasons and, in a film riddled with symbolism, worth some analysis. Na-mi wears her high-heeled sandals throughout the whole encounter (perhaps not so strange when engaging in coitus mid-air) but more unusually, when Young-jak tries to remove her underwear she tells him to leave it on and 'twist in from the side'. The refusal to remove her shoes or her underwear means a physical barrier is still there between the employee and his upper-class lover. When they arrive in Manila, Young-jak operates as her translator and driver, roles he had performed before when he worked for her family. She, like her mother before her, controls the relationship and fails to remove the markers of her financially and culturally dominant status. Na-mi, as the ultimate 'missy', is still utilising the power of youth and desirability that the neo-liberal moment has promoted for women – she may be rejecting one aspect of the dynamic but she is still embracing another. Alongside this, the shady Robert walks away from the whole affair untouched and, it is implied, will continue his dubious dealings with other partners.

The Taste of Money directly references a series of social and cultural debates that have taken place inside South Korea in the last decades. The film highlights the sexual, class and ethnic tensions that exist inside the state. Whilst the film's ending may repudiate the status quo, no genuine alternative is offered as a method of escape. A contrite Na-mi may be standing in her heels in the mud of the streets in Manila but in reality, the Southeast Asian female body has become the sacrificial victim to the awakening of her more affluent South Korean neighbours. Unlike the rest of her family, and it is implied the wider South Korean state, Young-jak and Na-mi have been awakened to their roles in the neo-liberal narrative and acknowledge their actions and symbolically apologise to the much-abused Eva and her children. However we are made aware that the discourse of governmental neo-liberalism continues without change. The message conveyed in the inclusion of the two early film versions of *The Housemaid* is therefore clear. The original *Housemaid* may have been set in 1960 but the story of class and gender inequality continues unimpeded.

Notes

1. See https://www.japantimes.co.jp/news/2018/04/22/asia-pacific/korean-air-boss-apologizes-hot-tempered-daughters-immature-behavior-says-will-resign-jobs/#.XBdocK10dPM
2. See https://www.imf.org/external/np/fad/inequality/

3. This characture is rather awkwardly played by film critic Darcy Paquet and the name is indeed a delibarate nod to the American director.

References

Abelman, Kathleen and McHugh, Nancy (2005), *South Korean Golden Age Melodrama*, Detroit: Wayne State University Press.

Bartky Lee, Sandra (2003), 'Foucault, femininity, and the modernization of patriarchal power', in R. Weitz (ed.), *The Politics of Women's Bodies*, Oxford: Oxford University Press, pp. 25–45.

Berlant, Lauren (2011), *Cruel Optimism*, Durham, NC: Duke University Press.

Brooks, Ann (2016), *Gendered Work in Asian Cities: The New Economy and Changing Labour Markets*, London and New York: Routledge.

Chiang, Min-hua (2007), *Contemporary South Korean Economy: Challenges And Prospects*, Hackensack, NJ: World Scientific.

Cho, Haejeong (2002), 'Living with Conflicting Subjectivities: Mother, Motherly Wife, and Sexy Woman in the Transition from Colonial-modern to Postmodern Korea', in L. Kendall (ed.), *Under Construction: The Gendering of Modernity, Class, and Consumption in the Republic of Korea*, Honolulu: University of Hawai'i Press, pp. 165–96.

Chung, In-Kyoung (2016), 'Internet Misogyny in a Post-Feminist Era', *Issues in Feminism*, vol. 16, no. 1, pp. 185–219.

Comaroff, Jean and Comaroff, John (2001), *Millennial Capitalism in the Culture of Neoliberalism*, Durham, NC: Duke University Press, pp. 1–56.

Eichengreen, Barry et al. (2015), *The Korean Economy: From a Miraculous Past to a Sustainable Future*, Cambridge, MA: Harvard University Press.

Elfving-Hwang, Joanna (2013), 'Cosmetic Surgery and Embodying the Moral Self in South Korean Popular Makeover Culture', *The Asia-Pacific Journal*, vol. 11, issue 24, no. 2, 17 June.

Fedorenko, Olga (2015), 'Politics of Sex Appeal in Advertising: Female creatives and post-feminist sensibility in South Korea', *Feminist Media Studies*, vol. 15, no. 3, pp. 474–91.

Fraser, Nancy (2009), 'Feminism, Capitalism and the Cunning of History', *New Left Review*, no. 56, pp. 97–117.

Gill, Rosalind (2008), 'Culture and Subjectivity in Neoliberal and Postfeminist Times', *Subjectivity*, vol. 25, no. 1 (December), pp. 432–45.

Gillespie, Graham (2016), 'Reading the "new world": neoliberalism in the South Korean gangster film', *Journal of Japanese and Korean Cinema*, vol. 8, no. 1, pp. 59–72.

Glenn, John (2018), *Foucault and the Post-Financial Crisis*, London and New York: Palgrave Macmillian.

Graff, Kaitlin, Murnen, Sarah and Smolak, Linda (2012), 'Too sexualised to be taken seriously? Perceptions of a girl in childlike vs. sexualising clothing', *Sex Roles*, vol. 66, nos. 11–12, pp. 764–75.

Guéguen, Nicolas (2015), 'High heels increase women's attractiveness', *Archives of Sex Behaviour*, no. 44, pp. 2227–35.

Guéguen, Nicolas (2011), 'The effect of women's suggestive clothing on men's behavior and judgment: a field study', *Psychological Reports*, no. 109, pp. 635–8.

Guéguen Nicolas and Stefan, Jordy (2015), 'Men's judgment and behavior toward women wearing high heels', *Journal of Human Behaviour in the Social Environment*, vol. 25, no. 5, pp. 416–25.

Haussmann, Ricardo, Tyson, Laura D. and Zahidi, Saadia (2010), The Global Gender Gap Report 2010, Geneva: World Economic Forum, http://www.weforum.org/reports/global-gender-gap-report-2010 (last accessed December 2018).

Hwang, Sun-Jae (2016), 'Public Pensions as the Great Equalizer? Decomposition of Old-Age Income Inequality in South Korea, 1998–2010', Journal of Aging & Social Policy, 2 April.

Inda, Jonathan Xavier (2008), Anthropologies of Modernity: Foucault, Govermentality and Life Politics, Oxford: Blackwell Publishing.

Jung, Jae-hee and Lee, Yoon-jung (2009), 'Cross-cultural examination of women's fashion and beauty magazine advertisements in the United States and South Korea', Clothing and Textiles Research Journal, no. 27, pp. 274–86.

Jung, Jae-hee, and Lennon, Sharron (2003), 'Body image, appearance self-schema, and media images', Family and Consumer Sciences Research Journal, no. 32, pp. 27–51

Kim, Ji-Yeon et al. (2009), 'The effects of body image satisfaction on obesity stress, weight control attitudes, and eating disorders among female junior high school students', Journal of the Korean Home Economics Association, no. 47, pp. 49–59.

Kim, Jinsook (2017), '#iamafeminist as the "mother tag": feminist identification and activism against misogyny on Twitter in South Korea', Feminist Media Studies, vol. 7, no. 5, pp. 804–20.

Kim, Jong-mi (2011), 'Is "the Missy" a New Femininity?', in R. Gill and C. Scharff (eds), New Femininities: Postfeminism, Neoliberalism and Subjectivity, London: Palgrave Macmillan, pp. 147–59.

Kweon, Soo Ae, Yoo, Joung Ja Kim and Kim, Eun Young (2014), 'A comparative study on body shape perception and satisfaction of Korean and Chinese female university students', Korean Journal of Human Ecology, no. 23, pp. 483–500.

Lee, Minwon (2006), 'Invisibility and Temporary Residence Status of Filipino Workers in South Korea', Journal for Cultural Research, vol. 10, no. 2, pp. 159–72.

Lee, Ji Young and Park, Hye-Jung (2013), 'Effects of self-esteem, physical appearance comparison, and media concern on sociocultural attitude toward appearance, body attitudes, and life satisfaction', Journal of the Korea Fashion & Costume Design Association, no. 15, pp. 1–17.

McGuigan, Jim (2014), 'The Neoliberal Self', Culture Unbound, vol. 6, pp. 223–40, http://www.cultureunbound.ep.liu.se (last accessed 11 November 2018).

Morris, Paul et al. (2013), 'High heels as supernormal stimuli: how wearing high heels affects judgments of female attractiveness', Evolutionary and Human Behaviour, no. 34, pp. 176–81.

Negra, Diane (2009), What a Girls Wants?: Fantasising the Reclamation of the Self in Postfeminism, London and New York: Routledge.

Nilsson, Jackob and Wallenstein, Sven-Olov (2012), Foucault, Biopolitics and Govermentality, Stockholm: Södertörn University Press.

Oh, John Kie-Chiang (1999), Korean Politics: The Quest for Democratization and Economic Development, Ithaca: Cornell University Press.

Park, Ji Hyun and Choi, T.-S. (2008), 'The effect of body image on self-esteem in adolescents', Korean Journal of Play Therapy, no. 11, pp. 117–29.

Scharff, Christina (2016), Repudaiating Feminism: Young Women in a Neoliberal World, London and New York: Routledge.

Shin, Chi-yun (2005), 'Two of a Kind: Gender and Friendship in Friend and Take Care of My Cat', in C. Shin and J. Stringer (eds), New Korean Cinema, Edinburgh: Edinburgh University Press, pp. 117–31.

Smith, Euclid (1999), 'High heels and evolution: natural selection, sexual selection and high heels', Psychology, Evolution, Gender, no. 30, pp. 245–77.

Smith, Euclid and Helms, Whitney (1999), 'Natural selection and high heels', *Foot Ankle International*, no. 20, pp. 55–7.

Wagner, Keith B. (2016), 'Endorsing upper-class refinement or critiquing extravagance and debt? The rise of neoliberal genre modification in contemporary South Korean cinema', *Critical Arts*, vol. 30, no. 1, pp. 117–38.

Wolf, Naomi (1992), *The Beauty Myth*, New York: HarperCollins.

Yea, Sallie (2015), *Trafficking Women in Korea: Filipina Migrant Entertainers*, London and New York: Routledge.

Chapter 17

It's gotta be the shoes: Nike in the Spike-o-sphere

Jeff Scheible

Oscar Jordans, Oscar Jordans

On the eve of the 2019 Academy Awards, in which he would go on to win his first non-honorary Oscar, filmmaker Spike Lee uploaded a five-part post to Instagram showing off his new gold 'Oscar Jordans'. The post opens with a thirty-second video that frames Lee waist-up in a medium shot, wearing a black baseball cap, thick-framed black glasses and a black hoodie from his own streetwear line displaying the year 1619 (a reference to the four-hundredth anniversary of the first slaves from Africa being brought to Virginia). Lines of Beverly Hills palm trees dot the background. As he holds the two gold Nikes on both sides of his face, Lee says: 'Shout out to my main man Michael Jordan. Commissioned Tinker Hatfield to design these gold Oscar Jordans. Ooooh, red carpet tomorrow night. Tomorrow night. What up what up.' He steps closer to the camera, swerves the shoes around, slides them back and forth in the air, and shows off the sides and backs as he urges his followers: 'Look at that, look at that. Look at that, look at that. Jordans. Gotta be the shoes. Gotta be the shoes. Oscars Jordans, Oscar Jordans. Oscar Jordans. Thank you Michael, thank you Tinker. Brand Jordan. 40 Acres. What up.' Accompanying this video are four photos revealing the shoes from different angles: lying on a wooden floor on their sides; from behind, soles to the ground; the gold tip of one artfully placed to the right of a black shoebox. The final photo shows Lee holding up both gold Jordans, dressed in layered tee-shirts advertising his upcoming film *Da 5 Bloods* (USA, 2020), which he would commence shooting in Southeast Asia the next month.

Figure 17.1 Mookie with Oscar, in hang time pose

This is only one of a few of Lee's posts featuring the Oscar Jordans. The first content Lee posted the day after actually winning his Academy Award for *BlacKkKlansman*'s screenplay (USA, 2018) is an illustration of himself as the Mookie character he played in *Do the Right Thing* (USA, 1989). Mookie appears in the same 'hang time' pose as the Michael Jordan silhouette featured on Air Jordan shoes, which Mookie also wears in the image himself, staging a playful *mise en abyme*. Rather than the basketball that Jordan holds in the iconic silhouette, Mookie holds an Oscar above his head. In accompanying text, Lee wrote, 'BROOKLYN WINS. BROOKLYN WINS. BROOKLYN WINS. MOOKIE WITH OSCAR.'

Two posts later is a photographic still life in which the gold Oscar sits next to his left foot. Lee holds his fist just above his foot, which is in a gold Jordan. His fist is positioned next to the head of the Oscar, sporting the brass-knuckle LOVE ring famously worn by Radio Raheem in *Do the Right Thing* – becoming something of a symbolic, solemn tribute to black lives lost to racial injustices. Another two Instagram posts further on, we see Samuel L. Jackson holding Lee up in his arms – a photo that went viral after Jackson called Lee to the stage to accept his Oscar for Best Original Screenplay. In the image, Lee wears a purple suit and hat, and his knees are bent with his Jordans suspended behind him in mid-air, reminiscent of the Nikes suspended in mid-air that we see in the iconic silhouette of Jordan in his signature hang time move, seemingly defying gravity.

Spike Lee's habitual use of Instagram opens up a line of inquiry of particular relevance to understanding his unique career and 'brand', formed in the intersections of African American culture, independent cinema, art, commerce and the urban politics of New York City, a cross-section that no other filmmaker occupies in quite the same manner. The series of relations among and allusions within Lee's posts described above offer a glimpse of the ways in which Lee creates what I refer to in my chapter's title as the 'Spike-o-sphere'. The term Spike-o-sphere identifies the extra-cinematic universe in which figures from Lee's movies take on lives beyond film frames and narrative boundaries, distinctions between celebrities, characters and places blur, a recurring set of references and iconography circulate fluidly across media, and wearable merchandise is paramount. In a moment when Hollywood's dominant mode of production entails transmedial storytelling, franchising and the constant remaking and updating of superhero worlds, Spike Lee has, over several decades, steadily created his own dynamic, paracinematic universe that both parallels this logic yet resists some of its core tenets by retaining at its centre the distinct idea of the auteur – precisely what transmedial storytelling and postmodern textuality are often viewed to have obliterated. Select iconography and objects recur throughout this intertextual Spike-o-sphere: references to Brooklyn, Radio Raheem's LOVE-HATE brass knuckle rings, the colour purple and Prince memorabilia and, above all, Nike Air Jordans.

My main goal in this chapter is to trace the history and explore the significance of Nikes within this auteurist mediascape that Lee has cultivated for three decades and counting. I focus primarily on the beginning of his professional career and its current moment (the late 1980s and the late 2010s) because there are particularly strong affinities between these moments both in American culture and in Lee's work, which are intimately bound up with one another. Racial, social and political tensions then and now are quite pronounced. As Ed Guerrero notes in his BFI volume on *Do the Right Thing*, the film was released amidst fiery 'culture wars', which saw

> sharply exploding controversies in the realms of American art and cultural production, as the nation's political right wing (coincident with a worldwide upsurge of religious fundamentalism) became politically visible and increasingly vocal about policing issues of 'decency' in the arts, humanities and popular forms of cultural production and consumption. (Guerrero 2001: 13)

Meanwhile, Lee's influential role in reshaping the terrain of the representation of race in American cinema is frequently recalled in the late 2010s as #BlackLivesMatter and unrest over ongoing racial injustices in Trump-era America leave their marks on contemporary cultural production. As various critics have observed, black film and media in the US has entered what is arguably its most vibrant, diverse phase yet. In this context, the cinematic history that has led to this moment is gaining increased recognition through programming, restoration and scholarship alike.

If the central goal here is to look at Lee's relationship with Nike, a secondary goal is to suggest that this case study offers an opportunity to think about how the subject and object of cinema studies might be understood as displaced from the text of the film and into other media configurations. Lee's February 2019 Instagram posts in particular suggest that it would behove us to better understand cinema in our social media age by considering cinematic paratexts such as a filmmaker's Instagram presence. Film scholars have yet to fully explore the ramifications of such new entanglements of media that cinema finds itself in today. How do filmmakers, who make livings by telling stories in images, tell other stories in images when left to their own (mobile) devices? To what extent does social media allow visual artists to be creatively unburdened by collaborative constraints and financial pressures? Might the singular personality communicatively established through an Instagram or Twitter account in fact reinvigorate the supposedly old-fashioned idea of the filmmaker as auteur? While I don't take on such general questions too explicitly in this chapter, they are nevertheless some critical methodological concerns in the back of my mind that I hope the description above invites us to consider.

Few if any filmmakers of comparable clout are more active on Instagram than Spike Lee. With nearly 4,000 posts as of April 2019, he has uploaded more content to the platform than other notable filmmaker-'grammers Ava DuVernay (with nearly 1,000 posts), Michael Moore (613), Barry Jenkins (500), Jordan Peele (427), Xavier Dolan (424), Darren Aronofsky (368), Miranda July (321), Michel Gondry (185), Alfonso Cuarón (123), Martin Scorsese (95) and Agnès Varda (82). In fact, Lee's posts outnumber the total of all these directors' posts combined. The content of his posts ranges widely from politicised snapshots of *New York Daily News* front pages and touristic snapshots from shoots in progress to commemorations of his previous films' anniversaries – and with so many films spanning a thirty-three-year-long career, there are plenty of milestones to celebrate. Lee's extensive use of the social media platform therefore feeds into his long-running and critically ambivalent status as a heavily promotional filmmaker, and relatedly what Jerome Christensen (1991) referred to as his 'corporate populism', an appraisal which remains relevant to revisit today, nearly thirty years after he and W. J. T. Mitchell debated *Do the Right Thing*'s politics and violence in the pages of *Critical Inquiry* (1990).

Lee's February 2019 Jordans posts most explicitly reference *Do the Right Thing* (*DtRT*), often considered the filmmaker's masterpiece, celebrating its thirtieth anniversary. When *BlacKkKlansman* received the 2019 Academy Award nomination for Best Picture, critics recalled *DtRT*'s failure to be nominated in this category in 1990, despite many proclamations that it was the best film of the year. (While presenting the Best Original Score Oscar during the telecast, actress Kim Basinger defiantly called out the Academy for snubbing Lee's film.) The parallels between the two moments were all the more pronounced given that *Driving Miss Daisy* (Bruce Beresford, USA, 1989) won Best Picture in 1990, and *Green Book* (Peter Farrelly, USA, 2018), a film presenting a similar white fantasy of racial reconciliation, was up – and went on to win – against *BlacKkKlansman* in 2019, much to Lee's frustration. As he succinctly put it in an interview afterwards: 'Every time someone is driving somebody, I lose.'[1] Recent efforts to diversify the Academy following controversial #OscarsSoWhite protests seemed to not be potent enough to sway the tone-deaf ears of the Academy's white majority. *BlacKkKlansman*'s screenplay win is nevertheless a positive sign of recognition, whether or not it was symbolic compensation for years-long neglect.

Lee materially referenced *Do the Right Thing* at the 2019 ceremony by wearing Raheem's LOVE/HATE brass-knuckle rings. Jackson's presentation of the award to Lee built another bridge to the thirty-year-old film, which was the first in a trio of Lee's films that would bring the star fame. As if keeping in line with his character, Mister Señor Love Daddy, the radio host who served as *DtRT*'s omniscient narrator, Jackson appropriately now took the mic to announce Lee's long overdue award. The image Lee shared of his Nikes suspended in mid-air as he was being embraced by Jackson could almost be viewed as a belated, right-handed response of LOVE to the HATE that fuels *Do the Right Thing*'s climactic moment, when the camera lingers on Raheem's Nikes dangling in mid-air as he is killed in chokehold by the police.

The Spike and Mike commercials

I want to return to the parallels between these complex moments and the question of footwear in *Do the Right Thing,* but before doing so it is important to recall Lee's history with the Nike corporation and to note that the references running through Lee's Oscar Jordans Instagram posts in fact predate his 1989 film. Indeed, Lee established his influential, ongoing partnership with Nike even earlier, in conjunction with his first feature, *She's Gotta Have It* (1986).

She's Gotta Have It – which Lee re-made thirty years later into a Netflix TV series, further expanding the Spike-o-sphere – details the romantic escapades of Nola Darling (Tracy Camilla Johns), a sexually liberated woman who openly

Figure 17.2 Mars Blackmon introduced in *She's Gotta Have It*

juggles non-exclusive sexual relationships with three different men. Lee plays one of these men: Mars Blackmon, the funniest but most boyish and irresponsible of Nola's suitors, who doesn't yet have a career established but has a firmly established urban style. As he points out later in the film when Nola's three suitors meet at a Thanksgiving dinner she hosts, he has $50 sneakers but no job. When Mars is introduced in the film, he is objectified through close-ups on individual parts of his attire: an arrow symbol shaved into the back of his head; a belt spelling his name in capital letters; a Brooklyn hat; a bike; and his Nikes. This metonymical introduction – Lee's very first on-screen appearance in any film – foretells the chain of slippages between apparel (in particular shoes), brand, name and identity that characterise and trouble Lee's place within and beyond the Spike-o-sphere.

After the film introduces Mars's character, Nola invites him into her apartment and says to him, 'there's something about you'. Mars asks, 'Good or bad?' She concedes that she hasn't figured it out yet, to which he replies, 'you'll let me know' five times. As the spectator soon discovers, this repetition of phrases is one of Mars's trademarks, teetering a thin line between being endearing and grating, or 'good' and 'bad'. This verbal pattern is also the site of a transferral between Mars's character and Lee himself: the repetition of 'Brooklyn Wins' three times in his Instagram post immediately following his Oscar win, for example, while visually depicting his Mookie character from *Do the Right Thing*, verbally echoes his Mars character from *She's Gotta Have It* – as do the multiple phrases he repeats throughout his thirty-second video showing off his Gold Oscar Jordans.

In a later scene in the film that echoes Mars's introduction but with key distinctions, Mars and Nola make love. This time Nola is divided into parts, but through close-ups on body parts (breasts, belly button, foot) rather than the commodities through which we are primarily introduced to Mars. The sexual difference of the camera's look is emphasised when, as Nola's foot slides down Mars's leg, we hear him yell 'no' and 'stop' while she tries removing his sneaker from his foot with her own foot. Even during intercourse, Mars refuses to disassociate from his Jordans. For Mars, as with several characters throughout Lee's films, personal identity is intimately tied to consumer artefacts, particularly clothing, so much so that by 1990 Lee opened his own store, Spike's Joint, in Fort Greene, Brooklyn. 'A Spike Lee Joint' is also of course the phrase he uses in his films' closing credits, thus blurring the boundaries between his artistic signature and the retail space where fans could buy film-themed merchandise. Discussing how *Do the Right Thing* would influence fashion trends throughout the summer following its release, Douglas Kellner observed that Lee 'not only depicts a society in which cultural identity is produced through style and consumption but contributes to this trend with both his films and commercial activity' (Keller 1997: 76). Though Spike's Joint closed in 1997 it still exists online, reflecting the digital transition various outlets made into the new millennium.

The lovemaking scene between Mars and Nola in *She's Gotta Have It* inadvertently ignited a long partnership between Lee and Nike, which in a sense Lee, like Mars, still insists on wearing. Jim Riswold, the former creative director of the shoe brand's ad agency, Wieden + Kennedy, recounts seeing *She's Gotta Have It* with the agency's president in Portland:

> The movie is about three men who pursue the same woman, and there was this Mars Blackmon character played by Spike, who when he has his chance to sleep with the woman of his dreams, he won't take his Air Jordans off, and it was like, that's an idea, that's an advertising campaign.[2]

Lee was then hired to make a series of commercials for Nike with Michael Jordan.

Their two debut TV commercials, for the Air Jordan III, aired in 1988. Both commercials are shot in black and white, like *She's Gotta Have It*, and in both Lee reprises his role as Mars. The first commercial opens on Lee: his arm hugging a basketball hoop, Mars chain around his neck and Brooklyn hat on his head. He says, 'Do you know who the best player in the game is? Me. Mars Blackmon. And I'm way above the rim, demonstrating some serious hang time. Very serious. Do you know how I get up for my game? Do you know? Do you know? Do you know?' As he answers his question, repeating 'Air Jordan' three times, the camera descends to reveal Lee's feet (wearing Jordans) resting

Figure 17.3 Mars standing on Jordan's shoulders, Hang Time Air Jordan III commercial

on top of Michael Jordan's shoulders. Lee's voice continues, 'Mike. What's up?' Jordan shakes his head and walks towards the camera, which has moved back, leaving Lee hanging on the rim of the basketball net. With fast-paced, callow petulance, Mars says: 'Aw money, money. Why you wanna do that to me? Why you leave me hanging?' As Mars remains suspended from the net, Jordan shoots a ball through the hoop. Lee makes some noises, laughs a bit, and says, 'Mike. That's cold man.' Without Jordan having uttered a word and without Lee having moved from the net, the commercial cuts to a red logo of Jordan's iconic hang time silhouette and accompanying text that reads 'Air Jordan from Nike'.

'Cover', the second commercial, released for the same shoe, opens with a rapid montage of Jordan's feet as he dribbles a ball on a court. Lee then talks in the foreground: 'Mars Blackmon here again, you know, nobody in the world can cover my main man Michael Jordan. Nobody nobody nobody. Telling you it's impossible impossible impossible impossible impossible.' As Lee repeats his words, we see Jordan repeatedly dunking balls in the net. Jordan then walks up to Lee and puts one hand over his mouth, with his other hand on his shoulder, delivering the punchline: 'However it's easy to cover Mars Blackmon.' These first two commercials establish Jordan and Lee as a variation on a familiar comedic duo: Mars is the fast-talking eccentric to Jordan's silent but fast-moving straight man. The congruities between Lee's speech and Jordan's actions are emphasised by the quick-paced editing, which contrasts Mars's reiterative phrasing with repeated shots of Jordan dunking, rhythmically equating Jordan's gift with the basketball with Lee's hip way with words.

A subsequent popular Spike and Mike commercial is 'Can/Can't', where Mars repeatedly tells the viewer you can buy an Air Jordan but you can't shoot hoops like Mike. (The sports drink Gatorade would team with Jordan and go on to explicitly disavow this message with their ubiquitous and catchy 'Be Like Mike' commercial in 1992, which became a motto throughout the decade.) Another spot even brings back actress Tracy Camilla Johns from *She's Gotta Have It* to reprise her role as Nola Darling, having left her other suitors and fallen in love with Jordan, not, as she declares, because of his athletic skill but because of his shoes. A later ad, for the Jordan IX in 1994, was released after Jordan retired intermittently from basketball to play baseball and makes fun of Jordan's lesser abilities in the sport; we see Mars pair with a series of baseball stars who each humorously concede that 'he's trying'. These commercials cemented Jordan's and Lee's reputations into the 1990s as 'the two public figures most associated with Nike sports shoes', as Krin Gabbard has claimed (Gabbard 2000: 377).

The social function of these television commercials was a representative point of contention in a heated scholarly debate between W. J. T. Mitchell and Jerome Christensen that unfolded in a trio of articles published in 1990 and 1991 in the pre-eminent humanities journal *Critical Inquiry*. Mitchell published a thoughtful essay reflecting on the question of 'public art' in *Do the Right Thing* – how the film itself circulated as a work of public art that was widely discussed across popular culture and also how the film is *about* the question of public art itself. For Mitchell, the 'Wall of Fame' in Sal's Pizzeria, upon which Sal (Danny Aiello) hangs framed pictures of famous Italian Americans and which Buggin' Out (Giancarlo Esposito) takes issue with for excluding blacks, 'exemplifies the central contradictions of public art' (Mitchell 1990: 893). Noting that visual references to black culture adorn the neighbourhood outside the pizzeria, Mitchell speculates on why this is not enough for Buggin' Out:

> The public spaces accessible to blacks are *only* public, and that only in the special way that the sphere of commercial-industrial publicity (a sphere that includes, by the way, movies themselves) is available to blacks. They are, like the public spaces in which black athletes and entertainers appear, rarely owned by blacks themselves; they are reminders that black public figures are by and large the 'property' of a white-owned corporation – whether a professional sports franchise, a recording company, or a film distributor. (Ibid.: 894)

Jerome Christensen published a response to Mitchell's essay, accusing his analysis of letting Lee's 'corporate populism' off the hook. Christensen insists, 'Doing the right reading of *Do the Right Thing* means appraising its impure effects' (Christensen 1991: 591). His prime example of 'impure effect' is Lee's relationship with Nike. Recounting how Lee and Nike became imbricated, he writes of the moment in the film in which the white, brownstone-owning Clifton unknowingly steps on Buggin' Out's Nikes. Living up to his name, Buggin' Out complains, 'Not only did you knock me down but you stepped on my brand new, white Air Jordans I just bought.' Christensen observes:

> Like a projectile, the brand name shatters the glass of realism and momentarily moves the film into the inebriating hyperreality of product fetishism. The problem of cleaning the dirt from the Air Jordans and erasing the insult to Buggin' Out's self-esteem becomes an important motif in the film, contributing to, if not purely causing the violence of the confrontation in the pizzeria. Meanwhile, after the film, outside the theater, away from the TV, shoes are bought. Many Air Jordans. Some with money earned by the sale of drugs. Shoes are stolen. Some from the dead bodies of black youths, who have been killed without any other narrative justification except their possession of Nikes and because someone's gotta have them. (Christensen 1991: 591)

Christensen's harsh stance echoes conservative backlash against Spike Lee and Michael Jordan in the early 1990s, when various pundits accused the two black celebrities of being complicit with if not responsible for street violence that erupted over expensive sports shoes in many urban communities. Sneaker violence became a flashpoint of popular media hysteria, most notoriously encapsulated in a *Sports Illustrated* cover from May 1990 that featured a pair of black hands holding a basketball shoe with alarmingly large, capital-lettered font, 'YOUR SNEAKERS OR YOUR LIFE'. The story inside the pages of the magazine is bookended with familiar Mars Blackmon quotes from Lee's Air Jordan commercials. It begins, 'Is it the shoes? . . . Money, it's gotta be the shoes!' and it closes with 'Do you know? Do you know? Do you know?' (Telander 1990: 36). The article quotes a *New York Post* columnist who wrote representatively of mounting resentment towards Lee: 'While Spike Lee watches Michael Jordan (or at least his shoes) dunk all over the world, parents around the country are watching their kids get mugged, or even killed, over the same sneakers Lee and Jordan are promoting' (Ibid.: 44).

The logic of Lee's filmed work being held responsible for real-life off-screen violence bears a striking resemblance to debates that took place in the early 1970s related to blaxploitation, the last time black cinema was at the centre of broader cultural conversations in the US. Backlash against blaxploitation was strong, and films produced at the time were viewed by figures such as civil rights activist Reverend Jesse Jackson as an 'unthinking commercial for the consumption of dangerous drugs, when other media were prevented from such advertising', as Ed Guerrero puts it (Guerrero 1993: 102). (Jackson's organization PUSH would go on to lead a boycott against Nike, demanding greater presence of black executives on its board and more substantial engagement with the African American community in 1990 [Hume 1990: 59].) Responding to outcries against blaxploitation, musician Curtis Mayfield, who recorded the soundtrack album for *Super Fly* (Gordon Parks Jr, USA, 1972) offered the famous rejoinder: 'The way you clean up the film is by cleaning up the streets. The music and movies of today are about conditions that exist. You change the music and movies by changing the conditions' (Guerrero 1993: 102). Lee's responses two decades later contained notable echoes of Mayfield's, suggesting that placing the blame on Jordan and himself drew on and fed into racist anxieties, while targeting two black men and displacing the conversation from the more important issue at hand: the broader social inequalities and systemic problems of which sneaker crimes were merely one of many symptoms. Illustrative of the unique double-binds in which African American cinema often gets caught, *Do the Right Thing* was equally criticized for *not* depicting drug use; several critics felt that Lee's Bed Stuy (Bedford-Stuyvesant) depicted a sterilised fantasy that had erased all signs of drug-related problems known to afflict the Brooklyn neighbourhood. Compounding these racial anxieties unearthed by *Do the Right Thing*, Lee and Nike were the broader culture wars raging at the time, wherein figures such as Michael Medved were attacking cinema itself for a great deal of society's ills.

Mitchell returned Christensen's critique of his essay with a delightfully sarcastic response, accusing him of knee-jerk Marxism while not paying close enough attention to the nuance in the details of Lee's work, missing the ambiguity and critique embedded within both *Do the Right Thing* and his Nike commercials. He amusingly writes, 'Christensen has discovered that Spike Lee is a capitalist. This disappoints him' (Mitchell 1991: 597). Mitchell continues:

> Christensen evidently hasn't seen the commercials Lee actually made for Nike or he might have noticed that the commercials themselves are critical of product fetishism, and satirize the notion that the purchase of Air Jordans will transform the owner into Michael Jordan … Lee's Nike commercials need to be seen, not labelled. […] Of course one can argue that all these ironic and critical gestures are simply co-opted by the medium of television and the genre of the corporate commercial. This argument saves a lot of time; one needn't look at the offending object, much less think about it. The label or trademark tells all. This is fine, but it hardly amounts to a *critique* of anything, and it is not an alternative to corporate populism, but an instance of its deepest mystification. (Mitchell 1991: 606–7)

Mitchell thus takes the critique of Spike Lee's work as an opportunity to make a methodological case for the value of a cultural studies inflected mode of close textual analysis, attuned to ways in which a single text does polysemous and often contradictory work. Debate about Lee's relationship with Nike was far from confined to the pages of *Critical Inquiry*. A range of scholars, public intellectuals and journalists at the time took sides. Paul Gilroy, for example, a leading scholar of black studies, wrote an essay on Lee articulating a point of view to some extent aligned with Christensen's, but foregrounding the detrimental racial connotations of the filmmaker's commercial work. He writes that with Mars Blackmon

> Lee has set the power of street style and speech to work not just in the service of an imagined racial community but an imaginary blackness which exists exclusively to further the interests of corporate America. Whether or not these streetwise products actually induce young black men to murder one another, there *are* unresolved moral and political questions involved in our racial heroes endorsing overpriced shoes, even while wearing a minstrel mask. (Gilroy 1993: 189)

Indeed, it is important to probe the question of the extent to which Nike commodifies blackness through Lee as opposed to the extent to which Lee and Nike have more of a 'symbiotic' relationship as Robert Goldman and Stephen Papson have claimed (Goldman and Papson, 1998). Beyond Nike helping Lee become a public figure in American culture far more familiar than most other independent filmmakers, Lee also certainly helped Nike become the leading shoe brand in the country; he was a vital part of the company's strategy to expand their advertising into television and to edge the company above Reebok and Adidas, their competitors going into the 1980s, by anchoring an idea of the athletic shoe into urban style and hip-hop culture, far beyond the sports market where it had previously been confined. Equally, as various other critics have suggested, it is generative to probe the extent to which Lee's black presence (imaginary, real and/or performed) serves to displace the optic of race from Michael Jordan in the Spike and Mike commercials (Goldman and Papson 1998: 27; Andrews 1996).

Such debates get to the heart of the difficulty of talking not only about Lee's relationship with Nike but also about race in American culture, suggesting why it would be insufficient to dismiss Lee's entanglements with the corporation through a Marxist critique of commodity fetishism. Lee's commercials promote Nike at the same time that they are self-consciously critical of the falsity of the work that commercials do in coupling unrealistic expectations and impossible fantasies with consumption. Lee's playfulness – which includes Mars's overdone verbal patter as well as the content of the patter ('You can do this; you can't do this'; 'Impossible, impossible,

impossible . . .') – undercut the construction of such fantasies and desires. As Goldman and Papson note

> Nike commercials playfully raise the usually unspoken assumptions concerning the relationship between commodities and identity so that Nike can distance itself from such philistine attitudes. In this way, Nike disavows the spectacular function of the shoe. It both joins and separates the superstar's performance from its product. Nike openly acknowledges its product will not endow us with the power to magically perform like Jordan, even while teasing that 'it's gotta be the shoes'. (Goldman and Papson 1998: 49)

The irony in Nike's disavowal is that though the shoes are of course unable to grant their wearers superhuman powers, there is extensive and often largely unacknowledged scientific research that goes into the cutting-edge design of their shoes. One of Lee's commercials that Mitchell references shows Douglas Kirkpatrick, a white Air Force lieutenant and member of the American Institute of Aeronautics and Astronautics, as a nerdy professor with a chalkboard on the basketball court trying to explain to Mars how Jordan defies gravity. Jordan silently and slowly turns his head to the camera, clearly not interested in having his skills scientifically theorised, locking the viewer into an identificatory dismissal of the professor's overly intellectual explanation. In slighting the effort to actually study Jordan's movement, the commercial's humour casually displaces the very real work done by the NIKE Sport Research Laboratory team of scientists, engineers and designers drawing on biomechanics, anatomy and physiology who have meticulously studied how to best tailor shoes for effective play on the court and in the game. The 2017 episode of the Netflix documentary series *Abstract: The Art of Design* on Tinker Hatfield, the former architect and pole-vaulter who became Nike's most legendary designer and worked on most of the Air Jordans, including Lee's recent gold pairs, offers a glimpse into the science behind the shoes, as do publications in Nike's own *Sport Research Review*.

Nike's brand perception itself is more broadly emblematic of the playful contradictions staged in Lee's commercials between the messages they promote and the products they sell. Their commercials often advocate socially progressive values, such as in Lee's colourful 1992 'Play Together' ad, a thirty-second spot promoting racial harmony shot in Los Angeles after the Rodney King beating and before the subsequent riots following the police officers' acquittal, though aired after the riots. Stylistically, it directly mimics *Do the Right Thing*'s infamous Brechtian racial-slur montage: a series of white basketball players face the camera spouting racist thoughts against blacks followed by a series of black players reciting anti-white epithets. In *Do the Right Thing*, Jackson's Mister Señor Love Daddy interrupts the sequence, addressing those in it to 'cool off'. Here, Lee (not playing Mars for a change) is the one to break up the fight: 'Hold up. If we gonna live together, we gotta play together. The mo' colors, the mo' better.' Highlighting the 'woke' messages in ads such as this one, several critics have sought to claim that while constructing a socially progressive brand identity, Nike hypocritically distracts public scrutiny from the corporation's exploitative employment of workers in Asian sweatshops.

Since Lee's late 1980s advertisements, Nike has continuously absorbed such critiques while maintaining its edgy image and courting controversy, seemingly willing to take risks by taking sides, most recently through making American football quarterback Colin Kaepernick the face of their 'Just Do It' thirty-year anniversary campaign. In 2016, Kaepernick garnered extensive national attention for protesting police brutality and racial injustice in the US by sitting out the customary national anthem played at the start of each NFL game; instead of standing with a hand across his chest like other players, he got in the habit of symbolically kneeling. Kaepernick opted out of his contract with the San Francisco 49ers and remained unsigned by the NFL, who were unwilling to support him. He was repeatedly a target of Donald Trump's bigoted remarks throughout Trump's election campaign and early presidency, a familiar icon via reference to which Trump could rouse anti-black sentiments of his supposedly patriotic base of supporters. Amidst mounting racial tensions surrounding Kaepernick's defiance of the NFL's traditions Nike symbolically worked with the ousted athlete. In response, politically conservative Americans launched widespread boycotts and protests beginning 4 September 2018 in which they burned their Nike apparel and shared thousands of videos featuring sneakers engulfed in flames across social media.

Nikes are burning

It would be instructive to situate these shoe-burning videos in relation to the media ecology of the Spike-o-sphere. *BlacKkKlansman* was released in the US on 10 August 2018, almost exactly one year after the white supremacist Unite the Right rally in Charlottesville, Virginia – a flashpoint in the recent string of anti-black demonstrations to which Kaepernick was directing the American public's attention. Lee's film was therefore released less than four weeks before the shoe-burning protest phenomenon and was the eighth highest-grossing movie in the domestic box office the week the protests occurred. Indicating the level of hype his new film was receiving, the filmmaker also appeared on the 20 August 2018 cover of *TIME Magazine*, in conjunction with the feature story, itself conflating Lee's filmmaking with athleticism: 'Spike Lee's Long Game'. Thus Lee was very prominently back at the centre of a national conversation about race, much like he was at the end of the 1980s. The Nike-burning protests that would happen less than two weeks after Lee graced *TIME*'s cover could, as such, be viewed as not only about Kaepernick but about the ongoing polarisation of feelings about race in American culture, feelings regarding which Lee has, for better or worse, become a primary commentator – in his cinematic work, on social media, and through his partnership with Nike.

Perhaps most striking about the sneaker-burning is its reliance on and circulation of densely layered symbolism, a tangled semiotic cluster of objects, gestures and collectives, which one also finds in Lee's work: Nikes, fire, property destruction, hate speech. Discourse about the Spike-o-sphere, like the sneaker-burning videos, tends to focus on the moral and ethical dimensions of the actions displayed. Did Buggin' Out over-react when the white yuppie Clifton soiled his Air Jordans? Did Mookie 'do the right thing' in setting fire to Sal's Pizzeria? Was it wrong for Mookie to then take the money he was owed by Sal the morning after? Is Lee indirectly responsible for the deaths of teens who killed themselves for overpriced shoes, or is it OK since Lee's collaboration with Nike helped fund his creative work, which explores racial tensions in America without offering palatable answers? Was Colin Kaepernick doing the right thing by kneeling during the national anthem? Were the people who burned Nikes in fact really doing Nike's business any harm if they presumably already owned the shoes being burned – or, for that matter, if they bought them?

Focusing locally on the question of the 'right thing' – whether done by Lee, Mookie, Mars, Jordan, Nike, Kaepernick, the president, the police or the public, and whether in 1989 or in 2019 – perhaps makes it too easy to flatten interrelated events into singular moments, obscuring more nuanced questions that one could ask about their affective entanglement. What if we instead considered the multiple interchanges of iconographies and gestures that one finds across these moments and texts? They are particularly suggestive of an idea of 'America' as a family of concepts, some compatible and some incompatible. On one hand, it designates what Benedict Anderson has called an 'imagined community' (Anderson 1983), whereby people separated by thousands of miles, living in different states, take part in reading the same magazines, following the same football games, watching the same commercials, wearing the same footwear, talking about the same films. They experience cultural events that give them a shared sense of identity and a sense of belonging to a nation state. In this America, racial codes and tensions are affixed to virtually all levels of shared experiences, and the white community's composite, imagined 'America' in many respects looks quite different than the black community's 'America'. In an America outside of quotation marks, on the other hand, one not only imagined through shared rituals and texts, blacks are both routinely and disproportionately victimised and criminalised.

In this same America, select African Americans are turned into heroes and champions – like Michael Jordan and, sometimes, Spike Lee – admired for their talent and often forced into positions where they function to help white Americans pretend that racism is not a problem, since these select few have been able to achieve great success. It is precisely the cinematisation of this fantasy that one finds in race-themed Oscar-winning 'best pictures'.

As Cheryl Cole writes:

> Understanding [Michael] Jordan's position in national culture and the implication of his embodiment in national fantasies and anxieties which dominate 1980s and 1990s America, requires that we consider what it means that America, a political body, and Nike, a meta- or trans-national body, are given form through an affective figure like Jordan. (Cole 1996: 371)

Indeed, a figure like Jordan, whose name became interchangeable with a shoe and nearly synonymous with a corporation, comes to occupy an impossible position where he both compensates for and contradicts the systemic injustices faced by the black community more broadly. Paired with Mars in the early Spike and Mike commercials, Jordan's role in mediating national fantasies and anxieties about race is not entirely clear. Several writers have argued that Mars's coding as black serves to deflect our attention from Jordan's race, configuring him as a body that transcends raced codings or is race-neutral – a position similar to that held by earlier black celebrity athlete O. J. Simpson in American popular culture throughout the 1970s and 1980s. Simpson's often-quoted line 'I'm not black, I'm O. J.' certainly resonates with Jordan's own perceived racelessness and the position he too played as a popular black athlete who crossed over with white fans. However, unlike the way in which Simpson was notoriously only gawked at by white onlookers in the groundbreaking television commercial he did running through an airport for Hertz rental cars, to make television audiences forget about Simpson's blackness, Jordan's pairing with Lee is more ambivalent as it arguably reinforces his racial difference at the same time.[3] Moreover, what does it mean to pair real-life Jordan with fictitious Mookie? And how do we retrospectively read Mookie's cartoonish-pattering sidekick to Jordan's straight man when Jordan reprises his on-screen appearance as himself in the blockbuster *Space Jam* (Joe Pytka, USA, 1996) just a few years later alongside an animated Bugs Bunny? From this perspective one surely could see how in these commercials Lee does revive something resembling the 'minstrel mask' that Gilroy accuses him of donning, playing into a long tradition in American popular entertainment of the black performer in caricature for white pleasure, casting aside racial anxieties with the reinscription of clearly delineated power dynamics (Gilroy 1993: 189).

There is no moment from Lee's filmography that better encapsulates the ambivalent symbolism of the role that Nike plays in the Spike-o-sphere more than the death of Radio Raheem in *Do the Right Thing*. Looking back on Christensen's text it seems striking that he identifies the climax of the film, like many other critics at the time, as the destruction of property that Mookie instigates, rather than the police brutality depicted immediately before, which prompts Mookie's protest. The destruction of a human life at the hands of the police is undoubtedly more upsetting than the destruction of a pizzeria. It is particularly suggestive that Christensen does not address Raheem's death, for it surely inconveniences his argument about Lee's corporate populism. When Raheem is killed at the end of the film, Lee quickly cuts to his Nikes dangling in air, unable to reach the ground because he is in chokehold by the police. Though fleeting, given the importance of Air Jordans earlier in the film, the image and its symbolism has an effect of being burnt into the spectator's memory. The most unsettling moment in the film, it could hardly be taken as a straightforward endorsement of the brand. At best, the Nikes might symbolise Raheem's innocence. Yet the image intersects with too many other connotations to just be left at that. Ed Guerrero has rightly noted the image's deep historical resonance, functioning as 'a gruesome metonym for lynching' (Guerrero 2001: 78). As Kerr Huston observes, the close-up cut to Raheem's shoes is more than just that too:

> It is also, when taken in context, a bald reference to Jordan, and it is, if unexpected, terribly powerful. In a perversion of Jordan's autonomous grace, Lee shows a powerful man suspended entirely against his will, and fatally unable to return to earth. Raheem's murder is thus doubly difficult for (black) spectators to gaze upon because it is pictured in a way that perverts Jordan's singular grace and agility. (Huston 2004: 643)

The cut to the Nikes manages to channel one of the most iconic images of popular culture at the time – Jordan's silhouette in hang time – and generates an affective surplus that cannot be distilled into a singular meaning. It draws on the grisly histories of American racism in the routine lynching of blacks by whites, the aspirations and achievements represented by Michael Jordan's athletic prowess (certainly giving Jordan's famous hang time a darker connotation) and puts these into critical tension with one another. It calls forth earlier racial frictions within the film between Buggin' Out and Clifton regarding the tri-angulation of race, cultural identity and gentrification. On top of this all, the image simultaneously forces us out of the diegetic fiction to consider Lee's very real and ambivalent relationship with Nike.

Beyond the internal levels of meaning one might find layered in Raheem's dangling shoes, the scene has gone on to have several lives in the future too, refusing to allow its textual containment. Not only might one find traces of it in the picture Lee posted on Instagram of Jackson lifting Lee in the air after winning an Oscar, but Raheem's dangling Nikes more explicitly return in a reappropriation Lee made of the scene, 'Radio Raheem and the Gentle Giant', which he uploaded to his personal YouTube page in July 2014. In this 59-second clip Lee intercuts the scene of Raheem's murder with footage from the viral cellphone video of 43-year-old black New Yorker Eric Garner being killed in chokehold by police earlier that month. He shared a re-edited version again in 2020, now including George Floyd, called '3 Brothers'. The parallels between fact and fiction, he demonstrates, are strong and unnerving. Lee's critics might view these videos as more online self-promotion by the filmmaker, accusing him of reappropriating footage of material too sensitive to be decontextualised; they might say that he did not 'do the right thing'. Advocates of Lee might view the videos as necessary engagements with the problem of police brutality, tragic reflections on life imitating art, or powerful reminders of the enduring injustices faced by the black community in the US. Either way, Lee proves that he'll always be Mars: repeating himself whether we like it or not.

Notes

1. Available at <https://mynewsla.com/hollywood/2019/02/24/every-time-somebody-is-driving-somebody-i-lose-spike-lee-says/> (last accessed 31 July 2019).
2. Available at <https://www.complex.com/sneakers/2015/03/mars-blackmon-michael-jordan-interview> (last accessed 31 July 2019).
3. See Ezra Edelman's *OJ: Made in America* (2016) for insightful contextualisation of the politics of race in these Hertz commercials.

References

Anderson, Benedict (1983), *Imagined Communities. Reflections on the Origin and Spread of Nationalism*, London: Verso.

Andrews, David L. (1996), 'The fact(s) of Michael Jordan's blackness: Excavating a floating racial signifier', *Sociology of Sport Journal*, vol. 13, no. 2, pp. 125–58.

Christensen, Jerome (1991), 'Spike Lee, Corporate Populist', *Critical Inquiry*, vol. 17, no. 3, pp. 582–95.

Cole, Cheryl (1996), 'American Jordan: P.L.A.Y., Consensus, and Punishment', *Sociology of Sport Journal*, vol. 13, no. 4, pp. 366–97.

Gabbard, Krin (2000), 'Race and Reappropriation: Spike Lee Meets Aaron Copland', *American Music*, vol. 18, no. 4, pp. 370–90.

Gilroy, Paul (1993), 'Spiking the argument. Spike Lee and the limits of racial community', in P. Gilroy, *Small Acts: Thoughts on the Politics of Black Culture*, London: Serpent's Tail, pp. 183–91.

Goldman, Robert and Papson, Stephen (1998), *Nike Culture. The Sign of the Swoosh*, London: Sage Publications.

Guerrero, Ed (2001), *Do the Right Thing*, London: BFI Film Classics.

Guerrero, Ed (1993), *Framing Blackness: The African American Image in Film*, Philadelphia: Temple University Press.

Hume, Scott (1990), 'Boycott of Nike ignored', *Advertising Age*, 29 October, p. 59.

Huston, Kerr (2004), 'Athletic Iconography in Spike Lee's Early Feature Films', *African American Review*, vol. 38, no. 4, pp. 637–49.

Jones, Riley (2015), 'How Mars Blackmon Became the Face of Jordan Brand Will Surprise You', 20 March, <https://www.complex.com/sneakers/2015/03/mars-blackmon-michael-jordan-interview> (last accessed 31 July 2019).

Kellner, Douglas (1997), 'Aesthetics, Ethics, and Politics in the Films of Spike Lee', in M. A. Reid (ed.), *Spike Lee's Do the Right Thing*, Cambridge: Cambridge University Press, pp. 73–106.

Mitchell, W. J. T. (1991), 'Seeing *Do the Right Thing*', *Critical Inquiry*, vol. 17, no. 3, pp. 596–608.

Mitchell, W. J. T. (1990), 'The Violence of Public Art: *Do the Right Thing*', *Critical Inquiry*, vol. 16, no. 4, pp. 880–99.

Telander, Rick (1990), 'Senseless. In America's cities, kids are killing kids over sneakers and other sports apparel favored by drug dealers. Who's to blame?', *Sports Illustrated*, 13 May, pp. 36–49.

Chapter 18

'Nice shoes': Will Smith, mid-2000s (post) racial discourse and the symbolic significance of shoes in *I, Robot* and *The Pursuit of Happyness*

Hannah Hamad

'Nice shoes.' With this clipped line of dialogue so ends an early scene in Alex Proyas' 2004 sci-fi blockbuster *I, Robot*, adapted (extremely liberally) from its famous source material by iconic science fiction author Isaac Asimov (1950). In the scene in question police detective Del Spooner (Will Smith) has been negotiating a difference of opinion about the social role of robots in mid twenty-first century America with his immediate superior Lt. John Bergin (Chi McBride), following a street altercation between Spooner and a robot earlier that day. Spooner, in error, had taken the robot to be a criminal and attempted to arrest it, only to be corrected in no uncertain terms by the robot's angry owner. Intending, it seems, to have the final word on the matter, Bergin calls Spooner back as he is exiting the office. However, Bergin thinks better of it, capitulates to Spooner's stubbornness and instead redirects his and the audience's attention away from robots and towards Spooner's shoes with this admiring and implicitly envious compliment. 'Nice shoes.'

By this point in the film, the audience has already been cued to notice, admire and covet Spooner's very deliberately placed and prominently showcased footwear. For the duration of *I, Robot* Smith's character is conspicuously and purposely dressed in this high-end pair of Chuck Taylor Converse All Star basketball shoes. Specifically, and very noticeably, they are brand new, mint condition, leather upper high-topped sneakers – a premium model in the range of Converse shoes that were released into the real world market in 2004, the same year that the film, set in the near future of 2035, was released in cinemas (Peterson 2004). Very obviously, the visual prominence of Spooner's Chuck Taylor shoes to the *mise en scène* of *I, Robot* is due to a corporate product placement agreement between Twentieth Century Fox Film and Converse (Lehu 2007: 9–10). The latter capitalises on the presence of their product on the feet of the star of choice of the former to sell more shoes. The star, Will Smith, was at that time one of the most bankable stars in Hollywood. In this way, this act of product placement makes a contribution, however minor, towards maintaining the status of Converse as the largest shoe company in the world (Banet-Weiser 2012: 100).[1] Further, it is not only the presence of the Chuck Taylor All Stars on Smith's feet that is significant here, but also the fact that the shoes are embedded within the larger context of Spooner's identity (especially at the intersection of blackness and masculinity) and characterisation, and the fact that his relationship to them, as expounded further below in an analysis of the key scene that cements our understanding of the detective protagonist's feelings about his shoes, is affective.

This chapter will contextualise the symbolic significance of shoes as they pertain to the mid-2000s stardom of Will Smith. Beginning with a discussion of the meanings underpinning Smith's character's fetishisation of his Converse trainers in *I, Robot*, it will then go on to interrogate the semiotic power of shoes in his subsequent film *The Pursuit of Happyness* (Gabriele Muccino, USA, 2006). *The Pursuit of Happyness* was released at a time when Smith's bankability, marquee value and box office pulling power were at their all-time height. In fact, the mid-2000s saw his career hit its peak in these respects, with the success of this film in 2006, in the previous two years of *Hitch* (Andy Tennant, USA, 2005) and the aforementioned *I, Robot*, and then the following year of *I Am Legend* (Francis Lawrence, USA, 2007). This strong box office run over this period of time contributed to Smith becoming the highest paid actor in Hollywood in 2008 (Rose 2014).

The first of my theoretical and conceptual starting points for the argument being made here about post-racial discourse and the symbolic significance of shoes in the stardom of Will Smith comes from Stella Bruzzi's foundational writing on clothing and identity in cinema, in which she argues that, in film, 'clothing makes a significant intervention in the representation and interpretation of identity' (Bruzzi 1997: xviii) – specifically in the case of Will Smith, at the intersection of race, class and masculinity, as the two case study analyses will illustrate. Relatedly, in focusing specifically on shoes I also build on and extend Sarah Gilligan's illuminating discussion of race, masculinity and clothing in the stardom of Will Smith, continuing the conversation about this intersection that she began when she noted that '[d]espite Smith's popularity with audiences, the intersection of Smith, black masculinity and fashion does not appear to have been the subject of extended academic attention' (Gilligan 2015: 171). Correspondingly, this chapter will continue the analysis of *I, Robot* that commenced at the outset, before moving the discussion on to the significance of shoes in relation to 'bootstrap' aspirationalism in *The Pursuit of Happyness*.

Blackness, masculinity and Chuck Taylor Converse All Stars in *I, Robot*

As an upshot of an interview with a brand representative from Converse, media and culture scholar Sarah Banet-Weiser, in her authoritative study of the politics of ambivalence in early twenty-first-century brand culture, explains Converse's 'conviction that authenticity within branding is not so much a cultivated tangible object as something that emerges from an affective relationship, one that is part of an organic development of culture' (Banet-Weiser 2012: 257). Correspondingly, in *I, Robot* 'Will Smith['s character] does not restrict himself to merely wearing Converse shoes, but clearly expresses his personal preference for them' (Lehu 2007: 65–6). However, there is more going on here than just relatively straightforward product placement. Importantly, there is symbolic semiotic signification that is taking place through these particular shoes in this particular representational and discursive context, and via the mid-2000s stardom of Will Smith. The shoes are signifying as part of Smith's star text in some quite specific ways at the discursive intersection of blackness and masculinity, as the following analysis makes clear.

By the time the shoes make their first appearance on screen, black masculinity has in fact already begun to be configured in this film in some quite particular ways. The configuration of black masculinity at the film's outset serves to invoke the discourse of race via superficial sartorial cues and intertextual references to black popular culture. Specifically, basketball and the association of this sport with high-achieving black athletes is signified via the shoes. Furthermore, icons of black popular culture are referenced, specifically Stevie Wonder, via the music playing on Spooner's sound system (Hamad 2015), and Paul Robeson, via the fetishisation of Spooner's naked body in the preceding shower scene that invokes famous nude photographs of the earlier Hollywood star (Palmer 2011; Dyer 2004 [1986]). All these racially charged signifiers are invoked only, ultimately, to negotiate the position that race is irrelevant to Spooner's characterisation, his narrative, his identity and to the social world of humans in 2035. This kind of signifying practice and ideological sleight of hand was common in mid-2000s (the early dawn of the Obama era) cultural negotiations of what had correspondingly come to be understood and termed as post-racial discourse. And Will Smith, especially in the mid-2000s, was Hollywood's poster boy for its various filmic negotiations of this post-racial hegemony (Hamad 2015). This peaked when he was named Hollywood's most bankable star of the year in 2008, following the annual poll of film exhibitors conducted by Quigley Publishing for the International Motion

Picture Almanac ('Top Ten Moneymaking Stars of the Past 82 Years' 2014) – a long established and respected, if not necessarily authoritative or methodologically knowable industry measure for determining star power at the US box office. This, of course, was the year that Barack Obama made history by becoming the first black American to be elected to the US presidency.[2] It was an event that unsurprisingly prematurely anchored and cemented discourses circulating to the effect that America had now established a new status quo in which it was no longer necessary to see or discuss race and that race relations as a social problem were now a part of American history, rather than a part of contemporary American life. Smith's stardom at that time embodied the idea that America had transcended race and racial strife in myriad ways and, as expounded in the ensuing discussions of *I, Robot* and *The Pursuit of Happyness*, one of these ways was via symbolic signification through footwear that, in the depicted contexts, is imbued with politically charged meaning.

As *I, Robot* prepares to introduce the Chuck Taylor Converse All Star shoes as a corollary to Spooner's character, an aerial shot looking directly down from the ceiling upon the interior of Spooner's Chicago apartment shows him picking up a shopping bag that has been sitting on an armchair in the centre of frame, before retrieving a black-and-white cardboard box from within it. Cutting to a frontal mid-shot, the camera then gradually zooms closer and closer in towards Spooner, who discards the bag and opens the box. The instantly recognisable logo of the Chuck Taylor Converse All Star shoe (a navy blue five-point star encircled by red lettering) is now fully visible on the top side of the box, so that we know instantly, through brand recognition, just before Spooner produces and presents the shoe to camera, what the box will contain.[3] The first part of the shoe that we see is the signature diamond-patterned rubber sole of the right shoe, before Spooner turns it top side up to reveal the immaculately white-laced black leather upper high-top sneaker, which he takes a moment to gaze upon before the shot cuts to a close up of the left shoe, now on Spooner's foot, being double knotted.

Then, the camera whizzes up to the detective's smirking face, just prior to his utterance of the line 'a thing of beauty' as he pays admiring tribute to his prized new footwear before leaving the apartment through the front door. In a subsequent scene at the home of his grandmother, known to Spooner as 'GG' (who, the film strongly implies, has raised him, thus adhering to popular cinema's well-worn tropes of black matriarchs and fatherless black families), she quickly spies the shoes he is wearing and asks him with manifestly apparent bewilderment, 'Boy, *what* is that on your feet?' Spooner elevates his right leg for his grandmother, the camera and the audience,

Figures 18.1 and 18.2 Blackness and masculinity are collapsed into the sartorial signifier of Del Spooner's Chuck Taylor Converse All Stars in *I, Robot*

and proudly informs her, much to her evident amusement, that they are 'Converse All Stars. Vintage. 2004.'

Thus, Spooner fetishises these shoes. This is something that Sarah Gilligan views as part of *I, Robot*'s discursive project to redirect the myth of phallic power away from the fetishisation of the male body and towards the fetishisation of the clothes and accessories of Will Smith's character (Gilligan 2015: 172; Tolliver 2015). Viewed from another perspective though, Spooner and his relationship to his branded sports shoes bears comparison to cognate examples of this kind of cinematic commodification of blackness via shoes, such as Michael Jordan (playing himself) and his Nike Air Jordans in *Space Jam* (Joe Pytka, USA, 1996),[4] but also Buggin' Out and his (again) Nike Air Jordans in *Do the Right Thing* (Spike Lee, USA, 1989). Stella Bruzzi highlights the significance of this latter example, which she describes as a 'quintessential example of the fetishisation of the ostensibly insignificant object' that nonetheless becomes charged with meaning in the act of fetishisation (Bruzzi 1997: 108). She contextualises the scene in question, explaining that 'one of Buggin' Out's Air Jordan Nike trainers is soiled when a white neighbour accidentally runs over it with his bicycle', and goes on to highlight what the stakes of this moment are for the intersection of class and race when she states that '[a]t over $80 a pair, these Nikes are not purely arbitrary signs randomly appropriated, but are status symbols because of their economic value' (Ibid.). Hence, the stakes of Buggin' Out's relationship to his shoes are raised with regard to the semiotic power of these shoes to signify in relation both to the performance of economic power (at odds with the social reality of it for the character in question) and to some of the racial tension that exists between black and white Americans in the depicted context of *Do the Right Thing*.

Bruzzi further notes that 'Buggin' Out's Air Jordans are shot in extreme, reverential close-up as he repairs the damage with some whitener' (Ibid.), the significance of which she understands in relation to what black cultural studies scholar Kobena Mercer famously termed as 'defiant dandyism' (Mercer 1994: 120), which he elucidates as a black sartorial act of 'fronting out oppression by the artful manipulation of appearance' (Ibid.). Paraphrasing Mercer, Bruzzi writes that this 'has historically been the underpinning feature of black subcultural styles' (Bruzzi 1997: 108), specifically that 'flashy clothes', encompassing shoes, 'are used in the art of impression management to defy the assumption that to be poor one necessarily has to "show" it' (Mercer 1994: 120). However, also significant here with regard to the racial charge carried by these shoes, is the very fact of their whiteness, the related fact of their whiteness as a perceived marker of elevated social status for Buggin' Out (broadly in line with Dyer's influential treatise on whiteness as invisible racial privilege [1997]), and also the ritual whitening of these dirt-sullied (blackened) shoes that this character performs. In the context of the history of American race relations, and in the more particular context of the cultural history of American performance traditions, the connotative significance of the use of whitener as shoe polish in this scene cannot be overstated. This is due of course to the purpose served by black shoe polish in the history and practice of blackface minstrelsy, whereby it would be applied to the faces of white performers to aid their performative mimicry of African Americans,[5] mostly famously practiced in American film in *The Jazz Singer* (Alan Crosland, USA, 1927). Given that *Do The Right Thing* is a Spike Lee film and that Lee would go on to interrogate and unpack the charged racial politics and racist tropes and practices of blackface minstrelsy in his later film *Bamboozled* (2000), the fact that he here reverses the visual terms of the discourse surrounding the social power differential between black and white Americans and the differently respective relationships of black and white Americans to the connoted meanings of shoe polish seems both conscious and meaningful.

'Bootstrap' aspirationalism and black masculinity in *The Pursuit of Happyness*

The wearing of clothes, and the wearing of shoes in particular, is often an aspirational act for characters such as Buggin' Out in *Do the Right Thing*, among others. This is certainly the case in Smith's subsequent vehicle *The Pursuit of Happyness*, in which Smith plays Chris Gardner, a struggling self-employed San Francisco medical equipment salesman in early 1980s Reagan's America, whose wife Linda (Thandie Newton) absconds, leaving him to support himself and their son Christopher (Jaden Smith) solo as he strives to effect a transition in his increasingly precarious social status, by securing a highly coveted but unpaid internship with the overwhelmingly white and wealthy stock brokerage firm Dean Witter. This he does in a bid to become successful by the standards of Reagan-era consumerism, materialism and entrepreneurialism, and by combining his doggedness and industriousness with determined capitalisation on his strong mathematical and interpersonal abilities and skills. Against all the odds, with no relevant qualifications or experience and in highly unfavourable interview circumstances, Chris is awarded the sole job available to a member of his twenty-strong cohort of interns on completion of their programme and evaluation of their learning. Unbeknownst to him, as in the meantime he had struggled financially to the point of having become homeless, he was streets ahead of his peers in the eyes of his prospective employers. Chris's success is thus presented to us as having been inevitable, albeit according to the false cultural logic of a purportedly pure meritocracy. This logic wilfully glosses over what Sut Jhally and Justin Lewis's research into the context and reception of arguably the most quintessential depiction of black American Reagan-era aspirationalism *The Cosby Show* (NBC 1984–92) revealed to be the clear 'disparity between the upwardly mobile position of black people on television [and, where our example is concerned, film] and the acutely disadvantaged position of many black people' in 1980s American society (Jhally and Lewis 1992: 71). Expounding upon the nature of this disadvantage in the period in question, Jhally and Lewis continue:

> The economic system effectively subjugates most black people. African Americans, having been placed at the bottom of the economic pile, are forced to struggle against inequalities in material and educational resources. In the current economic and political system, few can win such a struggle. Free market capitalism, the organizing principle of this system, allows the United States to forgo racist principles while maintaining a dress of white hegemony. (Ibid.: 72)

It is therefore crucial to understanding the insidiousness of this film and what is ideologically at stake here to see and recognise the significance of Chris's blackness and to acknowledge the structural inequalities that were negatively impacting upon black people in America in the depicted period. These inequalities however, according to the cultural logic of the film, do not apply to Chris. His insalubrious circumstances at the outset of the film's timeline are rather presented to us as having been merely the upshot of a particularly acute run of bad luck.

The Pursuit of Happyness is a singularly egregious example of a film that attempts to negotiate the hegemony of the American Dream, while wilfully glossing over the Reagan-era structural inequalities (some of them tantamount to an outright attack on African Americans and the modest social gains achieved for them in light of the then recent civil rights movement of the mid-twentieth century) of the depicted period, so as not to undermine the ideological myopia and mythic tyranny of its narrative of 'bootstrap' aspirationalism. Token gestures are made to the political backdrop in which this narrative of individualism unfolds insofar as Chris is at one point depicted watching news media reportage of Ronald Reagan addressing the nation about the poor state of the US economy. However, much like the superficiality of the markers of Del Spooner's blackness in *I, Robot*, the film's gestures towards the racialised economic realities of Reagan's America are invoked only to be dismissed via Chris's narrative of individualist triumph.

American film scholar and authority on American national myths in cinema Julie Levinson differentiates what she calls 'the American success myth' from the larger ideological project of the American Dream, proffering that the success myth operates to narrativise this ideology. Thinking specifically about American cinema, she highlights that '[t]he movies' particular contribution to the American idea of success has been to codify, perpetuate, amplify, and sometimes challenge that idea' (Levinson 2012: 1). Thinking even more specifically about *The Pursuit of Happyness*, Levinson remarks that the film 'has all the familiar signposts of a bootstrap story' (Ibid.: 24). However, despite directly invoking the ubiquitous American Dream shoe metaphor (whereby aspiring beneficiaries of the American Dream are said to effect their own upward social mobility by 'pulling themselves up by their bootstraps') as a means of characterising the film, at no point in her astute interrogation of its post-racial adherence to the master narrative of the American success myth does she connect this metaphor to the key moment in the film in which Chris loses his shoe. I would henceforth argue that shoes are an important part of the codification of the American Dream and the success myth, both within American films (including and especially this one) but also far beyond, in that shoes permeate and pervade discursive practices that negotiate this ideology via the omnipresence in American cultural discourse of the ubiquitous 'bootstrap' metaphor, used as indicated above to refer to the enterprisingly individualistic and industrious means by which Americans must effect their own upward social mobility if they are to achieve their manifest destiny. In other words: they must pull themselves up by their bootstraps. The symbolic significance of shoes to the American success myth therefore cannot be overstated, and herein lies the relevance of shoes to the codification of the success myth narrative in *The Pursuit of Happyness*: Chris's shoes, much like the rest of the suit of clothes that he wears to work at Dean Witter, are a symbolic signifier of his aspirationalism. It is therefore meaningful that arguably the most symbolically significant of Chris's many make-or-break moments in the film comes in the aforementioned scene involving the distressing loss of one of Chris's shoes in a road traffic accident.

On his way to work at Dean Witter, early on in his unpaid internship at the firm, Chris spies the thief of one of his precious bone density scanning machines (his sales of which provide his entire income, from which he must support himself and his young son), and he clocks that the thief is still in possession of the machine. He bolts across the road, dodging traffic in his attempt to retrieve his property. Then he tears down the pavement, dodging pedestrians as he goes. Seeing the thief cross back over the road, he likewise chases back after him, only to be mown down by an oncoming vehicle that ploughs right into him. He is shaken and sore, but seemingly uninjured. Righting himself he bends over and picks up his things. As he does so, a high angle shot looking down at him reveals that he is no longer in possession of his left shoe. Realising this himself as the initial shock of the accident starts to subside, Chris asks 'Where's my shoe?' of the driver that hit him. Becoming irrationally angry, he yells 'YOU KNOCKED OFF MY SHOE!' He gets down on his knees, scrabbling on the ground to look for it, his frustration mounting: 'Where's my damned shoe?! . . . Did you see it?! I lost my shoe!' Capitulating to its loss, he despairingly lets his head drop onto his arm on the ground, before getting up and walking away. Incredulous, the driver yells after him 'Hey you just got hit by a car, go to the hospital!' Chris scoffs at this. 'I gotta go to work! I'm in a competitive internship at Dean Witter!' Chris strides back to his office, wearing only one shoe, and stoically tolerates the sniggers and jibes of his fellow interns as he proceeds to carry on with his day's work in the absence of his shoe.

The symbolic significance of Chris's shoe in this moment is twofold, in line both with Mercer's notion of 'defiant dandyism', and with the metaphorical logic of the 'bootstrap' aspirationalism so central to American success myth narratives. Chris has only one set of smart clothes and one pair of smart shoes. With these accoutrements he defies the reality of his economic status in order to perform an inhabitation of black masculinity that transcends the reality

Figure 18.3 'Where's my shoe?!' Chris Gardner loses a key signifier of his 'bootstrap' aspirationalism

of that status. However, unlike the examples of defiant dandyism discussed by Mercer and Bruzzi, this is neither flamboyance and flashiness for their own sake, nor is it counter-hegemonic in either intent or effect. Rather, it is aspirational – a tactic employed in the spirit of the survival of the fittest logic of market capitalism, in a goal-oriented manner, intended instead to play a part in effecting his upward social mobility in hegemonic line with the dominant ideology of Reagan's America. As aforementioned, Chris's shoes symbolise his bootstrap aspirationalism, so in losing a shoe which he cannot simply replace (as presumably his peers on the internship programme could), the coherence of his performance of socio-economic success is undermined, and the likely success of his attempt at upward social mobility is rendered instantly more precarious. How can he pull himself up by his bootstraps if he only has one to pull? Presented as only the latest incident in Chris's run of bad luck, the lost shoe is nonetheless the closest that the film actually comes to acknowledging that Chris's blackness, and the extant poverty that has thus far accompanied him in life, might actually hinder his chances of success relative to those of his peers, albeit this acknowledgement is symbolic and therefore implicit, and thus much more easily surmounted without undermining the individualist tenets of the American success myth.

Conclusion

In different ways then, as the discussions above of these two case study sites of analysis make clear, shoes are visibly prominent in the *mise en scène* of both *I, Robot* and *The Pursuit of Happyness,* while serving an ideologically loaded communicative function with respect to the negotiation of post-racial discourse in both films. Just as Del Spooner's Chuck Taylor Converse All Stars play their part in the larger representational landscape of *I, Robot* to at once mark and commodify the character's blackness while glossing over the extent to which race might inform his experience of his social world, so does Chris Gardner's lost shoe play its own part in negotiating the exceptionality of his achievements as a socio-economically beleaguered black man in Reagan's America. More significantly in terms of post-racial discourse though, it simultaneously negotiates the notion that there are no social circumstances that cannot be surmounted by individual enterprise and effort. In other words, in both films the protagonists' shoes operate at once to signify race but also to transcend it.

As these symptomatic examples from these two key films in the mid-2000s oeuvre of Will Smith – the most important Hollywood star of that period – have demonstrated and illustrated, shoes can and do have the potential to be charged with political and ideological meaning in how they signify in relation to character, narrative, star persona and, most importantly, identity. Specifically, in the case of this moment in Will Smith's star career, shoes have a key communicative function at the intersection of blackness, masculinity and class – a function that enables Smith's star text to successfully negotiate the cultural logic of post-racial America at the dawn of the Obama era.

Notes

1. According to Sarah Banet-Weiser, in the early twenty-first century Converse was selling 55 million pairs of shoes per year (Banet-Weiser 2012: 100).
2. For more on mid-2000s intersections between the stardom of Will Smith and the rise to political prominence of Barack Obama, see Bacal (2009) and Lobalzo-Wright (2017).
3. For more on the iconicity of the Chuck Taylor Converse All Star shoe, see Muellerschoen and Steinfeld (1997) and https://www.chucksconnection/icon.html
4. *Space Jam* was based on a series of Nike commercials that had featured basketball star Michael Jordan and Warner Bros cartoon character Bugs Bunny performing together to advertise Nike shoes. The production of this film was seen, and came to be remembered, as a highly significant moment in the history of movie product placement. As Naomi Klein wrote in her classic book on brand culture *No Logo,* 'It was a historic moment in the branding of culture, completely inverting the traditionally fraught relationship between art and commerce: a shoe company and an ad agency huffing and puffing that a Hollywood movie would sully the purity of their commercials' (Klein 1999: 58). On the commodification of blackness via the relationship between the black male athlete and a branded sports shoe, see McDonald and Andrews (2001).
5. For more on the politics and practice of blackface minstrelsy in the United States see Lott (1995) and Johnson (2012).

References

Asimov, Isaac (1950), *I, Robot*, New York: Gnome Press.

Bacal, Edward D. (2009), 'On the Obama-Ization of Will Smith', *CineAction*, no. 77, pp. 50–2.

Banet-Weiser, Sarah (2012), *AuthenticTM: The Politics of Ambivalence in a Brand Culture*, New York and London: New York University Press.

Bruzzi, Stella (1997), *Undressing Cinema: Clothing and Identity in the Movies*, London and New York: Routledge.

Dyer, Richard (2004 [1986]), *Heavenly Bodies: Film Stars and Society* (2nd edition), London and New York: Routledge.

Dyer, Richard (1997), *White*, London and New York: Routledge.

Gilligan, Sarah (2015), 'Fragmenting the Black Male Body: Will Smith, Masculinity, Clothing and Desire', *Fashion Theory*, vol. 16, no. 2, pp. 171–2.

Hamad, Hannah (2015), 'Eddie Murphy's Baby Mama Drama and Smith Family Values: The (Post-) Racial Familial Politics of Hollywood Celebrity Couples', in S. Cobb and N. Ewen (eds), *First Comes Love: Power Couples, Celebrity Kinship and Cultural Politics*, New York and London: Bloomsbury Academic, pp. 116–32.

Jhally, Sut and Lewis, Justin (1992), *Enlightened Racism: The Cosby Show, Audiences, and the Myth of the American Dream*, Boulder, San Francisco and Oxford: Westview Press.

Johnson, Stephen (ed.) (2012), *Burnt Cork: Traditions and Legacies of Blackface Minstrelsy*, Amherst and Boston: University of Massachusetts Press.

Klein, Naomi (1999), *No Logo: Taking Aim at the Brand Bullies*, New York: Random House/Picador.

Lehu, Jean-Marc (2007), *Branded Entertainment: Product Placement and Brand Strategy in the Entertainment Business*, London and Philadelphia: Kogan Page.

Levinson, Julie (2012), *The American Success Myth on Film*, Basingstoke and New York: Palgrave Macmillan.

Lobalzo-Wright, Julie (2017), *Crossover Stardom: Popular Male Music Stars in American Cinema*, New York and London: Bloomsbury.

Lott, Eric (1995), *Love and Theft: Blackface Minstrelsy and the American Working Class*, Oxford and New York: Oxford University Press.

McDonald, Mary G. and Andrews, David L. (2001), 'Michael Jordan: Corporate Sport and Postmodern Celebrityhood', in D. L. Andrews and S. J. Jackson (eds), *Sport Stars: The Cultural Politics of Sporting Celebrity*, London and New York: Routledge, pp. 20–35.

Mercer, Kobena (1996), 'Just Looking For Trouble: Robert Mapplethorpe and Fantasies of Race', in H. A. Baker Jr, M. Diawara and R. H. Lindeborg (eds), *Black British Cultural Studies: A Reader*, Chicago: University of Chicago Press, pp. 278–92.

Mercer, Kobena (1994), *Welcome to the Jungle: New Positions in Black Cultural Studies*, London and New York: Routledge.

Muellerschoen, Mon and Steinfeld, Peter (1997), *Classics: The Best the World Has to Offer*, Los Angeles: General Publishing Group, Inc.

Palmer, Lorrie (2011), 'Black Man/White Machine: Will Smith Crosses Over', *The Velvet Light Trap*, no. 67, pp. 28–40.

Peterson, Hal (2004), '*I, Robot*', *The Chucks Connection*. Available online: https://www.chucksconnection.com/irobot.html (last accessed 31 May 2019).

Rose, Lacey (2014), 'Hollywood's Best Paid Stars', *Forbes*. Available online: https://www.forbes.com/2007/02/13/actor-actress-oscar-tech-media-cx_lr_0213actor_slide.html#2549868a3515 (last accessed 28 September 2014).

Tolliver, Willie, Jr (2015), 'Transcending Paul Poitier: *Six Degrees of Separation* and the Construction of Will Smith', in I. G. Strachan and M. Mask (eds), *Poitier Revisited: Reconsidering a Black Icon in the Obama Age*, London and New York: Bloomsbury, pp. 253–70.

'Top Ten Moneymaking Stars of the Past 82 Years' (2014), *The 2014 International Motion Picture Almanac*, La Jolla, CA: Quigley Publishing. Available online: http://www.quigley-publishing.com/MPAlmanac/Top10_lists.html (last accessed 10 August 2014).

Chapter 19

'Whoa! Look at all her Louboutins!' Girlhood and shoes in the films of Sofia Coppola

Fiona Handyside

> Only women and gay men can tell the difference between a Manolo.
> Blahnik and a Jimmy Choo.
>
> Camille Paglia, 'The Stiletto Heel'

Sofia Coppola's 2013 film *The Bling Ring*, based on Nancy Jo Sales's *Vanity Fair* 2010 article 'The Suspects Wore Louboutins', shows us the eponymous gang composed of five teen girls, and a lone teen boy, entering celebrities' houses and stealing their clothes, jewellery and shoes. As the title of Sales's article documenting the real-life crimes Coppola lightly fictionalises demonstrates, branded designer shoes are among the most iconic and desirable of the goods the gang take. The credit sequence of the film confirms the importance and significance of Louboutin shoes to the teens and their desire to experience, literally rather than metaphorically, what it is like to walk in someone else's shoes (as long as that someone else is a celebrity).

Following the title card, the film breaks into four rapid shots of the credit sequence which are all of shoes, placing shoes front and centre of the story and its exploration of a group of teens fascinated by celebrity, consumerism and image. The first shot, which lasts the longest at more than two seconds, is a left-right panning shot of shoes in which we can just make out the dark sprawling signature 'Louboutin' on the inside of the shoe (ironically, the trademark red soles are hidden). The shoes are displayed as if they are on racks in a shoe shop, toes facing forwards, and organised by colour and pattern. Altogether we can see fourteen pairs of high-heeled, pointed-toe shoes that pop with colour, glitter and accessories (the shoes themselves are bejewelled and accessorised as if they too are celebrities). This shot functions as a kind of establishing shot, turning these shoes into something akin to a landscape, as the following three shots are all brief, each one lasting barely a second, and consists of a close-up of a section of the shoe shelf we have seen in the first shot. The camera moves throughout the sequence, beginning a left-right pan over the first two shots, then a right–left pan, then back to a left–right pan, imitating the rapid glance of the hyperlinked digital world in which more images of things are always available to be looked at and then swiped past, in contrast to the contemplative gaze associated with the art connoisseur. The teens' recognition of, and desire for, these Louboutins is thus placed directly into a complex politics of taste. While such a large collection could, in other circumstances, be considered an act of curation and the desire to acquire the objects wise investment or display of cultural knowledge, here it is marked as merely acquisitive, potentially greedily excessive. This association of the shoes with bad taste is continued as Coppola uses a bright garish yellow Sub Comic caption font for her credits. The names of the actors playing Marc, Rebecca and Sam – Israel Broussard, Katie Chang and Taissa Farmiga – are superimposed over the first two shots in the sequence, and the names of the actors playing the other three members of the Bling Ring, Chloe, Emily and Nicki – Claire Julien, Georgia Rock and Emma Watson – over the fourth shot.

Shoes come prior to any other objects in the sequence. They are the objects Coppola aligns with her teen cast through superimposing their names over them, prioritising the shoes over other accoutrements of celebrity and aspects of the story we see in the rest of the sequence naming the adult cast and crew, such as close-ups of jewellery, the gang's Facebook pages, Marc attending court and celebrities posing on the red carpet. As the camera pans over a glittering diamond necklace that spells out 'rich bitch' in pink capitals, the credit 'written and directed by Sofia Coppola' appears on the screen, displayed so that the words 'rich bitch' bifurcate the credit and thus precede Coppola's name. This typical deployment of Coppola's dry wit nevertheless confirms for us we are correct to assume special connections between the names displayed in the credit sequence and the goods on display. Furthermore, while Coppola's title card jokily plays with her fame and image, it also shows how she is such a 'rich bitch' she is above the greedy, grasping busy-ness of the teens' relation to shoes. Coppola is a 'rich bitch' who would never need to steal anything, and doesn't need 'bling' to affirm her celebrity status, alerting us to the race and class bias behind notions of good taste and suitable behaviour.

The term bling as slang for jewellery and, by extension, markers of ostentatious wealth, originates from black hip-hop communities where showy displays of jewels are used to signify, and perhaps exaggerate, cultural rank and social power. These spectacles curry favour within materialist cultures that have for decades excluded black communities and derided their 'acquis-itiveness' on racist grounds. As Roopali Mukherjee explains, commodity consumption thus emerges as a conflicted site in which goods are used to assert political subjectivity, even while these efforts are met with ridicule and censure (Mukherjee 2012: 117). As Stephen Gundle further notes, the term bling is

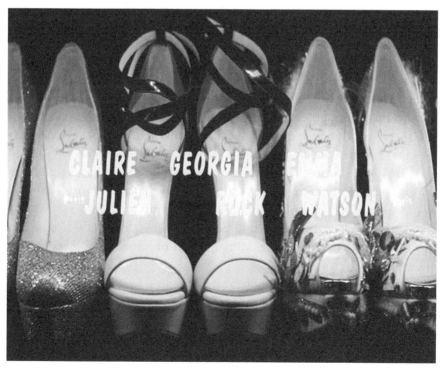

Figures 19.1 and 19.2 *The Bling Ring*'s credit sequence shows cast members' names superimposed over shoes

associated with a trashy, bad-taste glamour aesthetic, which has hidden racial and class associations (Gundle 2008: 331). The teenagers of *The Bling Ring*, all of whom are coded as white, appropriate black hip-hop and R&B culture without consequence. Although Katie Chang, who plays Rebecca Ahn, is part Korean, the film represents her as just another white middle-class girl, whereas the real-life bling ring included Diane Tamayo, an illegal immigrant who was threatened with deportation. Coppola's teens can play with a 'bling' lifestyle without inciting any of the legal or social issues an explicitly black or Latina identity would evoke.[1] Nevertheless, the teens' investment in celebrity and commodity culture as a symbolic means to assert their personhood operates in a world that allows its most privileged citizens, such as Coppola herself, to not need such devices for political and social power, and which judges such activity as being in poor taste.

The bright colours and striking patterns of the Louboutin shoes offer a sensory feast for the eyes, while the repetitive styling of the high heels and the signature allows for the quick brand recognition necessary for teens to emulate and achieve a celebrity look. As Sales's article title makes clear, it's not any old pair of shoes this group are stealing, but Louboutins: the brand name functions to mark these objects out as something more than (or rather *other* than) mere practical clothing for the feet. While Coppola's film title removes the direct reference to designer shoes, her credit sequence deftly inserts glamorous Louboutin shoes right at the start of the film and links them solidly back to the brand identity of the group and their fascination with/need for the glamorous accoutrements of the celebrity lifestyle. The rapid camera movement and cutting gives this sequence a hyper, kinetic energy, imitating the adrenalin buzz of a shopping spree or a crime haul. It showcases the shoes as beautiful, glittering objects, to be acquired quickly in a momentary ecstatic sweep, and the knowledge that allows the girls to identify them so efficiently as desirable is formatted in a culture that privileges speed, vision, commodities and surface over deliberation, thought, people and depth. This rapid sequence, lasting just three seconds of screen time, functions to give us important information about the roles of shoes in this story and perhaps in the Coppola universe more generally, which is a sympathetic illumination of the cultural links between girlhood, leisure/crime and shoes.

Some critics found the film shallow. For Jeffrey Lyles *The Bling Ring* was 'a film as vapid and empty as its subjects and inspiration' (Lyles 2013), and Melissa Anderson argued it was 'remote, repetitive . . . [and] as insubstantial as the reality TV stars name-checked (and burgled) throughout' (Anderson 2013), while Jeff Beck wrote, '*The Bling Ring* is the most superficial film I've seen [. . .] There's so little here in the way of substance. . .' (Beck 2013: 14). Such accusations of frivolity and superficiality are frequent in critical reactions to Coppola's work, most notably her 2006 film *Marie Antoinette*, the teen queen biopic, which was infamously greeted with boos following its press screening at the Cannes Film Festival.[2] Not coincidentally, this film too shows us a teen girl indulging in the delights of designer shoes: anachronistically, the shoes Marie Antoinette (Kirsten Dunst) has in her closets have high heels, alongside one rogue pair of Converse high-tops. The heels are the work of designer Manolo Blahnik, at the suggestion of the film's costume designer Milano Canonero (Diamond 2011: 209). It is my contention, however, that these films – both in spite of and through their apparent shallowness – deliver complex critical commentary on contemporary relations between the representation of teenage girls and the perpetuation of a glamorised consumer capitalism in the face of massive social inequalities. Rather than these films seeing intense interest in the tiny differences that mark a Louboutin from a Blahnik from a Jimmy Choo as indicative of teen girls' stupidity and crassness, they show us how teen girls are a product of a stupid and crass system that rewards their investment in gaining and performing such knowledge. It is not that the shoes cover up a more substantial politics, whether that of the suffering that led to the French Revolution (an event *Marie Antoinette* sidelines) or the racial and class divides of contemporary Los Angeles (left implicit in the white, beige and cream suburban houses lived in by Coppola's middle-class teens, serviced by Mexican maids only ever present in the background of the shot). Rather, designer shoes *are* the substantial politics, the prize fetish object of a system that, while offering girls some power and agency outside traditional gender roles, still depends on class, race and gender difference to continue.

In an interview with Kent Jones at the Lincoln Film Center promoting *The Bling Ring*, Coppola says she never expected to make a true crime story movie, and Jones replies, 'maybe you could argue that *Marie Antoinette* is kind of a true crime story. People plundered and pillaged a nation.' Coppola replies, to general laughter, 'Uh yeah, I didn't think of that, I've heard of comparisons because of the amount of shoes, but I didn't think about the crime aspect' (Coppola 2013). Coppola's acknowledgment that *Marie Antoinette* and *The Bling Ring* are both in some ways true crime stories about shoes positions her teen girl subjects as criminal in their pursuit of luxury designer shoes. Indeed, Coppola's films show us how the crime of acquiring (excessive amounts of) shoes emerges effortlessly and naturally out of the worlds these girls find themselves in, whether that be as the queen of an absolute monarch at Versailles in eighteenth-century France or as a wannabe reality TV star in twenty-first-century Los Angeles.

Just as *The Bling Ring* provides its audience with a montage sequence in which shoes play an important part, so too does *Marie Antoinette*. Described by Heidi Brevik-Zender as 'perhaps the most significant transhistorical fashion moment in the film' (Brevik-Zender 2011: 13), the shoe montage takes place within a two-minute-forty-second-long music video that also includes fans, pastries, wigs, silk swatches, small dogs, card games, jewellery, hairdressing and champagne. The soundtrack to this sequence is the song 'I Want Candy', a 1982 hit for New Wave band Bow Wow Wow whose lead singer, Annabella, was, like Marie Antoinette, a teenager. This use of a teen girl voice from the 1980s on the soundtrack, able to clearly articulate her desire, contrasts with the stifled court world the 1770s-based Marie Antoinette operates in. After all, the event that triggers this sequence is Marie Antoinette's distress that her sister-in-law has given birth while she is still unable to consummate her marriage with her husband and fulfil her expected wifely duty of providing an heir. The soundtrack and the images work together to offer the cinematic Marie Antoinette as imagined by Coppola the opportunity to express a teen girl desire for 'candy' of various sorts; a desire that emerges from a world in which teenage girls have precious little political power.

The sequence opens with a left–right pan across five brightly coloured and heavily decorated shoes (two pairs light blue, and one pair each of pink, bright yellow, dark blue; trimmed with bows, ribbons, diamonds and fur). As the pan stops, hands reach in and grab the shoes. Starting the whole sequence with shoes echoes the prominent position shoes occupy in *The Bling Ring* credit sequence, and the alacrity with which shoes are grabbed suggests they are a sweet comfort in the same way as the actual confectionary we see consumed later in the sequence. We see shoes featured on two subsequent occasions in the sequence. First, a series of beribboned shoeboxes are filmed from above and opened to reveal the gorgeous confections within. This flurry of opening shoeboxes concludes on a shot of pink-shoe-clad feet wriggling in apparent delight; the ground-level shot also captures a full champagne coupe and a plate of delicate pink macarons placed on the floor, creating a symphony in shades of pink and yellow that seal shoes' place in the world of teen girl pleasures alongside food and drink. Just as shoes can be practical, but here are transformed into fantastical objects, so too the everyday world of nourishment is converted into luxurious sparkling wine and indulgent sugary treats. Second, we have a quick overhead frozen photomontage of eight pairs of shoes. In the first image, the shoes are neatly lined up; in the second, the shoes have moved on the diagonal; in the third, the shoes have fallen and one pair has been removed. This still photomontage technique in which human action is suggested but not shown recalls and references the layouts used in high fashion magazines such as *Vogue* and *Harper's Bazaar* in the 1950s (for more on this see Sellars 1995). Such images also reflect these magazines' artistic directors' fascination with the mechanical techniques of the American avant-garde, such as montage and the stylistic application of surrealism and modernism, reclaiming even the

Figure 19.3 Marie Antoinette's lavender blue Converse high-tops sit alongside Manolo Blahnik-designed high heels

sterile rational world of the International Style for the allegedly superficial and frivolous world of the girl who likes shoes.

Brevik-Zender discusses the significance of possibly the most memorable shot in this sequence. The opening panning shot is followed by a shot that foregrounds a pair of ankles in blue stockings and feet clad in light blue silk shoes with blue and diamond bows; in the background, unworn, are a very similar pair of pink silk shoes and a lavender coloured pair of Converse high-tops.

The scene depends for its frisson on our instinctive recognition of the blurred timelines this represents. For the early 2000s audience watching *Marie Antoinette* on its initial release, the most likely association of Converse trainers was with the 1990s musical style known as grunge, whose bands dressed in a unisex uniform of flannel shirts, beanie hats, ripped jeans and Converse shoes (a look easily imitated by fans). The music and the clothes became identified with 'Generation X', or 'slackers', young people coming of age in the 1990s and allegedly without the secure futures of their baby-boomer parents. The connection between grunge, Converse and youthful alienation and disaffection was sealed by the mass-syndicated pictures of Kurt Cobain from grunge band Nirvana following his suicide. Photographs circulated of his dead body in his garage, his Converse shoes clearly visible in close-up (Strong 2011: 3). Converse trainers thus connote youthful disaffection and rebellion.

Furthermore, in their unisex appeal and practical use, they vividly contrast with the high heels which, while beautiful, only confirm the restrictions of Marie Antoinette's gendered existence (such shoes would not be suitable for any kind of athletic activity or farm work, although she attempts a fantasised version of the latter which only subjects her to ridicule).[3]

Yet, as Brevik-Zender explains, deeper brand knowledge gives this scene further resonance:

> the Converse high-tops that viewers read as anachronistically modern were, in fact, invented as basketball shoes in 1917, and enjoyed the first of their many waves of popularity when marketing genius Chuck Taylor attached his name to them in the 1920s [...] By contrast [...] the opulent costume shoes featured throughout were designed by contemporary haute couture footwear guru Manolo Blahnik, who today sells his pricey stilettos, dubbed Manolos, with similar self-branding prowess. (Brevik Zender 2011: 13)

Brevik-Zender's careful reading here shows how shoe brands play with notions of historic authenticity. Neither shoe belongs to a historically accurate portrayal of eighteenth-century Versailles, although the blue silk shoes look the part far more than the high-tops. Yet the high-tops are the more antiquated pair of shoes, coming from the 1920s rather than the 2000s. Coppola's girlishly playful decision to leave in the Converse that was allegedly placed in the frame as a joke by her brother[4], whose second unit filmed the entire montage sequence, speaks also to the film's more serious project of questioning anyone's ability to represent accurately what the historic Marie Antoinette's existence was like, and the extent to which we can judge her (permitted) extravagance as criminal greed.

Coppola's display of glorious, manic, delirious quantities of shoes, provides a neat illumination of the lyrics of British post-punk band Gang of Four's 'Natural's Not In It', which talk of leisure as a problem to be solved by shopping. The music plays over the beginning of *Marie Antoinette* as a maid slips a pink silk shoe onto Marie Antoinette/Kirsten Dunst's foot while she eats cake. Girls are shaped in a culture that imagines them as fulfilling the problem of how to fill in their leisure time by buying/robbing things. In Coppola's world, it is hard to tell the difference between the two. The Bling Ring refer interchangeably to 'shopping' and 'robbing'. In the opening credit sequence, Rebecca exclaims 'Let's go shopping', as she slides open a glass door, whereas later Nicki, smoking a roll-up cigarette, will impatiently say, 'Let's go to Paris's. I want to rob.' Marie Antoinette is lectured by Count Mercy (Steve Coogan), her advisor, on the worsening bread shortage in France, but all she can think to suggest is asking the court jeweller to stop supplying diamond necklaces. Although the film has Marie Antoinette explicitly deny she uttered the words 'let them eat cake' in response to her starving population, it shows a (criminal?) lack of awareness about her privileged position and excessive consumption. Acquiring things is constructed as a rush of feeling, a whirl of heightened emotions and fun, in which longer-term issues are ignored. Coppola's most memorable shoe images in both films are montage sequences filmed as if they are music videos, with the sassy jingle of Bow Wow Wow's 'I Want Candy' or the abrasive metal of Sleigh Bells' 'Crown on the Ground'. These exciting sequences make use of the all the devices of cinema – colour, movement, sound, light – to offer thrilling and absorbing sensual revelry. These shoes are (cinematic) art before they are practical footwear, and the girls experience the shoes as a joyful indulgence rather than anticipating the consequences of how they acquired them. So 'natural' is the role of shoes in this girl culture that perhaps it doesn't even feel like a crime simply to go out and get them, regardless of the broader social impact and context.

As Christoph Lindner argues, shoes have played an important role in critical theory as they are objects that blend art and consumerism. He quotes Fredric Jameson's famous comparison of Van Gogh's 1886 painting *A Pair of Shoes*, which speaks to us of a whole life world, and Andy Warhol's early 1980s screen print series *Diamond Dust Shoes*, which are 'a random collection of dead objects' (Lindner 2015: 237). Lindner argues that Jameson's inquiry no longer seems edgy or vital, as postmodernism's flatness and superficiality is accepted as part of everyday life. Coppola's shoes in both *Marie Antoinette* and *The Bling Ring* move beyond Jameson's account of the art-object shoe into an emotional relation to the designer shoe. Designer shoes are commodities, but in this world, they function in a way more akin to art, channelling affects of energy and excitement into repetitive and boring lives but without the prestige and power connoisseurship bestows. *Marie Antoinette* shows Versailles as a place of complex and baroque rituals that stifle spontaneity and freedom. On her first morning in Versailles, Marie Antoinette shivers, naked, while ladies-in-waiting bicker over who has the right to handle her clothes. The young princess denounces the actions as ridiculous, only for her to be chastised by the curt rejoinder that 'this is Versailles!', the very location demanding and justifying the grotesque parody of domestic bliss. In *The Bling Ring*, Nicki, Emily and Sam's mother, Laurie's (Leslie Mann) attempts at spiritual home-schooling via an Angelina Jolie vision board is undermined by their obvious lack of interest. 'What is most special about Angelina Jolie?' asks Laurie. 'Her husband?' asks Sam and the girls giggle and smirk. 'How much longer are we doing this?' asks Nicki, staring at her mobile phone. These girls see shoes as neither items to buy nor objects to admire, but as effective and affective strategies in the creation of a more exciting and thrilling life beyond these boring routines. Now what matters is how shoes make you feel, and to feel right, you need the right shoe.

The acquisition of knowledge

The Bling Ring shows us both the significance of the designer shoe as an index of a celebrity lifestyle and the importance of being able to distinguish between different designer brands. As suggested by the Camille Paglia quotation I cite at the beginning of the chapter, the film shows how sexuality and gender impact on the production of this knowledge; unlike Paglia, however, it also emphasises the importance of youth to this dynamic. The Bling Ring are teenagers, well versed in digital culture and able to exploit it to carry out their crimes. The film deploys a series of montages between internet sites showing celebrities and identifying the various components of their outfits, including their shoes; to internet sites showing celebrity addresses; to google maps allowing the precise locating of the house; to footage of the teens breaking and entering, as if the actions all follow seamlessly from one to the other. All these various orders of behaviour and knowledge are created by and deployed within a digital celebrity-oriented culture that the teens navigate with ease. Other institutions – school, the family – are pushed to the edges of the frame, as the knowledge and values they inculcate are less important in navigating this world, and the teen girls seem barely aware of the fact they are committing crimes. The one character in the film who feels less at ease, and who worries during the house break-ins, constantly repeating 'let's get the fuck out of here', is Marc. Less socially confident than the girls, more worried about his looks, and gay, Marc's relationship to designer shoes develops differently to that of the girls in the gang – Rebecca, Nicki, Sam, Chloe and Emily. Whereas for the girls the shoes underline their knowing and glamorous performance of an idealised femininity, ready to be photographed and uploaded to social media, for Marc the shoes remain hidden. He wears a bright pink pair of Paris Hilton's high heels just once, posing in them for the girls, and drawing their laughter as they say 'If only the guys at school could see you now!' The shoes then get packed away in the attic at his parents' house; the next time we see them is when they are carted away as evidence during a police raid as Marc cries to his mother. Even though all the teens in *The Bling Ring* covet designer shoes and use their knowledge to acquire them, the film shows how they are able to use and enjoy them differently along lines marked by class, gender and sexual difference.

In the metropolitan, urban environment of contemporary Los Angeles it is, above all, teen girls who have the geographical proximity and sociocultural knowhow to be able to acquire these celebrity-owned branded shoes, and parlay this acquisition into cool cultural capital which in turn offers them the ability to brand and celebritise themselves. The film shows how designer shoes become part of a dense network of branded celebrity identities, each shoring up the other in a system where intensities and affects shift rapidly through mediated digital encounters. Knowing what brand these shoes are, which celebrities wear which brands, and therefore wearing precisely this pair of shoes and not others, and then letting as many people as possible know that you know these things through the image of yourself wearing these shoes being broadcast via the various channels available on the internet, creates an enhanced and improved self-worth. This worth manifests both in the sense of a more secure and happier existence and in the sense of being able to monetise one's own personal brand. The fact that these girls committed crimes to boost their self-esteem is not ignored by the film and we see them being arrested and put on trial. However, as suits the gendered dynamic I discuss above, it is only Marc we see imprisoned, wearing an orange uniform and being chained to a fellow prisoner. In contrast, the film finishes on an image of Nicki proclaiming her website address. At the very start of the film, before the story circles back to one year earlier, it is Nicki we have seen earnestly proclaiming to multiple cameras that she will use her experience to grow and become a better person; that she 'may lead a country one day, for all I know.' The film shows how the girls' relationship to designer fashion, especially designer shoes, far from being criminal and aberrant, is actually promoted and glamorised in contemporary Los Angeles and the digital culture that emanates from it.

The Bling Ring rapidly introduces us to how this shoe knowledge is produced within teen culture, when ten minutes into the film we see Marc and Rebecca cementing their new friendship by browsing through magazines featuring celebrities while sitting on the floor in her bedroom. As the two of them swap information about their lives – their ambitions, their parents' jobs, their schooling – they also discuss celebrity styles, carefully and minutely detailing their looks. Rebecca comments about a female celebrity, 'that's so cute. I love that dress. I love Chanel', and Marc replies, 'yeah, and the shoes, but she needs better hair extensions' to which Rebecca responds, 'I know, right?' She leans in slightly for a better look at the shoes in the photo and turns to Marc. 'Are those Prada?' Marc confidently responds 'Miu Miu.' Rebecca replies, 'Really? Wow' and it seems that it is this moment of Marc proving his knowledge of shoes that seals his role within the group as style advisor. He works in a similar fashion to a celebrity stylist, advising the girls on the correct combinations of accessories, shoes, patterns and prints to perform the look of celebrity teen girlhood. Marc's knowledge marks him as out-of-step with mainstream male culture (and presumably as homosexual) but includes him in the girl friendship circle.

Alison Winch has demonstrated that many contemporary films that display a postfeminist sensibility explore the ramifications of girlfriend culture for teen girl identity. Winch explains that these films pinpoint the 'normative cruelties' that are displayed in girl friendships, where the 'many girls survey the many girls' in what Winch calls the gynaeoptican (Winch 2013: 64). Girls advise each other on the correct way to behave and the correct way to look in a culture that exhorts bodily surveillance from its girl subjects. *The Bling Ring* shows how for these teen girls, friendship norms become imbricated with celebrity culture, so that the 'girlfriend gaze' takes on a further twist where it acquires knowledge of designer goods, most especially here shoes, and promotes this knowledge as essential to the correct performance of girlhood. This means that the criminality that fuels the acquisition of these shoes, far from being subversive or transgressive, in fact shores up the norms of teen girl culture.

The teen girl in this film is thus shown to be a key shaper and subject of consumer and popular culture. Maryn Wilkinson argues that teen girls are tasked with the affective labour of producing the informational and cultural content of the commodity. This includes all the activities involved in defining and fixing artistic and cultural standards, fashions, tastes, norms and public opinion. As Wilkinson explains, such

> immaterial labor demands a process of mass intellectuality and constant self-valorization; a general knowledge that is produced collectively, through communication, productive cooperation and collective learning, which is then taken on by the 'subjectivities' it produces, to reproduce that very knowledge. [...]The films [*The Bling Ring* and *Spring Breakers*] suggest that it is precisely this general knowledge that allows its actors to transgress so easily; to just resituate, extend, and apply that knowledge elsewhere, because it is already theirs for the making, and taking. (Wilkinson 2017)

In fact, the knowledge we see deployed as central to giving the commodity informational and cultural content concerns shoes. They are turned from being merely one fashion item among many to being the core content of celebrity teen girlhood. While Marc's branded shoe knowledge (distinguishing Prada from Miu Miu) is demonstrated early on, the notion that this knowledge is key to performance of successful teen femininity is shown in a section of the film where all five girls from the gang and Marc are shown in Paris Hilton's mansion. The significance of shoes is signalled as they occupy a special room accessed via a door in Hilton's walk-in wardrobe: a closet within a closet. This topographical arrangement reinforces the notion that shoes contain a secret power that can be unleashed through knowledge. The film viewer as well as the group gets to enjoy the sheer volume of Hilton's shoe collection as the camera pans around shelves filled with brightly coloured high heels, ordered by colour (the scene was filmed at the real-life location, after Coppola managed to orchestrate a meeting with Hilton at the latter's birthday party). The shoes are organised more as spectacle than as practical items, their organisation along shelves recalling the phantasmagoria of the urban window display as discussed by Walter Benjamin in his work on the city of Paris's growth as the epicentre of modernity and its concomitant promotion of the pleasures of shopping. Arranged over multiple shelves in a display ordered by colour, the shoes look more as if they are there for the buying/taking than as if they are part of a functional everyday wardrobe. We join the girls exclaiming over the shoes and examining their heels, bows and straps as they scream excitedly, 'Woah, look at her Louboutins!'

Sam wanders over to the black shoes and begins looking at them, finally picking up a black shoe with a slender stiletto heel and flipping it over to reveal Paris's signature. 'Oh my God! She's got her own line! Look!' Sam then spots a leopard print pair on the other side of the closet, saying 'I'll take these Loubies', before murmuring 'can't wear them though', as they have discovered Hilton has size eleven feet. The only member of the gang whose feet they fit is Marc, who poses for them while wearing a bright pink pair, wobbling slightly uncertainly on the enormous heels. Indeed, the discovery that Hilton has such big feet and that only Marc is able to wear the shoes as they are too big for all the girls doesn't at all diminish their pleasure in the act of finding them in Hilton's wardrobe. Access to these particular designer shoes has both allowed for the fulfilment of a relatively conventional relationship to a shoe (I would like to own this shoe and wear it), but also a whole intense affective rush of closeness to a celebrity. Hilton's unfeminine big feet are an unexpected flaw in a beautiful celebrity who appears the epitome of Barbie-doll femininity with her slender figure, long blonde hair and blue eyes. Knowing her feet are big is a piece of intimate knowledge gained from a tactile handling of her shoes, a movement beyond the image and into the materiality of the shoe itself. Such shifts from image to object are vital to a theory of designer shoes developing here as being neither art nor commodity but affect-carrier, an intimacy also underlined in giving the shoes the casual nickname of 'Loubies'.

In this world, the priorities and fantasies of teen girls rule. Digital celebrity culture appeals to them and takes their desires seriously. The teen girls produce themselves as suitable for incorporation into this culture through their ability to acquire its goods and understand their significance and importance. Designer shoes thus operate as a mechanism for a not-so subtle demarcation of inclusion and exclusion. Elizabeth Wissinger has coined the term 'glamour labour' to describe the cultural construction of the body in contemporary Western culture (Wissinger 2015: 3). Glamour labour involves working on the physical body and its multiple manifestations as image across digital media. It covers the physical areas of diet, exercise and grooming, but also operates as a virtual mode, such as keeping up with fashion magazines and watching awards shows, distinguishing between multiple brands, cultivating friendships and fun and manipulating photo filters, so as to maintain a cool image on social and networked media. Several scholars have discussed the aesthetic labour involved in maintaining a desirable body; the difference with Wissinger's use of the term glamour labour is that it fuses the physical and virtual aspects of bodywork in pursuit of the fashionable ideal. Glamour labour describes the process through which life, work and appearance blend together, and are made part of what is promoted as the good life. The current era of live streaming, taking selfies, geolocating and living online has intensified the pull of glamour labour, so that it is no longer the preserve of fashion models or female celebrities, although these lines of work make glamour labour seem attractive and desirable.

The virtual knowledge that glamour labour requires is gleaned not via prolonged study or educational effort but rather through a technique of skimming through multiple websites from various magazines, entertainment channels, paparazzi images, Twitter feeds and social media. *The Bling Ring* shows us some of the work of glamour labour and imitates this technique of skimming through multiple media forms and formats, editing together static surveillance footage, hand-held camera close-ups on objects, documentary-style talking heads, reality TV and red carpet images of celebrities, actual news footage and art-cinema techniques of slow zooms and locked-down camera positions on near-static tableaux. The fleeting engagement with any one style or form is the point. This is a world in which knowledge must be gained on the fly, from skimming a surface. The girls acquire their understanding of designer shoe brands in an economy that ensures this information is quickly and easily accessible. As Sara Pesce explains, the twenty-first century has seen a revolution in the availability and use of luxury fashion goods and high fashion's 'impact on the desires and behaviours of "ordinary people" has [...] become ubiquitous' (Pesce 2015: 7). Couture houses pursue ambivalent and contra-dictory policies of democratising luxury, constructing a global middle-market through producing lower-cost accessories (shoes, handbags, sunglasses, perfume), while at the same time extending the system of dressing Hollywood stars and provocative publicity campaigns. The luxury goods industry infiltrates much of the media these teens consume, so that brand knowledge becomes a basic and essential tool in navigating the world they inhabit, shaped as it is by celebrity culture and consumer capitalism. The couture houses, now run by large corporations, work hard to ensure that such knowledge is accessible in the fleeting moments that teens deign to give them, while also endowing such knowledge with the mystique of celebrity associations and elitist lifestyles and the affects of joy and happiness.

Furthermore, Coppola's films themselves play a role in this process of expanding shoe knowledge and recognition. In twenty-first century screen culture, Nick Rees-Roberts argues, the fashion industry has moved from a niche use of media aimed at fashion insiders to the commercially profitable hybrid concepts of 'motion content' and 'branded entertainment'. Meanwhile, Hilary Radner, cited by Rees-Roberts, identifies the fashion film as a feature film that transcends product placement to embed narrative within an elaborate consumer environment, self-consciously playing upon the attraction fashion and style may hold for a potential audience in its conception and promotion (Rees-Roberts 2018: 13). For example, the *Sex and the City* TV series (1998–2004) and feature film franchise (Michael Patrick King, USA, 2008 & 2010) regularly showed the four main characters, especially Carrie (Sarah Jessica Parker), wearing Manolo Blahnik heels. The synergy between the shoes and the series reached an apogee in the 2008 movie when it featured close-ups of Manolo Blahnik heels used as a prop to replace a diamond ring in a marriage proposal. *Marie Antoinette* and *The Bling Ring*, with their ability to take us into the real locations where these shoes are worn (Versailles and Hilton's home), hyperbolic brand name checking and cameo appearances, are themselves part of this screen culture in which part of the audience's pleasure is derived from the sense that they are gaining insider knowledge about designer shoes and the people who wear them.

Conclusion

These shoes, in their excess and connotations of a life of leisure and ease, invite critical opprobrium on both the girls who buy/borrow/steal and wear them, and the films that show us girls enjoying doing just that. *The Bling Ring* and *Marie Antoinette* construct a rhetoric of shoes that shows how they work to associate successful femininity with contradictory and paradoxical traits of luxury, glamour, leisure, excess, criminality, transgression and knowledge. In both films, teen girls desire beautiful high-heeled shoes – objects marked as for female-identified bodies. In both films, these shoes are figured as excessive as the camera pans over multitudes of pairs. In contrast to Cinderella or Dorothy, whose relationship to shoes is vital to their iconic performances of girlhood, these girls don't have a relation to one special, magical shoe; rather, they covet multiple shoes produced by named, earth-bound designers. Rachel Moseley explains how postfeminist culture deploys the supernatural to enable a precarious balancing act between glamour and power in the construction of idealised femininity. Historically, the etymology of the word glamour means 'enchantment, spell', and associates femininity with mystery, physical allure and power. In the recurrent figure of the teen witch, found in films and television programmes such as *Charmed* (1998–2006), *The Craft* (Andrew Fleming, USA, 1996) and *Sabrina, the Teenage Witch* (1996–2003), charmed sparkle signifies the coincidence of the witches' femininity and power. 'While they often dramatize contemporary anxieties around the conjunction of gender and power, the common-sense meaning of the word "glamour" is securely in place, with power, danger and difference safely contained on the spectacular surface of the text' (Moseley 2002: 422).

The power of Cinderella's and Dorothy's shoes is explained through their supernatural aura, which partially relies also on their uniqueness – only the correct owner can get full benefit from the shoe. We have no such story to attach to the multiple shoes of Marie Antoinette and Paris Hilton, and without this alibi for their power the glamour of the shoes tips towards criminality and greed. The disgraced Queen Marie Antoinette and the fame-hungry Bling Ring celetoids offer a more threatening and more mocked version of teen girlhood than witches. Contemporary girls and women are exhorted to participate in a gendered beauty and celebrity culture in which high heels figure as the epitome of glamour, but they are judged as their delight in these shoes is found excessive and vulgar, not leavened by a bit of magic sparkle. In Coppola's films, shoes become an object that shows how the very qualities girls are encouraged to cultivate, such as prettiness, interest in fashion and appearance, indulging in trivial gossip about celebrities and acquiring enough knowledge to imitate their style, become the defects for which they are judged and punished. In such a double bind these girls do not so much abandon morality as dismiss it as irrelevant hypocrisy. It is not surprising from this perspective that we never see Coppola's Marie Antoinette at the guillotine; nor do we see the Bling Ring girls endure prison. Such reckonings are beyond the universe these films describe. Fascinated by the glamour, the sparkle, the quasi-impossible heights of shoes, Coppola's camera pans over them, offering audiences a glimpse of why they are so desirable for her girl subjects and, within the film world at least, both the characters and the audience are allowed to enjoy them without condemnation.

Notes

1. For various accounts of Coppola's omission of Diane Tamayo's story, see Meagan Hatcher-Mays, 'How Sofia Coppola Whitewashed The Bling Ring' *Jezebel*, 20 June 2013; Muna Mire and Isabelle Nastasia, 'Sofia Coppola and the Unbearable Whiteness of The Bling Ring', *mic.com*, 4 July 2013; Jorge Rivas, 'The Immigrant You Won't See in Sofia Coppola's Bling Ring', *ColorLines*, 13 June 2013.

2. See for example the debate between Manohla Dargis and A.O.Scott in *The New York Times* on 25 May 2006 about Coppola's decision to remove Marie Antoinette's bloody death from her film, and whether the film rises above pastiche.
3. Founded in 1908 by Marquis Mills Converse in Malden, Massachusetts, the Converse Rubber Shoe Company has produced variants on the Converse high-tops since 1917. Their golden period was the 1940s–1960s, when they dominated the sports market and they were also worn by such iconic figures of youth rebellion as James Dean and the Jets in *West Side Story* (Wise and Robbins, USA, 1961). By the 1990s and grunge their association with youthful counter-culture was well established. Following management changes (the brand was bought by Nike in 2001), the company now concentrates on fashion and creativity over sport uses of the shoe. See Katya Foreman, 'Converse Shoes: In the All-Star Game', *BBC.com*, 21 October 2014. Converse shoes continue to connote cool, rebellious youth, and now have (feminist) associations with rejection of oppressive fashion norms in celebrity culture, such as Kristin Stewart's decision to wear Converse on the red carpet (despite her stylist apparently begging her not to). See for example Sally Holmes, 'The Definitive Guide to Kristin Stewart's Ten Pairs of Sneakers', *The Cut*, 21 November 2012; Anon, 'Kristin Stewart: 7 Things we can learn from this Reluctant Style Icon', *Marie-Claire.co.uk*, 9 July 2014.
4. 'Why was that? Yeah, he [Roman] shot the whole "I Want Candy" montage and he just saw that there [the trainers] and put it in for me for fun. He just shot a bunch of stuff and left that in for fun because he thought I would like it, and then when I was editing we decided to leave it in.' Todd Gilchrist, 'Interview: Sofia Coppola', *IGN*, 17 October 2006.

References

Anderson, Melissa (2013), 'We'll Always Have Paris', *Artforum*.
Anon (2014), 'Kristin Stewart: 7 Things we can learn from this Reluctant Style Icon', *Marie-Claire.co.uk*, 9 July.
Beck, Jeff (2013), 'The Bling Ring', *The Examiner*.
Benjamin, Walter (2006), *The Writer of Modern Life: Essays on Charles Baudelaire*, in M. Jennings (ed.), Cambridge, MA: Belknap Press.
Brevik-Zender, Heidi (2011), 'Let them wear Manolos: Fashion, Walter Benjamin, and Sofia Coppola's *Marie Antoinette*', *Camera Obscura*, vol. 78, no. 26 (3), pp. 1–33.
Coppola, Sofia (2013), 'Summer Talks: The Bling Ring', Film Society of Lincoln Center, New York, http://www.filmlinc.org/daily/summer talks-sofia- coppola- on- the-bling-ring
Dargis, Manohla (2006), 'Under the Spell of Royal Ritual', *New York Times*.
Diamond, Diana (2011), 'Sofia Coppola's *Marie Antoinette*: Costumes, Girl Power and Feminism', in A. Munich (ed.), *Fashion and Film*, Bloomington and Indianapolis: Indiana University Press, pp. 203–31.
Foreman, Katya (2014), 'Converse Shoes: In the All-Star Game' *BBC.com*, 21 October.
Gilchrist, Todd (2006), 'Interview: Sofia Coppola', *IGN*, http://uk.ign.com/articles/2006/10/17/interview-sofia-coppola
Gundle, Stephen (2008), *Glamour: A History*, Oxford: Oxford University Press.
Hatcher-Mays, Meagan (2013), 'How Sofia Coppola Whitewashed *The Bling Ring*', *Jezebel*, 20 June.

Holmes, Sally (2012), 'The Definitive Guide to Kristin Stewart's Ten Pairs of Sneakers', *The Cut*, 21 November.

Lindner, Christoph (2015), 'The Oblique Art of Shoes: Popular Culture, Aesthetic Pleasure, and the Humanities', *Journal of Cultural Research*, vol. 19, no. 3, pp. 233–47.

Lyles, Jeffrey (2013), 'The Bling Ring', *Lyles Movie Files* https://lylesmoviefiles.com/2013/11/14/review-the-bling-ring/

Mire, Muna and Nastasia, Isabelle (2013), 'Sofia Coppola and the Unbearable Whiteness of *The Bling Ring*', *mic.com*, 4 July.

Moseley, Rachel (2002), 'Glamorous Witchcraft: Gender and Magic in Teen Film and Television', *Screen*, vol. 44, no. 3, pp. 403–22.

Mukherjee, Roopali (2012), 'Diamonds (Are From Sierra Leone): Bling and the Promise of Consumer Citizenship', in R. Mukherjee and S. Banet-Weiser (eds), *Commodity Activism: Consumer Resistance in Neoliberal Times*, New York: New York University Press, pp. 114–33.

Paglia, Camille (2013), 'The Stiletto Heel', https://www.moma.org/interactives/exhibitions/2013/designandviolence/the-stiletto-heel/

Pesce, Sara (2015), 'Ripping off Hollywood celebrities: Sofia Coppola's *The Bling Ring*, luxury fashion and self-branding in California', *Film, Fashion and Consumption*, vol. 4, no. 1, pp. 5–24.

Rees-Roberts, Nick (2018), *Fashion Film: Art and Advertising in the Digital Age*, London: Bloomsbury.

Rivas, Jorge (2013), 'The Immigrant You Won't See in Sofia Coppola's *Bling Ring*', *ColorLines*, 13 June.

Scott, Anthony (2006), 'Holding Up a Mirror to Hollywood', *New York Times*.

Sellars, Susan (1995), 'How Long Has This Been Going On? *Harper's Bazaar, Funny Face* and the Construction of the Modernist Woman', *Visible Language*, vol. 29, no. 1, pp. 13–35.

Strong, Catherine (2011), *Grunge, Music and Memory*, Farnham: Ashgate.

Wilkinson, Maryn (2017), 'Leisure/Crime, Immaterial Labor, and the Performance of the Teenage Girl in Harmony Korine's *Spring Breakers* (2012) and Sofia Coppola's *The Bling Ring* (2013)', *Journal of Feminist Scholarship*, vol. 12, no. 12, pp. 20–37.

Winch, Alison (2013), *Girlfriends and Postfeminist Sisterhood*, Basingstoke: Palgrave.

Wissinger, Elizabeth (2015), *This Year's Model: Fashion, Media, and the Making of Glamour*, New York: New York University Press.

Chapter 20

Isabelle's espadrilles, or, *les chaussures d'Huppert*

Catherine Wheatley

> A lady is known by her shoes.
>
> Isabelle Huppert in *Greta*

In an early sequence of Mia Hansen-Løve's 2016 film, *L'Avenir/Things to Come*, Nathalie Chazeaux, the philosophy teacher played by Isabelle Huppert, is asked by her students to set them a topic for debate. Nathalie sits perched at her desk as she ponders their request. She is in her late fifties or early sixties, dressed in a printed blouse, blue denim straight-leg jeans and tan leather court shoes with a thick, mid-height heel. Her tan suede Gérard Darel jacket is thrown over the back of her chair.

Having seemingly come to a decision, Nathalie stands and descends the platform on which her desk is posed, placing her left foot down first then her right. Her hip juts and she wobbles, almost imperceptibly: the movement is slightly too fast, impatient, throwing her gently off-balance. Once down, she begins pacing between the rows of student desks. The camera traces her movements. On the soundtrack we hear her stern, clear voice, quoting Rousseau, and the dull thud of her metal-tipped heels on the wooden floor. Her voice says what it is supposed to – it speaks to the students – but her footsteps speak of distraction, restlessness: a desire or a need to move. Moments later she strides from the room, exasperated: her pace picks up as her heels hit the marble corridor and their sound transforms into a series of sharp metallic blows. The camera lingers at the threshold of the classroom, unable to keep up. We cut away.

Watching Isabelle Huppert descend from her desk, I am momentarily stopped. There is something about that brief wobble, about the too-loud sound of footsteps, a sound that threatens to drown out speech that unsettles me, asking me to look again, to *check my experience*. Surely this strange combination of noises is no accident on the part of Hansen-Løve and her sound designer Vincent Vatoux, who are clearly very aware of the impact of sound (their previous collaboration, *Eden*, was set in the world of French house music and devotes several sequences to showing the process of sound mixing). So why, to borrow a phrase from the philosopher Stanley Cavell, did they think to do it *like that*? Why does it *matter*? What are the implications of this moment for our understanding of the film and its motivations more broadly? In short, what can we learn from *les chaussures d'Huppert*?

Attention to detail

'I understand it to be, let me say, a natural vision of film that every motion and station, in particular every human posture and gesture, however glancing, has its poetry, or you may say its lucidity' (Cavell 2005b: 96). So writes Cavell, in an essay entitled 'The Thought of Movies'. Here, Cavell points us towards those '*apparently insignificant moments* in whose power a part of the power of the film rests' (Ibid.: 94, my emphasis): what he terms 'the ordinary' or 'the missable' (2005a: 11). On screen, any detail – however brief or small – may hold, in Andrew Klevan's words, 'a wealth of significance ... may adjust our way of seeing everything else in the film' (Klevan 2011: 51). For Klevan, Cavell's criticism takes the form of a 'disclosure of the everyday': of revealing or uncovering what was always before our eyes (or ears!), of seeing a new aspect of something familiar. He writes:

> Unlike most contemporary forms of textual scholarship which derives meaning from a work's origins, its historical, cultural or national context, Cavell's criticism emphasises those meanings that are *discovered* during *this* moment of engagement with the text ... It tends not to rely on information or facts ... in order to propose a 'truth' and instead stresses 're-sponsiveness' as a way of learning (about something). (Ibid.: 35, emphasis in original)

Something of this process is captured in Ludwig Wittgenstein's observation in point eighty-nine of the *Philosophical Investigations*, where he writes: 'We want to understand something that is already in plain view. For this is what we seem in some sense not to understand' (Wittgenstein 1958). According to both Cavell and Klevan, film continuously reminds us of this because it presents people, places and objects in plain view. The trick, then, is to pay attention to what is before us, avoiding the assumption that we can apply ready-made frameworks or theoretical approaches to film to yield meaning, and allowing the film to speak first. We must strive to understand, to be responsive, both to what is in the film and our own experience of it. There is a moral imperative to this revelation of the everyday, since, when we miss the things before us, we fail to pay attention to the world that surrounds us and by extension to our experience of it. The result is that our lives go not exactly unexamined, but that we miss them, they are lost to us. Klevan makes an astute connection between the missable and the dismissible – to miss something is a failure to appreciate it. 'We may simply miss a moment, it may simply pass us by, but we may also think we have seen a moment, seen all there is to see' (Klevan 2011: 60). Thinking about this problem of oversight, Cavell quotes Henry James on 'The Art of Fiction':

> The power to guess the unseen in the seen, to trace the implications of things, to judge the whole piece by the pattern, the condition of feeling life in general so completely that you are well on your way to knowing any particular corner of it – this cluster of gifts may almost be said to constitute experience … Therefore, if I should certainly say to a novice, 'Write from experience and experience only', I should feel this was a rather tantalising monition if I were not careful immediately to add, 'Try to be one of the people on whom nothing is lost'. (Cavell 1984: 6)

In response to this quote, Cavell asks that we allow ourselves to be momentarily stopped, turning away from whatever our surface preoccupations may be and turning our experience to itself. Coming to attention (Cavell 1981: 10).

From face to feet

Isabelle Huppert is one of the most celebrated actresses in French cinema, and one of the most prolific. Since her feature film debut in *Faustine et le bel été* (Nina Companeez, France, 1972) she has made more than 140 films and continues to release two or three a year. Across this body of work, she has developed a distinctive star persona. In an article analysing Huppert's celebrity, Michelle Royer refers to the actress's 'mystery, intellectualism, authenticity and impertinence'. Royer emphasises what she refers to as Huppert's 'secretive nature', pointing to a set of terms that circulate around her image: 'discretion, intelligence, independence, risk-taking, rebellion, singularity, distance, froideur, sexuality, perversity and versatility' (Royer 2015: 153). Likewise, in an overview of Huppert's career for *Sight & Sound*, Ginette Vincendeau describes the actress as 'cerebral', 'intellectual', 'cool' and 'masochistic', characterised by 'opacity, intellectualism and authenticity' (Vincendeau 2006). She divides Huppert's film roles into the 'melancholic' in which her 'sad, pale face is frequently awash with tears', and the 'cerebral-perverse core' established by an early role in Claude Chabrol's 1978 film *Violette* (Ibid.). David Bordwell, in his *New Biographical Dictionary of Film*, calls her 'wistful', 'watchful', 'pale' and 'numb' (Bordwell 2002: 420). The scholar Tony McKibbin sees her entire output as being characterised by listlessness. 'As we look over her career', he writes, 'we see the way Huppert so often lacks motivation. We notice that a sense of purpose which could give one's life meaning is replaced by a bored, petulant gesture that undermines the lives of others' (McKibbin 2005: 17).

These perceptions of Huppert are largely based on her performances. Interviewers frequently comment on the star's charm, wit and warmth in person (James 2016: 18). In character, however, there is a deliberate blankness to Huppert. The director Claude Chabrol once said of her that she had an 'invaluable gift of being able to convey emotional upheaval without any change of facial expression' (LaSalle 2012: 81). Since her face gives little away, camera and spectator alike are forced to scrutinise her for signs of an inner life. So it is common in Huppert's films for the camera to move in close, searching for the 'concentrated micro-expressions', that reveal what she is thinking or feeling (Álvarez-López and Martin 2018b). As it does so, it stills the film. As Laura Mulvey explains:

> The close-up has always provided a mechanism of delay, slowing cinema down into contemplation of the human face, allowing for a moment of possession in which the image is extracted, whatever the narrative rationalisation may be, from the flow of a story. Furthermore, the close-up necessarily limits movement, not only due to the constricted space of the framing, but also due to the privileged lighting with which the star's face is usually enhanced. (Mulvey 2005: 163–4)

Little wonder that Huppert has come to be associated with stillness, passivity, boredom: her presence literally halts film's forward trajectory. Hence, perhaps, so many of her films are part of the genre of predominantly European, auteur-driven cinema that is referred to as 'slow cinema'.

And yet close attention to Huppert's body of work reveals a more complex relationship to movement and stasis than popular and scholarly analyses of her stardom suggest. In a brilliant video-essay, 'I furrow my own film inside those I pass through', Adrian Martin and Cristina Álvarez-López break down Huppert's performances into their contingent parts, contrasting those frequent close-ups of Huppert – inscrutable, restrained – with footage of what they refer to as her tendency towards 'restless movement, vigorous action and physical exertion' (2018b). In these sequences, Huppert is framed in medium close-up or long shot, her whole body visible against the backdrop she inhabits. She is no longer a face, but a figure. Crucially, she is a figure in motion. In an excerpt from *Malina* (Werner Schroeter, Germany/Austria, 1991) she ferociously staggers through the rooms of her writer's apartment, her cream suede court shoes striking the parquet flooring; tipping, unbalanced on her heels, and righting herself. Several sequences from *The Lacemaker* (Claude Goretta, Switzerland/France/Germany, 1977) see her clambering over sand dunes in chunky boots and crunching across the pebble beach in flat, unflattering sandals or bare feet. In footage from *La cérémonie* (Claude Chabrol, France, 1995) she stomps and bops around in clunky Buffalo trainers. The camera follows her, caught up in her maelstrom of activity.

There are other scenes we could point to beyond those that Álvarez-López and Martin isolate. Huppert careering around the roller rink on skates as prostitute Ella Watson in *Heaven's Gate* (Michael Cimino, USA, 1980); stalking on patent stilettos through concrete-floored offices of her high-tech games company as Michèle Leblanc in *Elle* (Paul Verhoeven, France/Germany, 2016); skittering across a motorway in Victorian-style lace-up boots as matriarch Marthe in *Home* (Ursula Meier, Switzerland/France/Germany, 2008). The shoes that Huppert wears in all these sequences reveal something about her characters that her face conceals. This revelation takes place on a surface level: Marthe's steampunk boots, set alongside her long, unbrushed hair and tiny, retro dresses, suggest she is an unconventional mother and a free spirit, just as Michèle Leblanc's unfeasibly high heels, the pointed, glossy 'power pumps' sported by powerful screen businesswomen such as Alicia Florrick in *The Good Wife* and Jessica Pearson in *Suits*, announce her as a corporate mover and shaker. But there is something more fundamental about how Huppert inhabits these items of costume. Huppert's shoes do not merely tell us something about the character's tastes, disposable income and lifestyle, for instance. These shoes shape their wearer's very being.

In heels, a woman's pelvis – Huppert's pelvis – is tilted forwards, her calves are elongated, her arches are elevated and her ankles appear slimmer. The very effort of wearing them – whittling one's heels down to tiny points, forcing wide toes into acute angles, courting slips and sprained ankles, sacrificing one's ability to flee – is a statement to the world. As Mary Karr writes, 'every pair of excruciating heels also telegraphs a subtle masochism: that is, I am a woman who can not only take an ass-whipping; *to draw your gaze, I'll inflict one on myself*' (Karr 2016, my emphasis). Just so, the black ballet pumps Huppert sports as Erika Kohut in *The Piano Teacher* (Michael Haneke, Austria/France/Germany, 2001) force her feet out slightly, giving her a slight waddle. In these shoes she is lumpen, earthbound. They are commercial variants on technical shoes made for tough women – dancers whose feet can take a beating. But their soles are fine and unsupportive. They are literally *thin-skinned*. They have no grip to them, so that when Erika staggers out on to the frictionless surface of an ice rink in pursuit of her former lover she slips and sprawls, becoming childlike, exposed. In both *Elle* and *The Piano Teacher*, Huppert's shoes reinforce her star image: they signal self-inflicted suffering, discipline, precision and a tacit vulnerability. But they also stress the discrepancies between the two roles: the heels raising her up, the ballet pumps bringing her down to earth.

Huppert notoriously does not like to rehearse or overprepare for her roles. 'Movies work on immediate feeling, something you can never expect,' she tells Mick LaSalle. 'I like to be late when I arrive in the morning. I like to be quick . . . I don't want to think too much. I'm very, very fast' (LaSalle 2012: 23–4). We might say she approaches her roles on the hoof. Indeed, in an interview with Lisbeth Koutchoumoff, Huppert claims: 'I enter into a character's skin through the feet. Wearing high heels or flat shoes hugely defines a role. For Jeanne in Chabrol's *The Ceremony*, the type of high-heeled trainers I was wearing determined how I played the part' (Koutchoumoff 1998).

For Bernard Stiegler 'everything begins with the feet' (Stiegler 1998: 112). For Huppert 'it is all in the shoes'. In both cases, shoes are the pathway to thought. Shahidha Bari puts it eloquently when she writes that:

> in their shod state, human beings find their footing, figuratively, as well as literally. They make sense of the world, reckoning with its physical conditions and testing their ability to master it. Our shoes allow us to realise that potential. In them, we traverse all manner of terrain at unexpected speeds and to unimaginable ends. (Bari 2019: 139)

Huppert's characters are thinking, feeling. We know this from their shoes (which change with every character) as much as their faces (which, after all are all the same, since they are all the face of Huppert). The shoes, we might say, are the place where actor and character meet.

Huppert's own shoes are often the subject of media commentary. Off-screen profiles of the actress frequently comment on Huppert's choice of footwear, contrasting her high heels with her tiny frame and imbuing both with a synecdochal significance: Huppert's shoes are the embodiment of French chic. Huppert is small – five foot, three inches – and very slight. At public events she shows a preference for vertiginous yet sturdy heels by designers such as Christian Louboutin and Giuseppe Zanotti, which lend her glamour and height while emphasising, by contrast, her thinness and fragility.

The director Guillaume Nicloux seems to make reference to Huppert's own tastes in his *Valley of Love* (France, 2015), in which Huppert plays an actress named Isabelle. The film pauses on several occasions to take in her feet – clad sometimes in hiking boots or sandals appropriate to the Death Valley setting, but also, more jarringly, high strappy sandals that lend a wiggle to her walk incongruous to the wild backdrop or down-at-heel motel where her character stays.

Strikingly, too, the film opens with Huppert/Isabelle striding purposefully into shot, before the camera takes off in pursuit of her. Huppert's shoes are vehicles, setting her – and whatever film she inhabits – in motion. Often, too, they announce her. In *Amour* (Michael Haneke, France, 2012), for instance,

Figure 20.1 Huppert at Cannes, 2015

we twice hear the sound of her suede, heeled boots striking the parquet flooring before we see her. In the hushed confines of her parents' apartment, in which the elderly pair pad or shuffle around in leather slippers that make the barest of thwumps against the floor, the percussive sound of her clipped strides is violent, intrusive. The camera speeds up to follow her trajectory through the space. She ruptures the peace. Undoubtedly it says something about the kind of films Huppert makes that she spends so much time moving across the polished wooden surfaces of expensive-looking apartments. But it also seems to chime with her off-screen persona that she is an icon not of stasis, but of movement. As Mick LaSalle puts it, Huppert's production rate is so high, her energies so seemingly inexhaustible, that 'it is difficult to keep up with her, frankly' (LaSalle 2012: 24).[1]

A busy body

L'Avenir (2016) is a film that plays on Huppert's *busyness*. At its heart is a desire to hold back, or outrun, time. It details a period in the life of Nathalie Chazeaux, who we met in the opening passage of this essay. After a brief prequel set at the Breton coast, the film introduces us to latter-day Nathalie, now a teacher and author-editor of a prestigious textbook and book series, living in Paris, married to fellow philosopher Heinz (André Marcon), mother to two adult children. She has an elderly mother who is difficult and disruptive and early in the film Nathalie takes the decision to put her into a home. A chance encounter with former student Fabien (Roman Kolinka) revives their friendship at the same time that Heinz announces he is leaving her for another woman. While clearing out the Breton cottage she and Heinz have shared Nathalie learns her mother has gone on hunger strike, and returns to Paris. Her publishers inform her that the textbook and book series will be discontinued; shortly afterwards, her mother dies. Nathalie goes to stay with Fabien and his friends in the mountains, but finds herself out of step with their radical thinking and returns to Paris, upset. At the film's end, Nathalie's daughter has given birth to a grandchild. After a brief visit to Fabien, which seems to leave a profound impression on him, she returns to her home, and we leave her cradling the infant.

As Nathalie Chazeaux, Huppert wears eight different pairs of shoes, which range from boots through plimsolls and espadrilles to heels. She also – briefly – goes barefoot. When we first meet her at the start of the film the action is set in the early 2000s and Nathalie is at the Brittany coast for a family holiday, crunching over gravelled paths in tall gumboots. In the present, she initially sports tasteful tan court shoes that clip over paving stones and over the sterile, smooth spaces of classrooms, her publishing house and her small but elegant apartment (Nathalie keeps her shoes on inside her flat, which, lined with books, looks more like a library or an office than a family home). They stand in contrast with the bouncy trainers her millennial students wear, or the low-heeled sandals preferred by her daughter. But Nathalie herself has two pairs of espadrilles, one made of tan suede and rope, with open toes and ankle straps; the other black and chunkier, with an embossed leather T-bar down the middle (the latter pair are slightly smarter), and as the film progresses these become her preferred choice of footwear.

We first see Nathalie wearing her brown espadrilles while she is teaching a class outside in a park (there is a strike on: Nathalie is presumably avoiding the picket lines). She sits with her students on a grassy hillside; the camera moves languidly around them as they talk about truth and art. Nathalie receives a phone call, informing her of an unspecified crisis to do with her elderly mother, and stands, rather ungracefully, excusing herself to her students as she half-hobbles, half-shuffles, down the hill and out of shot. In the subsequent scene she is running awkwardly, slowing to walk, running again, her rubber soles slapping against the paving stone, her ankles wobbling slightly. These espadrilles provide the stability of flat soles, but their height, and delicate ankle ties makes her flight a precarious endeavour. At home, that evening, she flings these heavy, disproportionately large shoes – still on her

Figure 20.2 Nathalie wears brown espadrilles while teaching in the park

feet – onto the table, exhausted, then slowly plants them back on the floor as she listens to her husband telling her he is leaving her. In the next shot, she is asleep in the park, her espadrilles still on her feet. Later, when she learns of her mother's death Nathalie will once more tear over the Paris streets in these shoes.

The espadrilles mark a middle ground for Nathalie between the court shoes that she sports in earlier scenes, and the white Superga plimsolls she wears in subsequent scenes at the Breton coast with Heinz and in the mountains with Fabien. They are more relaxed than the former, more stylish than the latter. Espadrilles are named after esparto, the wiry grass used for producing the rope soles, but the high wedge style that Nathalie wears was first developed by French fashion designer Yves Saint Laurent in the 1970s. These shoes speak, then, to both toughness and elegance, practicality and Gallic chic. As Maxine Eggenberger writes in an article entitled 'How to wear Espadrilles like A French Girl': 'these are beloved by the French almost as much as ballet pumps [and] can give any outfit an air of effortless cool' (Eggenberger 2019).

Her espadrilles reinforce Huppert's star image (cool, insouciant, effortless) at the same time as they tell us something about Nathalie (stylish, practical, but not a woman who spends too long thinking about her clothes – after all, she has higher pursuits to consider). As Summer Brennan recounts, early twentieth-century suffragettes were constantly criticised for their shoes: when they wore flat shoes appropriate for marching, they were mocked as ugly and unfeminine; when they wore the more fashionable higher-heeled styles of the day, they were dismissed as unserious or overly sexed (Brennan 2019: 22). When one follows these arguments to their logical conclusion, one realises that 'sensible' shoes are unfeminine and 'feminine' shoes are not sensible . . . therefore, 'to be feminine is to be without sense' (Ibid.: 23). Such critiques continue to hold sway in the present age (Freeman 2013). Sensible and feminine all at once, Nathalie's espadrilles are in many ways a perfect compromise between heels and flats, well suited to a modern woman philosopher.

They also tell us something about Nathalie's environment. Open-toed, relatively flimsy, these are shoes for summer – or perhaps better, for summer in the city. At the coast, in the mountains, Nathalie goes barefoot, or wears plimsolls better suited to walking through fields and over rocks. Later, when she returns to the mountains in December, she wears high, fur-lined boots. In a film that is vague about the passage of time, Nathalie's espadrilles root us in a particular season. But more than this, they take on a metaphorical significance. Nathalie – newly single after twenty-five years of marriage, approaching retirement, her adult children having flown the nest – is moving from one state of stability to somewhere new, from summer to autumn, or indeed autumn to winter (as the film's ending suggests). The espadrilles link the trans-seasonal to the transitional.

Nathalie's shoes bear her forward. This is true for all of Huppert's roles, but perhaps nowhere is it more significant than in *L'Avenir*. We first meet Nathalie at sea, on a boat cutting through the waves. As the film progresses we see her in trains and buses and cars. Her conversations with Fabien take place as they stroll together through Paris parks. Nathalie runs for taxis, springs over rocky beaches and hikes through fields. For a philosophy teacher, it is surprising how rarely she is at rest. Even at the film's close, she stands – she doesn't sit – in elegant black heeled shoes, as she rocks her grandchild.

Figure 20.3 Nathalie's shoes bear her forward

This final sequence never fails to move me to tears. Lifting her sobbing grandchild from his bassinette, Nathalie pulls him close to her and begins to sing 'À la claire fontaine' to the baby that she cradles. The sound of her voice overlays the occasional tap of her heel on parquet as she shifts her weight, jostling him up and down, traversing the room. As the soundtrack shifts delicately to The Fleetwoods' a cappella version of 'Unchained Melody' (one of only three pieces of non-diegetic music in the film), the camera moves across the threshold to the room, taking in the almost empty living room of Nathalie's flat. Her children are barely visible in the lower left corner on the frame; the overall impression is of her absence. Watching it again, it strikes me that I can no longer hear Nathalie's shoes – not the squelch of her bare feet over sand, or the slapping of rubber on pavement, nor the crisp crumpling of plimsolls over dry grasses. Nathalie has lost her career, her mother and her marriage. Her children have left home and at least one has started their own family. She has said a final goodbye to Fabien and even given away her cat. She has stopped running. Has she given up? Passed on the baton to the next generation? It is a very restful moment, one that brings a powerful sense of relief, but also of loss. And yet – and yet! – as the closing credits appear on screen, the camera pulls back further, allowing us a final glimpse of Nathalie, swaying. Instead of the shot we might expect, the close-up that leaves us to ponder the inscrutability of Huppert's face at this ambivalent moment, we see that Nathalie is still moving, and she is still shod.

Nathalie still has places to be. She may have paused for breath, but she has not come to a halt.

The future

Summer Brennan writes of the particular relationship between women and shoes and the stories they tell:

> The story of a person's shoes is the story of her function in society, and our footprints are the marks we leave, where we've been and the direction we're going … Pain, pleasure, desire, status, blood: these are the refrains in the songs of women, as we strut, hobble, dance and walk through this man-made labyrinth we call the world. (Brennan 2019: 28)

Huppert's shoes exist for the most part in what Cavell would call the realm of the ordinary. In and of themselves they are unremarkable. Neither *L'Avenir* nor any of the other films mentioned in this essay could be said to be in any way *about* shoes. They do not even play a central role (in the way that, say, Dorothy's ruby slippers do). But by allowing myself to be stopped by that early sequence in *L'Avenir*, by coming to focus on the sound of Nathalie's shoes, the ways in which they affect her movement and gesture, I am afforded a deeper understanding of both character and film. The piece – the shoe – allows me to glimpse the whole.

The shoes that Huppert sports as Nathalie deepen and expand my understanding of the character – of who she is and where she might be going. Thinking about them allows me, additionally, to gain a more nuanced view of Huppert as a star and a performer, to understand that her repertoire expands beyond stillness, passivity and micro-gesture. That in fact it is premised just as much upon movement, activity and the use of her whole body - starting with the feet. Arguably her finest performances are those in which the full range of her abilities is deployed, allowing her to play on the tension between the two opposing forces that structure her work. After all, as Laura Mulvey has it, stillness is at the heart of screen movement:

> the great achievement of star performance is an ability to maintain a fundamental contradiction in balance: the fusion of energy with a stillness of display. However energetic a star's movement might seem to be, behind it lies an intensely controlled stillness and an ability to pose for the camera. Reminiscent, figuratively, of the way that the illusion of movement is derived from still frames, so star performance depends on pose, moments of almost invisible stillness, in which the body is displayed for the spectator's visual pleasure through the mediation of the camera. (Mulvey 2005: 162)

But perhaps what Huppert's shoes teach me most of all is that female stardom and performance need not slow film, as Mulvey argues. Women can also move film, setting it in motion.

For Cavell, 'the most significant films in the history of the art of film will be found to be those that most significantly discover and declare the nature of the medium' (Cavell 1996: 122). Let's rephrase this: the most significant discoveries are those that also discover the nature of the medium. While Huppert's shoes are revelatory of her, they are also revelatory of the medium. This discovery is not declamatory, or even remarkable: we already know, don't we, that film is always – inextricably – moving forward, towards an ending over which we have no control. But rather than resisting this momentum, as Mulvey would have us do, by pausing, rewinding, replaying, stopping, applying the brakes to scrutinise the female face, why not do as Huppert does? We cannot stop time, as Nathalie learns. Why not then run, arms outstretched – on clogs, gumboots, moccasins, mules, plimsolls, pumps, stilettos and, yes, espadrilles – towards the future?

Note

1. Huppert's apparent ability to juggle two or three projects at once is parodied to comic effect in an episode of the French series *Dix pour cent/Call My Agent*.

References

Álvarez-López, Cristina, and Martin, Adrian (2018a), 'Isabelle Huppert: The Absent One', *The Third Rail*, issue 10, available at http: https://thirdrailquarterly.org/isabelle-huppert-the-absent-one

Álvarez-López, Cristina, and Martin, Adrian (2018b), 'I furrow my own film through those I pass through' (video essay), *The Third Rail*, issue 10, available at http: https://thirdrailquarterly.org/isabelle-huppert-the-absent-one

Bari, Shahidha (2019), *Dressed: The Secret Life of Clothes*, London: Jonathan Cape.

Birchall, Bridget (2005), 'From nude to metteuse-en-scène: Isabelle Huppert, image and desire in *La Dentellière* (Goretta, 1977) and *La Pianiste* (Haneke, 2001)', *Studies in French Cinema*, vol. 5, no. 1, pp. 5–15.

Bordwell, David (2002), *The New Biographical Dictionary of Film*, London: Little, Brown.

Brennan, Summer (2019), *High Heel*, London: Bloomsbury.

Cavell, Stanley (2005a), *Philosophy the Day After Tomorrow*, Cambridge, MA: Harvard University Press.

Cavell, Stanley (2005b), 'The Thought of Movies', in W. Rothman (ed.), *Cavell on Film*, New York: State University of New York Press.

Cavell, Stanley (1996), *Contesting Tears: The Melodrama of The Unknown Woman*, Chigaco: University of Chicago Press.

Cavell, Stanley (1984), *Themes out of School: Effects and Causes*, San Fransicso: North Point Press.

Cavell, Stanley (1981), *Pursuits of Happiness: The Hollywood Comedy of Remarriage*, Cambridge, MA: Harvard University Press.

Eggenberger, Maxine (2019), 'How To Wear Espadrilles Like A French Girl', *WhoWhatWear*, 2 July, available at http: https://www.whowhatwear.co.uk/how-to-wear-espadrilles

Freeman, Hadley (2013), 'Can a feminist wear high heels', *Guardian* (online edition), 28 January, available at http: https://www.theguardian.com/fashion/2013/jan/28/can-feminist-wear-high-heels

Garber, Megan (2016), 'The Good Clothes', *The Atlantic* (online edition), 16 May, available at http: https://www.theatlantic.com/entertainment/archive/2016/05/the-good-clothes/481614/

James, Nick (2016), 'The Interview: Isabelle Huppert', *Sight & Sound*, vol. 25, no. 9, pp.18–23.

Joudet, Murielle (2018), *Isabelle Huppert: Vivre ne nous regarde pas*, Paris: Éditions Capricci.

Karr, Mary (2016), 'Uninvent This: High Maintenance', *New Yorker*, 16 May, available at http: https://newyorker.com/magazine/2016/05/16

Klevan, Andrew (2011), 'Notes on Stanley Cavell and Philosophical Film Criticism', in H. Carel and G. Tuck (eds), *New Takes in Film-Philosophy*, Basingstoke: Palgrave Macmillan, pp. 48–64.

Koutchoumoff, Lisbeth (1998), 'Isabelle Huppert: "Je rentre dans chacun de mes rôles par les pieds"', *Le Temps*, 31 July, available at http: https://www.letemps.ch/culture/isabelle-huppert-rentre-chacun-roles-pieds

LaSalle, Mick (2012), *The Beauty of the Real: What Hollywood Can Learn from Contemporary French Actresses*, Stanford: Stanford University Press.

McKibbin, Tony (2005), 'The chaos of the organs: Isabelle Huppert's reverse Pygmalionism', *Studies in French Cinema*, vol. 5, no. 2, pp. 17–26.

Mulvey, Laura (2005), *Death 24x a Second*, London: Reaktion.

Orr, John (2014), 'Stranded: stardom and the free-fall movie in French cinema, 1985–2003', *Studies in French Cinema*, vol. 4, no. 2, pp. 103–11.

Royer, Michelle (2015), 'Mystère, intellectualisme, authenticité et impertinence: Isabelle Huppert en jeu', *Australian Journal of French Studies*, vol. 52, no. 2, pp. 149–61.

Stiegler, Bernard (1998), *Technics and Time*, trans. R. Beardsworth and G. Collins, Stanford: Stanford University Press.

Vincendeau, Ginette (2006), 'Isabelle Huppert: The Big Chill', *Sight & Sound*, vol. 16, no. 12, pp. 36–9.

Wittgenstein, Ludwig (1958), *Philosophical Investigations*, trans. G. E. Anscombe, New York: Macmillan.

Index

300 (2007), 143, 144–6
2046 (2004), 206

Abbas, Ackbar, 210
Academy of Motion Picture Arts and Sciences,
    65, 233
Addams, Jane, 39
Africa, and economic liberalisation,
    193, 194
African American cinema, 231–2, 238–9
African Americans
    and blaxploitation, 238–9
    shoeshining, 7–8
    and structural inequalities, 254–5
    and white performers' mimicry, 253
    see also Mammy Two-Shoes
agency, 185, 189, 192
Álvarez-López, Cristina, 282
Ambrosio Studios, Turin, 27
American Dream, 2, 255–6
American Film Company (AFC), 126, 127
American in Paris, An (1951), 72
Americanisation, 130
Amor pedestre (1914), 26–36
Amour (2012), 284–5
Andersen, Hans Christian, 68, 69
animation, Hollywood, 103–22
Arthur, Paul, 207
Aschenputtel (*Cinderella*) (1922), 57
Asimov, Isaac, 248
Astaire, Fred, 2, 7–8, 10
Australia (2008), 132
auteurism, 231, 232
avant-garde, 31–2
Avenir, L' (2016), 279–80, 285–90
Avery, Tex, 111, 114–16

Bacall, Lauren, 94, 95, 97–8, 131
Balides, Constance, 40, 47
Band Wagon, The (1953), 7–8, 74
Banet-Weiser, Sarah, 250
bare feet, 6, 10, 141, 143, 183, 184, 191, 193, 219
Bari, Shahidha, 1, 6, 284
Barker, Jennifer, 143–4
Barthes, Roland, 155, 168
Basi, Le (1915), 26
Battleship Potemkin (1925), 10
Baum, L. Frank, 50, 52, 53
Benjamin, Walter, 2, 3, 273
Bergman, Ingrid, 132
Berlant, Lauren, 222
Bettelheim, Bruno, 55, 57
Bettinson, Gary, 203, 210
Betz, Mark, 204, 206
Beugnet, Martine, 99
Birds, The (1963), 167–8
black film and media, 231–2, 238–9; *see also*
    African Americans
black masculinity
    I, Robot, 250–3
    The Pursuit of Happyness, 254–7
Black Narcissus (1947), 69, 71, 75
BlacKkKlansman (2018), 230, 232–3, 242
Blahnik, Manolo, 265, 268, 275
Bling Ring, The (2013), 261–4, 265, 266, 269
Blot, The (1921), 39, 41, 42–7
boots, and masculinity, 148–63
Bordwell, David, 281
Borom Sarret (1963), 185–7
Bourne, Matthew, 74, 75
Brennan, Summer, 11, 287, 289
Brevik-Zender, Heidi, 265, 267, 268
Bruzzi, Stella, 160, 249, 252–3

Burkina Faso, 193, 194
Bush, Kate, 76

Cannes Film Festival, 10, 265, 285
castration anxiety, 10, 140, 145
Cavell, Stanley, 280–1, 289, 290
celebrity culture, 261, 264, 270–1, 272, 273
cérémonie, La (1995), 283, 284
Chabrol, Claude, 281, 282
chaebŏl, 215
Chaplin, Charlie, 2, 9, 19, 128
Children of Heaven (1997), 5, 6
Chow, Rey, 210
Christensen, Jerome, 232, 238, 239–40, 245
chthonicity, 138, 141, 144, 145
Cinderella (1899, 1912), 49–58, 276
Cinderella (fictional character/narrative), 40, 96,
    104, 106
CinemaScope, 95, 96, 98, 121
Cinémathèque française, 21
class
    and consumer culture, 216–17, 218
    and early film audiences, 19–20
    South Korea, 215
classical music, 69, 108–9
close-ups, 10, 22, 35
    Marnie, 171, 174, 177
    Mulvey on, 282
    Shoes, 40
    Sullivan's Travels, 83
clothing
    as class marker, 98
    fetishism, 252–3
    In the Mood for Love (2000), 199
    and the parergon, 81, 83, 90
    and power relations, 188, 192–3
    and sexual identity, 101
    The Taste of Money, 217, 219
    see also costume
Cocteau, Jean, 68
Cohan, Steven, 149, 153, 154
Cohen, Lisa, 95, 96, 97, 117, 121
Cole, Cheryl, 244
colonialism
    legacies of, 187
    and otherness, 183–5
    see also post-colonialism
commercials *see* TV commercials, Air Jordan III
consumer culture, 40, 254, 261–2, 272, 273
    and the fashion film, 275
    and post-colonialism, 187, 190, 193–4
    The Taste of Money, 216–17
    see also fetishism

Converse shoes, 250, 267–8
    product placement, 248–9
    and symbolic signification, 251–2, 258
Cooper, Gary, 159, 160–1
Coppola, Sofia, 261–77
corporate crime films, 214, 215
Cosby Show, The (NBC 1984–92), 254
costume, in silent film, 29, 33–4
costume designers, 63, 126–7, 265; *see also*
        Hollywood Costume exhibition
    cowboy boots, 126–7, 155; *see also Midnight*
        Cowboy (1969)

Dadié, Bernard, 180, 183–4, 185
Damnés de la terre, Les, (1961/1963), 184–5
Davidson, Hilary, 68, 71, 76
Davidson, Ruth, 2
Davies, Marion, 128
Day in the Life of a Pair of Legs, A, 28–9
De Lauretis, Teresa, 148, 149, 150
Derrida, Jacques, 13, 79–89, 91–2
Dietrich, Marlene, 160
Dior, Christian, 131
Disney, Walt, 71, 104, 108, 111, 112, 119
Do the Right Thing (1989), 230, 232, 234, 235,
        237–9, 241–2, 245, 252–4
Doane, Mary Ann, 28, 33
Driving Miss Daisy (1989), 233
Dumb Girl Of Portici, The (1916), 38–9
Dundes, Alan, 53
Dürrenmatt, Friedrich, 191, 192, 193
Dyer, Richard, 96, 97, 141, 155

editing, 23, 237, 274
Eggenberger, Maxine, 287
Elle (2016), 283
Entr'acte (1924), 29–30
erotic thrillers, 11
espadrilles, 286–7, 288
everyday, the, 280–1
Evita (1996), 132
Extremities (1913), 28, 29

Fabre, Marcel, 26–36
Fairbanks, Douglas, 126, 127, 128
fairy tales, 'animation' of shoes, 105
Family Shoe, The (1931), 105–6, 107
Fanon, Frantz, 2, 180, 183, 184–5
fashion, and modernity, 3, 4, 131; *see also*
        costume
Faustine et le bel été (1972), 281
Feet (1986), 26
Feet and Hands (1915), 29

female sexuality
    as masquerade, 166
    The Taste of Money, 218, 221
Ferragamo, Salvatore, 125–34
fetishism, 2–4, 39, 168
    and close-ups, 35
    commodity, 3–4, 11
    product, 238, 252–3
    sexual, 11, 137
    see also castration anxiety
film noir, 11, 34
Fleischer Studios, 106, 112
Florence, 131
Floyd, Kevin, 157
Fokine, Michel, 69
Foot Love (1996), 26
Footloose (1984), 1
Ford, Charles, 19
framing, 27, 28, 30, 32
Francisci, Pietro, 139, 141, 143
Frayling, Christopher, 62–3
Freud, Sigmund, 2, 11, 56–7, 60, 140, 145
Frusta, Arrigo, 29
Fury of Hercules, The (1962), 142
Futurism, 26, 30–2

Gaines, Jane, 28, 33–4
gangster film genre, 216
Garland, Judy, 63, 64, 133–4
Garner, Eric, 246
gay liberation movement, 156
Gay Shoe Clerk, The (1903), 10, 35
gaze, 139–40, 175
gender performance, 10, 149, 150, 157
George Eastman Museum, 21
gestures, in silent film, 28, 33
Gilbert, John, 128
Gill, Rosalind, 220
Gilligan, Sarah, 249, 252
Gilroy, Paul, 240, 244
Girl, The (2012), 177
Gladiator (2000), 144
glamour, and power, 275–6
glamour labour, 273–4
Glass Slipper, The (1938), 55
Gold Rush, The (1925), 9
Gone with the Wind (1939), 62, 121
Grable, Betty, 94, 95, 97–8
Graham, Winston, 169
Great Depression, 112
Green Book (2018), 233
Greenberg, Adrian Adolph, 64
Grimm, Jacob and Wilhelm, 57, 68, 106, 110

grunge, 267
Gucci, Guccio, 129
Guerrero, Ed, 231, 239, 245
gun violence, US protest, 6
Gundle, Stephen, 262–4

Hansen-Løve, Mia, 279
hapticity, 143–4
Heaven's Gate (1980), 283
Hedren, Tippi, 166, 167, 176–7
Heidegger, Martin, 2, 9, 79, 80, 81, 84–5, 87, 92
Hepburn, Audrey, 131–2
Hercules (1958), 137–41
Hercules (2014), 143
Hercules Unchained (1959), 141
Herron, Stella Wynne, 39–40
high heels, 34–5, 96, 98, 101–2, 189
    Ferragamo's design, 132
    In the Mood for Love, 201, 202, 204
    The Taste of Money, 214, 217, 218, 221
    see also stilettos
Hitchcock, Alfred, 1, 14, 154, 166–79, 172, 176–7
Holiday for Shoestrings (1946), 108–9, 111
Hollywood, studio system, 64, 126
Hollywood Costume, V&A exhibition, 62–7, 167
Home (2008), 283
homophobia, 159, 162
Hong Kong, 210–11
Hop – The Devil's Brew (1916), 38
Housemaid, The (1960), 215
Housemaid, The (2010), 213, 216–17, 218, 219
How to Marry a Millionaire (1953), 94–102
Huppert, Isabelle, 279–91
Huston, Kerr, 245
Hyènes (1992), 191–4
Hypocrites (1915), 46

I, Robot (2004), 248–9, 250–3, 255
Immortals (2011), 143
In the Mood for Love (2000), 198–212
individualism, 255, 256
Inge, William, 152
Instagram, 229, 230–1, 232
International Monetary Fund (IMF), 191, 215, 216
intertextuality, 95, 98
Italian Futurism, 26, 30–2

Jacobowitz, Florence, 176
Jameson, Fredric, 269
jazz, 108
Jazz Singer, The (1927), 253

Jephcott, Pearl, 75
Jhally, Sut, 254
Johnson, Catherine, 94, 96, 97
Jolly Little Elves (1934), 108, 113
Jordan, Michael, 229, 230, 235, 236–7, 238, 239,
    241, 244
Journey to Italy/Viaggio in Italia (1954), 132
Judy Garland Museum, Minnesota, 65

Kaepernick, Colin, 242
Kidman, Nicole, 132
Kids in the Shoe, The (1935), 105–6, 108, 112
Klevan, Andrew, 280–1
Konkle, Amanda, 95, 96, 97, 98
Korda, Alexander, 68–9, 70
Kosofsky Sedgwick, Eve, 159, 162

labour, 2–3, 7, 14
Lacemaker, The (1977), 282–3
Landis, Deborah Nadoolman *see* Nadoolman
    Landis, Deborah
Langer, Mark, 112
Lantz, Walter, 108
LaSalle, Mick, 284, 285
Lee, Spike, 229–46
Lehman, Christopher, 120–1
Leuvielle, Gabriel-Maximillien *see* Linder, Max
Levinson, Julie, 255
Lewis, Justin, 254
Linder, Max, 18–24
Lindner, Christopher, 269
Lista, Giovanni, 29, 31–2
Literary Digest, 42
Lives of a Bengal Lancer, The (1935), 149, 158–61
Logan, Joshua, 152
Louboutin shoes, 261–2, 264, 273, 284
Love Afoot (2015), 27
luxury goods industry, 274

Macdonald, Kevin, 69
Madonna, 132
magic shoes, 54–7
male gaze *see* gaze
Malina (1991), 282
Mambéty, Djibril Diop, 191, 192, 194
Mammy Two-Shoes, 103, 116–21
Marie Antoinette (2006), 264–9
Marinetti, Filippo Tommaso, 26, 30, 31
Marks, Laura, 143–4
Marnie (1964), 166–79
Martin, Adrian, 282
Martin, Phyllis, 182, 187

Marx, Karl, 2, 3
masculinity
    desublimised, 156, 159
    ideal, 150–4, 160
    in sword-and-sandals films, 136–7, 139–41,
        143, 145
    see also black masculinity; queer masculinity
masquerade, 81, 166
Massa, Steve, 27
material culture, footwear as, 182–5
Matter of Life and Death, A (1946), 69–70
Max collectionne les chaussures, 21
Max et les escarpins, 21
Max Sets the Style (1912), 18, 20–4
Max's Feet are Pinched, 21
May, Theresa, 2
McKibben, Tony, 281–2
Méliès, Georges, 10, 50–1
memorials, shoes as, 6
memory, 207–8, 209
Mercer, Kobena, 253, 256
Meshes of the Afternoon, (1943), 30
MGM, 64, 65, 116–21
Midnight Cowboy (1969), 155–8
Miller, Frank, 144
Minnelli, Vincente, 72, 74
mise en scène, 10, 39, 100, 192
    La Noire de . . ., 188
    Marnie, 166
Mitchell, W. J. T., 232, 237–8, 239–40
Monroe, Marilyn, 94–102, 131–2
montage, 265–6, 268, 269, 270
Morocco (1930), 160
Motion Picture Magazine, 38
Motion Picture News, 40
Mulvey, Laura, 35, 99, 100–1, 139, 282, 290
Murdoch, Iris, 166, 167, 170–1, 173, 177

Nadoolman Landis, Deborah, 62, 64, 65, 126, 167
Napoli, Joe, 64
Nazism, 5, 6
Neale, Steven, 141, 150, 154, 161
Negri, Pola, 127, 128
neo-liberalism, 215, 218, 220
Nicloux, Guillaume, 284
Night and Fog (1956), 6
Nikes, 9, 229, 230, 233–4, 242–6, 253
    commercials, 235–7, 238, 239–41
    protest against, 242–3
    see also Converse shoes
La Noire de . . . (1966), 187–91
Now Voyager (1942), 95

Obama, Barack, 251
Oberon, Merle, 69
objects, drama of, 32
Oedipal narratives, 148, 149–51, 161
Over the Chafing Dish (1911), 28, 29

Packard, Chris, 157–8
Paglia, Camilla, 261, 270
pairing, 84–6
Papachristophorou, Marilena, 104–5
Parchesky, Jennifer, 40–1, 44
parergon, 81–6, 88, 89, 90
Peachy Cobbler, The (1950), 111, 114–16
Pedestrian Love (1986), 26
peplum films *see* sword-and-sandals films
Perez, Manuel Fernandez *see* Fabre, Marcel
Perrault, Charles, 50, 53, 104
phenomenology, 103
Photograph Taken from Our Area Window, A, 28
Piano Teacher, The (2001), 283
Pickford, Mary and Lottie, 127
Picnic (1955), 151–4, 160
Place-Verghnes, Floriane, 115
plastic surgery, 216, 220
Playing Footsie (2000), 26
pointure, 91–2
post-colonialism
    and consumer culture, 187, 190, 193–4
    and power relations, 185–7, 190–1
postfeminism, 220, 271, 275
Postman Always Rings Twice, The (1946), 132
post-racial discourse, 250–1, 255, 258
Powell, Michael, 68–71, 73, 75–6
Prada, Mario, 129
Pressburger, Emeric, 68–9, 71, 73, 76
Pretty Woman (1990), 9, 56
product placement, 248–9, 250
Proyas, Alex, 248
psychoanalytic theory, 55, 57, 96, 115; *see also*
    Freud, Sigmund
Pucci, Emilio, 130
Pursuit of Happyness, The (2006), 249, 254–7

queer masculinity, 155

Rabinowitz, Paula, 6, 8, 169
Rachmaninov, 69
Randolph, Lillian, 116
Red Shoes, The (1948), 9, 11, 66–77
Rees-Roberts, Nick, 274–5
Reid, Richard Colvin, 8
resistance, 189–90, 195

Robinson, Sally, 162
Rogers, Ginger, 2, 10
Roman sandals *see* sword-and-sandals films
Rome, 131
Royer, Michelle, 281
Rushdie, Salman, 53, 54

sabotage, 8, 51
Sadoul, Georges, 19, 20–1
Sales, Nancy Jo, 261, 264
    sandals, 104, 127, 133; *see also* sword-and-
        sandals films
Sang-Soo, Im, 213, 215
Schapiro, Meyer, 84–5, 87
Schlesinger, John, 155
Schulberg, Budd, 4
Schwartz, Stephen, 66
Sedgwick, Eve Kosofsky *see* Kosofsky
        Sedgwick, Eve
Sembene, Ousmane, 185, 187, 191
Sensation Seekers (1927), 46
Sex and the City 2, 57–8
Sex and the City (TV and film), 1, 11, 57, 217, 275
She's Gotta Have It (1986), 233–5
shoe production, animation, 109–13; *see also*
        Ferragamo, Salvatore
Shoemaker and the Elves, The (1935), 106–8,
        109–10
Shoes (1916), 38, 39–47
shoeshining, 7–8
Show People (1928), 128
Sight & Sound (magazine), 281
Silverman, Kaja, 95, 98, 101, 168
Simpson, O.J., 244
Single White Female (1992), 11, 12
Sitney, P. Adams, 30
Slide, Anthony, 38–9
slippers, 35, 104, 141, 161, 171
    animation, 120
    In the Mood for Love, 201–3, 207–9, 211
Smith, George Albert, 28
Smith, Will, 248–58
Smithsonian Museum, Washington, 66
sneakers, 104, 242
Sobchack, Vivian, 140, 143–4
social inequality, 41, 43
social mobility, 3, 40–1, 255–6, 257
social problem films, 40
soundtrack, 285
    L'Avenir, 279, 290
South Korea, 213–14, 215
    women immigrants to, 222, 223

Space Jam (1996), 252
Spartacus (TV; 2010–13), 143
spectatorship, 35, 99, 100–1, 139–40, 150
Stamp, Shelley, 45–6, 47
Stewart, Kristen, 10
Stiegler, Bernard, 1, 5, 284
stilettos, 8, 10, 11, 12, 283
Story of a Pair of Boots, The (1910), 29
Story of Lulu Told by her Feet (1910), 29
Story of the Boots Told (1908), 28
Street, Sarah, 168–9, 177
Sturges, Preston, 78–93
suffragettes, 287
Sullivan's Travels (1941), 78–93
surveillance, 149, 221, 272, 274
Swing Time (1936), 7
sword-and-sandals films, 136–47
synedoche, 30, 32

tap dancing, 7, 10
Tarantino, Quentin, 39
Tasker, Yvonne, 141, 162
Taste of Money, The (2012), 213–26
Technicolor, 53, 64, 69
teen culture *see Bling Ring, The* (2013)
Thaïs (1917), 32
Thief of Baghdad, The (1924), 127
Things to Come, 279–80, 285–90
Thomas, Rhys, 64–5, 66
Tom and Jerry cartoons, 103, 116–21
Too Wise Wives (1921), 38
touch *see* hapticity
Traffic in Souls (1913), 40
true crime stories, 265
Trump, Donald, 231, 242
Turim, Maureen, 6, 10, 16
Turner, Lana, 132
TV commercials, Air Jordan III, 235–7, 238,
    239–41
Twentieth Century Fox Film, 248

Valley of Love (2015), 284
Van Gogh, Vincent, *Old Shoes with Laces*, 2, 9,
    80, 81, 84–6, 91, 269
Vanity Fair (magazine), 261
Velocità (1930), 32
Victoria and Albert Museum, London,
    62–7
Vidal-Naquet, Pierre, 138–9
Violette (1978), 281
Virginian, The (1929), 160
Vitrotti, Giovanni, 29

war films, 158–61
wardrobe director, role of, 126
Warhol, Andy, 269
Warner, Kent, 65
Warner Brothers, 109, 112
Weber, Lois, 38–47
Wells, Paul, 103, 114–15
Westerns, 156
Whitten, David O., 112
Wilkinson, Maryn, 272
Winch, Alison, 271–2
Wissinger, Elizabeth, 273
Wittgenstein, Ludwig, 280
Wizard of Oz, The (1939), 49–50, 57–9,
    68
    V&A costume exhibition, 62–7
Wolf, Naomi, 2, 11, 216–17
women
    and misogyny, 162
    in post-war Britain, 70, 75, 76
Wong, Kar-wai, 198, 200, 206, 210
Wretched of the Earth, The (1961/1963),
    184–5

Yankee Dood It (1956), 112–14
Young, Clara Kimball, 28

Zaidi, Muntadhar al-, 8

EU Authorised Representative:

Easy Access System Europe Mustamäe tee 50, 10621 Tallinn, Estonia

gpsr.requests@easproject.com

Printed and bound by CPI Group (UK) Ltd, Croydon, CR0 4YY

20/05/2025

01876627-0001